WLM 228 STR

F4.7
PAY
37

28

EXETER MENTAL HEALTH UNI
MEDICAL LIBRARY REF·

MEDICAL LIBRARY
WONFORD HOUSE HOSPITAL
DRYDEN ROAD
EXETER EX2 5AF

3209692985
Exeter University Library

Stress in Health Professionals

WILEY SERIES ON STUDIES IN OCCUPATIONAL STRESS

Series Editors

Professor Cary L. Cooper
Department of Management Sciences,
University of Manchester
Institute of Science and Technology

Professor S. V. Kasl
Department of Epidemiology,
School of Medicine,
Yale University

Stress at Work
Edited by Cary L. Cooper and Roy Payne

White Collar and Professional Stress
Edited by Cary L. Cooper and Judi Marshall

Stress, Work Design and Productivity
Edited by E. N. Corlett and J. Richardson

A Behavioural Approach to the Management of Stress
H. R. Beech, L. E. Burns and B. F. Sheffield

Living Abroad: Personal Adjustment and Personnel Policy in the Overseas Setting
Ingemar Torbiorn

The Mechanisms of Job Stress and Strain
John R. P. French, Jr., Robert D. Caplan and R. Van Harrison

Noise and Society
Edited by Dylan M. Jones and Antony J. Chapman

Job Stress and Blue Collar Work
Edited by Cary L. Cooper and Michael Smith

Stress and Health: Issues in Research Methodology
Edited by Stan V. Kasl and Cary L. Cooper

Stress in Health Professionals
Edited by Roy Payne and Jenny Firth-Cozens

Further titles in preparation

Stress in Health Professionals

Edited by

Roy Payne
Manchester Business School

and

Jenny Firth-Cozens
Sheffield University

JOHN WILEY & SONS
Chichester · New York · Brisbane · Toronto · Singapore

Copyright © 1987 by John Wiley & Sons Ltd.

All rights reserved.

No part of this book may be reproduced by any means, or transmitted, or translated into a machine language without the written permission of the publisher

Library of Congress Cataloging-in-Publication Data:
Stress in health professionals.
  (Wiley series on studies in occupational stress)
  1. Medical personnel—Job stress. I. Payne, Roy.
II. Firth-Cozens, Jenny. III. Series. [DNLM: 1. Health
Manpower. 2. Stress, Psychological. WM 172 S91535]
R690.S78   1987   610.69   87-8122

ISBN 0 471 91254 9

British Library Cataloguing in Publication Data:
Stress in health professionals.—(Wiley
  series on studies in occupational stress).
  1. Medical personnel—Job stress
  I. Payne, R. L.   II. Firth-Cozens, Jenny
  610.69′01′9   R690

ISBN 0 471 91254 9

Typeset by Witwell Ltd, Liverpool
Printed and bound in Great Britain by Anchor Brendon, Colchester

List of Contributors

LILLIAN CARTWRIGHT	California School of Professional Psychology, 1900 Addison Street, Berkeley, California, USA
JENNY FIRTH-COZENS	MRC/ESRC Social and Applied Psychology Unit, Department of Psychology, University of Sheffield, UK
MIKE FITTER	MRC/ESRC Social and Applied Psychology Unit, Department of Psychology, The University of Sheffield, UK
JOHN HOWIE	Department of General Practice, University of Edinburgh, 20 West Richmond Street, Edinburgh, UK
JOHN M. IVANCEVICH	Department of Management, College of Business Administration, University of Houston, Texas, USA
TODD D. JICK	Harvard Business School, Harvard University, Boston, Mass., USA
GRAHAM JONES	Department of Phyical Education and Sports Science, University of Loughborough, Leicestershire, UK
GERRY KENT	Department of Psychiatry, University of Sheffield, Royal Hallamshire Hospital, Glossop Road, Sheffield, UK
ANITA LEVINSON	Napier College, Edinburgh, UK
FRANK MARGISON	Department of Psychiatry, Manchester Royal Infirmary, Gaskell House, Swinton Grove, Manchester, UK

MICHAEL T. MATTESON *Department of Management, College of Business Administration, University of Houston, Texas, USA*

ROY PAYNE *Manchester Business School, Manchester University, Manchester, UK*

MIKE PORTER *Department of General Practice, University of Edinburgh, 20 West Richmond Street, Edinburgh, UK*

ANDREE RUSHTON *Social Worker and Author, London, UK*

STEPHEN C. SCHEIBER *American Board of Psychiatry and Neurologyine Deerfield, Illinois, USA*

SOPHIE THOMSON *Department of Psychology, Jenner Wing, St. George's Hospital Medical School, Cranmer Terrace, Tooting, London, UK*

Contents

Editorial Foreword to the Series... ix
Preface xi
Introduction.. xv

PART I   THE MEDICAL PROFESSION

1. **The stresses of medical training** 3
    Jenny Firth-Cozens

2. **Stress in physicians** 23
    Stephen C. Scheiber

3. **Stress and the general practitioner** 45
    A.M.D. Porter, J.G.C. Howie, and A. Levinson

4. **Occupational stress in women physicians** 71
    Lillian Kaufman Cartwright

5. **Stress in surgeons** 89
    Roy Payne

6. **Stress in psychiatrists** 107
    Frank R. Margison

PART II   NON-MEDICAL HEALTH PROFESSIONALS

7. **Stress amongst dentists**... 127
    Gerry Kent

8. **Stress in staff working with mentally handicapped people**............ 151
    Sophie Thomson

9. **Stress amongst social workers**.. 167
    Andrée Rushton

10. **Stress in psychiatric nursing**.. 189
    J. Graham Jones

11. The impact of new technology on nurses and patients 211
    Mike Fitter

12. Medical technologists and laboratory technicians: sources of stress and coping strategies 231
    John M. Ivancevich and Michael T. Matteson

PART III THE HOSPITAL AS A CONTEXT

13. Managing and coping with budget-cut stress in hospitals 259
    Todd D. Jick

Conclusion 271
Index 285

Editorial Foreword to the Series

This book, *Stress in Health Professionals*, is the eleventh (11) book in the series of *Studies in Occupational Stress*. The main objective of this series of books is to bring together the leading international psychologists and occupational health researchers to report on their work on various aspects of occupational stress and health. The series will include a number of books on original research and theory in each of the areas described in the initial volume, such as Blue Collar Stressors, The Interface Between the Work Environment and the Family, Individual Differences in Stress Reactions, The Person–Environment Fit Model, Behavioural Modification and Stress Reduction, Stress and the Socio-technical Environment, The Stressful Effects of Retirement and Unemployment and many other topics of interest in understanding stress in the workplace.

We hope these books will appeal to a broad spectrum of readers—to academic researchers and postgraduate students in applied and occupational psychology and sociology, occupational medicine, management, personnel, etc.—and to practitioners working in industry, the occupational medical field, mental health specialists, social workers, personnel officers, and others interested in the health of the individual worker.

CARY L. COOPER,
*University of Manchester Institute of
Science and Technology (UK)*
STANISLAV V. KASL,
Yale University

Preface

It is 25 years since the *Journal of Social Issues* published a complete issue on 'Work, Health and Satisfaction' (French *et al.*, 1962). Its articles not only heralded the future strategy for the voluminous works of the Institute of Social Research at the University of Michigan, but perhaps unwittingly they signalled the start of a growth industry: occupational stress. The growth in occupational stress research is, of course, only part of a larger intellectual enterprise concerned with understanding how stress affects the maturation and survival of humans and animals, and Selye must be accorded recognition as *a* founder, if not *the* founder of this field.

During that 25 years research has been carried out on a wide range of occupations, but it is only during recent years that books have begun to appear which deal with strain in specific occupational groups. Shostak (1980) wrote a book on blue-collar workers; Cooper and Marshall (1980) edited one on white-collar workers; and more recently Skevington (1984) has edited a volume on nurses. This is not to say that books have not been published on specific occupational groups before, but they have usually been monographs on particular research studies such as Becker *et al.*'s (1962) classic study on doctors, or Fineman's (1985) study of a social work department.

The appearance of books on specific occupational groups is a sign that there is now sufficient research available to make a consideration worthwhile both theoretically and practically. This is one motivation for the present volume on health professionals, but a second reason is that these professionals face an occupational stressor which is not part of most other occupations. Health professionals process people, and they deal with them in situations which have the profoundest implications for any human being: those involving death and suffering. McCue (1986) expresses the problem for physicians, but it applies to all those responsible for the care of the sick:

> complaining about one's job is an activity enjoyed by all—regardless of nationality, race and sex, economic, cultural and educational status—except physicians. . . . The 'conspiracy of silence' isolates physicians who are troubled by aspects of their work and makes it difficult for maladapted and impaired physicians to seek non-judgmental advice and counseling.

The origins of the evocative term 'burnout' by Maslach (1976) has begun to make inroads into that conspiracy and has certainly inspired an increase into research in all the human service professions. Some professions, however, have had much more attention than others and this is reflected in the balance of chapters in *Stress in Health Professionals*.

After an Introduction by the editors which presents a general framework for looking at occupational stress, and details the justification for producing a book on health professionals, the book is divided into three parts. Part I contains six chapters which review different aspects of the large volume of research concerning members of the medical profession, but which also reflect larger issues faced by health care workers more generally. The first chapter is by Firth-Cozens and deals with the considerable literature on the stresses experienced during medical training. The next is by Scheiber and concentrates on what is known about research on physicians in the United States. Chapter 3 provides an international comparison, with Porter, Howie and Levinson reviewing the stresses faced by General Practitioners in Britain. Neither the health professions generally nor occupational stress research in particular has escaped the general prejudice that exists against women in most societies and we have tried to redress this imbalance by inviting Cartwright to focus on the pressures that a career in medicine creates for women.

The last two chapters in Part I concern medical specialities which face their practitioners with very different kinds of stresses, and which have received far less attention than physicians and medical students. Payne presents research on stress amongst surgeons in Chapter 5 and Margison concentrates on the social and psychological dynamics of practising psychiatry. The absence of important specialities such as obstetrics and gynaecology, internal medicine, anaesthetics, and pathology is a reflection of what remains to be done rather than a belief that they do not all contain their unique stressors.

Part II concentrates on professions who have not had medical training. It starts with a chapter by Kent on dentists, who have long been regarded as members of a stressful profession because of their reported high suicide rates; his careful review of the quite extensive research on dentists begins to question this myth. Given the large amount of research that now exists on nurses generally, and the knowledge that J. Wiley & Sons had recently published a book on nurses (Skevington, 1984), we decided to concentrate on groups who had not been widely studied. Thus Thomson's chapter on staff working with the mentally handicapped reflects this decision, and the same strategy determined the choice of Jones's chapter on psychiatric nursing, especially since both these areas are commonly regarded as the Cinderallas of the health services. In Chapter 9 Rushton deals with the stresses met by social workers struggling to repair the damage of societies caught in the turbulence of economic and cultural change. The technological changes occurring in those societies also have their impact and Fitter considers the effects of the use of new technology in nursing. The stresses generated by the complexity of new technology, the hazards of new diseases, and the problems of working in a status hierarchy determined by another profession (medicine) produce unique strain for medical technologists too and these are discussed by Ivancevich and Matteson in Chapter 12, which brings Part II to a close.

Part III contains only one chapter, by Jick, who eloquently outlines the difficulties which hospitals face in dealing with the problems of budget cuts alongside the increasing sophistication of a technology which allows lives to be saved, but at such an economic cost that doctors and administrators begin to face the most complex ethical decisions. As Jick's chapter shows, there is no readily available anaesthetic for organizational surgery.

We as editors have the last, but not final, say in the conclusion where we summarize the main themes in the book and indicate some gaps in the state of the art, knowledge and methods.

December 1986
Roy Payne
Jenny Firth-Cozens

REFERENCES

Becker, H. S., Geer, B., Hughes, E. C. and Strauss, A. L. (1961). *Boys in White: Student Culture in a Medical School*, University of Chicago Press, Chicago.
Cooper, C. L. and Marshall, J. (1980). *White Collar and Professional Stress*, Wiley, Chichester.
Fineman, S. (1985). *Social Work Stress and Intervention*, Gower, London.
French, J. R. P., Kahn R. L. and Mann F. C. (1962). Work, health and satisfaction. *Journal of Social Issues*, XVIII, (3), 1–129.
Maslach, C. (1976). Burned out. *Human Behavior*, 5, 16–22.
McCue, J. D. (1986). Doctors and stress: is there really a problem? *Hospital Practice*, March 30, 7–16.
Shostak, A. B. (1980). *Blue-collar Stress*, Addison-Wesley, Reading, Mass.
Skevington, S. (1984). *Understanding Nurses: the Social Psychology of Nursing*, Wiley, Chichester.

Introduction

THE CONCEPT OF STRESS

In everyday speech the word stress can refer to an event that causes physical or psychological pain, or it can refer to the pain itself. Most writers are now beginning to recognize that it is necessary to distinguish cause from effect, and are beginning to follow the analogy from engineering that the effects of an external *stress* (or stressor) results in *strain*. With human beings this slightly oversimplifies the situation since the environment may be causing little stress for a person, but they may nevertheless claim to feel very strained. This is because they themselves may be the source of their own stress. They may set themselves unattainable goals or standards of behaviour, and continually failing to achieve them can lead to guilt, low self-esteem and strain. An interest in stress from this intra-individual point of view has largely been the interest of clinical psychology and psychiatry. Occupational psychology has focused more on the role of the psycho-social environment in creating stress which the person has to cope with, over and above any psycho-dynamic problems of the kind described above. Since this is a book about the occuption—health professionals—we will follow the conventional stress–strain framework, but wish to recognize that this is a somewhat arbitrary way of drawing a boundary about a person. This is recognized in the recent trend for clinical and occupational psychology to begin to work more closely with each other (Broadbent, 1985; Firth, 1985).

What is already clear from the brief exposition above is that 'stress' refers to a *process* that takes place over time (Pearlin *et al.*, 1982). One of the major reasons that stress is a growing research area is the need to understand the role it plays in the onset, or maintenance of mechanisms which lead to diseases. Figure 1 is taken from Kagan and Levi (1974) and emphasizes that disease is the important outcome state and that it is a process that takes place over a considerable period of time. The large number of feedback loops, and the general box 'interacting variables' also suggests the complexity of the process.

Figure 2 presents a framework which closely follows that described in Figure 1, but it provides examples of some of the major constructs used by occupational psychologists in investigating stress at work. Figure 2 is a modification from Payne (1980). This framework follows the conventional stress–strain assumptions. Stressors occur in the Objective Environment and in the present

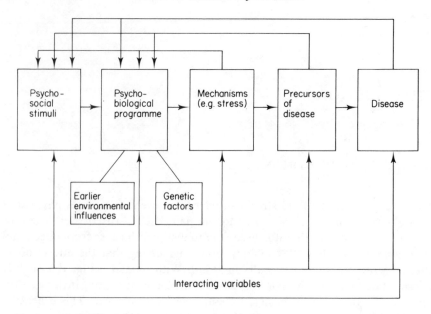

Figure 1 A framework for understanding psycho-social stress and health. From Kagan and Levi (1974). Reprinted by permission Pergamon Press

model stressors are defined as demands which arise from the job a person does. The overall stressfulness of the objective environment, however, is determined by the number and strength of the constraints which exist in meeting those demands. Thus two consultant surgeons may be asked to perform the same number of operations per annum, but one has few resources, poor equipment and poor working conditions whilst the other has plenty of resources, the best equipment and excellent working conditions. The first consultant is much more stressed than the second. One thing that may help the stressed surgeon to cope, however, is the quality of support they receive from the people around them; other colleagues, the patients and their relatives, the administration. As it happens, most aspects of our environment can be either supports or constraints: a good boss helps, a poor boss hinders. Thus it is the balance that exists between demands, supports and constraints which determines the overall stressfulness of the environment.

Whilst this is a relatively simple framework it helps to explain why highly demanding jobs may not be stressful overall. Chief executives of companies, for example, have demanding jobs, but since they can control resources and constraints they can considerably reduce the effects of those demands. Indeed, if mortality and morbidity is analysed by occupational level it is those in the jobs at the lowest levels (e.g. machine minding) that have the highest rates of morbidity and mortality, and the highest rates of sickness absence (Fletcher and Payne,

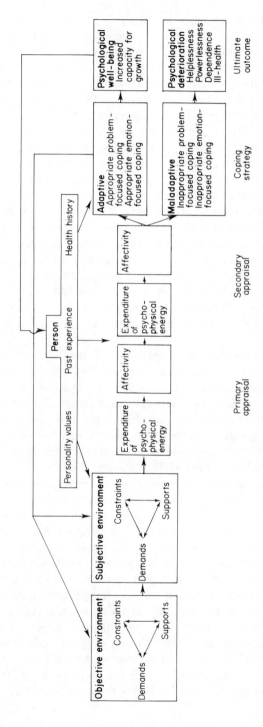

Figure 2 A stress-strain-coping framework. Reprinted by permission J. Wiley & Sons

1980). This general pattern also holds within health service professions themselves, and these sort of data appear in the main body of the book.

It is also worth noting that low constraint, high support environments provide a person with a high degree of control. Control is now regarded as an important way of decreasing the effects of stressors, and the role of job autonomy/discretion/control is a developing area of research (Karasek, 1979; Fisher, 1986). A review of the role of social support in stress is available in Cohen and Wills (1985).

The second box in Figure 2 is labelled the Subjective environment, and it again contains the same three variables: demands, supports, constraints. There is also a direct line connecting the Person box with the Subjective environment to indicate that personality, beliefs and past experiences will influence how the objective environment is actually perceived.

Imagine two social workers working from the same office. One has grown up in a very stable, caring environment and has good relationships with family and friends. The other has come from a very unstable home and has always found the world a threatening place so that it is difficult to put trust in other people. The first may empathize with the problems of their clients and find the caseload heavy, but bearable. The second may over-identify and fail to trust in the support of, say, senior colleagues, even when it is readily available to both of them. The same 'objective environment' produces very different 'subjective environments'.

Depue and Monroe (1986) note that over 50 per cent of illnesses are experienced by less than 25 per cent of the population and they emphasize the important roles that personality, affective states such as anxiety and depression, chronic illnesses and enduring life difficulties have on reactions to stresses (e.g. life events) that occur in the environment. Highly anxious people, for example, not only report more symptoms of strain, but also see their environment as more demanding, and this effect has to be considered when testing models of the stress–strain type based on self-report data (Payne, 1986).

So far we have characterized the environment in a very global way, but people have come to see their environment the way it is because of the different events that occur in it. The framework in Figure 2 portrays this ongoing aspect of the stress process by indicating that the person is always appraising the environment to try and predict its consequences for them. According to Lazarus (1966) there are two steps in this continuous appraisal process. At Primary Appraisal the person is trying to decide if the environment subjectively perceived has negative (or positive) implications for them. Of course, this appraisal might be distorted by all sorts of unconscious, irrational forces which might make the person feel unnecessarily strained, or unwisely safe, but whatever happens this process is followed by Secondary Appraisal where the person has to decide what actions are possible and appropriate to the situation as appraised. Let us return briefly to a surgeon who is stressed because of having poor resources. One surgeon might make a primary appraisal that this is not threatening anyway. 'I can cope,

I always have.' The secondary appraisal that follows might be, 'I'll just soldier on', i.e. do nothing. This may work, or it may lead to cutting corners which may lead to the spread of infections or other errors. Another surgeon might see this potential threat at the stage of primary appraisal and decide to mount a campaign for increasing resources (secondary appraisal). Both parts of the appraisal process consist of (a) the expenditure of physical and psychological energy and (b) emotional experiences (ranging from positive to negative) which indicate the degree of stress, and anticipations of the costs of coping with it.

Once the secondary appraisal has been made the person needs to take action to put the decision into practice. These patterns of actions have come to be called coping responses and they form the next stage of the stress process. In Figure 2 two alternatives are presented. They are Adaptive Coping processes and Maladaptive Coping processes. It is difficult, in principle, to argue that any particular form of coping is necessarily bad. Even drugs might work for some people, in some situations.

The search for good theories of coping processes, and measures of them is not as well developed as is needed to understand the consequences of stressful environments (Lazarus and Folkman, 1984) but the broad classification of strategies into those that concentrate on practical problem-solving, and those that rely largely on emotion focused, or psychological techniques, is a useful summary of two important ways in which people cope. Major issues in the coping literature are (a) the role of the environment in determining choice of strategy, and (b) whether people are relatively consistent, or not, in the strategy they adopt to solve similar problems over different situations and times. The continuous interaction which takes place between the person and the situation, which is portrayed in Figure 2 by the use of feedback loops, indicates why the search for consistent styles of coping has proved more difficult than originally imagined. Situations change, people create new ways of coping or learn to accept conditions as bearable which at other times they might have thought as quite unbearable.

As in Figure 1 the two final boxes of Figure 2 indicate the long-term consequences of the stress process: successful coping leads to health and well-being, and inappropriate coping, whether it is problem-focused or emotion-focused, may lead to physical and psychological ill-health.

A true appreciation of the effects of environmental stress on a person's health and well-being would require a detailed life history. There are virtually no studies of this nature in occupational psychology though those by George Vaillant (1977) are very much in that tradition. Many studies of occupational stress consist of trying to understand the effects of particular life events which are job related such as promotion, job change, demotion or job loss, and these studies involve the assumption that the job is playing some part in the differences that are found. A variation on the latter approach is to get people to indicate the nature and strengths of stressors in their work environment and then to relate these to levels of psychological strain or mental health. Again, the assumption is that those with higher levels of symptoms are in the more stressful jobs. Both these sorts of studies may also assess people's personalities and beliefs (e.g. the degree to which people believe they are in control of events that happen to them) to see how they relate to symptom levels. They may also assess coping styles to see if those with similar coping styles have fewer symptoms given a similarly stressful environment. It can be seen from these brief descriptions that much of the research on occupational stress does not measure Objective Stress, but relies on perceptions or Subjective Stress. This background is relevant because in designing this book we asked the authors of the different chapters to try to achieve three objectives, and they focus on the three main elements in the stress model: stressors, strain and coping. The authors were asked to:

(1) Indicate how much strain there is in the occupation to get an idea of the size of the problem.
(2) Identify the major sources of stress indicating which are the most common.
(3) Suggest what can be done to reduce or remove these stressors.

As indicated, the data on strain, sources and coping patterns are largely self-report data, though there are some observational studies, a few personal accounts, some physiological data and statistics on mortality and morbidity which supplement the evidence on these three topics. There are some studies on health professionals which attempt to test what are implicitly causal models and these are included for those occupations where they exist. The basic focus of the book, however, is to answer these three questions, acknowledging that the complexity of the stress process will in the future face us with much more searching challenges. (Depue and Monroe, 1986).

WHY CHOOSE HEALTH PROFESSIONALS?

The National Health Service is the largest employer in Britain, and health professionals in the rest of Europe and the USA represent a huge proportion of workers both in public employment and in private practice. The health professions showed their largest growth during the 1960s and early 1970s but real numbers began to fall over the last decade. Being the largest professional group is a sufficient reason for giving them consideration, but they also have special reasons for being more stressed than some other professional groups. The strain of dealing with clients face-to-face has been recognized in many groups of workers and is seen as one of the most important aspects of 'burnout' (Maslach, 1982). However, within the health field the stress created by such interactions may well be exaggerated by the involvement of deformity, physical suffering and sometimes death. The fact that many of these workers have not only to witness considerable suffering but also to inflict it through tests and medical procedures makes their interactions with clients very different from other professional groups. For health professionals such as doctors, nurses and dentists, some of these procedures are invasive of the person, giving 'contact' an altogether more extreme definition.

Several studies of occupational stress have found a greater relationship between occupational stress and responsibility for people, rather than for objects (Caplan et al., 1975). However, unlike many other professions, wrong decisions by health professionals may lead to the exacerbation of the disease or even to the patients' death: such responsibility has a finality shared by few other professions. It is not difficult to imagine a spiral of increasing responsibility leading to increasing stress which in turn may create difficulties in decision-making which may make the responsibility more difficult to tolerate, and so on. Certainly, Friedman et al. (1971) have demonstrated the association between sleep loss and cognitive functioning in junior residents, and it is clear cognitive problems, including impaired decision-making, concentration loss and memory loss, are a feature of distress occurring in the occupational environment (Firth and Shapiro, 1986).

A particular stress for health professionals is that their own stress may affect the very focus of their role, the patient. Patient–helper communication itself may be affected by the helper's own levels of strain, especially by withdrawal as a patient approaches death (Stewart et al., 1982). Thus the issue of stress for these workers becomes crucial for patient care itself.

Although many jobs have hazards and health risks, the possibility of infection passing to members of the health professions is sometimes less preventable than other occupational threats to well-being. Moreover, new strains of viral illness such as AIDS add to the risk of contamination. Apart from these invisible hazards, members of some groups, such as social workers, casualy nurses and workers in psychiatry and mental handicap, suffer physical injury and even death from their clients (Murray, 1985). Although such a risk is present for police and prison officers, for them violence is expected and they have been given appropriate training which is rare for other health professionals. There is less conflict and therefore clearer guides for action when workers are not expected to help the person involved but only to restrain them.

All professionals have suffered the risk that they can be sued for negligence. However, for those in the health services the threat of litigation has increased dramatically since the mid-seventies, leading to changed and restricted practices which are not always to the advantage of the patients. Although it is unarguable that negligence should be actionable, it is undoubtedly easier to avoid for, say, architects or lawyers, than within the medical field where uncertainty and risk exist, often to some considerable degree.

Most of the occupational stress research uses questionnaire assessments and these are always likely to be affected by a person's defences against anxiety

(Lawrence et al., 1982). It would be predicted that defences would be particularly strong concerning anxiety-provoking issues such as death, disease and deformity (Firth and Morrison, 1986)—what Philip Larkin called 'the costly aversion of the eyes to death'—and it has been suggested that professions, such as nursing, are organized in such a way as to maintain defences against such anxieties (Menzies, 1960). This is achieved by having rules about 'not getting involved with the patient' and by keeping 'professionally detached'. The possible presence of such defences presents a special problem for research into the stressors and strains of health work and adds to the methodological problems which exist in organizational stress investigations more generally.

A second research issue, highlighted by Depue and Monroe (1986), is the role of individual differences in the experience of life stress. While there are undoubtedly the same large individual differences amongst health professionals as there are in any other group, it has been suggested by Malan (1979) that people who choose to be helpers may well have particular characteristics arising from a need to make good the unresolved difficulties of early childhood.

Whilst the focus of this book is on stress, it must be acknowledged that there are also great satisfactions experienced by the holders of these jobs (Cartwright, 1978). They are able to help, and to be needed and valued by society. Moreover, most health jobs offer an unusual variety of experience, a high utilization of skills and intellectual challenge. For this reason, while there are distinct occupational hazards in the health professions, it is likely that there are equally distinct satisfactions which may, to some extent counter the potential sources of emotional distress.

Describing similarities between health professions which distinguish them from other groups of workers does not, of course, imply that the various occupations that are subsumed under this general heading face identical stressors and strains, nor enjoy the same levels of satisfaction. Despite their overall similarities there are some very clear differences.

Perhaps the most basic difference, and the one most often referred to in salary negotiations, is that of financial rewards. The differential between, say, junior and even qualified nurses on the one hand, and general practitioners and dentists on the other is undeniable. This comes originally from the length of training that was perceived necessary for the various professions, but as jobs such as nursing and medical technology become more and more specialized, longer training is required and increasingly involves degree level courses. Then the differentials themselves may become more obvious sources of dissatisfactions which in turn may create tensions in relationships between members of multi-disciplinary teams.

With salaries goes status, and both will provide satisfactions particularly to the professions at the top of the health hierarchy. The latter reflects (we refuse to say inevitably) the usual sex differences, with a preponderance of males in the higher paid, higher status jobs at the top of the triangle, and predominantly females in the lower status professions. Although this pattern is repeated within each individual profession, the overall effect is to produce very distinct sex differences between them which is likely to create variety in the experiences of strain.

Despite the fact that many health service jobs require shiftwork, there are clearly differences between the demands placed upon the different professions concerned. For example, jobs such as nursing, physiotherapy and surgery make far more physical demands than social work or general practice. Moreover the number of hours worked by individuals, and the amount of patient contact involved, varies enormously.

On the other side of the coin, the satisfactions gained through the ability to help relieve suffering and illness and to save life will vary enormously according to both the role played and the types of patient contact that is involved. Thus Parkes (1982) showed the differences in perceived strain in nurses moving between surgical and medical wards and female and male patients. These differences are likely to be even greater when one compares the satisfactions involved in work with mentally handicapped adults held in security hospitals compared say, with the high turnover and bustle of a maternity ward.

Because of this huge variety of jobs gathered under the umbrella title of 'the health professions', there will obviously be a large number of apparent gaps in any book which attempts to consider the stressors and strains experienced by their members. To tackle, for example, the current difficulties in nursing alone would require some dozen chapters to look at intensive care, psychiatric, health visiting, midwifery, cancer care, renal units, surgery, and so on. Rather than be too general in our coverage of each profession, we have chosen to represent a cross-section of groups to illustrate the problems and satisfactions currently emphasized by each, and to tackle in more depth the problems of one profession, medicine, in order to illustrate wider issues which will apply to some extent to each profession; for example, training, legal liability, the position of women, physical demands and life-and-death decisions, mental illness, and so on.

We are aware of the professions unrepresented specifically by this book—physiotherapy, clinical psychology, occupational therapy, radiography, several branches of nursing, etc.—but hope that many of the issues they face and the research issues involved in their assessment bear sufficient similarity to other professions treated in the book that conclusions can be drawn about these 'missing' professions. Thus Part I of the book looks at general issues of stress in health care via a detailed look at the medical profession; Part II looks at the particular stressors and strains of a variety of other health professions; and Part III considers the ways financial cut-backs create organizational stress for all health workers, and describes methods to introduce such changes with fewer deleterious results.

REFERENCES

Broadbent, D. E. (1985). The clinical impact of job design, *British Journal of Clinical Psychology*, **24**, 33-44.
Caplan, R. D., Cobb, S., French, J. R. P., Jr., Van Harrison, R. and Pinneau, S. R. (1975). *Job Demands and Worker Health*, National Institute of Occupational Safety and Health, Washington DC.
Cartwright, L. K. (1978). Career satisfaction and role harmony in a sample of young women physicians, *Journal of Vocational Behaviour*, **12**, 184-96.
Cohen, S. and Wills, T. A. (1985). Stress, social support and the buffering hypothesis, *Psychological Bulletin*, **98**, 310-57.
Depue, R. A. and Monroe, S. M. (1986). Conceptualization and measurement of human disorders in life stress research: the problem of chronic disturbance, *Psychological Bulletin*, **9**, 36-51.
Firth, J. (1985). Personal meanings of occupational stress: cases from the clinic, *Journal of Occupational Psychology*, **58**, 139-48.
Firth, J. and Morrison, L. (1986). What stresses health professionals? A coding system for their answers, *British Journal of Clinical Psychology*, **25**, 309-10.
Firth, J. and Shapiro, D. A. (1986). An evaluation of psychotherapy for job related distress, *Journal of Occupational Psychology*, **59**, 111-19.
Fisher, S. (1986). *Stress and Strategy*, Lawrence Erlbaum Associates, London.
Fletcher, B. (C). and Payne, R. L. (1980). Stress and work: a review and theoretical framework, Part 1, *Personnel Review*, **9**, 1, 19-29.
Friedman, R. C., Bigger, J. T. and Kornfeld, D. S. (1971). The intern and sleep loss, *New England Journal of Medicine*, **285**, 201-3.
Kagan, A. and Levi, F. (1974). Health and environment—psychosocial stimuli: a review, *Social Science and Medicine*, **8**, 225-41.
Karasek, R. J. (1979). Job demands, job decision latitude and mental strain: implications for job redesign, *Administrative Science Quarterly*, **24**, 285-308.
Lawrence, W. G., Cullen, J., Foster, M., Mayer, H., Wisner, A. and De Wolff, C. (1982). *Physical and Psychological Stress at Work*. Report compiled for the European Foundation for the Improvement of Living and Working Conditions.
Lazarus, R. S. (1966). *Psychological Stress and the Coping Process*, McGraw-Hill, New York.
Lazarus, R. and Folkman, S. (1984). *Stress, Appraisal and Coping*, Springer-Verlag, New York.
Malan, D. H. (1979). *Individual Psychotherapy and the Science of Psycho-dynamics*, Butterworths, London.
Maslach, C. (1982). *Burn-out—The Cost of Caring*, Prentice-Hall, Englewood Cliffs.
Menzies, I. E. P. (1960). Nurses under stress, *International Nursing Review*, **7**, 9-16.
Murray, N. (1985). Occupational hazards, *Community Care*, September, 14-15.
Parkes, K. R. (1982). Occupational stress among student nurses: a natural experiment, *Journal of Applied Psychology*, **67**, 784-96.
Payne, R. (1980). Organizational stress and social support. In C. L. Cooper and R. Payne (eds) *Current Concerns in Occupational Stress*, J. Wiley, London.
Payne, R. L. (1986). A longitudinal study of psychological well-being of unemployed men and the mediating effect of neuroticism. SAPU Memo no. 778. Sheffield University.
Stewart, B. E., Meyerowitz, B. E., Jackson, L. E., Yarkin, K. L. and Harvey, J. H. (1982). Psychological stress associated with out-patient oncology nursing, *Cancer Nursing*, **4**, 383-7.
Vaillant, G. (1977). *Adaptation to Life*, Little, Brown, Boston.

PART I

The Medical Profession

Stress in Health Professionals
Edited by R. Payne and J. Firth-Cozens
© 1987 John Wiley & Sons Ltd

Chapter 1
The Stresses of Medical Training

Jenny Firth-Cozens

It has been widely reported that the practice of medicine contains sources of stress which can create risks to the mental health of those who are qualified and to those who are still in training. The stress-related problems encountered by those already qualified—alcohol and drug abuse, divorce, and depression—are described in other parts of this book. This chapter considers the levels of strain and sources of stress within medical education, the ways these sources may interact with the individual student, and the possible role this plays in producing the impaired physician. Finally it considers the ways strain levels may be reduced.

HOW STRAINED ARE MEDICAL STUDENTS?

An unusual feature of studies which estimate strain in the medical profession is that instruments or interviews are often used which provide psychiatric diagnoses rather than those which report simply levels of perceived stress without diagnosis, which are found in studies taking place within other occupations. This sets the area rather separate to the rest of the occupational stress literature (indeed, it is usually reported in medical rather than occupational journals) and makes comparisons between groups more problematic. It also allows reports of medical strain to be described in terms which sound more severe than 'stress' or 'strain'—terms such as 'depression', 'alcoholism', 'hypochondriasis' and 'schizophrenia'.

The difficulties involved both in measuring strain and in agreeing levels of psychiatric illness within a population are as apparent in the medical student literature as they are elsewhere. Thus we find estimations ranging from Heath *et al.* (1958) who reported finding that 75 of 100 cases in a student health service, which saw largely medical students, were schizophrenic; to Saslow (1956) who reported only 4 per cent psychosis in medical students referred for psychotherapy. Whilst part of these differences may be accounted for by appropriate non-referral of psychotic cases for psychotherapy, it is more likely to reflect the general difficulties inherent in making accurate psychiatric diagnoses (Katz, Cole and Lowry, 1969). In studies which report upon the general population of medical students, estimations of psychiatric levels of distress range from that of Mitchell *et al.* (1983) who found that first year medical students taking part in their study had scale averages which were within the normal range on all measures; to Lloyd and Gartrell (1984) who reported up to one-quarter could be estimated as suffering from a level of distress equalling some form of psychiatric morbidity. This wide range of findings may be due to different means of assessment, to differences in populations, to low response rates and to differences between medical schools.

Assessment of strain in medical students has been by psychiatric interview or questionnaire, by general well-being questionnaires, by analyses of student health records, or by instruments specifically designed to measure feelings of stress within this particular population. Saslow (1956) reported the interviewing by a psychiatry lecturer of one entire year of students. Following these interviews a number of them referred themselves for 'obviously needed psychotherapy' and these, added to those already receiving psychotherapy, represented 26 per cent of the course. The interviewing was not designed as an evaluation and it is possible that it stimulated a need which may otherwise not have surfaced. On the other hand, as the author points out, the fact that the initial interviews were not directed to case-finding may have resulted in the proportion of students requesting treatment being an under-estimation of real need. The estimate is, however, very similar to Bojar (1971) who reported that 25 per cent of students seek psychiatric help before graduation from medical school.

After the entire class had volunteered as subjects, Pitts, Winokur and Stewart (1961) gave structured psychiatric interviews to a random selection of 40 students, all but five being male, at their medical school. They found that six (15 per cent) of these students received a psychiatric diagnosis including manic-depressive cases, anxiety reaction and chronic alcoholism with histories ranging from six months to twelve years.

That so many of the students in the Pitts *et al.* study volunteered and that even six of them were open enough to describe their symptoms (and the psychiatric histories of their families) to a member of the faculty, shows that in the United States, even in 1961, there was a climate of acceptance towards such problems, possibly greater than that persisting in other countries. In Britain, for example, Salmons (1983) consulted medical student records for the past 25 years at one university and found that only 2.4 per cent had been reported as developing a psychiatric disorder severe enough to cause loss of time from the course, and 1 per cent required hospitalization. She notes, however, that total psychiatric morbidity was likely to be considerably higher since students are often treated for their problems in ways which may not be entered on student records.

Lloyd and Gartrell (1984) used the Hopkins Symptom Checklist (HSCL) to identify the extent of psychiatric symptomatology, or 'distress', within their medical school. Of the 39 per cent of students who replied to their questionnaire, levels of distress were reported around the midpoint between those found in the general population and those of psychiatric patients. Scores were particularly elevated on the scales of obsessive-compulsive symptomatology and interpersonal sensitivity. These areas may reflect true morbidity; alternatively they may be seen as an almost inevitable part of a medical role: checking and re-checking where a mistake may mean death, and being sensitive to the constant face-to-face evaluation of both staff and patients. Correlations between the HSCL and a questionnaire of perceived stress covering various areas of the medical student role were high (0.59) indicating that the psychiatric measures and those of stress as found in the bulk of the occupational literature, were highly related. The authors concluded that their findings were congruent with earlier reports such as those mentioned above, and estimated that between 15 and 25 per cent of medical students met the criteria for a psychiatric diagnosis.

Against these findings comes the report by Mitchell et al. (1983), mentioned earlier, that first year students' mean scores on three psychiatric questionnaires (the MMPI, the Beck Depression Inventory and the State-Trait-Anxiety Measure) were all within the normal range. The difficulty with this study, as with many of the other questionnaire surveys, is that response rates were low, at around 38 per cent, only one university was investigated, and mean scores tend to obscure the possibility that a larger than normal proportion of students may be suffering uncomfortably high levels of symptomatology.

These criticisms were to some extent tackled in a longitudinal study by Firth (1986) who paid fourth year medical students at three British provincial universities £2 to complete a large questionnaire which included the 12-item version of the General Health Questionnaire (GHQ-12), a measure of perceived strain used in a number of occupational studies. This measure can be used both to assess and compare average levels of distress within and between populations and as a means of estimating proportions of psychiatric cases—those who would be likely to receive a psychiatric diagnosis in a clinical interview (Henderson et al., 1979; Banks, 1983). She obtained 318 replies, a response rate of 78.5 per cent, perhaps because of the small payment or perhaps due to what appeared to be a distinct concern in a large number of students that the question of strain in both students and doctors should begin to be tackled in the UK. Despite this the author, who is clinically trained, received several notes written on the backs of questionnaires requesting help, outside of the faculty, for symptoms which often seemed severe. It appeared that the toleration of psychiatric symptomatology within the medical profession is still presumed, at least by some students, to be low.

The author found that mean strain levels amongst medical students (11.66 on the GHQ-12) were considerably higher than comparable groups within the normal population (8.67). More important was the finding that, using a highly conservative cut-off score as an estimation of psychiatric caseness, 30 per cent of students fell into this category compared with 9.1 per cent found in a comparable sample of young employed men and women. The three universities produced significantly different mean scores, with the largest faculty producing the highest mean (12.24), but the proportion of 'cases' at each establishment, though following the pattern of these overall means, did not differ significantly. Although these results cannot be generalized to all students, the differences between these schools were small and this negates to some extent the possibility that the students or the courses were atypical. The high return rate of this study makes its findings particularly important, though a recent epidemiological survey found that those who did not respond tended to be more depressed than those who did (Vernon, Roberts and Lees, 1984).

The results of this study are very much in line with those of Lloyd and Gartrell (1984), of Saslow (1956) and others over the years, despite differences in methodology and response rates. It is, however, possible that all these reports are simply illustrations of high strain levels in students as a whole rather than in medical students alone. Entering university is usually the first step away from the parental home and with it come disturbances to social support, to eating and sleeping patterns, to social and sexual pressures, on top of the demand for sustained intellectual work. It is a time of both physical and emotional transition and, as such, many of the psychosocial disturbances that are picked up by psychiatric assessment may be no more than 'normal' response to such transitions rather than any actual morbidity.

Few studies exist which compare medical to other groups of students, possibly because the programmes followed by different graduate and professional groups are so very different. However, Heins, Fahey and Leiden (1984), comparing reactions to a variety of common student stressors such as 'time stress', 'fear of failure', 'future career' and 'competition', found that medical students perceived these areas as not significantly more stressful than their peers in law or psychology or chemistry. At the same time, medical students did report having less sleep, and less time for recreation, for personal care and to spend with friends than any of the other groups of students. Unfortunately, the authors did not use any standardized test to see whether the groups were clinically different in any way.

Saslow, Counts and Du Bois (1951) reported that while up to 25 per cent of medical student classes were found to require psychiatric assistance, by the same test 18 per cent of dental students and 23 per cent of entering freshmen were similarly identified. They concluded that there were no major differences between student groups at their university.

Contrary to these findings, Bjorksten *et al.* (1983) compared medical students at their university with other health orientated student groups (dentists, pharmacists, nurses and allied professions) and found the medical students perceiving a wide range of problems significantly more intensely than the other groups. Similarly, in a previously unreported pilot study of 44 psychology students, Firth found that mean GHQ-12 scores for this group were above those of the general population but lower than those of the medical students referred to earlier ($t = 1.57$, $p < 0.06$), and that the percentage of potential psychiatric cases within the group was significantly lower than the medical students ($\chi^2 = 6.95$, $p < 0.01$). It seems from these studies that medical students suffer similar problems to other students, but suffer more intensely.

Evidence of student strain has also been provided by data showing alcohol and drug abuse, and it has been suggested that education concerning their use during training may lower the rates for later physician impairment (AMA Council on Mental Health, 1973). The availability of drugs to young physicians linked with the need to be awake or asleep at irregular hours would on the face of it make them a particularly vulnerable group. However, here again the literature is far from conclusive.

Differences between universities are, it seems, large: Lipp *et al.* (1972) in a survey of four schools found that between 16 per cent in Nebraska to 70 per cent in San Francisco had used marijuana at some time, and this range is very illustrative of surveys overall (McAuliffe, Rohman and Wechsler, 1984). This emphasizes the need in all studies of stress in the health professions generally to sample a range of centres rather than just one.

Thomas, Luber and Smith (1977), in a cross-sectional study of medical students from one mid-western university, classified 10 per cent to be problem drinkers with drinking patterns fairly consistent over the years. So far as drug use was concerned, about a quarter of their senior students felt it to be definitely a problem among medical students; 10 per cent of students reported using hashish over 12 times and 5 per cent amphetamines over 12 times; 4 per cent reported receiving treatment for drug problems. While 18 per cent of freshmen used tobacco, this proportion had increased to 40 per cent by their senior years. With a response rate of only 35 per cent and only one university being studied, it is difficult to generalize from these figures; however, since non-respondents have been reported as having more pathology than respondents (Vernon, Roberts and Lee, 1984), and since mid-western universities seem to show lower levels than those in New York or the west coast, and since drug and alcohol use is likely to be under-estimated from a social desirability viewpoint, the results may well be conservative and certainly appear to be in line with other studies surveyed by McAuliffe *et al.* (1984). However, they do not answer the question of whether or not medical students are particularly at risk when compared with other student groups.

In a comparative study between samples of medical and law students' use of marijuana, Slaby, Lieb and Schwartz (1972), found no differences between the groups. Similarly in a cross-sectional survey of alcohol and drug use in samples of physicians and students, it was found that both groups showed little difference from non-medical populations and medical students clearly drank less than most other student professional groups (McAuliffe, Rohman and Wechsler, 1984). On the whole the authors did not find strain to be significantly related to drinking, and considered that it may have been emphasized too strongly in explaining later physician impairment. They concluded that young physicians and medical students were healthy non-smokers and generally light drinkers.

Drinking, however, takes time and it has been shown that medical students have very little spare time compared with other student groups (Heins, Fahey and Leiden, 1984). The administration of drugs, on the other hand, can be extremely fast and in this way could be seen as a greater risk than alcohol, especially when linked to their later availability either by self-prescription or because of high professional incomes. Drug use trends tend to follow fashion and there is no reason why medical students should be immune to this. However until recently, it was apparently assumed by most researchers that opiate use was unlikely. In one of the few studies which did address the issue, Rochford, Grant and La Vigne (1977) reported that 7 per cent of freshmen medical students in their survey had tried opiates at least once. More recently, McAuliffe, Rohman and Wechsler, (1984) found the percentage to have increased among both students and young physicians, and medical students were as likely or more likely to use opiates than other professional students. Cocaine was found to be the second most commonly used recreational drug by both medical and nursing students and by young physicians, with up to 21 per cent having tried it. These proportions were consistent with impaired-physician committee reports of cocaine-addicted physicians.

Overall, the conclusions of McAuliffe, Rohman and Wechsler, (1984) were that drug use in this population 'should not be viewed with great alarm'. However, they point out that their recreational drug use has increased substantially over the past 20 years and the use of opiates and cocaine make the risks of addiction greater, especially in a population where self-prescription will be available. The accessibility of these drugs to young physicians together with the worldwide increase in heroin and cocaine abuse, makes it particularly important for future surveys to continue to seek data in this area.

Suicide rates have been reported as being particularly high in students (Parnell, 1951), but their use as an indicator of the strain within a professional group is fraught with difficulties similar to those discussed in other chapters of this book; the principal one being the relatively small sizes of the groups concerned. In her 25-year survey of psychiatric morbidity in the Birmingham medical school, Salmons (1983) found only three suicides, all men, which is close to the figure Rook (1959) gives for students generally at seven non-Oxbridge universities. However, in the States, Pepitone-Arreola-Rockwell, Rockwell and Core (1981) reported elevated suicide rates in women medical students of three to four times that of age-mates in the general population. Hamilton *et al.*'s (1983) study of suicide in law students (described more fully in Cartwright's chapter) provides some contrast to this by finding that the rates of suicide for both male and female law students were very low, significantly more so than their age-mates in the general population.

In conclusion there is considerable evidence that medical students are suffering levels of distress which are higher than those of the general population. Moreover, there are some indications that this strain may be higher than that suffered by students generally.

SOURCES OF STRESS

Stress is seen in a transactional or 'ecological' sense (Huebner, Royer and Morrel, 1981) as a mismatch between an individual's perceived and actual capabilities, and the perceived and actual demands of the environment. Reductions to strain can therefore be achieved either at the environmental or the individual level. This section considers the sources of stress that medical students see existing within their roles.

Medical students are subject to all the stressors of other student groups: examinations, information overload, financial difficulties, and career worries. However, they perceive these problems to be of greater intensity than do other student health professionals (Bjorksten et al., 1983). On top of these, they are subject to areas unique to their training: they are under constant face-to-face evaluation; involved with death, disease and suffering; confronted with difficult ethical issues; and expected to perform at times intimate physical examinations of patients at an age when their own sexual development is still relatively immature (Mudd and Siegel, 1969). Moreover, they are on duty for longer hours and take far fewer holidays. Certainly medical students report themselves to be subject to more sources of stress than other students (Alexander and Haldane, 1979).

A number of studies have considered the sources of stress in medical school, some by asking the students to name the stressors (Huebner, Royer and Moore, 1981; Alexander and Haldane, 1979; Firth, 1986) and others providing questionnaires compiled from other studies or from stressors named by those attending student counselling services (Coburn and Jovaisas, 1975; Lloyd and Gartrell, 1983).

Huebner, Royer and Morrel (1981) used a 'brainstorming' session by a group of students and staff to provide lists of situations identified as stressful. These lists plus those of previous research were pooled and consolidated to produce an inventory. It was found that for students overall a shortage of time for family and friends and information overload were scored and ranked as the most problematic areas, followed by the difficulty involved in determining an acceptable level of performance. For women students, the lack of available role models was by far the greatest source of stress.

Generally, Huebner et al. found that pre-clinical years were reported as less problematic than clinical years. In Britain, Alexander and Haldane (1979) also reported first year as the least stressful with the most difficult period being second and third years, the transition period from pre-clinical to clinical work. In a previous study at the same university, Alexander, Ogston and Douglas (1972) had described students' first experiences with patients as 'extremely stressful'.

Time pressure and overload were found to be important areas of stress in a number of other studies (for example, Edwards and Zimet, 1976; Lloyd and Gartrell, 1983), and certainly medical students report having less time for all recreational, personal and social activities than other groups of students (Heins, Fahey and Leiden, 1984). In Britain, Firth (1986), coding fourth year students' descriptions of recent stressful events within their training, found that less than 3 per cent of incidents concerned overwork. However, this may be because the wording of the question, in terms of 'an event', precluded those which had become a part of life, and which to some extent are experienced by all students. The events described were, on the whole, more illustrative of the especial difficulties experienced by medical students alone.

In this study, students were given questionnaires at the commencement of their psychiatry placements, and thus the largest source of stress reported (20 per cent) concerned talking (or failing to talk) to patients, 90 per cent of whom were psychiatric. Descriptions were often vivid and reflected both a fear of madness, often linked with identification, and a sense of powerlessness and frustration that these patients were so difficult to help. The following answers illustrate this category of event.

> Talking to psychiatric patients—rather frightening—I've tended to get rather anxious as to how I would cope; I have difficulty (more than I have had with physically ill patients) in not letting myself get down and to brood about psychiatric patients and to shake it off, when I am away from the wards. Psychiatry tends to make me introspective and anxious about myself. Also, I am not patient with my own progress at learning to cope with new situations.

> Meeting a chronic schizophrenic girl of my own age who seems to have so little going for her in life. Her mother can no longer cope with her and she rarely is visited by any of her family. I feel I can identify with her at her more lucid times and that she can be an extremely likeable person. The thought that there is so little to offer this girl is upsetting, frustrating and it gives me a feeling of helplessness. With other chronic patients I have met I have been able to accept their situation but being able to identify with this girl makes this a problem for me.

Although a few students described incidents where talking to non-psychiatric patients was a problem, this category on the whole reflected the current placement. In another section of the questionnaire which asked students what they liked best about their role as medical students, 'talking to patients' was the largest category (37.7 per cent), and this to some extent might explain the frustration experienced when students were faced with psychiatric patients who often far from welcomed their attention.

'Effects on Private Life' was the second most reported category (11.9 per cent) and reflected reports of strained or broken relationships, being treated as 'a doctor', difficulties with finances, or having to live in degrading hospital conditions. For example:

On a weekend visit home I was approached by an uncle who told me that he hadn't been well and had passed blood per rectum. He suggested he had piles but was seeking some reassurance from me. I felt too close to the situation to raise the possibility of cancer and felt that I'd been put on the spot as a *'doctor'*.

I was competing with a friend for a house job and it was a problem deciding whether to discuss and aid each other or to keep any helpful information/thoughts to myself.

This was the only area that significant differences occurred between the proportion of men (13.4 per cent) and women (7.9 per cent) describing an event within the category. Perhaps women have given up so much of their 'private life' already in order to take part in such a long training, that the more 'trivial' day-to-day effects upon them are no longer seen worthy of reporting.

Events which fell into the category of 'Presenting Cases' represented 11.6 per cent of the total and rather illustrated the popular image of the medical student struggling to perform on ward rounds, usually with inadequate knowledge, a frowning consultant and competitive peers. For example:

Whilst on Professional Surgical Unit each student had to give a 10 minute talk on a subject set by a doctor from the unit and present it to students and doctors. Following the talk comments were made by the staff of PSU which were mainly derogatory regardless of effort and content. This was a problem in that my talk was 3 weeks before our 3rd year exams and took much preparation. I was appalled at the way senior staff members criticised our efforts. I approached it with the impression that seeing I had made some effort I would cope. However, I was criticised, as expected, to some extent, but was prepared to ignore it as I realised the rat-race that takes place in this department.

A ward-round with a rather old-fashioned physician, with houseman, registrar, senior house officer, sister plus nurses. It was stressful because I was constantly asked questions (very difficult to answer even when you know the answer) and being humiliated for not knowing or giving the correct response.

The final large category (10.2 per cent) was 'Dealing with Death and Suffering', where events produced feelings of inadequacy and powerlessness. For example:

Talking to and checking in terminally ill patient one day. Tending to his incontinence. Next day seeing patient within half an hour of his death on the ward. I was unhappy that anyone should die in such a distressed and uncomfortable manner, and in such noisy and impersonal surroundings. There seemed to be no dignity, or peace, in dying in hospital. Why did terminally ill patient die in hospital and not peacefully at home?

Although a question concerning difficulties in coping with death and suffering is often included in questionnaire studies, it is not reported as being a significant problem to students. It seems, however, from this study, that if students are asked simply to report events, this category represents one of the main difficulties. Perhaps this methodology allows defences to be lowered and real fears to be discussed somewhat better than direct questions (Firth and Morrison, 1986).

Three areas of the coding scheme—Relationships with Consultants (5.0 per cent), Relationships with Other Doctors (3.3 per cent), and Feeling the Medical Professional Has Failed (4.3 per cent)—produced the highest mean level of feelings and in some ways reflect a single theme of conflict that they were becoming part of a profession and being taught by mentors at times far less than perfect. These descriptions seemed to represent a struggle to retain ideals and to ward off the process of socialization which had perhaps affected those above them. For example:

> A ward round, on a surgical firm I was attached to, was carried out in such a way that I felt very annoyed with the consultant and distressed for the patients concerned. The ward round consisting of about 9 people (5 medical students) went round the patients, and left a trail of very upset, worried people behind it. The consultant, casually broke very serious news to several patients, without showing any concern nor waiting to answer questions. One patient was told he would probably have to have his leg amputated, which obviously upset him, but he tried to pretend not to be bothered and yet as we moved on to the next bed, he hung his head and started to cry. It was a problem in that it was done so callously and that the whole group of us walked on leaving him. I was dying to drop back and comfort several patients especially the one mentioned above. But what worried me was the sudden impact that the consultant was not atypical.

> Attitude of certain doctors particularly consultants of the 'old school' towards patients. In particular a consultant making a patient look a fool due to his assumption of knowledge of the patient of the way in which a CNS examination is carried out. The patient was upset, and I was furious and upset. It aroused hatred in me towards the doctor and sadness that it happens all too often.

The other significant finding in the coding of events, was that 17.7 per cent of male students compared with 3.2 per cent of females reported having no stressful event occurring in the last month. Since women students were no more stressed overall than men, this seems to suggest either that women are more open in recognizing and reporting stressful incidents, or that they are indeed experiencing more sources of stress within their role, but have learnt to cope with them in a more efficient way than their male counterparts.

In summary, the sources of stress experienced by medical students reflect those of overload and lack of time shared by (but possibly to a greater extent than) most university students, alongside those often special to medical students of powerlessness in the face of death and suffering, constant evaluation and conflicts of idealism. These latter experiences may be shared by others in the health professions, but rarely for so long and with so little chance of recuperation.

INDIVIDUAL DIFFERENCES AND MEDICAL STUDENT STRAIN

Taking strain as the experience of a mismatch between an individual's perceived and actual capabilities, and the perceived and actual demands of the environment, any consideration of ways to reduce this mismatch must also look to the individual factors which help to create it.

In the last decade, medical school populations have included 'minority' populations in sufficient numbers to enable researchers to compare the experience of stress between different groups. Thus studies have considered the sources and levels of stress between men and women, between different ethnic groups or classes, the married and unmarried, students of different ages, etc. One of the first of these studies reported in 1975 found significant positive relationships between strain and several individual variables including sex, minority status, birth order, age and marital status (Coburn and Jovaisas, 1975). These and other areas of individual differences will be considered in this section.

Are women students more stressed than men?

Most US studies have reported higher levels of perceived strain in female students when compared with their male counterparts, whether they report use of mental health services (Davidson, 1978), or assessments by questionnaire (Lloyd and Gartrell, 1981; 1984). Since these differences do not appear on intake (Notman, Salt and Nadelson, 1984) but rather tend to appear and increase during the first half year (Lloyd and Gartrell, 1981) it seems they are due, at least in part, to the medical student environment itself.

In Britain, however, Firth (1985a) reported no differences in strain levels between male and female students in her sample. Similarly in the Salmon (1983) survey, no significant differences appeared in psychiatric morbidity and no female student was reported as committing suicide (although the numbers for both sexes may be artificially low since for much of the period covered by the survey, suicide remained an illegal act and so may have been reported as accidental death). This is in sharp contrast to the Pepitone-Arreola-Rockwell *et al.* (1981) study reported earlier, which found that the suicide rate of women medical students was up to 4 times the rate of age-mates. There does appear, therefore, to be a cross-cultural difference in the experience and perceptions of strain by women students in these two countries. Lloyd and Gartrell (1981) found that their women students reported more role conflict and described their families as being less supportive of their career choice. Perhaps therefore the differences between the countries lies in the fact that university education is on the whole free in Britain, unlike that of the United States, and so any personal conflicts about career choice will at least not be exacerbated by parental attitudes that 'it's a waste of money to educate a girl'.

Murphy, Nadelson and Notman (1984) found no differences between the sexes on the number of life events occurring prior to entry into medical school, nor on most of the types of stressful experiences occurring within the first year. However, female medical students were significantly more likely to report medical career conflicts than male students. Almost half the women in their sample reported stresses associated with being female at medical school, and this was particularly felt by those with a physician parent who, the authors suggest, may have entered with higher expectations of themselves or their schools.

Many of the issues raised by Cartwright in Chapter 4 are of course relevant to female medical students as well as to practitioners. The conflicts that face them concerning career and family (Murphy, Nadelson and Notman, 1984) the prejudice, and the lack of female role models at the top of the specialty (Huebner, Royer and Morrel, 1981), are all singular stressors facing the woman training for a medical career.

Ethnicity and socio-economic status

Coburn and Jovaisas (1975) reported that those of their students who were of minority status or lower SES backgrounds reported higher academic stress, though fewer social stresses such as loneliness. Nine years later Murphy, Nadelson and Notman (1984) found no differences between ethnic and SES groupings on the number of stressful life events occurring prior to entry, though not surprisingly those from minority ethnic groups showed a greater proportion of race-related problem areas (such as prejudice and danger of attack) outside of medical school. There were no differences between the groups on any of the stress variables within medical school, apart from 84 per cent of the minority students mentioning race-related stressors such as a lack of role models and general prejudice.

Career Choice

This area has already been touched upon in regard to the conflicts that present to women in terms of career or family. In addition, Schwartz *et al.* (1978) report findings which might suggest that students whose inclinations, had they not studied medicine, may have led them into a literary or artistic career, are particularly vulnerable to the signs and symptoms of strain and to 'the process of disillusionment'. These students expressed significantly more suicidal ideation and feelings of depersonalization, and grew generally more disillusioned with medicine than those who would have pursued a scientific career had they not studied medicine.

Early experience

It would not be surprising if a medical student who had lost a parent in the past few years through heart disease would find it particularly distressing to work as part of a cardiac arrest team. Equally understandable would be the upset felt at a consultant's over-harsh criticism by a student who had continually felt unable to meet his or her father's high standards. Such unresolved life experiences can easily be seen as creating stress when they interact with some aspect of the occupational role, and it has been argued that it does not matter how early these experiences occur so long as they are in some sense unresolved (Malan, 1979; Firth, 1985).

The complicated interactions that may occur between life history and the particular stressors of the clinical years are described in four case reports by Sacks et al. (1980). For example, one case described a woman who had an intense anxiety reaction when caring for a psychiatric patient whose mother was a professional. The conflicts and guilt that had arisen for her were linked to her own mother's giving up of a career to look after her, and her own determination to be a 'superwoman' physician, wife and mother. She feared her professional strivings might cause her to be an inadequate mother like her patient's. A second case described a male student who had panic attacks and became depressed and suicidal during his obstetrics-gynaecology placement. He subsequently reported feeling enraged at children's families during his paediatric clerkship and 'related this anger to his own family's neglect during his recent psychiatric difficulties, when they refused to be involved in his treatment'. The anger that he felt throughout his life towards his mother in particular had intensified during his obstetrics-gynaecology placement when he had to care for older women.

Two empirical studies have linked physician impairment to early relationships. In the Precursors Study begun in the 1940s by Thomas at the Johns Hopkins Hospital, it was reported (Thomas and Duszynski, 1974) that physicians who had subsequently committed suicide, suffered mental illness, or died from tumours, as students were more likely to describe their parents as lacking closeness. Similarly, early experience was related to later impairment by Vaillant, Sobowale and McArthur (1972).

The types of experiences which may interact with later occupational factors to create distress have been described by Firth (1985) in a case study paper on the personal meanings of occupational stress. These meanings may relate to any of a number of early individual experiences such as sibling rivalry, loss of a parent or sibling, conflicts over sexuality, feeling responsible for a parent's happiness, and anger and guilt at feeling loved only for what he or she could achieve. The empirical investigation of these perceived and actual early experiences is being explored longitudinally in medical students by Firth (1984).

It is suggested by some (for example, Malan, 1979) that the choice of a helping career itself is related to childhood experiences and may involve some sense of reparation or 'making good' of early traumas (Klein, 1957). Paris and Frank

(1983) have investigated this concept empirically by considering the number of illnesses and legal problems within the child's family for medical students and law students. They found that medical students were more likely to have experienced illness in the family during childhood and law students to have experienced legal problems. If it is true therefore that some medical students have unconsciously chosen their career to make good early wrongs, it is likely that they will find the wrongs persist and strain and disillusionment may well ensue. Vaillant, Sobowale and McArthur (1972) found that physicians were especially likely to have aspects of psychopathology if they had experienced an unhappy childhood. He considered these disturbed physicians had attempted to redress their own unmet needs by becoming the caretakers of others, perhaps at the expense of themselves.

WHAT IS TO BE DONE?

It has been remarked that medical training is a form of initiation rite, necessary to strengthen the fortitude of students so that they can operate under future pressure, to teach them discipline and sacrifice and to eliminate those unable to cope (Reidbord, 1983). Like many such rites some of the initiates may at times see the process as having its irrational aspects and being unnecessarily punishing. Although this was clear from some of the descriptions by students in the study by Firth (1986), there were also students who felt that the symptoms of strain were unacceptable in those training to be practitioners. For example:

> My colleagues and I have often discussed stress, alcoholism, suicide, depression, etc., in doctors and feel that much could be done in weeding out such people in the early stages of training, i.e. first year of Medical School. Let's face it; people who need handfuls of Valium to cope with an anatomy viva are in my opinion not really the type of person to undertake a career in such a stressful field without problems arising.

In the study by Alexander and Haldane (1979) the final year students in their sample unanimously felt that 'learning to cope with stress is an important ingredient in the training of a doctor'. Most of those involved in the training would undoubtedly agree with this; however, it is important that this essential feature of a medical education should in some form be taught, rather than left solely to a 'make-or-break' routine. If for no other reason than to increase academic or clinical excellence, it also seems important to reduce the environmental stressors to a level where they do not have a detrimental effect on the principal aspects of training, especially since more than half of Alexander and Haldane's sample considered that stress interfered with their work. In their survey they also found that: 92 per cent thought that students experiencing stress were not spotted sufficiently quickly by staff; 66 per cent agreed that faculty was not sufficiently interested in staff-student relationships; and 65 per cent that staff were insufficiently sensitive to the personal needs of students. Sixty per cent of students (particularly the men) felt that faculty should have shown more interest in those who had had to discontinue.

A variety of ways have been used, or at least suggested, in order to reduce the levels of strain experienced by a large proportion of the students. Some of these are aimed at altering the environmental stressors in some way, while others are intended to help the individual students find better ways of coping. In order to reduce the stress-inducing mismatch referred to earlier, both individual and environmental aspects should be tackled.

Selection

The problems of students who are finding it difficult to cope can of course be reduced in the future by more stringent selection procedures which look to personal strengths as well as academic, and this has been advocated in a survey of directors of admissions (Willer, Keill and Isada, 1984). The possibility of using psychiatrists to interview potential students, and the use of standardized psychological tests was suggested. However, unless it is proved that students who particularly suffer from stress make poor practitioners, it may be more humanizing for medical training to make attempts to heal its own casualties to some extent. That the more stressed student should be helped rather than excluded is suggested by the findings of Firth-Cozens (1987) in her follow-up of students who were now in their first post-graduate year. These showed that the 22 per cent of junior doctors consistently showing distress at both times of assessment were significantly more empathic than the 37 per cent with consistently low scores. Those for whom such help is insufficient are still able to choose to leave medicine, and the current drop-out rate in the US is around 1.8 per cent (Crowley, Etzel and Petersen, 1983) compared with 9 per cent in 1966 (Johnson and Hutchins, 1966). This reduction may be due to more rigorous selection, to better teaching and a reduction in stress-inducing factors, or to more toleration of difficulties on the part of the profession.

Environmental stressors

A shortage of time for socializing and having pleasure, as well as for rest, has been described by a number of reports to be the most difficult aspect of a student's life. As in any initiation rite, those who have completed the course often have increased enthusiasm in administering it to novices; however, while medical educators may be able to show that it is inalterably necessary for students to work so intensely for so long, it is necessary too that they should continually question this and attempt to find other methods. Reidbord (1983) suggests that, since medicine is a lifelong study, and it will always be impossible to know everything, it may sensibly reduce the students' hours and make their learning more enjoyable if they are taught, as Dr Johnson suggested, to know where to find information on a subject rather than to know the subject for themselves.

In response to the enormous amount of non-academic information that students need concerning courses, teachers, clerkships, accommodation, and so on, one university set up a student-run Medical Student Resource Centre to provide up to date student schedules and information (Weinstein, 1983). An additional approach is to provide facilities so that students can easily socialize during their free time, albeit briefly. This makes the leisure itself more rewarding and enhances social contact through the working time. Adsett (1968) recommended that schools provide good dining facilities and recreation areas in places easily accessible to both clinical and preclinical students, so that the younger group is exposed to and helped by the older one and the transition is not so fearful.

Inadequate feedback featured as a stressor in the Huebner, Royer and Morrel (1981) study. With such constant evaluation, it is especially necessary that some form of continued feedback be given to students both to enhance their academic and clinical work and to reduce the stress of uncertainty that arises, especially when evaluations are so often public and subject to all the ambiguities of multi-channel messages. The provision of regular staff–student functions may provide an important avenue for reducing the strain of evaluation and enables feedback to flow both ways informally. Formal provision for feedback to staff can come about by letting students participate directly in faculty decision-making and Weinstein (1983) reports the success of a committee on well-being of medical students and house staff convened to investigate the difficulties that arise and to influence the learning climate so that the educational experience might be enhanced.

Difficulties in dealing with death and suffering, including having to inflict pain upon others, although not reported as a significant area of stress in any of the US questionnaire studies, was a major reported area of stress in the Firth (1986) study which may indicate a source denied when asked about directly. Field (1984) considered that teaching on and around the subject of death had improved over the past few years but still may be largely ineffective. Lectures and large groups are unlikely to allow students to explore their natural fears about death, and Field suggests that this can best take place in small groups.

Teaching coping skills

Large group methods to teach ways of handling anxiety have been frequently used within the occupational field, with workers being taught the symptoms of stress, and shown ways of relaxation, anxiety management and methods of cognitive restructuring (Murphy, 1984). While their overall effectiveness in such a setting is open to doubt (Ganster et al., 1982), it is probable that this method would relieve students who recognize the symptoms in themselves and let them know that effective psychological methods are available to reduce their problems. This then can be achieved by small group situations and by student counselling services. Teaching students ways of handling anxiety would relieve the stress experienced in presenting on ward rounds and generally facing difficult and demanding situations, and methods of cognitive restructuring might be an effective way of handling the feelings of friction that arise in confrontations with consultants and other senior doctors. These methods and others have been used successfully to reduce psychological symptoms in a group of professional people suffering problems at work (Firth and Shapiro, 1986).

The need for a counselling service within a university has been described by a number of writers (for example, Lucas, 1976; Adsett, 1968) and most students in Alexander and Haldane's sample (1979) felt that such a service would be a very useful facility. Almost all of these agreed, however, that faculty should not be informed of the student's use of the service unless he or she wished for this. At the time of the study there was no such service and half of the students had approached a friend for help in time of difficulties, a quarter had used a family member, 7 per cent had consulted with a faculty member and 5 per cent with student health. It seems that, for the types of problems that may be related to early experience, professional counselling would frequently be necessary. If no such service is provided by the university, then all students should be provided with sources of professional help that exist within the locality and are independent of the faculty.

Some earlier reported areas of stress have been reduced, it seems, by changes in society itself. Thus being female or being part of a minority group are no longer so likely to create problems. Despite this, prejudice still exists and a procedure of positive discrimination to ensure that these students have representatives on staff-student committees may be one way of reducing this. Adsett (1968) has stressed the importance for students generally of role models within the faculty and the health service. It seems their lack continues to contribute to the difficulties experienced by these groups of students, and progress on this front is remarkably slow. Notman and Nadelson (1973) have presented a number of recommendations for ways to enable women students both to recognize and to take advantage of the possibilities of all medical careers. They suggest, for example, that flexible residency in all fields should be open to any student.

In conclusion there is no one cause of strain for medical students or for any other group; nor is there any one cure. The issue needs constantly tackling, however, not just for the sake of a better and more humanizing training (Kimball, 1973), but also for the future health of medical practitioners. Medical education takes five or six years of a young person's life and the stress that is involved, even if not severe, can clearly be seen as chronic. Two of the feelings most often aroused by stressful incidents are 'powerlessness' and 'frustration' (Firth, 1986) and, taken over a long period, these may well give rise in some students to the feelings of learned helplessness linked by Seligman (1974) to future depression (Reidbord, 1983). Many of the stressors producing these feelings can be reduced, especially if they are accompanied by a more general acceptance by staff and students that, unless longitudinal studies indicate otherwise, survival of the fittest in medicine may not necessarily be survival of the best.

REFERENCES

Adsett, C. A. (1968). Psychological health of medical students in relation to the medical education process, *Journal of Medical Education*, **43**, 728–34.
Alexander, D. A. and Haldane, J. D. (1979). Medical education: a student perspective, *Journal of Medical Education*, **13**, 336–41.
Alexander, D. A., Ogston, D. and Douglas, A. S. (1972). The influence of personality on student reactions to clinical experience, *Journal of Medical Education*, **47**, 652.
AMA Council on Mental Health (1973). The sick physician: impairment by psychiatric disorders, including alcoholism and drug dependence, *Journal of the American Medical Association*, **223**, 684–7.
Banks, M. H. (1983). Validation of the General Health Questionnaire in a young community sample, *Psychological Medicine*, **13**, 349–53.
Bjorksten, O., Sutherland, S., Miller, C. and Steward, T. (1983). Identification of medical student problems and comparison with those of other students, *Journal of Medical Education*, **58**, 759–67.
Bojar, S. (1971). Psychiatric problems of medical students. In G. B. Blaine and C. C. McArthur (eds), *Emotional Problems of the Student*, Appleton-Century-Crofts, New York.
Coburn, D. and Jovaisas, A. V. (1975). Perceived sources of stress among first-year medical students, *Journal of Medical Education*, **50**, 589–95.
Crowley, A. E., Etzel, S. I. and Petersen, E. S. (1983). Undergraduate medical education, *Journal of the American Medical Association*, **250**, 1509–97.
Davidson, V. M. (1978). Coping styles of women medical students, *Journal of Medical Education*, **53**, 902–7.
Edwards, M. T. and Zimet, C. N. (1976). Problems and concerns among medical students—1975, *Journal of Medical Education*, **51**, 619–25.
Field, D. (1984). Formal instruction in United Kingdom medical schools about death and dying, *Journal of Medical Education*, **18**, 429–34.
Firth, J. A. (1984). Vulnerability to occupational stress in doctors. SAPU memo No. 688.
Firth, J. A. (1985). Personal meanings of occupational stress: cases from the clinic, *Journal of Occupational Psychology*, **58**, 139–48.
Firth, J. A. (1986). Levels and sources of stress in medical students, *British Medical Journal*, **292**, 1177–80.
Firth, J. A. and Morrison, L. (1986). What stresses health professionals? A coding system for their answers, *British Journal of Clinical Psychology*, **25**, 309–10.
Firth, J. A. and Shapiro, D. A. (1986). An evaluation of psychotherapy for job-related distress, *Journal of Occupational Psychology*, **59**, 111–19.

Firth-Cozens, J. A., (1987). Emotional distress in junior house officers, *British Medical Journal*, in press.
Ganster, D. C., Mayes, B. T., Sime, W. E. and Tharp, G. D. (1982). Managing organizational stress: A field experiment, *Journal of Applied Psychology*, **67**, 533–42.
Hamilton, M. J., Pepitone-Arreola-Rockwell, F., Rockwell, D. and Whitlow, C. (1983). Thirty-five law student suicides, *Journal of Psychiatry and Law*, Fall, 335–44.
Heath, R. G., Leach, B. E., Byers, L. W., Wartens, S. and Feighley, C. A. (1958). Pharmacological and biological psychotherapy, *American Journal of Psychiatry*, **114**, 683.
Heins, M., Fahey, S. N. and Leiden, L. I. (1984). Perceived stress in medical, law and graduate students, *Journal of Medical Education*, **59**, 169–79.
Henderson, S., Duncan-Jones, P., Byrne, D. G., Scott, R. and Adcock, S. (1979). Psychiatric disorder in Canberra: a standardised study of prevalence, *Acta Psychiatrica Scandinavia*, **60**, 355–74.
Huebner, L. A., Royer, J. A. and Morrel, J. (1981). The assessment and remediation of dysfunctional stress in medical students, *Journal of Medical Education*, **56**, 547–58.
Johnson, D. G. and Hutchins, E. B. (1966). Doctor or dropout? A study of medical student attrition, *Journal of Medical Education*, **41**, 1107–1269.
Katz, M., Cole, J. O. and Lowry, H. A. (1969). Studies of the diagnostic process, *American Journal of Psychiatry*, **125**, 937–47.
Kimball, C. P. (1973). Medical education as a humanizing process, *Journal of Medical Education*, **48**, 71–77.
Klein, M. (1957). *Love, Hate and Reparation*. London: Tavistock.
Lipp, M., Tinklenberg, J., Benson, S., Melges, F., Taintor, Z. and Peterson, M. (1972). Medical student use of marihuana, alcohol and cigarettes: a study of four schools, *International Journal of Addications*, **7**, 141–52.
Lloyd, C. and Gartrell, N. K. (1981). Sex differences in student mental health, *American Journal of Psychiatry*, **138**, 1346–51.
Lloyd, C. and Gartrell, N. K. (1983). A further assessment of medical student stress, *Journal of Medical Education*, **58**, 964–7.
Lloyd, C. and Gartrell, N. K. (1984). Psychiatric symptoms in medical students, *Comprehensive Psychiatry*, **25**, 552–65.
Lucas, C. J. (1976). Psychological problems of students. *British Medical Journal*, **2**, 1431–3.
McAuliffe, W. E., Rohman, M., Fishman, P., Friedman, R., Wechsler, H., Saboroff, S. H. and Toth, D. (1984). Psychoactive drug use by young physicians, *Journal of Health and Social Behaviour*, **25**, 34–54.
McAuliffe, W. E., Rohman, M. and Wechsler, H. (1984). Alcohol, substance use and other risk-factors of impairment in a sample of physicians-in-training, *Advance in Alcohol and Substance Abuse*, **4**, 67–87.
Malan, D. H. (1979). *Individual Psychotherapy and the Science of Psycho-Dynamics*, Butterworths, London.
Mitchell, R. E., Matthews, J. R., Grandy, T. G. and Lupo, J. V. (1983). The question of stress among first-year medical students, *Journal of Medical Education*, **58**, 367–71.
Mudd, J. W. and Siegel, R. J. (1969). Sexuality—the experience and anxieties of medical students, *New England Journal of Medicine*, **281**, 1397–1403.
Murphy, J. M., Nadelson, C. C. and Notman, M. T. (1984). Factors influencing first-year medical students perceptions of stress, *Journal of Human Stress*, **10**, 165–73.
Murphy, L. R. (1984). Occupational stress management: a review and appraisal, *Journal of Occupational Psychology*, **57**, 1–15.

Notman, M. T. and Nadelson, C. C. (1973). Medicine: a career conflict for women, *American Journal of Psychiatry*, **130**, 1123-7.
Notman, M. T., Salt, P. and Nadelson, C. C. (1984). Stress and adaptation in medical students: who is most vulnerable? *Comprehensive Psychiatry*, **25**, 355-66.
Paris, J. and Frank, H. (1983). Psychological determinants of a medical career, *Canadian Journal of Psychiatry*, **28**, 354-7.
Parnell, R. W. (1951). Mortality and prolonged illness among Oxford undergraduates, *The Lancet*, **1**, 731.
Pepitone-Arreola-Rockwell, F., Rockwell, D. and Core, N. (1981). Fifty-two medical student suicides, *American Journal of Psychiatry*, **138**, 198-201.
Pitts, F. N., Winokur, G. and Stewart, M. A. (1961). Psychiatric syndromes, anxiety symptoms, and response to stress in medical students, *American Journal of Psychiatry*, **118**, 333-40.
Reidbord, S. P. (1983). Psychological perspectives on iatrogenic physician impairment, *The Pharos*, 2-8.
Rochford, J., Grant, I. and La Vigne, G. (1977). Medical students and drugs: further neuropsychological and use pattern considerations, *International Journal of Addictions*, **12**, 1057-65.
Rook, A. (1959). Student suicides, *British Medical Journal*, **1**, 599.
Sacks, M. H., Frosch, W. A., Kesselman, M. and Parker, L. (1980). Psychiatric problems in third-year medical students, *American Journal of Psychiatry*, **137**, 822-5.
Salmons, P. H. (1983). Psychiatric illness in medical students, *British Journal of Psychiatry*, **143**, 505-8.
Saslow, G. (1956). Psychiatric problems of medical students, *Journal of Medical Education*, **31**, 27-33.
Saslow, G., Counts, R. M. and Du Bois, P. H. (1951). Evaluation of a new psychiatric screening test, *Psychosomatic Medicine*. **13**, 244-53.
Schwartz, A. H., Schwartzburg, M., Lieb, J. and Slaby, A. E. (1978). Medical school and the process of disillusionment, *Medical Education*, **12**, 182-5.
Seligman, M. E. P. (1974). Depression and learned helplessness. In R. J. Friedman and M. M. Katz (eds) *The Psychology of Depression: Contemporary Theory and Research*, Winston & Sons, Washington, DC.
Slaby, A., Lieb, J. and Schwartz, A. (1972). Comparative study of the psychosocial correlates of drug use among medical and law students, *Journal of Medical Education*, **47**, 717-23.
Thomas, C. B. and Duszynski, K. R. (1974). Closeness to parents and the family constellation in a prospective study of five disease states: suicide, mental illness, malignant tumor, hypertension and coronary heart disease, *Johns Hopkins Medical Journal*, **134**, 251-70.
Thomas, R., Luber, S. A. and Smith, J. A. (1977). A survey of alcohol and drug use in medical students, *Diseases of the Nervous System*, **38**, 41-3.
Vaillant, G., Sobowale, N. C. and McArthur, C. (1972). Some psychological vulnerabilities of physicians, *New England Journal of Medicine*, **287**, 372-5.
Vernon, S. W., Roberts, R. E. and Lee, E. S. (1984). Ethnic status and participation in longitudinal health studies, *American Journal of Epidemiology*, **119**, 99-113.
Weinstein, H. M. (1983). A committee on well-being of medical students and house staff, *Journal of Medical Education*, **58**, 373-81.
Willer, B., Keill, S. and Isada, C. (1984). Survey of United States and Canadian medical schools on admissions and psychiatrically at-risk students, *Journal of Medical Education*, **59**, 928-36.

Chapter 2
Stress in Physicians

Stephen C. Scheiber

Medicine is a demanding mistress—any doctor who is unable to make the commitment necessary for the patient whenever he is needed is better off in some other field of endeavor. (Heimbach, 1976)

Medical school graduates are taught by instruction and example that the practice of medicine comes first in their lives and that all other obligations are secondary. Many thrive on this singular devotion while others are distressed.

George Bernard Shaw wrote in his preface to the *Doctor's Dilemma* about the long hours doctors must work and the strain caused by it: 'Why the impatient doctors do not become savage and unmanageable and the patient ones imbeciles. Perhaps they do to some extent.' (Shaw, 1931).

Not having personal free time, being on call and carrying a heavy workload were the most prevalent sources of dissatisfaction in the lives of 180 physicians who were alumni of the Case Western Reserve School of Medicine, studied by Mawardi (1979). Time factors were a major source of dissatisfaction in Mechanic's (1975) study of physicians in primary care settings. The adverse effects of time pressures and sleep deprivation as the leading cause of stress among interns and residents have been well documented. Such stresses lead to diminished ability to learn, adverse effects on the delivery of medical care and decreased capacity to respond to urgent problems (McCue, 1985).

Linn, *et al.* (1985) studied 211 physicians on the UCLA faculty: 91 per cent male, 75 per cent clinical faculty and 97 per cent specialists. They found as a group, physicians worked 52 hours per week with academic faculty working longer hours (60 ± 10.2) compared with clinical faculty (49 ± 14.5 hours). On a frequency scale of 1 (never) to 5 (very often), the most frequent source of stress was time pressures (3.2 ± 0.76), with academic faculty being more stressed than clinical faculty (3.45 compared with 3.11; $p = 0.005$).

The pressure of time is only one of many stresses encountered by physicians. For house officers, others that have been identified include financial worries, personal and professional identity issues, alienation from family and social networks, dissatisfaction with marital and family life, continuous dependency status, apprehensions about incompetency and an inability to balance personal and professional demands. (Pfifferling, 1983).

TIME PRESSURES BEGINNING IN POSTGRADUATE TRAINING

A twenty-six-year-old white male resident was on call every other night during a transitional year internship in an American university hospital. He averaged four hours of interrupted sleep and worked a twenty-hour work day when on call throughout the year. Two separate phone calls in the middle of the night while on duty are remembered with residual shame and guilt twenty-one years after successful completion of the internship.

A nurse on an inpatient service called at 2:00 a.m. She described her own addiction to phenobarbital. She rambled incoherently. She recited her story of her problem with drugs. She demonstrated slurred speech. She spoke of being depressed. After approximately one-half hour, she terminated the telephone conversation. When awakening the next morning for duty, the intern could only recall that he had received a call from a nurse about her addiction. He had no recollection of any of his responses. He did not know whether he had recommended seeking help for her problems nor whether he had made any appropriate responses to this cry for help.

This intern later in the same year received a call from a minimal care diagnostic unit from the charge nurse.

She described a patient whom he had never evaluated who was complaining of abdominal pain. The patient had no history of acute medical or surgical problems. The intern advised by phone without seeing the patient that the nurse should administer a non-narcotic analgesic. Two hours later, at 5:00 a.m., the nurse rang the intern again and reported the patient was still complaining of abdominal pain. This time the fatigued intern ordered a narcotic for pain relief, again without seeing the patient. When the intern awoke at 7:00 a.m. and started making his bedside rounds, he learned that the patient was in surgery for a ruptured bowel. The nurse had wisely called the attending physician, who saw the patient, diagnosed the problem, and arranged for the appropriate care.

The intern in each instance felt too ashamed by his sense of dereliction of duty to share his feelings of guilt for not arousing himself from his bed to perform his duties appropriately. The expectation of the intern was that he should be able to perform optimally whenever he was on duty and sleep deprivation was never viewed as reason for failing to perform optimally. Though every other day call is rare today, the work week for residents still exceeds eighty hours per week. McCue (1985) points out that the ritual of overwork relates to the view that the residency years are a time for intensive training for the difficult predicaments that physicians will face in practice. His claim that most practitioners have more time and resources to deal with them is supported by Linn et al's (1985) assessment of clinical faculty. The stress of sleep deprivation in internships continues in spite of Friedman *et al*'s (1971, 1973) elegant studies of how much less proficient the intern is in carrying out his duties when sleep deprived, e.g., ability to accurately interpret electrocardiographic findings in patients.

As Spears (1981) points out, the literature on physician impairment is long on identification of problems yet short on solutions. He demonstrates that it is possible to quantify the demands on time, to define a sensible work week, and to control an open-ended schedule. In designing a schedule for family physicians, he has arranged schedules such that all professional activities should ideally approximate 50 equivalent hours, should never exceed 60 equivalent hours on an accrued basis, and at no time should exceed 70 equivalent hours. To accomplish a 60-hour work week in a group practice, four physicians must be on staff. He cites Walker's (1980) differential characteristics of the professionals who thrive on long hours versus professionals who experience an 'overwork syndrome'. Those who thrive postpone thinking about problems, respond promptly to evidence of fatigue, avoid substance abuse, enjoy scheduled vacations, maintain stable domestic situations, are able to maintain friendships, engage in regular exercise and maintain a sense of humor.

In contrast, those professionals who experience an 'overwork syndrome' (syndromes abound in this literature, e.g. 'house officer syndrome' (Small, 1981), 'pre-residency syndrome', and 'physician burn-out syndrome', and so on) are characterized by ruminating about work problems, lengthening their work day to compensate for low productivity, consuming alcohol and drugs to escape stress, postponing vacations, being loners, remaining sedentary, having no outside interests, and being unable to laugh at one's self.

In spite of the rationality of decreasing the work overload and the overly long work week devoted to professional activities with an opportunity to enhance the health of the physician and increase quality care to patients, there is a continued resistance to implement such a plan for interns. Mizrahi (1984) points out that 'doctors ... quickly learn to interpret their behavior as moral and justifiable and believe the yoke of responsibility bears heavily on their shoulders and no one who has not experienced their pressured existence could possibly be a valid judge of their actions'. McCue (1985) points to additional reasons for resisting change. The pleasant memories of internships is one reason. The intern cited in the case above remembers his internships 21 years later with relish, guilt and shame notwithstanding. Also, McCue points out that the resident's education is related to the number of patients he cares for. However, he cautions that the demands for test ordering, consultation scheduling, and paperwork detract from time spent with patients and learning clinical skills, and learning in depth about disease processes and how they affect patients' lives. He urges distributing the responsibility for primary patient care throughout training and not concentrating it during internship.

In spite of the perception that fatigue is a major cause of stress, Werner and Korsch (1979) found that changing the night call at Children's Hospital, Los

Angeles, from every third to every fourth night, did not improve house staff morale. Their study group hypothesizes that fatigue serves to mask other sources of stress, such as new and overwhelming responsibility for patients, uncertainty about how to diagnose and treat patients, and uncertainty how well one is performing. They speculate that if some of these other stresses could be handled more effectively, patient care would not be so tiring. Modlin and Montes (1964) found that fatigability was usually related to lack of satisfying marital and family relationships, lack of satisfying participation in community affairs, lack of recreation and avocations, and the physicians' underlying neurotic conflict about medical practice.

PHYSICIAN BACKGROUNDS AND STRAIN

Werner and Korsch (1979) point out that interns whose personalities are well integrated and who have strong self-esteem may fair better than those with unresolved conflicts or vulnerabilities. They conclude that an individual with no major emotional difficulties, who has been able to adapt to stress, and whose culture holds humanitarian service and intellectual endeavors in high esteem, seems the ideal candidate for internship.

Those whose backgrounds fall short of this ideal are vulnerable to stress. Vaillant and Sobowale (1972) identified unstable childhood and adolescent adjustments as a critical variable in physicians with poor marriages, drug or alcohol abuse, or psychiatric difficulties. Only 15 per cent showed two or more psychiatric symptoms among those who had a stable childhood adjustment period. (Waring, 1974). Modlin and Montes (1964) in a study of physician addiction, describe early life adjustment problems as significant determinants in increasing risk for physician addiction. Waring (1974) reports that a family history of psychotic illness, a disturbed childhood, and a past history of psychiatric illness were major factors predisposing to illness in a group of doctors. He goes on to describe how personalities characterized by 'obsessionalism, lack of pleasure-seeking and feeling of indispensability' may predispose to affective disorder in midlife. Nadelson and Notman (1979) caution that 'the factors affecting vulnerability, distress, and symptom formation are complex: the nature, number, and magnitude of the stresses and individual personality factors and capacities must all be considered'.

Krakowski (1982) found that 100 per cent of 100 physicians who were polled randomly declared themselves 'compulsive personalities'. Eighty per cent met three of the five criteria for such a formal diagnosis and 20 per cent met four of the five criteria. The criteria include restricted ability to express warm and tender emotions, perfectionism, insistence that others submit to one's way of doing things, excessive devotion to work and productivity to the exclusion of pleasure and the value of interpersonal relationships and indecisiveness. Gabbard (1985) describes his findings of physician compulsiveness based on observations of those who attended the Menninger Foundation's sponsored workshops for physicians and their families in Colorado.

Gabbard characterized the physician's psychological makeup as a triad of compulsiveness consisting of doubt, guilt feelings, and an exaggerated sense of responsibility. In addition to a certain personality of being drawn to medicine, the compulsive traits are reinforced in a physician's training. Gabbard advises about the 'grand paradox: compulsiveness and excessive conscientiousness are character traits that are socially valuable but personally expensive. Society's meat is the physician's poison'. He then points out both the adaptive and maladaptive aspects of compulsive traits and focuses on the latter. These include:

> difficulty in relaxing, reluctance to take vacations from work, problems in allocating time to family, an inappropriate and excessive sense of responsibility for things beyond one's control, chronic feelings of 'not doing enough', difficulty setting limits, hypertrophied guilt feelings that interfere with a healthy pursuit of pleasure, and the confusion of selfishness with healthy self-interest.

He concludes with a caution that these ingrained patterns are difficult to change and that 'recognition in the physician reader will set him thinking about the consequences of these patterns in his own life'.

STRESSES AND PERSONAL MATURATION

In addition to time pressures, the resident is stressed by personal development issues. As Pfifferling (1983) has observed, whereas medical school has been often called 'delayed adolescence' and house staff training 'end of adolescence', he notes that adolescence is an opportune time for exploration, curiosity fulfillment and a period of intense personal growth. However, for the house officer there is no qualitative time to process his emerging identity. Using an anthropological model, he illustrates how a resident undergoes an initiation ritual without the time to reflect and learn from the sacrificial rites that he undertook.

Among the developmental tasks that must compete with the acquisition of a professional identity in the young adult are 'detachment from parents and a development of independence, maturation of sexual and ego identities, experimentation with community and society roles, and the development of the capacity for intimacy', according to Pfeiffer (1983).

Roeske, Clair and Brittain's (1986) study of 227 house officers (163 male, 62 female, 2 left category blank) indicates that female house officers are more openly concerned about personal and family developmental issues than their male counterparts. Forty-one house staff (18 per cent) felt anxious/depressed most (2 male, 4 female) or much (14 male, 19 female, 2 did not indicate sex) of the time. Of the 41 anxious/depressed group most or much of the time, the women represented 37 per cent of the female house staff and men 10 per cent of the male house staff. Suicidal ideation was reported most or much of the time by three house staff, all of whom were Caucasian women. In reviewing those house officers who are anxious and/or depressed, all of them felt they were not prepared for residency. For the women in this group, their principal concerns were a need for a personal life, conflicts between personal and professional life, and a self-perception that the woman was not prepared for the life of a house officer. Women experienced the need for emotional support and understanding, both through faculty and a personal relationship. The single women were particularly concerned about establishing a relationship with another person, a necessary condition for developing the capacity for intimacy. Married women expressed concerns about child care while questioning their future ability to get housekeepers or arrange for appropriate child care facilities.

The anxious and/or depressed male house officer was concerned about a diversity of issues that were more related to work conditions than personal growth issues. They included the quality of faculty teaching, faculty's interest and encouragement, work pressures and fatigue, and a need for personal time. Time with family is only mentioned by a few.

Roeske *et al.* found that women, more than men, were more likely to evaluate themselves for weakness or inadequacies whereas men looked outward to the educational system. Weinstein (1983) reports that the experience of a medical school ombudsman at Stanford revealed that the major concerns of house officers were in the area of academic issues. There was no mention whether there were any gender differences.

McCue (1985) points out that the major support group for house officers is their peer group and that few have ever had independent lives. He further maintains that the culture of the teaching hospital is insufficient for providing a milieu for interacting with non-medical people as a 'friend, neighbor, or spouse'.

STRESS AND THE MEDICAL MARRIAGE: THE MALE PHYSICIAN

Berman (1979), using Levinson's development model, examined stresses in the medical marriage beginning with the internship. She describes the stress of usually moving to a new location, often away from home. Usually the transition is to a 'wonderful internship which is absolutely in the worst area of the worst hospital in the worst city'. For both the graduating medical student and his spouse, this represents a loss of a social network and support systems. She suggests that the intern begins to lose a sense of adolescence and begins to move into a sense of power. This assumption contrasts with Weinstein's (1983) findings that house officers felt themselves to be a disenfranchised group who were neither students nor staff and felt like an 'orphan' group with no unified representation at a policy level. The Well-Being Committee at Stanford viewed the major house staff concern as a sense of powerlessness (Weinstein, 1983). For the spouse, however, Berman cites the frequent complaint, 'I thought it was going to be different when he finished medical school'.

With the earning of money for the first time, male physicians' wives often choose to begin their families. She stresses that age 30 is a particularly vulnerable time for stress in a marriage, especially for those married five to seven years. She cites one example, 'You work all your life to get where you are and now that you are there, what does it matter' blues. She points out that after all the devotion to becoming a doctor, one result is the shock that 'this is what you are going to be doing for 30 to 40 years'. Becoming a doctor leads to life changes, e.g. real money and real staus for the first time. For the male physician's spouse, she describes how living with an absent husband is no longer acceptable. At this point, the wife declares that she wants her own life, wants help and often threatens the physician husband if she does not get what she wants.

Berman then cites a particularly critical period for the male physician is in his forties. One typical issue for all people in their forties is the sense of loss of youth contrasted with the joy of power. She describes the physician as being 'drained, exhausted, and bored'. This is often a time for career specialty changes. This is also a time when divorce rates in physicians increase.

Berman stresses that during this period the female spouse re-examines her needs as well. With children growing up, the wife often feels less needed and examines 'what am I going to do with my life?'

Berman then examines the stresses of age 60 when most people are exploring retirement. However, physicians rarely retire, she contends. Instead, the stresses are more in relation to giving up power to the younger generation. Throughout her discussion, Berman urges the growth possibilities through each of these stages and transitions.

Bird (1979), in the same symposium on the Physician's Marriage: Joys and Sorrows, cites five danger signals in the medical marriage. These include when the male physician's spouse 'becomes painfully disillusioned or painfully deceived when she discovers that what she had perceived as strength in her strong, unafraid, efficient and unemotional husband really represents emotional control and detachment'. He describes how the physician husband, in response to his wife's anger and insistence that he be 'more emotional, more loving, more kind, more involved, and more sympathetic' becomes more emotionally distant. The same defenses used in the medical practice are used in the marriage, namely, denial and isolation of affect. The physician husband's emotional distance only enhances the spouse's anger and the response pattern by the husband is repeated.

Secondly, he warns of the wife's losing her identity, her feelings of self-worth, and her own individuality. This occurs when she does not cultivate her own individual interests but instead 'merges into her husband and the world of medicine'. Bird describes the worst scenario is one where 'all the spouse's activities as a housemaker, mother, wife, and person becomes subservient to the demands and needs of patients in the medical practice'.

Thirdly, Bird cautions about the stress relating from spouses' discovery that 'doctors are strange creatures'. (!) Unlike most people, they like to be around sick or dying people. He urges that wives not somaticize in order to gain their physician husband's attention. He cites how some wives experience intense negative feelings in the face of their fatigued husband's inability to respond to their needs and the spouse's failure to express their feelings for fear of being a 'bad patient'.

Fourthly, he warns about the stresses on a medical marriage resulting from the male physician who relates to his family in the same fashion as he does to his medical profession. He describes this type of doctor as autocratic and not one who engages in contemplative activity and who discourages discussion. Instead, he tries to run the household by issuing 'doctors orders'.

Lastly, he warns about doctors being poor patients and the tendency to treat themselves, particularly for symptoms of anxiety and depression, with drugs and alcohol. He also mentions enhanced sexual activity as an outlet for anxiety. He then asserts that doctors are 'not the world's best lovers'. He relates that physicians, in their commitment to the practice of medicine and their patients, do not 'place a high premium on the romantic arts'. Secondly, he cautions about the physician 'who imparts his practice into the living room, may also move into the bedroom, and create an atmosphere that is not conducive to lovemaking'. He concludes by urging that for the medical couple there be no clear limit on authority and responsibility of either spouse.

Miles, Krell and Lin's (1975) study of 20 physicians' wives who had been inpatients in British Columbia found the following: 90 per cent had a primary diagnosis of depression, 95 per cent had personality disorders of hysterical and passive-aggressive types, 90 per cent had a history of suicidal ideation or attempts, 54 per cent had significant drug and/or alcohol problems and they represented difficult ward management problems. More to the point of marital stress, he discovered a common pairing: a dependent, histrionic wife and an emotionally detached husband. Treatment was complex and difficult.

Martin discusses the common psychiatric difficulties of physicians and their families as depression, alcohol and drug dependency, and marital conflicts. He cites a common feature, namely, conflicts concerning unresolved dependency needs. He also points out that attempts at formal evaluation and treatment are met with denial and resistance. In spite of Berman's claim that physicians do not retire, Martin identifies special problems of many physicians around issues of retirement. Martin urges educational programs directed at all stages of professional development.

Glick and Borus (1984) in their report of thirteen male physicians and their spouses with emotional difficulties in themselves or their relationships, cites

Deckert, who claims male physicians, in selecting spouses, 'tend to use selective recruitment in seeking a marriage partner, with the aim of finding someone who will fit into the single-mindedness of the doctor's life style'. Glick elaborates on Berman's transitional period around age thirty by describing how the spouse often delays personal and material gratification and builds high expectations of the positive changes she hopes will occur at the end of training. In particular, he cites her hope that the physician husband, on completion of training, will settle down and devote more time to being a husband and provider. Borus (1982) has documented how the recently graduated physician is actively and eagerly exploring professional opportunities and, instead of redirecting energies towards his spouse and family, is focusing his energies on his practice. Such a conflict leads to the physician relying on his wife to 'run the family'. Glick points out that marital stresses revolve around status, power and priority issues. In the 25–35-year-old group, issues regarding competition over career priorities in dual career marriages and insufficient time devoted to the marriage may occur. In mid-life (35–50), he describes depression in the spouse or emotional problems of adolescent children as often the first experiences of marital disequilibrium. In the more traditional medical marriage (fifty years and over), he finds those spouses devoted to the role of 'doctor's wife' feel acutely alone when children grow up. Glick then goes on to describe specific therapeutic issues in treating the couple, such as the spouse's suspicion that the therapist will ally himself with the physician patient and will 'side with the husband and attend more to his needs because he is the professional and she is "just the spouse"'. Another issue is the physician viewing the therapist as a competitor and feeling 'one down' as a patient and tries to prove his own competency and denying his problems to the treating physician. Glick concludes that individual therapy for the troubled male physician is difficult and often ineffective and suggests that marital and/or family therapy may be the treatment of choice.

STRESS AND THE MEDICAL MARRIAGE: THE FEMALE PHYSICIAN

Nadelson and Notman (1983) examined stresses which are different for female physicians than male physicians. They cite Roscow and Rose (1972) in their study of physician divorces. The divorce rate for female physicians is higher than for male physicians and higher than for the general population. In contrast, the rate for male physicians is lower than for most male professionals and for men in general. The ratio of divorces for female physicians compared with male physicians is 3 to 2. More female physicians are single than male physicians. Comparative percentages are 31 per cent for the female and 8 per cent for the male physician.

Marwell, Rosenfeld and Speleman (1979) examined problems with geographical constraints for professional women in academia in the 1940s, 1950s and 1960s. In dual career marriages, the professional wife gave preference to her husband's career advancement. In a study of how physician spouses influence each other's career, Lorber (1982) suggests that older couples retain this trend whereas younger couples tend to make career decisions based on mutual needs.

One continued source of stress for the female spouse in a dual career medical marriage is the lack of symmetry in traditional marriages for assuming domestic chores. The female professional continues to assume 3/4 of child rearing and home care chores, even when both couples work (Szalgi, 1973). Heins *et al.* (1977) found that women physicians spend 90 per cent as much time in medical practice as men physicians while tending to assume full responsibility for home and family. Eisenberg (1983) urges that 'to the extent that marital roles take root in mutuality and sharing, men will benefit no less than women'.

Nadelson and Notman (1983) point out that women are in a different position than men in that they are traditionally expected to assume direct responsibility for their own parents and those of their spouses. This is an added stress during training and medical practice.

Nadelson, Notman and Lowenstein (1979), in a study of Harvard Medical School graduates, note that women physicians were particularly stressed by the pressures and desires to be with their children, obtaining suitable jobs for both partners, and other dual career issues. One such issue was the financial burden of providing good household help, particularly during training. As a result of these stresses, a larger number of women were working part-time or in positions they viewed as compromises. Women modify career plans more than men for family reasons.

Nadelson and Notman also note that women physicians appear to postpone childbearing until after training. Data on the particular stresses of this postponement are lacking.

A final indication of stress for the female physician compared with the male physician is the suicide data from Steppacher and Mausner's study (1974). They studied 530 deaths by suicide in a five-and-one-half year period: 489 male and 41 female physician suicides. They reported that the suicide rate for female physicians is three times that of the overall female population whereas for male physicians it is only 1.15 times that of the male population. They also document that 40 per cent of the physician suicides in this group of women were under forty compared with 20 per cent of the men. More physician suicides occurred among women than men during the training period and a substantial portion of the women were single.

FINANCIAL STRESS AND THE PHYSICIAN

The mean debt of graduates of American medical schools in 1984 was $26 496. Eighty-eight per cent of graduates incurred some debt before entering the internship year (Leeds, Cohen and Purcell, 1985). In 1985, the indebtedness averaged $29943. It was $25718 at public medical schools and $36417 at private schools. The indebted graduate is apprehensive about repayment. One result is that those students whose repayment of debts is not subsidized are likely to avoid primary care specialties in favor of becoming a subspecialist. Another effect is that students opt to enter salaried positions at an increasing rate rather than solo or group practice on a fee for service basis.

Reflective of the financial stresses of house officers was Weinstein's (1983) finding that house officers requested low cost counseling as one of three primary unmet needs. In addition, house officers wanted to attend graduate courses at Stanford University at no cost. Borenstein and Cook (1982), in recognition of the need to provide an affordable method of obtaining psychiatric help for house staff at UCLA, set up a program that provided evaluation and treatment free of charge. He did so 'to dispel the panic that trainees may feel in contemplating psychotherapy at a time when their educational debts may be mounting to astronomical proportions'. Those physician patients requiring long-term care were able to do so without having to face 'fiscal nightmares'. Using voluntary, fully-trained UCLA clinical faculty, he evolved a system whereby the physician-volunteer agreed to continue treatment on either a courtesy basis or at greatly reduced fees.

The stresses of finances which traditionally eased when a physician graduated from his residency are not so likely to diminish in the future practice of medicine. As Ginzberg (1985) observes, the following is likely to prevail:

(1) As the number of physicians increases and unless physicians can redirect monies from hospitals, physicians 'are certain to see their earnings reduced'.
(2) Physicians are likely to face new competition with hospitals.
(3) With hospitals likely to merge, convert (to skilled nursing beds), or close, recent graduates will have greater difficulties obtaining hospital appointments.
(4) Physicians will have fewer patient hours filled as per capita visits decline and the numbers of physicians and new health delivery forms increase.
(5) Fee increases will decline with government intervention to eliminate usual, customary and reasonable fee determinations.
(6) With large indebtedness and increasing malpractice premiums, recent graduates will opt for employment in corporate medicine.
(7) With decreased support of graduate medical education, teaching hospitals will come under increased financial pressures.

He concludes that 'the outlook for physicians has definitely taken a turn for the worse'.

With a trend toward medicine becoming a business versus a profession, physicians face the stress of the conflicting values of these two systems. With corporate medicine, the value of 'bottom line' profits for shareholders replaces the primary needs of patients. Cost accounting becomes the preoccupation of office business managers and hospital administrators. They, in turn, subtly, and increasingly blatantly, dictate medical decisions. As King (1985) points out, 'Business, under the profit motive, tries to create needs, to sell more and more goods and services. Medicine, as a true profession, tries to discern the real needs of the patient (without rationalization that might be quite justifiable)'. These are his conclusions in examining medicine as a trade or as a profession.

Linn et al. (1985) discovered that when physicians evaluated their work, family life, social relations, leisure activities, physical health, mental health, finances, and life in general, on a seven-point scale from terrible to delighted, physicians as well as the general population were least satisfied with finances. In comparing academic faculty with clinical faculty, the former were clearly less satisfied with the finances. The mean score for 56 academic physicians was 4.5 compared with 5.1 for the 155 clinical faculty ($p < 0.001$). Academic faculty were significantly more stressed than their clinical counterparts in their concerns about being able to make enough money or achieve or maintain a desirable lifestyle. The academic faculty also had significantly more concerns about what direction their career would take.

Such fiscal concerns of academic faculty members occur at a time when the funding of medical education has shifted from subsidies from research money and direct subsidy of education to patient care dollars. As academic faculty members are increasingly being pressed to earn greater proportions of their income from patient care, they are in more direct competition with private practitioners and are being forced away from teaching and research activities. The residents in graduate education are faced with less exposure to the full-time faculty and often have worried, tired, and at times, frenzied full-time faculty with whom to identify. Not a comforting prospect for a future physician! To complicate this picture, academic physicians are faced with the same prospects as their practitioner colleagues in receiving reduced reimbursements for their clinical services.

MALPRACTICE AND STRESS IN THE PHYSICIAN

The subject of liability insurance has received wide press in the United States and the rising premiums and the cancellation of liability policies is affecting not only the professions but also industry, services, government, recreation, and so on.

Among medical specialities, obstetrics and gynecology has been the most affected. Seventy-three per cent of the 24,500 members of the American College of Obstetricians and Gynecologists have been sued for malpractice. To escape soaring costs of malpractice, approximately 3000 obstetricians have abandoned this specialty. Neurosurgery is also a high risk malpractice specialty. In Long Island, New York, malpractice premiums for neurosurgeons have risen to $83 000 a year.

The threat of malpractice has altered the practice of medicine. Physicians are practicing 'defensive medicine'. This is reflected in the ordering of additional laboratory and radiological tests which otherwise would not be considered necessary. Such tests are ordered to protect the doctor from suit. This practice stands in the face of a conflicting demand to contain costs of medical care. Also, the fear of malpractice threatens to alter the patient–doctor relationship. Whereas the ideal of medical practice is to earn trust in this relationship, the practicing physician is compelled to view his patient as a future adversary in a courtroom proceeding. Not only does the threat of malpractice alter the practice of medicine and the availability of specialists, it adds significantly to the stress of the physician. This is masterfully documented in Charles and Kennedy's (1985) book, *Defendant: A Psychiatrist on Trial for Medical Malpractice*:

> My first feelings after being charged with medical malpractice were being utterly alone. Suddenly, I felt isolated from my colleagues and patients. Since then, I have learned, in the course of my own suit and trial and in the research I have conducted, that this feeling of aloneness is not at all unusual, that almost every physician accused of being negligent has a similar reaction. I also understand that what I experienced during the five-year span of my case—that it swallowed up my life completely, demanded constant attention and study, multiplied tensions and strain, generated a pattern of broken sleep and anxiety because I felt my integrity as a person and a physician had been damaged and might be permanently lost—are the common reactions of most doctors accused of negligence.

Further, in the introduction, they describe the anger physicians experience at the perceived injustice of the accusations against them. The physician's confidence is undermined and the pleasure they previously experienced in their practice is lost. With the practice of defensive medicine comes shame and guilt. Doctors feel a sense of 'helplessness about dealing successfully with a problem that has devastated so many of their colleagues'.

In describing the effects on doctors and patients, Charles and Kennedy speak of the profound ambivalence Americans have toward authority figures. They mention that doctors are a target of discontent by making too much money, spending insufficient time with patients and being arrogant, on the one hand, and expressing pride and affection in holding doctors in high esteem, on the other hand. They describe how malpractice litigation is sapping physicians' energies and deflecting them from practicing medicine the way they think they should practice, and how patients are the ultimate victims by absorbing the costs of increased premiums, by losing the benefits of the traditional doctor–patient relationship, by being shortchanged as beneficiaries of research on risky frontiers and for other subtle changes in the delivery of health care.

As for the stresses on physicians, they also speak of the tendency of physicians towards suppressing feelings and how physicians have been reluctant to discuss their malpractice experiences and how such suppression adversely affects the doctor's ability to provide optimal patient care.

Even those physicians who are ultimately found not at fault in negligence suits are adversely affected. They become anxious and indecisive. Others decide to retire. Charles and Kennedy cite one surgical departmental chairman, 'Doctors who are sued are never the same again, even after they have cleared their reputations in court. The problem is that they know that it might happen again at any time'.

The contamination of the doctor–patient relationship is summarized in their observation that the

> impossible demand that the relationship be both human and error-free deepens the alienation that doctors and patients already regretfully experience. As they become more defensive with each other, the heart of satisfactory medical treatment hardens. Both patients and physicians suffer as health care, in the name of awarding litigation, is routinized and depersonalized.

Charles, Wilbert and Franke (1985) go on to describe how extrinsic factors are increasingly interfering with clinical judgment. They suggest that such judgment is often 'affected by legal constraints, insurance regulations, legislative actions, or even the business practices of the new "health provider" medical managers'.

In their paper describing the effects of malpractice on individual practitioners, Charles *et al.* reported in one study that physicians who had been sued order more tests in 61.8 per cent of cases, stop performing certain procedures in 28.2 per cent of cases, and stop seeing certain kinds of patients in 41.8 per cent of cases. In a second study of physicians who had been sued, they found that 48.9 per cent refused to see certain types of patients, 42.9 per cent were thinking of retiring (a finding which may very well lead to Berman's reconsidering her contention that physicians do not retire), and 32 per cent were discouraging their children from becoming physicians. Charles *et al.* go on to describe that among physicians who had never been sued that even the threat of malpractice has led to 29.5 per cent no longer seeing certain patients, 59.6 per cent ordering more tests than were clinically indicated, and 32.6 per cent having stopped performing certain procedures. Even those who have never been sued also have been personally stressed. They suffer from decreased self-confidence (30.9 per cent), a loss of nerve in certain clinical situations (35.5 per cent), and indecision (26.3 per cent).

Recognizing the stress on the individual physician who may be sued, the next step would be to identify how widespread such a problem may be and how many physicians may be affected. Charles *et al.* studied the prevalence of the problem in Cook County and six counties in northern Illinois. They discovered that from 1977 to 1983 inclusive, of the 17714 practicing physicians, 9487 doctors had been named in a malpractice suit. In 1984, 3002 physicians were named as defendants, twice the number filed in 1979. As for outcome of suits, they cited that in 1984, for the first time in history, physicians won fewer than 70 per cent of their trials. Even though in 82 per cent of instances no indemnity was paid, expense payments amounted to $11233801. They also document the escalating monetary awards. Between 1975 and 1978, awards went from $26565 to $45187 on average. Awards of one million dollars or more increased from five in 1975 to 23 in 1978. In 1984 alone, the total amount of awards in medical malpractice trials amounted to $45040367 compared with $59182093 for the previous fourteen years. With the stakes so high, patients and lawyers are encouraged to sue.

Such statistics are impressive if not overwhelming. One conclusion is that the experience of malpractice suits and the threat thereof are major contributors to the stress of the American physician in the 1980s.

STRESS AND IMPAIRMENT

The practitioner of medicine faces many stresses, some of which have been illustrated in this chapter. Under what conditions may such stresses lead to impairment? The term impaired physician denotes doctors with psychiatric illness, alcoholism and/or abuse of other drugs and suicide (Scheiber and Doyle, 1983).

The best evidence that stress and impairment are related is in Friedman, Kornfield and Bigger's (1973) study of sleep deprivation in the internship. The interns reported that when sleep deprived, they felt significantly more fatigue and sadness and perceived themselves to develop numerous psychophysiological abnormalities. The psychological problems described included difficulty in thinking, depression, irritability, referentiality, depersonalization, inappropriate affect and recent memory deficit. Friedman *et al.* point out that the 'necessity for repression of rage, the inability to live up to standards of the "iron men" and intense feelings of loneliness probably explain the frequency with which depression was reported during the sleep deprived state'.

How prevalent is depression in the internship year? Valko and Clayton's (1975) study revealed that 30 per cent of interns suffered from depression. Depression generally occurred in the beginning of the year on a service with a higher number of working hours per week. Four of the 54 studied had suicidal ideation; three had a suicidal plan and six had marital difficulties with their depression. The depressed intern had a positive family history of depression, a family history of suicidal attempts and a positive past history for depression. The average duration of depression during the internship year was five months. The service on which the intern was most vulnerable to depression was one in which 63 per cent of the interns were working over 100 hours per week and four were working about 130 hours per week.

In Roeske, Clair and Brittain's (1986) study of residents, they found that between 16 and 24 per cent reported anxiety/depression most or much of the time through the first three years of postgraduate training.

Thomas (1976), in her study of graduates and non-graduates of the Johns Hopkins Medical School from 1948 to 1964, found that 3.7 per cent of 1337 subjects died prematurely; 3.1 per cent were graduates and 11.2 per cent non-graduates. Suicide was the most frequent cause (17 cases). Nine died in accidents including six involving airplane accidents. She found that incipient mental illness and emotional disturbance appeared to have significantly contributed to academic failure, poor performance during and after medical school and premature death. She believes that these students should be identified early in medical school as they are most vulnerable to stress and subsequent impairment. She urges that they receive help.

In Valko and Clayton's study, in response to the question, 'During your depression, what did you plan to do to help yourself?' the following responses were obtained: fourteen decided to wait, one saw a psychiatrist and one distracted himself with family and a girlfriend. Hence, identification of depression as a problem by the intern does not lead to help-seeking behaviors in spite of the acknowledgement by six of the interns that they felt hopeless, three felt helpless, and two feared losing their minds. Only six of sixteen depressed interns regarded the depression as abnormal.

The resistance of the physician to seeking help has been observed by many authors. The equating of psychiatric symptoms with a sign of weakness has been a common finding. Also, acknowledging psychiatric symptoms as part of an illness would challenge a physician's sense of omniscience, omnipotence and invulnerability. As Robinowitz (1983) points out, 'physicians may use their own knowledge and skills to defend themselves against their own anxiety about strength, body integrity, and dangers of illness and health'.

Prevention of physician morbidity and mortality was one of the goals of a study co-sponsored by the American Psychiatric Association and the American Medical Association. Those physicians who died a suicidal death were compared with a control group of those who died from natural causes. The report is based on 219 physicians who were reported to have killed themselves between 1982 and 1984. All but three deaths occurred between 1979 and early 1984. Of the original 219, family members and other survivors of 156 initially agreed to be interviewed. Thirteen later refused the interview, four turned out not to be suicides and two interviews were unattainable. Four ambiguous causes turned out to be suicides and one natural death control proved to be a suicide. Altogether, 142 interviews were obtained from survivors of suicide. Two control groups were interviewed: family members of those dying of natural causes (68) and those dying of ambiguous circumstances (33).

Of the 142 suicide cases, 129 were male physicians. The average age overall was 49.3. For female physicians, it was 43. Sixty-nine per cent of the entire group was married or living as married at the time of suicide. Only five of the thirteen female physicians were married.

Sixty per cent of physicians who killed themselves were not receiving treatment for mental health problems at the time of death (AMA Council, 1986). The results, according to Sargent (1986), 'implicated biological heredity and premorbid personality as causative factors of suicide. The stresses particular to life in medicine are seen as aggravating factors which may differentially affect women'. The twelve clues to impending death learned from this study in presuicidal physicians include prior suicide threats, chronic illness at time of death, a history of psychiatric treatment, self-prescribing drugs, prior suicide attempt, prior psychiatric hospitalization, violence to spouse, sexual problems in marriage, acknowledged drug abuse, smoking, blaming self for illness, and financial losses in the two years before death. Sargent reports that in the presuicidal phase, 'depression is the most prominent risk factor, though a recent professional, financial or personal loss may trigger the fatal act'. With suicide prevention as a goal, it is hoped that the profession can use this knowledge about high risk factors to achieve its goal.

COPING WITH DISTRESS

No discussion of distress is complete without discussing methods of coping. Tokarz, Bremer and Peters (1979) point out that distress is often generated by role ambiguity, periods of transition, responsibility beyond one's ability, alienation and social isolation, and sleep deprivation and a lack of regular exercise. They claim all are pertinent in the life of a resident.

First, Tokarz *et al.* urge that postgraduate training should include skills in recognizing and expressing feelings and personal needs. They then urge anticipatory guidance for promoting well-being, particularly for the lack of a defined role, rapid transitions, and the loss of a social network for the beginning house officer.

Tokarz *et al.* look to the program director and the departmental chairman to give visible support to house officers and to provide role models with which to identify, particularly humanistic ones. They stress the need for frequent communications between residents and faculty to express mutual expectations. Discussions should include careful evaluation of working hours, core curriculum, and a balance between responsibility and supervision. They also urge open communication with hospital administrators. Through house staff associations, they suggest that house officers negotiate with the hospital administrators time for expression of religion and the development of strong family and social ties. Tokarz *et al.* further argue for both faculty and residents to view mental health counseling as positive and non-punitive, 'a source of strength and to be sought out early in times of stress'.

For distresses related to financial worries, they support financial planning and practice management training, and favor residents learning the art of negotiating as patient advocates.

In orientation sessions, Tokarz *et al.* point out the importance of raising the consciousness of residents regarding their own health. Impairment prevention is a necessary part of the orientation for residents.

These authors discuss the advantages and impact of small groups for residents including support groups, experiential groups, women's groups, spouse groups, and Balint groups.

Tokarz *et al.* describe a variety of stress reduction techniques that can be helpful to the resident. They go on to describe a program to promote well-being. They stress the importance in the life of a physician to engage in personal assessment, values clarification, assessing one's current situation and prioritizing and obtaining goals.

McCue (1985) highlights interventions that can improve residency training. These include early recognition of problems, improved work conditions, and formal supports. The latter, he contends, should include financial, legal and medical advisers. He concludes with a plea for informal supports including a collegial and friendly environment.

In a similar fashion, when discussing the physician in practice, McCue (1982) urges honest discussions of the psychological difficulties of medical practice and discussing difficult encounters with patients.

In addition to group activities, self-assessment and action planning guides are available. One such is by Jaffe, Orioli and Scott (1984). To help identify sources of stress, they have developed a self-assessment stress map. Factors that are measured include work changes, work pressures, work satisfaction, personal changes, personal pressures, personal satisfactions, self-care, direct action, support seeking, situation mastery, adaptability, time management, self-esteem, positive outlook, personal power, connection, expression, compassion, physical symptoms, behavioral symptoms and emotional symptoms. After evaluating particular sources of stress, they then provide a workbook to help individuals discover new directions in dealing with particular stresses.

The work of promoting health awareness for physicians, if not begun early in life, would hopefully begin in medical school. Attention to enhancing coping skills in a systematic fashion has only recently begun. Much of this pioneering effort is being promoted by Dickstein and Elkes (1986) at Louisville. Their materials for medical students in their orientation to medical school include a philosophy of wellness, identifying stresses in medical school, advising about exercise, relaxation techniques, coping strategies and relationships, and nutritional suggestions among others.

With the burgeoning literature on such topics as stress, burn-out, and impairment in physicians, it is helpful in keeping these topics in perspective to review Linn *et al.*'s (1985) conclusions about the health status, job satisfaction, job stress and life satisfaction in their UCLA study. They report that the physician sample was as healthy or healthier than other population groups. The greatest work satisfaction for physicians was expressed with the diversity of patients seen as well as the personal gratification from patient care. They advise, 'clearly, not all stress is distress, and all physicians derive satisfaction from mastery of often difficult problems'. Indeed, they conclude, 'there is little in our data that suggests that our physician samples work longer hours, are more stressed, less satisfied, or in poorer health than other professional groups'.

Bittker (1978), in examining areas of prevention for the distressed physician, suggests that work must begin at the medical school level and that peer oriented self-help groups should be instituted at all levels of training and experience. He urges that at annual meetings of physicians, there should be a provision for an opportunity for physicians to join together in small groups in order to re-examine their professional identity, their lifestyle and their future. He also urges that alternatives to drug-seeking behaviors should be sought in dealing with stress. He mentions training or retraining constructive uses of leisure time such as wilderness, art or music appreciation, fitness programs, cultivating skills in such communication techniques as assertiveness training and peer counseling, and instruction in meditative equivalents. Lastly, he urges that the physicians' spouse is a welcome ally in helping the distressed physician. Bittker recommends spouse affinity groups as an excellent opportunity to bring into the home some very basic principles in mental health. He also believes that such groups will embrace total family orientation. He suggests that medical societies warrant sponsoring couple retreats that could be coordinated with continuing education programs. He concludes with 'in each one of us are planted seeds of positive functioning and help as well as the seeds of disaster. To eradicate the latter, we must cultivate the former'.

ACKNOWLEDGEMENT

Henry W. Brosin, MD, provided critical review of the manuscript.

REFERENCES

AMA Council on Scientific Affairs (1986). Results and Implications of the AMA–APA Physician Mortality Project: Stage II.
Asken, M. J. and Raham, D. C. (1983). Resident performance and sleep deprivation: a review, *Journal of Medical Education*, **58**, 382–7.
Berman, E. (1979). The physician's marriage: joys and sorrows: life transition points, *Facets*, Winter, 25–8.
Bird, H. W. (1979). The physician's marriage: joys and sorrows: spotting the danger signals, *Facets*, Summer, 18–20.

Bittker, T. E. (1978). The distressed physician: where do we go from here? *Arizona Medicine*, 35, 7–10.

Borenstein, D. B. and Cook, K. (1982). Impairment, prevention and the training years: a new mental health program at UCLA, *Journal of the American Medical Association*, 247, 2700–3.

Borus, J. F. (1982). The transition to practice, *Journal of Medical Education*, 57, 593–601.

Charles, S. C. and Kennedy, E. (1985). *Defendant: A Psychiatrist on Trial for Medical Malpractice*, Free Press, New York.

Charles, S. C., Wilbert, J. R. and Franke, K. J. (1985). Sued and non-sued physicians' self-reported reactions to malpractice litigation, *American Journal of Psychiatry*, 142, 437–40.

Charles, S. C., Wilbert, J. R. and Kennedy, E. C. (1984). Physicians' self-reported reactions to medical malpractice, *American Journal of Psychiatry*, 141, 563–5.

Cousins, N. (1981). Internship: preparation or hazing? *Journal of the American Medical Association*, 245, (4), 377.

Dickstein, L. and Elkes, J. (1986). A health awareness workshop: enhancing coping skills in medical students. In C. D. Scott and J. Hawk (eds), *Heal Thyself, The Health of Health Care Professionals*, Essi Systems, San Francisco.

Eisenberg, C. (1983). Women as physicians, *Journal of Medical Education*, 58, 534–41.

Friedman, R. C., Bigger, T. J. and Kornfield, D. S. (1971). The intern and sleep loss, *New England Journal of Medicine*, 285, 201–3.

Friedman, R. C., Kornfield, D. S. and Bigger, T. J. (1973). Psychological problems associated with sleep deprivation in interns, *Journal of Medical Education*, 48, 436–41.

Gabbard, G. O. (1985). The role of compulsiveness in the normal physician, *Journal of the American Medical Association*, 254, 2926–9.

Ginzberg, E. (1985). What lies ahead for American physicians: one economist's view, *Journal of the American Medical Association*, 253, 2878–9.

Glick, I. D. and Borus, J. F. (1984). Marital and family therapy for troubled physicians and their wives: a bridge over troubled waters, *Journal of the American Medical Association*, 251, 1855–8.

Heimbach, D. (1976). Why the clinical clerkship: a statement to students, *Pharos*, 39, 103–5.

Heins, M., Smock, M., Martindale, L. *et al.* (1973). Psychological problems associated with sleep deprivation, *Journal of Medical Education*, 48, 436–41.

Heins, M., Smock, M., Martindale, L. *et al.* (1977). A profile of the woman physician, *Journal of the American Medical Association*, 32, 21–6.

Jaffe, D. T., Orioli, E. M. and Scott, C. D. (1984). *Essi Systems Stress Map: Personal Exploration*, Essi Systems, San Francisco.

King, L. S. (1985). Medicine-trade or profession, *Journal of the American Medical Association*, 253, 2709–10.

Krakowski, A. (1982). Stress in the practice of medicine II: stresses and strains, *Psychotherapy and Psychosomatics*, 38, 11–23.

Leeds, M. P., Cohen, S. N. and Purcell, G. Jr. (1985). Competition and cost in graduate medical education: should we train unsalaried residents and fellows? *Journal of the American Medical Association*, 254, 2787–9.

Linn, L. S., Yager, J., Cope, D. and Leake, B. (1985). Health status, job satisfaction, and life satisfaction among academic and clinical faculty, *Journal of the American Medical Association*, 254, 2775–82.

Lorber, J. (1982). How physician spouses influence each other's career, *Journal of the American Medical Women's Association*, 37, 21–6.

Marwell, G., Rosenfeld, R. and Speleman, S. (1979). Geographic constraints on women's careers in academia, *Science*, **285**, 1225-31.
Mawardi, B. H. (1979). Satisfactions, dissatisfactions and causes of stress in medical practice, *Journal of the American Medical Association*, **241**, 1483-6.
McCue, J. D. (1982). The effects of stress on physicians and their medical practice, *New England Journal of Medicine*, **306**, 458-63.
McCue, J. D. (1985). The distress of internship: causes and prevention, *New England Journal of Medicine*, **312**, 449-52.
Mechanic, D. (1975). The organization of medical practice and practice orientations among physicians in prepaid and non-prepaid primary care settings, *Medical Care*, **13**, 189-204.
Miles, J. E., Krell, R. and Lin, T. Y. (1975). The doctor's wife: mental illness and marital pattern, *International Journal of Psychiatry in Medicine*, **6**, 481-7.
Mizrahi, T. (1984). Managing medical mistakes: ideology, insularity and accountability among internists-in-training, *Social Science and Medicine*, **19**, 135-46.
Modlin, H. C. and Montes, A. (1964). Narcotic addiction in physicians, *American Journal of Psychiatry*, **121**, 358-65.
Nadelson, C. and Notman, M. (1979). Adaptation to stress in physicians. In E. Shapiro and L. Lowenstein (eds), *Becoming a Physician*, Ballinger Publishing Company, Cambridge.
Nadelson, C. and Notman, M. (1983). What is different for women physicians? In S. C. Scheiber and B. B. Doyle (eds), *The Impaired Physician* New York, Plenum.
Nadelson, C., Notman, M. and Lowenstein, P. (1979). The practice pattern, life styles and stresses of women and men entering medicine: a follow up study of Harvard Medical School graduates from 1967 to 1977, *Journal of the American Medical Women's Association*, **34**, 400-6.
Nelson, F. G. and Henry, W. F. (1978). Psychosocial factors seen as problems by family practice residents and their spouses, *Journal of Family Practice*, **6**, 581-9.
Pfeiffer, R. J. (1983). Early development in the medical student, *Mayo Clinic Proceedings*, **58**, 127-34.
Pfifferling, J. H. (1983). Coping with residency distress, *Resident and Staff Physician*, **29**, 105-11.
Robinowitz, C. B. (1983). The physician as a patient. In S. C. Scheiber and B. B. Doyle (eds), *The Impaired Physician*, Plenum, New York.
Roeske, N. C. A., Clair, D. and Brittain, H. (1986). A study of anxiety/depression, and adaptive behaviour of medical students, house staff and spouse/partners. A paper presented at the annual meeting of the American College of Psychiatrists, Marco Island.
Rosow, I. and Rose, K. D. (1972). Divorce among doctors, *Journal of Marriage and Family*, **34**, 587-98.
Sargent, D. A. (1986). Physician suicide. A paper presented at the annual meeting of the American College of Psychiatrists, Marco Island.
Scheiber, S. C. and Doyle, B. B. (1983). *The Impaired Physician*, Plenum, New York.
Shaw, G. B. (1931). The doctor's dilemma. In *The Complete Works of George Bernard Shaw*, London.
Small, G. W. (1981). House officer stress syndrome. *Psychosomatics*, **22**, 860-69.
Spears, B. W. (1981). A time management system for prevention physician impairment, *Journal of Family Practice*, **13**, 75-80.
Steppacher, R. C. and Mausner, J. S. (1974). Suicide in male and female physicians, *Journal of the American Medical Association*, **228**, 323-8.
Szalgi, A. (ed). (1973). *The Use of Time: Daily Activities of Urban and Suburban*

Populations in Twelve Counties, Mouton Publishing, The Hague.
Thomas, C. V. (1976). What becomes of medical students: the dark side, *Johns Hopkins Medical Journal*, **138**, 185-95.
Tokarz, P., Bremer, W. and Peters, K. (1979). *Beyond Survival*, American Medical Association, Chicago.
Vaillant, G. C. and Sobowale, N. (1972). Some psychological vulnerabilities of physicians, *New England Journal of Medicine*, **287**, 372-5.
Valko, R. J. and Clayton, R. J. (1975). Depression in the internship, *Diseases of the Nervous System*, **36**, 26-9.
Walker, J. I. (1980). Prescription for the stressed physician, *Behavioural Medicine*, **7**, 13.
Waring, E. M. (1974). Psychiatric illness in physicians: a review, *Comprehensive Psychiatry*, **15**, 519-30.
Weinstein, H. M. (1983). A committee on well-being of medical students and house staff, *Journal of Medical Education*, **58**, 373-81.
Werner, E. R. and Korsch, B. M. (1979). Professionalization during pediatric internship: attitudes, adaptation, and interpersonal skills. In E. C. Shapiro and L. M. Lowenstein (eds), *Becoming a Physician: Development of Attitudes in Medicine*, Ballinger Publishing Company, Cambridge.
Wilkinson, R. T., Tyler, P. D. and Varey, C. A. (1975). Duty hours of young hospital doctors: effects on the quality of work, *Journal of Occupational Psychology*, **48**, 219-29.

Stress in Health Professionals
Edited by R. Payne and J. Firth-Cozens
© 1987 John Wiley & Sons Ltd

Chapter 3

Stress and the General Practitioner

A. M. D. Porter, J. G. R. Howie and A. Levinson

INTRODUCTION

Two comments about general practitioners illustrate the divergent stereotypes that people hold about family doctors: 'He's off playing golf', and 'I don't want to bother the busy doctor'. At one extreme, general practitioners are believed to lead leisurely working lives with plenty of opportunity to engage in their own interests; at the other extreme, they are seen as worn down by the incessant demands of their patients, and as having little time to themselves or their families. Medical practitioners as an occupational group are known to have significantly raised standardized mortality rates for suicide and cirrhosis of the liver, but there is no evidence to suggest that these raised SMRs are caused by the stresses and strains of being a doctor. Furthermore, there is no data specific to general practitioners.

The first part of this chapter reviews the information about general practitioners' work, and does so within the context of a theoretical model that we used in a research programme on patterns of work, stress and quality of care. The second part of the chapter describes the initial stages of this research programme, which has been limited to validating our research instruments. It concludes with a discussion of potential developments.

Both in carrying out our research, and in writing this chapter, we have become aware of the different perspectives and interests of doctors and behavioural scientists. We have found the collaboration to be stimulting and productive. We hope that what we have written will make sense to people with equally different backgrounds and interests.

1 THE THEORETICAL MODEL AND LITERATURE REVIEW

The Theoretical Model

As newcomers to the field of stress research, our initial review of the literature suggested that there were two distinct traditions. There were studies of occupational stress (for example: French and Caplan, 1973; Warr and Wall, 1975; Cooper and Payne, 1978; Murrell, 1978), and studies of life events (for example: Dohrenwend and Dohrenwend, 1974, 1981; Brown and Harries, 1978). More recently, there was some indication that there was beginning to be some convergence of the two traditions (Payne, Jick and Burke, 1982).

Figure 1 presents the simplified theoretical model of the effects of stress on general practitioners with which we began. Stressors or loads are experienced by the individual doctor and the extent to which she or he feels psychologically impaired (or possibly enlivened) depends on the interplay of various personal characteristics and on the level of social support. Physiological changes may also take place as a load is experienced. In response to the strain imposed by the load, the individual may adopt various social, psychological and physiological coping mechanisms, which again will depend on the influence of personal and social factors. It is these coping mechanisms that, in general practice, are likely to play an important part in determining the quality of patient care. Mental and/or physical ill-health may develop when either the coping mechanisms are insufficient to relieve the load, or when an ineffective coping process continues over such a period of time that the body or mind becomes exhausted.

During the course of our research we have become aware of the oversimplification of such a model, but have still found it useful when introducing our work to mixed audiences. Figure 2 presents a more sophisticated model, and takes particular notice of feedback loops (Cox, 1981). Thus, for example, a general practitioner may feel himself getting pressured during a busy surgery and change his behaviour with patients so that he works faster, thereby relieving the strain of work overload. This behavioural change may take place before significant psychological or physiological changes occur.

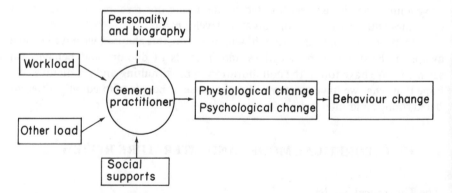

Figure 1 Simplified theoretical model for effects of stress on a general practitioner. Reproduced by permission of Oxford University Press from Porter, Howie and Levinson (1985)

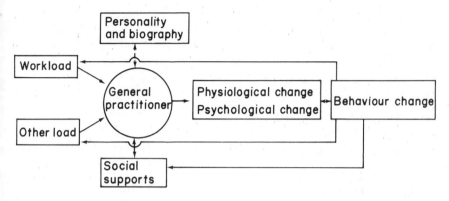

Figure 2 Theoretical model for effects of stress on a general practitioner with feedback loops

Work Stressors

Most studies of occupational stress focus on features like work overload, job ambiguity or conflict, work tedium, repetitiveness and poor environment.

Work overload (or pressure of work) in manual workers has been found to be associated with speeding up, and with errors, tension and anger (Sales, 1970). It is one stressor commonly reported by professional employees and appears to be the stressor most commonly reported by general practitioners, and their patients. Two comments serve to illustrate this aspect of stress: 'Doctors today are overworked. If they had fewer patients they could give them more time.' This is one example of the most common criticism of general practitioners made by Ann Cartwright's lay respondents in her 1964 survey of general practice in England and Wales (Cartwright, 1967). 'Not enough time—ever—to do one's work adequately and still have time to live a normal family life.' Twenty per cent of general practitioners in Cartwright's 1977 survey (Cartwright and Anderson, 1981) shared this feeling of lack of time, the second most commonly mentioned frustration.

Ann Cartwright's 1964 study was the first systematic survey of general practitioners' and patients' views about general practice. It is particularly interesting because it was carried out just a few months before general practitioners were threatening to leave the NHS because they were dissatisfied with the terms and conditions of their NHS contract. The solution to the crisis came with the 'Charter for the Family Doctor Service' (BMA, 1965) which, amongst other things, awarded pay increases, and instituted special 'incentive' payments for group practice, ancillary help, and night and weekend work.

The Doctors' Charter changed the face of British General Practice, and in 1977 Ann Cartwright set out to describe the views and experiences of both patients and doctors eleven years after the implementation of the Charter and,

Table 1

Percent of general practitioners finding the following frustrating:	1964 (%)	(n)	1977 (%)	(n)
Inadequate time to do work properly	20	(408)	27	(356)
Lack of leisure/free time	25	(408)	8	(356)

Percent of patients who felt their doctor was 'not so good' about:				
Always visiting when asked	3	(1168)	13	(569)
Keeping people waiting	17	(1069)	21	(671)
Taking time and not hurrying you	6	(1237)	14	(712)
Listening to what you say	3	(1260)	7	(715)
Explaining things to you fully	16	(1168)	23	(692)

Adapted from Table 6 and Table 3 in Cartwright, and Anderson (1981) by permission of Tavistock Publications

where possible, to make comparisons with the 1964 study. Table 1 presents some of her findings. The evidence suggests that in the process of solving the problems of pay and of free time, general practitioners have created the problem of having to get through the work in a more structured timetable, with more deadlines to meet. It seems reasonable to hypothesize that as general practitioners feel overloaded, particularly by trying to fit too much work into a defined amount of time, that they will begin to feel tense and irritable, and they will speed up. They are certainly giving the impression to patients of hurrying, of not listening, and of not taking time to explain things properly. They may also make mistakes in diagnosis and treatment.

More recently, Erica Bates (1982) has found that 'physical overwork' was the main stress that medicine placed on a sample of Australian general practitioners; and Morrice (1984) has reported that 87 per cent of a sample of Aberdeen general practitioners responding to a questionnaire said that they experienced 'periods of exhaustion'. Horobin and McIntosh's (1983) survey of 50 Scottish Highland general practitioners found that shortage of time was an important problem for 'urban' doctors but not for rural doctors—who found the distance from hospital services a greater difficulty.

Armstrong (1985) has recently traced the organizational developments of general practice and noted the increasing preoccupation with time. This preoccupation is well illustrated by the focus of much general practice research in the 1960s and 1970s into workload studies. If work overload is the source of stress that practitioners most commonly identify in themselves, any study of stress should examine the volume of work to be carried out, the nature of the work to be done and the constraints on re-timetabling.

McDonald and McLean (1971) found that the average working week in southeast Scotland was 39 hours (with a range of 26–53 hours) and that 76 hours were spent 'on call' (with a range of 37–102 hours). Butler, in his 1980 review, estimated that the average working week lay between 35 to 42 hours (with a range of 25–55 hours).

In another Scottish study, the average north-east Scotland general practitioner was consulted on 180 occasions in a typical week (Richardson et al., 1973). This figure is slightly lower than those reported elsewhere, approximately 200–210 (Hodgkin, 1973; Fry, 1972). Most studies suggest that consultation rates have been falling over the last 15 years or so (Howie, 1977). A home visiting rate of about 55 visits per week was noted in the early 1970s (Vardy, 1972; McDonald and McLean, 1971; Marsh, McNay and Whewell, 1972), while more recent evidence suggests that the figure is now nearer 40 visits per doctor per week (Gray, 1978; Howie and Porter, 1985).

'Indirect' services (defined as services provided other than at a face-to-face consultation between patient and doctor) have generally received scant attention but may contribute substantially to workload and stress. In his review of 'Patterns of Work' in general practice, Howie (1977) arrived at a figure of some 1.7 indirect consultations per patient per year. Given a list size of 2000 patients, this would be about 70 indirect consultations per week, and about 27 of these would be telephone contacts between doctor and patient. An additional two to seven calls per week would also be received from a hospital or other agency.

Most studies have suggested that from 5.5 to 6.0 minutes is the average time that patients spend with their doctor in the surgery face-to-face (Howie, 1977). Doctors spend slightly longer in the patient's home, and travelling takes an average of 5–10 minutes per patient, a figure that may be surprisingly similar irrespective of whether the doctor has a city or rural practice (Buchan and Richardson, 1973). While six minutes may seem a very short time, it has to be put in the context of continuing care, so that five consultations in as many weeks would imply a total consultation time for an episode of illness of half an hour. Asking the patient to come back is a commonly used strategy, and about 60 per cent of consultations are 'doctor-initiated' in this way, but the variation between doctors is large (Morrell and Nicholson, 1974; Richardson et al., 1973). We believe that this strategy is used more at times of workload stress.

One study (Williams, 1970) also looked at work done outside the practice and suggested that 25 per cent of doctors spent 4–8 hours per week on paid work outside the practice, and a further 25 per cent of doctors spent more than eight hours on outside paid work. It is perhaps worth noting that general practitioners' pay awards are based on the expectation that general practitioners will make up their pay to 'consultant' levels by engaging in paid non-practice work.

Increases in practice workload were the basis of a recent appeal by general practice negotiators to the Doctors and Dentists Review Body on Pay and Remuneration:

The profession argued that the workload of GMPs (general medical practitioners) is particularly affected by changes in the state of the economy, by social problems, and by cutbacks in expenditure on the NHS and on local authority social services. We were again told that the elderly form an increasing proportion of all patients. Unemployment and other effects of general economic downturn were also said to have an adverse effect on the health of the nation, the impact of which is felt first at GMP level. We were told that cash limits and other financial constraints had led hospitals to trim the level of their services with a further shift in the burden of care onto the GMP. The Health Departments, on the other hand, told us that they had no reliable evidence of a systematic, general increase in the workload of GMPs, although they accepted that financial constraints on the hospital service and cutbacks in social services are probably having some effect. (Para 93: Workload and Stress. *Review Body Report*, 1981).

However, as the Review Body itself noted, practice list sizes have been falling, the home visiting rate has been falling, general practitioners are increasingly being supported by primary health care team staff, and fewer practitioners are doing night and week-end work.

The issue of incentives in general practice is a key topic for future research and evaluation because the present structure and financing of general practice rewards doctors for having large lists and for working fast—neither of which may be in the best interests of doctors or their patients.

As this summary has suggested, the range of activities and the time spent on them varies considerably between doctors, and these variations seem to remain fairly consistent for individual doctors over time. Butler's review (1980) of list size and number of patients per doctor was unable to reach any firm conclusion about the relationship between list size and time spent with patients, and suggests that differences were likely to be due to personal style. In an attempt to clarify some of these issues, Wilkin and Metcalfe's study (1984) of 190 general practitioners suggested that 16 per cent of these general practitioners spent less than 12 hours per week seeing patients, and 15 per cent spent more than 28 hours (the range was five hours to 46 hours). They found positive correlations between list size and number of consultations (0.44, $n = 199$) and the amount of time spent in patient contact. They also found negative correlations between list size and consultation rates, average consultation times, and the amount of time devoted to each patient per year (no correlation coefficients quoted).

The literature also suggests other sources of work stress. The changing responsibilities and relationships concurrent with the development of primary health care teams (Bowling, 1981; Gilmore, Bruce and Hunt, 1974) might be expected to cause the stress associated with *job ambiguity and conflict*. This is an important point to bear in mind as one solution to the problem of work overload might be to extend the work of the nurse, and health visitor (Stilwell, 1982), or to introduce 'new' members of the team—for example the clinical psychologist, the marriage guidance counsellor, or the social worker (Reedy, 1977).

The frequency of minor illness and of social problems presented to the general practitioner, particularly if perceived as trivial (Cartwright and Anderson 1981), may create the stress associated with *tedium and repetitiveness*. Indeed, David Mechanic comments that

> the average (English) doctor responds to his growing practice and increasing demands on his time ... by practicing at a different pace and style. Such a pattern of work requires doctors to practice on an assembly line basis, which diminishes the unique satisfactions possible in general practice. (Mechanic, 1968).

At the other extreme, the risk of missing the rare but life threatening illness, and the more common responsibility of caring for people (and their families) during terminal illness may impose the stress of *responsibility for others*.

For those general practitioners providing out-of-hours cover, the loss and disruption of sleep may be similar to the stress associated with *long working hours or shift work* (Stevenson, 1982).

Karasek's work on *job decision latitude* is an important concept to apply to general practice (Karasek, 1979). To outside observers, general practitioners would appear to experience high intellectual responsibility, high skill levels, high decision authority and high personal schedule freedom. In comparison with other members of the primary health care team, general practitioners do experience considerable job decision latitude. Whether general practitioners themselves *feel* that they have this latitude, or if they feel that they have less latitude than other doctors of equal experience, is uncertain. The distinction between objective and subjective experience is crucial for our understanding of this factor in the aetiology of doctors' stress.

Other Stressors and Social Supports

Stress at work is only one source of stress. Family and leisure commitments and responsibilities may serve both as supports and as stressors. Although supports have proved to be important as moderator variables in the experience of life events (Cobb, 1976; Gore, 1978; Jenkins, Mann and Belsey, 1981; Henderson *et al.*, 1978), research into work stress has seldom incorporated the contribution of family and leisure as supports or stressors. For example, in general practice, the very latitude of the job may enable the practitioner to fit many different activities into the working day, but the constraints of surgery and clinic timetabling may lead to stress if personal and family commitments take longer than expected, or if family commitments are squeezed out by a long-running surgery. Furthermore, unforeseen or unplanned events may seriously disrupt a carefully timetabled day, thereby leading to feelings of strain. We believe that studies of occupational stress should incorporate non-work stressors and supports, particularly as more men and women are more committed to both. General practice is particularly interesting in that 50 per cent of medical undergraduates are now women, and many of them want to follow a career in general practice.

The model presented in Figure 1 suggests that 'social supports' are separate from loads. In fact, most factors that create stress can also act as supports so that the two are inseparable. Indeed, it may be that many people go to work to get away from stressful family or domestic difficulties and responsibilities. The distinction between them is, however, analytically useful.

It should also be noted that an individual stressor may not be stressful on its own, but a combination of stressors may be (Pearlin et al., 1981), and that the duration of a stressor may also be important (Fletcher and Payne, 1980).

Personality, Biography and Attitudes

People's perception of and response to stressors is mediated, not just by social supports but also by personality, biography and attitudes. Most researchers emphasize the importance of personality on an individual's response to stressors and to strain, but there is no agreed model on which to base work on general practitioners. The work of Jenkins et al. (1971) and Rosenman et al. (1970) on the relationship between stress, Type A/Type B personality and heart disease would appear to be intuitively relevant to studies of stress on all types of doctor, and suggests that general practitioners with Type A personalities may organize their day differently, and may perceive and respond to work overload differently to general practitioners with Type B personalities. For example, Type A doctors may take on more outside commitments, and be more actively involved in running the practice. They may perceive more stressors but self-record low levels of pressure as part of a denial of that pressure. They may be more impatient with patients who arrive late, and find it difficult to involve themselves in family life. They will probably respond to feelings of workload pressure by working faster, while Type B doctors may consciously slow down, relax and take their time.

Others have found that an ability to be flexible appears to moderate certain stressors, while proneness to anxiety and dependence on other people to maintain self-esteem may increase the effect of stressors (French and Caplan, 1973). All three of these may affect how general practitioners organize their days and respond to stress. Kyriacou and Sutcliffe (1979) have argued that an individual's concept of his control over his environment may be important in determining the level of perceived stress. This 'level of control' factor obviously has an important link with Karasek's 'job decision latitude' factor. A further factor which seems to have been unexplored in the literature but which may be relevant to general practice is the individual general practitioner's willingness to take risks or his preference to avoid them. Such a concept is intuitively closely tied up with how doctors handle uncertainty, and Budner's instrument for measuring 'tolerance/intolerance of ambiguity' may be appropriate for use with general practitioners (Budner, 1962).

Age, experience, gender and family structure are also likely to affect the way that practitioners organize their days and respond to stressors.

Attitudinal factors have not been studied in any detail in general practice. Apart from Cartwright's work (which did provide some information on those aspects of practice work that general practitioners found frustrating, and this probably crosses the border from workload into attitudes), little research has been carried out into this influence on general practitioners. David Mechanic's work (1972) is one exception. He described general practitioners 'social orientations to medical care' and categorized them into high, medium high, medium low and low scores. The scores were derived from a set of 'social problems' which the practitioner was asked to comment on in terms of their propriety for consulting the doctor. About a quarter of respondent general practitioners scored 'high', and slightly more than a third scored 'medium high'. Thirty-seven per cent of doctors scored low or medium low. Almost half of British practitioners were either 'not very satisfied' or 'quite dissatisfied' with general practice, and 24 per cent felt that 50 per cent or more of patient consultations were trivial, unnecessary or inappropriate. The British general practitioners provided a stark contrast to USA general practitioners—only about 20–25 per cent of USA practitioners scored low or medium low on 'social orientation', only 4 per cent expressed feelings of dissatisfaction, and only 9–13 per cent felt that 50 per cent or more consultations were trivial or inappropriate.

At one point in this comparative study, Mechanic draws attention to the demise of US general practitioners but notes their comparatively greater satisfaction with working conditions. He comments:

> Those American doctors who continue to maintain a practice of wide scope appear to function with greater gratification than their British counterparts, who have a much narrower general orientation which seems to exaggerate the disparity between the scientific orientation of medical schools and their own daily practice.

Elsewhere, Mechanic presents a more detailed picture of the characteristics of British general practitioners and their 'orientations' which confirms the impression that practitioners with high 'social orientation' are more likely to be more satisfied than low scorers, and less likely to consider consultations as 'trivial or inappropriate'. He goes on to make the interesting observation that 'high social orientation' is not necessarily incompatible with technical orientation (defined in terms of diagnostic use of diagnostic procedures), and he categorizes GPs into four groups:

Withdrawers (low technical, low social orientation)
Technicians (high technical, low social)
Counsellors (low technical, high social)
Moderns (high technical, high social)

As one would expect, the withdrawer or technician practitioners were least satisfied with general practice and more likely to complain that 50 per cent or more of consultations were for trivia. Many of the 'technicians' were young general practitioners.

Remembering Mechanic's earlier comment on the scientific orientation of medical schools, his conclusion to this paper contains the following comment: 'It is interesting to note that the technicians have not had, on the average, less training specific to social science and psychiatry than other groups' (Mechanic, 1970). Like many other studies, it would appear that medical school confirms existing attitudes and does little to change them or introduce new attitudes. There is a large literature on the attitudes of medical students, all of which tends to support this finding, but it is perhaps surprising that none of it has been extended into doctors' professional careers.

No one has attempted to develop Mechanic's work, nor has it been repeated more recently to see if attitudes have changed. However, Ann Cartwright's work does give some idea of changes in doctors' frustrations over time. Reference has already been made to some of the results of Cartwright's comparisons of her 1964 and 1977 respondents (Cartwright and Anderson, 1981). Perhaps surprisingly, given the low morale of general practitioners in 1964 and the many changes that had taken place by 1977, there was little difference in general practitioners' assessments of the extent to which they enjoyed their work. In both her studies only about 10 per cent said that they were not enjoying their work. Of particular relevance to the concept of 'job decision latitude', the proportion of respondents who specifically mentioned that they enjoyed 'being their own master' and having 'freedom and independence' changed from 10 to 26 per cent. And yet during those 15 years, many practitioners had moved from single-handed practices in shopfront premises to group practices in purpose-built local authority owned health centres. Who were these general practitioners comparing themselves with? Maybe the fact that hospital practice had become increasingly subject to government and union intervention during the 1970s has made general practitioners appreciate their independent contract status all the more.

As far as frustrations were concerned, 40 per cent of Cartwright and Anderson's general practitioners felt frustrated by trivial and inappropriate consultations, compared with 48 per cent in 1964. About a quarter of general practitioners in both the 1964 and the 1977 surveys felt that 50 per cent or more surgery consultations were trivial, unnecessary or inappropriate. These figures correspond closely with Mechanic's findings, and suggest that there had been little attitudinal or orientation change between 1964 and 1977.

The section on the theoretical model drew attention to certain personality traits which have been shown to play a part in the stress process. The only work we know of which has attempted to apply some of the standard personality inventories to general practitioners has been carried out within this Department of General Practice, and none of it has yet been published. There is a need for more research into the relationship between 'orientations', attitudes and personality.

We should also note that both Mechanic and Cartwright found that younger general practitioners were more likely to hold 'social orientations' about their work, and to be interested in 'whole person' medicine and health promotion. Given the number of young recruits into general practice since the Charter, it is surprising that the proportion of general practitioners feeling frustrated by trivial and inappropriate consultations had hardly changed by 1977. Does something happen to general practitioners as they grow older which changes their orientations? Do their personalities change too?

Psychological changes

The psychological experience of strain can be measured over different time periods, and may at times be difficult to disassociate from personality. 'Now' feelings or present mood are of obvious importance; for example: tension and fatigue. (Mackay *et al.*, 1978; Mackay, 1980). But more medium-term feelings of low self-esteem, well being, and anxiety (Warr, 1978; Warr, Cook and Wall, 1979) are also of relevance.

Physiological Changes

Most studies of stress have examined the health of individuals experiencing stress, and measured physiological changes which may be indicative of greater risk of ill-health. No work in this area has been published from general practice, and while such research may well be relevant, at this stage in our work on general practitioners we have been more interested in job performance and quality of care than in the physiological functioning of the doctor, which we do not see as being easily assessed. Obviously the two should not be separated out as it is unlikely that a sick doctor (particularly if depressed or mentally ill) will be performing well, but we have mostly chosen to leave (for the present) the more physiological measures of response to stress.

Behavioural Changes

Of greater concern to us than physiological changes, is the measurement of behavioural responses or coping mechanisms that doctors utilize when they feel stressed or threatened by stress. Do they speed up or slow down? Do they become more irritable and short-tempered with patients? Less empathetic and less interested? Do they listen less and explain less? Do they prescribe more and refer more?

What evidence there is suggests that short consultation times are associated with higher prescribing levels (Hughes, 1983). More recent research suggests that short consulting times are associated with increased prescribing of antibiotics, while longer consultation times are associated with increased identification of psycho-social problems and with increased prescribing of psychotropic drugs (Morrell, 1986). This is consistent with the earlier work of Raynes and Cairns (1980).

Mechanic (1974) attempted to relate degree of frustration with quality of job performance and he reports significant associations between frustration and performance indicators based on the taking of short cuts. Unfortunately the methods are open to criticism, but he suggests that 'frustrated doctors tend to be poorer doctors and are willing to take undesirable short cuts'.

Melville has studied the job satisfaction of general practitioners and quality of prescribing (Melville, 1980), and she suggests that low job satisfaction is associated with higher levels of prescribing of certain drugs with potential adverse side effects. She herself is quick to note that, whilst job satisfaction appears to be closely correlated with frustration, our understanding of why some general practitioners feel frustrated is inadequate. She suggests two broad reasons: first, some individuals might have personality characteristics and attitudes which are not ideally matched to the requirements of general practice work; and second, certain aspects of the general practitioner's task could lead to dissatisfaction. Melville also points out, however, that few studies of job satisfaction have demonstrated any relationship between performance and satisfaction.

Grol et al. (1985) have recently found that positive feelings about work (satisfaction, feeling at ease) correlated with more oppenness to patients (Pearson correlation 0.29, n = 57), more attention to psychosocial aspects of the complaints (0.28). Negative feelings (frustration, tension, lack of time) correlated with a high prescription rate (0.44), and with giving little explanation to patients (0.19).

2 THE EDINBURGH STUDY AND FUTURE DEVELOPMENTS

Aims of the Edinburgh Study

The long-term aim of this study is to describe and analyse the relationships between workload, stress, job performance and quality of care in general practice. The short-term aim was:

> To develop measures of the pressure under which general practitioners consult, within the framework of the stressors and mediating factors that affect general practitioners during their working day (Porter, Howie and Levinson, 1985).

The research data presented represents three study days on each of 18 doctors working in three group practices in Edinburgh. All the practices were 'training' practices, and two took undergraduate students on attachment.

Developing the Instruments

The development of measures of load and pressure of work involved four stages:

(1) Measurement of workload and other loads.
(2) Measurement of mediating or intervening factors (personality, biography, attitudes/orientation, and social supports).
(3) Measurement of self-perceived pressure and stress.
(4) Measurement of physiological changes.

(1) Measurement of workload and other loads

The following types of activities were identified:

(a) *Activities internal to the practice:*

surgeries, including interruptions and phone calls
home visits
on call commitments
night work
administration: notes, letters, other phone calls, internal meetings, etc.
teaching
research

(b) *Activities external to the practice:*

other NHS commitments, hospital appointments, etc.
insurance work
industrial health work
committee work
teaching/lecturing/publishing

(c) *Family and personal commitments.* A daily diary card was devised (Figure 3) on which general practitioners recorded, first thing in the morning, details of their 'anticipated commitments', and their subjective rating of the 'unbreakability' of each commitment. Unforeseen or unplanned commitments and activities were recorded on the right-hand side of the inside page.

Information on workload and work-flow during surgery sessions was collected using 'patient time cards' which were usable with appointment and non-appointment surgery sessions (Figure 4).

DEPARTMENT OF GENERAL PRACTICE UNIVERSITY OF EDINBURGH STRESS STUDY	Time	Anticipated commitments (please be as detailed as possible)		New or changed commitments	Time	What are your feelings of pressure just now?
			Unbreakability (0-4)			(bored-optimal-v.press.)
Doctor _____	8.00–	–	–	–	–8.00	0-1-2-3-4-5-6
Practice _____	9.00–	–	–	–	–9.00	0-1-2-3-4-5-6
Date _____	10.00–	–	–	–	–10.00	0-1-2-3-4-5-6
Were you on call last night? Yes/No	11.00–	–	–	–	–11.00	0-1-2-3-4-5-6
No. of telephone calls received _____	12.00–	–	–	–	–12.00	0-1-2-3-4-5-6
How many of these were between 11.00 pm and 7.00 am? _____	1.00pm–	–	–	–	–1.00pm	0-1-2-3-4-5-6
No. of times you were out _____	2.00–	–	–	–	–2.00	0-1-2-3-4-5-6
How many of these were between 11.00 pm and 7.00 am? _____	3.00–	–	–	–	–3.00	0-1-2-3-4-5-6
Are you on call tonight? Yes/No	4.00–	–	–	–	–4.00	0-1-2-3-4-5-6
How would you assess your background stress level?	5.00–	–	–	–	–5.00	0-1-2-3-4-5-6
(relaxed ... av ... stressed)	6.00–	–	–	–	–6.00	0-1-2-3-4-5-6
0-1-2-3-4-5-6	7.00–	–	–	–	–7.00	0-1-2-3-4-5-6
(Time now _____)	8.00–	–	–	–	–8.00	0-1-2-3-4-5-6

Figure 3 Daily diary card for general practitioners to record anticipated and unforeseen commitments and their subjective rating of breakability. Right-hand portion shows the system used to record self-perceived pressure of work at half-hourly intervals. 0 = snoozing; 1 = idle/bored; 2 = coasting/relaxed; 3 = optimal/stimulated; 4 = stretched; 5 = hurried; 6 = hectic/frantic. Reproduced by permission of Oxford University Press from Porter, Howie and Levinson (1985)

```
NAME _____

DATE _____

To see Dr _____

Appointment Time            _____

       (Time cancelled_____)

Time arrived at Reception   _____


    PLEASE TAKE THIS CARD WITH
         YOU TO THE DOCTOR

Time entered GP's Surgery   _____

Time left Surgery           _____

To see nurse?              Yes/No

If seen again by GP:

Time began                  _____
Time finished               _____
```

Figure 4 'Time card' used to collect information on workload and work-flow. Reproduced by permission of Oxford University Press from Porter, Howie and Levinson (1985)

General practitioners were initially issued with a small pad on which to record the number of times they were interrupted by telephone calls or people coming into the room. This information was felt to be important as it might indicate disturbance of the smooth running of the surgery session. The method of data collection was abandoned when it became apparent from discussion with the general practitioners that it was being unreliably completed. A new way of collecting this data has subsequently been incorporated into a revised version of the 'patient time card'.

Night-work was recorded by the general practitioner on the front of the diary card (Figure 3), and included details of the number of phone calls at different times of the night and the number of times the doctor went out.

Interviews were held with the general practitioners in two of the practices on two occasions, and with the general practitioners of the third practice on one occasion. The purpose of these interviews was: (a) to check the reliability of the information contained in the self-completed diary card, (b) to collect information on sources of stress other than pressure, and (c) to identify practical problems encountered during the use of the research instruments. All interviews were conducted using a semi-structured questionnaire, and all interviews took place either at the end of a recording day or on the subsequent morning.

(2) Measurement of mediating factors

Personality. The participating general practitioners completed two personality inventories, one relating to Type A/Type B personality (Bortner, 1969), and one which measured 'intolerance of ambiguity' (Budner, 1962).

Age, gender, attitudes and orientation. Information was collected on age and gender, but the decision to incorporate an instrument to measure attitudes and orientation came too late to be included into the first phase of the project's development.

(3) Measurement of self-perceived pressure and stress

A measure of pressure was developed which used an instrument attached to the diary card (Figure 3) on which the general practitioner made half-hourly recordings of self-perceived pressure on a seven-point scale, where:

0 = snoozing
1 = idle/bored
2 = coasting/relaxed
3 = optimal/stimulated
4 = stretched
5 = hurried
6 = hectic/frantic

As can be seen from the scale, the words indicated how pressured the doctors felt. 'Pressure' was selected because, being one component of potential stress, it was more suited to a single visual-analogue scale. Doctors were reminded to complete the 'pressure' scale by setting a buzzer to ring every half-hour. Contrary to what might be supposed, no doctor found this activity to be a cause of pressure or stress, and the doctors themselves said that half-hourly intervals were preferable to hourly because they gave a better representation of the pressures experienced.

The general practitioners were also asked to complete, before and after each surgery session, the Nottingham Stress Adjective Check List (SACL) which measured self-reported stress and arousal (Mackay *et al.*, 1978; Cox and Mackay, 1985). The SACL has been validated and used in a variety of settings (Watts, Cox and Robson, 1983; Pringle, Robins and Brown, 1984), and it provided a measure of stress against which the experimental 'pressure' scale could be compared. The SACL was shortened slightly to make it more acceptable to general practitioners.

A third measure of stress was devised to measure 'background stress level' which was defined as:

0 = relaxed/not a care in the world, to
↓
6 = very stressed.

The doctor was asked to complete this scale first thing in the morning of his/her recording day.

Results

(1) Measurement of daily loads

Table 2 gives details of the anticipated and new/changed commitments entered by the 18 general practitioners on their diary cards during 52 recording days

Table 2 Anticipated commitments recorded by all 18 general practitioners over 52 days

Activity	Number of entries	Hours taken	(% of allocated hours)
Within practice			
Surgeries	87	163	(48)
Calls	49	112	(33)
Clinics	5	9	(3)
Meetings	11	9	(3)
Administration	21	15	(4)
Teaching	3	5	(1)
Research	—	—	
Interviews	2	2	
Outside practice			
Hospital work	2	3	(1)
Other clinic work	1	1	
Industrial health and medicals	5	6	(2)
Committee work	—	—	
Meetings/conferences	3	1	
Teaching	—	—	
Research	—	—	
Writing	3	3	(1)
Other	1	?	
Personal commitments	30	12	(4)
Total	223		
Total allocated time		341	(100)
Total unallocated time		72	
Total day time (allowing for half-days)		414	

Reproduced by permission of Oxford University Press from Porter, Howie and Levinson (1985)

(excluding night work from 6 p.m., and weekends). Eighty-three per cent of the time during which the doctors recorded their activities was classifiable into the pre-selected headings.

Direct patient care accounted for 83 per cent of the allocated time, about 28 hours per week (sixteen hours per week surgery time, eleven hours per week on calls, and one hour on clinics). Practice-related work (meetings and administration) accounted for a further two hours per week. Activities outside the practice accounted for a further 2.5 hours per week of allocated time, of which personal commitments accounted for almost half.

Unplanned activities or changes in expected commitments were recorded on 16 occasions. Eighteen per cent of surgeries were constrained by another commitment at the end of the session.

The average consultation rate during 66 surgery sesions (for which there was 'patient-flow' data) was 7.0 patients per hour, with a range of 3.8 to 11.5 patients per hour. The average time doctors spent with patients during these surgeries was 7.2 minutes per patient with the range from 3.7 to 12.5.

The interviews that were conducted revealed that 'administrative' activities like writing letters and writing up case-notes were not seen as 'commitments'. The interviews also revealed that there were 14 administrative events which had caused difficulties, 17 professional, medical, or inter-personal events which had caused difficulties, and 15 personal commitments/events which had caused difficulties. None of these had been recorded on the diary card, and a new 'end-of-day' questionnaire has been designed to replace the interview, and is currently being piloted.

(2) The measurement of mediating factors

Personality. Only 15 of the original 18 general practitioners were available to complete the two personality inventories. These two instruments were significantly correlated ($r = 0.55, p < 0.05$) which made intuitive sense as Type A people want to feel in control and are thought not to tolerate ambiguity well. Neither instrument correlated directly with frequency of feelings of pressure (per cent of scores > 4), but Table 3 does suggest that extreme Type A personalities

Table 3 Personality of doctors and pressure scores

	No. of doctors	Percent of average pressure scores > 4
Type A high scorers	2	38
Type A low scorers	5	28
Type B high scorers	6	27
Type B low scorers	2	13

are more likely to report feelings of stress than extreme Type B personalities. However, considerable caution should be taken given that only four of the 15 doctors fell into these two categories.

(3) Measurement of self-perceived pressure and stress

Table 4 summarizes the 'pressure' levels that general practitioners recorded on their diary cards over the 52 recording days—excluding night work from 6 p.m. Nearly a half of the 863 recordings were scores of 3, and a quarter were of 4 and over.

The average score for all doctors was 3.0 and the range ran from 2.3 to 3.7, but this fails to illustrate the variation between doctors. Three doctors used scores of 4 and over on less than 10 per cent of their half-hourly recordings (one doctor never recorded 4 or over), whereas two doctors used scores of 4 and over on more than 50 per cent of their recordings.

Self-perceived 'stress' and 'arousal' (using the SACL) was recorded by doctors on a total of 110 occasions. The average stress score was 4.7 and there was a wide range of average 'stress' values per doctor. Three doctors had average stress scores of zero, while one doctor had an average score of 10 (Maximum: 14).

Table 5 gives the correlation coefficients between the measure of pressure and the SACL measures of stress and arousal. There was a statistically significant, but not particularly strong, correlation between pressure and SACL stress. Table 6 shows the correlation coefficients between pressure and stress for the three

Table 4 Diary card 'pressure' scores recorded by all 18 general practitioners over 52 days (excluding night work)

Pressure score	Practice A (%) ($n = 260$)	Practice B (%) ($n = 215$)	Practice C (%) ($n = 388$)	Total (%) ($n = 863$)
0	3.3	0.8	0.3	1.1
1	5.1	3.1	3.4	3.7
2	19.1	35.0	25.3	26.6
3	57.2	39.0	38.4	43.2
4	12.6	15.4	20.1	17.0
5	2.8	6.9	11.1	7.8
6	0	0	1.0	0.5
Average pressure scores	2.9	2.9	3.1	

Reproduced by permission of Oxford University Press from Porter, Howie and Levinson (1985)

n = number of observations.
Differences in number of scores of 4 and over:
χ^2 (B versus C) = 7.79 ($p < 0.01$)
χ^2 (A versus C) = 20.56 ($p < 0.001$)
χ^2 (B versus A) = 3.24 ($p > 0.05$)

Table 5 Correlations between pressure, stress and arousal
(110 observations)*

	Pressure	Stress	Arousal
Pressure	1	—	—
Stress	0.51 ($p = 0.001$)	1	—
Arousal	0.08 (ns)	−0.25 ($p = 0.01$)	1

* Missing data = 22.
ns = not significant.
Reproduced by permission of Oxford University Press from Porter, Howie and Levinson (1985)

practices for each set of recording days. While there was a correlation between pressure and stress in two of the practices, this did not hold for Practice A. However, when correlation coefficients were calculated on one of the doctors in Practice A it was found that his ratings were negatively correlated and that the other doctors were similar to the doctors in the other two practices.

Self-reported feelings of pressure correlated with surgery consultation rates ($r = 0.43$, $n = 58$), but there was no correlation between these variables when the three practices were analysed separately. It was observed, however, that the practice with the slowest consultation rate (5.9 patients per hour) recorded the lowest proportion of pressure scores of 4 and over (15 per cent). The practice

Table 6 Correlation between self-reported 'pressure' scale on diary card and self-reported stress on the stress adjective check-list, by practice and by day

	Day	Number of observations	Correlation coefficient (r)	Significance level
Practice A*	1	10	−0.29	ns
	2	12	0.39	ns
	3	9	0.37	ns
	Total	31	−0.06	ns
Practice B	1	—	—	—
	2	—	—	—
	3	14	0.72	$p < 0.01$
	Total	14	0.72	$p < 0.01$
Practice C	1	23	0.52	$p < 0.01$
	2	23	0.62	$p < 0.001$
	3	19	0.82	$p < 0.001$
	Total	65	0.64	$p < 0.001$
Full totals		110	0.50	$p < 0.001$
*Practice A				
Dr V		12	−0.59	$p < 0.05$
Other doctors		19	0.53	$p < 0.01$

ns = not significant.

with the fastest consultation rate (8.0 patients per hour) recorded the highest proportion of pressure scores of 4 and over (32 per cent).

3. CONCLUSION

It is not possible, on the basis of published evidence, to make comparisons between the stressfulness of general practice and the stressfulness of other jobs. Indeed, it is probably unwise to consider making such comparisons as there is no valid and reliable way of measuring the relative importance of the various factors that explain why people respond so differently to stress. Our awareness of these complexities and difficulties has restricted our thinking to making longitudinal comparisons of stress levels in the one individual, and to examining changes in the content and style of practice as a general practitioner becomes stressed.

Intuitively it would seem unlikely that general practice is any more or less stressful than other clinical jobs or other 'caring' professions, and that the stress that practitioners experience is probably closely related to the expectations they have of the job. However, there are aspects of the job that have now been documented as causing general practitioners to experience levels of tension and stress beyond levels that are simply stimulating—work overload being the most well described. More research is required to describe the extent of tension and stress, and practitioners methods of coping. A number of related questions and topics follow:

(1) Does tension and stress affect the quality of care provided by general practitioners, and adversely affect their health and well-being?
(2) Are the stresses and strains inherent in the job, or can organizational and structural changes be made to ease the strains without detriment to the quality and quantity of patient care?
(3) Little work has been done on the ways that general practitioners cope with stress, indicating an important area for future research.
(4) Little attention has been given to the selection, training and preparation of general practitioners for the job. Some years ago, one young doctor who had just entered general practice returned to his medical school to demand his money back as he had been so inadequately prepared for the job. While there is little doubt that the development of Departments of General Practice in medical schools and of postgraduate general practice training schemes have begun to provide a better education for general practitioners, there have been few attempts to identify the cognitive and emotional, organizational and social skills needed by practitioners. A key area for further work is the postgraduate experience of housemen, senior housemen, registrars and trainee general practitioners.

(5) Closely related to this are the opportunities for personal change. If doctors who commonly express feelings of tension are also those who exhibit low social orientation and frustration, and are less flexible and less tolerant of ambiguity, then opportunities for personal change may be small.

(6) Finally, and possibly most important for the future of general practice and patient care, is the changing relationship between work and family life. Almost 50 per cent of medical graduates are women and about 50 per cent of all graduates enter general practice. Little is known about the experience of women in the medical labour market, the work that women general practitioners do, their experience of working in a traditionally male profession, or about the ways in which they organize their practice and family commitments. Similarly, little thought or research has been given to the changing role of young male general practitioners if they assume greater family responsibilities.

There is little doubt that workers in the health and welfare services have been subject to considerable external threat over the last few years. Although less subject to government activities, general practice has not been immune from these events. If the public's and the profession's expectation of high quality primary care are to be realized, there will have to be changes in the organization and financing of primary care, in general practitioners' education and training, and in their attitudes and orientations. A sound research programme into stress in general practitioners should provide both the informed basis on which appropriate developments can take place, and the means by which assessment of changes can be made.

REFERENCES

Armstrong, D. (1985). Space and time in British General Practice, *Social Science and Medicine*, **20**, 659–66.

Bates, E. (1982). Doctors and their spouses speak: stress in medical practice, *Sociology of Health and Illness*, **4**, 1, 25–39.

Bortner, R. W. (1969). A short rating scale as a potential measure of Pattern A behaviour, *J. Chron. Dis.*, **22**, 87–91.

Bowling, A. (1981). *Delegation in General Practice—a Study of Doctors and Nurses*. Tavistock, London.

British Medical Association (1965). Charter for the Family Doctor Service. *Br. Med. J.* Supplement, 1, 89.

Brown, G. W. and Harris, T. (1978). *Social Origins of Depression*. Tavistock, London.

Buchan, I. C. and Richardson, I. M. (1973). *Time Study of Consultations in General Practice*. Scottish Health Service Studies: SHHD.

Budner, S. (1962). Intolerance of ambiguity as a personality variable, *J. of Personality*, **30**, 29–50.

Butler, J. R. (1980). *How Many Patients*? Occasional Papers on Social Administration, 64. Bedford Square Press, London.

Cartwright, A. (1967). *Patients and Their Doctors*. Routledge & Kegan Paul, London.
Cartwright, A. and Anderson, R. (1981). *General Practice Revisited*. Tavistock, London.
Cobb, S. (1976). Social support as a mediator of life stress, *Psychosomatic Medicine*, 38, 300-14.
Cooper, C. L. and Payne, R. (eds) (1978). *Stress at Work*. Wiley, Chichester.
Cox, T. (1981). *Stress*. Macmillan.
Cox, T. and Mackay, C. (1985). The measurement of self-reported stress and arousal, *Br. J. Psychol.*, 76, 183-6.
Dohrenwend, B. S. and Dohrenwend, B. P. (1974). *Stressful Life Events: The Nature and Effects*. Wiley, New York.
Dohrenwend, B. S. and Dohrenwend, B. P. (1981). *Stressful Life Events and their Contexts*. Prodist, New York.
French, J. R. P. and Caplan, R. D. (1973). Organisational stress and individual strain. In *The Failure of Success*, ed. A. J. Marrow, Amacom.
Fletcher, B. C. and Payne, R. L. (1980). Stress and work, *Personal Review*, 9, 1, 19-29 and 9, 2, 5-8.
Fry, J. (1972). Twenty-one years of general practice—changing patterns, *J. Roy. Coll. Gen. Practit.*, 22, 521-8.
Gilmore, M., Bruce, N. and Hunt M. (1974). *The Work of the Nursing Team in General Practice*. Council for Education and Training of Health Visitors, London.
Gore, S. (1978). The effect of social support in moderating the health consequences of unemployment, *J. Health and Soc. Behav.*, 19, 157-65.
Gray, D. J. Pereira (1978). Feeling at home. *J. Roy. Coll. Gen. Practit.*, 28, 6-17.
Grol *et al.* (1985). Work satisfaction of general practitioners and the quality of patient care, *Family Practice*, 2, 128-35.
Henderson, S. *et al.* (1978). The patient's primary group. *Br J. Psychiatry*, 132, 74-86.
Hodgkin, G. K. (1973). Evaluation the doctor's work, *J. Roy. Coll. Gen. Practit.*, 23, 759-67.
Horobin, G. and McIntosh, J. (1983). Time, risk and routine in general practice, *Sociology of Health and Illness*, 5, 3, 312-31.
Howie, J. G. R. (1977). 'Patterns of work'. *Trends in General Practice*, Royal College of General Practitioners. BMJ, London.
Howie, J. G. R. and Porter, A. M. D. (1985). Provision of primary care in the United Kingdom, *Oxford Textbook of Public Health*, Vol. 2.
Hughes, D. (1983). Consultation length and outcome in two group general practices. *J. Roy. Coll. Gen. Practit.*, 33, 143-7.
Jenkins, C. D. *et al.* (1971). Association of coronary-prone behaviour scores with recurrence of coronary heart disease, *J. Chronic Diseases*, 24, 601-11.
Jenkins, R., Mann, A. H. and Belsey, E. (1981). The background, design and use of a short interview to assess social stress and support in research and clinical settings, *Soc. Sci. and Med.*, 15E, 195-203.
Karasek, R. A. (1979). Job demands, job decision latitude, and mental strain: Implications for job redesign, *Administrative Science Quarterly*, 24, 285-308.
Kyriacou, C. and Sutcliffe, J. (1979). A note on teacher stress and locus of control, *J. Occupational Psychology*, 52, 227-8.
McDonald, A. and McLean, I. G. (1971). Study of the work of general practitioners, *Practitioner*, 207, 608.
Mackay, C. J. (1980). The measurement of mood and psychophysiological activity using self-report techniques. In I. Martin and P. H. Venables (eds), *Techniques in psychophysiology*. Chichester, Wiley.
Mackay, C., Cox, T., Burrows, G. and Lazzerini, T. (1978). An inventory for the measurement of self-reported stress and arousal. *Br. J. Soc. Clin. Psychol.*, 17, 283-4.

Marsh, G. N., McNay, R. A. and Whewell, J. (1972). Survey of home visiting by general practitioners in North-East England. *Br. Med. J.*, **1**, 487–92.

Mechanic, D. (1968). General medical practice in England and Wales: its organization and future. *New England J. Med.*, **279**, 680–9.

Mechanic, D. (1970). Practice orientations among general medical practitioners in England and Wales. *Medical Care*, **8**, 15–25.

Mechanic, D. (1972). General Medical Practice: some comparisons between the work of primary care physicians in the United States and England and Wales. *Public Expectations and Health Care*. Wiley, New York.

Mechanic, D. (1974). *Politics, Medicine and Social Science*, Wiley, New York.

Melville, A. (1980). Job satisfaction in general practice: implications for prescribing. *Soc. Sci. and Med.*, **14A**, 495–9.

Morrell, D. C., Evans, M. E., Morris R. W. *et al.* (1986). The 'five minute' consultation; effect of time constraint on clinical context and patient satisfaction, *Br. Med. J.*, **292**, 870–873.

Morrell, D. C. and Nicholson, S. (1974). Measuring the results of changes in the method of delivering primary medical care—a cautionary tale. *J. Roy. Coll. Gen. Practit.*, **24**, 111–18.

Morrice, J. K. W. (1984). Job stress and burnout. *Bulletin of the Royal College of Psychiatrists*, **8**, 3, 45–6.

Murrell, H. (1978). *Work Stress and Mental Strain*. Work Research Unit, Department of Employment. Occasional Paper No 6.

Payne, R., Jick, T. D. and Burke, R. J. (1982). Whither stress research? An Agenda for the 1980s. *J. Occupational Behaviour*, **3**, 131–45.

Pearlin, L. I. *et al.* (1981). The stress process. *J. Health and Soc. Behav.*, **22**, 337–56.

Porter, A. M. D., Howie, J. G. R. and Levinson, A. (1985). Measurement of stress as it affects the work of the general practitioner. *Family Practice*, **2**, 136–46.

Pringle, M., Robins, S. and Brown, G. (1984). Assessing the consultation: method for measuring changes in patient stress and arousal, *BMJ*, **288**, 1657–8.

Raynes, N. V. and Cairns, V. (1980). Factors contributing to the length of general practice consultations, *J. Roy. Coll. Gen. Practit.*, **30**, 496.

Reedy, B. L. E. C. (1977). The Health Team. *Trends in General Practice*. Roy, Coll. Gen. Practit., BMJ, London.

Review Body on Doctors' and Dentists' Remuneration (1981). Eleventh Report. Cmnd 8239. HMSO.

Richardson, I. M. *et al.* (1973). A study of general practitioner consultations in North-East Scotland, *J. Roy. Coll. Gen. Practit.*, 23, 132–42.

Rosenman, R. H. *et al.* (1970). Coronary heart disease in the western collaborative group study, *J. Chronic Diseases*, **23**, 173–90.

Sales, S. M. (1970). Some effects of role overload and role underload, *Organisational Behaviour and Human Performance*, **5**, 597–608.

Stevenson, J. S. K. (1982). Advantages of deputising services: a personal view. *Br. Med. J.*, **284**, 947–9.

Stilwell, B. (1982). The nurse practitioner at work. *Nursing Times*, 27 Oct., 1799–1803.

Vardy, P. I. (1972). How many patients? *J. Roy. Coll. Gen. Practit.*, **22**, 848–

Warr, P. B. and Wall, T. D. (1975). *Work and Well Being*. Penguin.

Warr, P. B. (1978). A study of psychological well-being. *Br. J. Psychol.*, **69**, 111–21.

Warr, P. B., Cook, J. D. and Wall, T. D. (1979). Scales for the measurement of some work attitudes and aspects of psychological well-being, *J. Occupational Psychology*, **52**, 129–48.

Watts, C., Cox, T. and Robson, J. (1983). Morningness—Eveningness and diurnal variations in self-reported mood, *J. of Psychology*, **113**, 251–6.

Wilkin, D. and Metcalfe, D. H. H. (1984). List size and patient contact in general medical practice, *BMJ*, **289**, 1501-5.

Williams, W. D. (1970). A study of general practitioners' work load in South Wales 1965-1966. Reports from General Practice No 12, *J. Roy. Coll. Gen. Practit.*, **19**, Suppl No 1.

Stress in Health Professionals
Edited by R. Payne and J. Firth-Cozens
© 1987 John Wiley & Sons Ltd

Chapter 4

Occupational Stress in Women Physicians

Lillian Kaufman Cartwright

Medicine can be a demanding and a rewarding profession. At all stages of the career—from entry to retirement—there are challenges, conflicts, and opportunities for all physicians, both men and women (Cartwright, 1979a). Three areas of research will be considered within the chapter. First it will present salient demographic information which permits analysis of gender differences in occupational stress. Changes relevant to women's role in medicine will be discussed as well as evolutionary shifts in the profession itself.

Second, several interrelated questions about occupational gender differences will be addressed: Are there different sources of stress for men and women? Is the severity of problems different? Do problems manifest themselves in different symptom patterns? What part does timing in the occupational and personal life cycle play in symptom formation?

Last, recommendations concerning the alleviation of gender-related occupational stress will be delineated. Guidelines for educational policy and program development will be discussed. These suggestions take into account changes within the profession as well as external and internal barriers impeding the assumption of leadership roles by women. Let us begin by identifying the significant changes of the last decade and a half as they relate to women and to the profession.

WHAT HAS CHANGED? WHAT HAS REMAINED THE SAME?

Entry

In the United States, the women's movement and accompanying antibias legislation significantly affected the number of women entering the general labor force, increasing the number of working women to 43 per cent in 1983. This figure compares with 39.6 per cent in Britain, 38.4 per cent in West Germany, and 34.2 per cent in Italy (US Bureau of Census, 1984).

These movements have also led to a significant increase in the number of women entering medicine. Currently, 31.8 per cent of total enrollment in the 127 US medical schools are women. This figure represents more than three times as many women as attended in 1969 when enrollment approximated 9 per cent (Turner, 1985). Also, it appears that more older women are among the accepted applicants (Turner, 1985; Kaplan, 1982).

Although female applications and acceptances to medical school have burgeoned in the last decade, it will take several more decades before the gender ratio of practicing physicians will be affected substantially. In 1982, there were approximately 64,000 women doctors or less than 13 per cent of all physicians (Eiler, 1983). Some predict it will take thirty more years before women will comprise 25 per cent of the practicing work-force. At that time they will still be a minority.

Speciality Choice

Are women choosing different specialities than they did in the past? Although a few reports found greater convergence between men and women (cf. McGrath and Zimet (1977) and Weisman *et al.* (1980)), more recent investigations find women choosing the same specialities they did in the past, for practically the same reasons (Berquist *et al.*, 1985; Bonar, Watson, and Koestler, 1982; Ferner and Woodward, 1982; and Zimny and Shelton, 1982).

Current national statistics reflecting residency choice indicate that in 1983 the greatest number of women entered Internal Medicine, Pediatrics, Obstetrics/Gynecology, Family Practice, and Psychiatry (in that order). The lowest number of women residents entered Aerospace Medicine, Urology, Orthopedic Surgery, and Thoracic Surgery. In looking at the proportion of women *vis-à-vis* men residents, women represented 24.3 per cent of the resident force; however, there were considerably more of them in Pediatrics (46.5 per cent), Child Psychiatry (42.6 per cent), Dermatology (37.5 per cent), and Obstetrics/Gynecology (36.5 per cent) (Turner, 1985). These proportions do not suggest radical change from past choice except for the specialty of Obstetrics/Gynecology where women have more than doubled their percentage since 1975 when 15 per cent were women. Women are still concentrated in the lower-status and traditionally nuturant, primary care specialties (Bauder-Nishita, 1980).

Why are women not choosing the more prestigious and higher paying specialties? Berquist *et al.* (1985) found that women gave significantly more weight to three motivational factors that entered into specialty choices: patient contact, the family, and working fewer hours. The majority of men, 70 per cent in this midwestern sample, expected to make over $75 000 a year while only 43 per cent of the women expected that same income.

Davidson (1979) accounts for the differential specialty concentration of women as resulting from a combination of (1) sex-role compatibility, (2) time pressures, (3) formal organizational structure of the specialties and (4) informal social pressures. She argues that free choice of specialty is a mirage and substitutes the concept of 'choice by constraint'. She states that when women seem to be making choices they really are making accommodations based on maximizing role compatibility and minimizing conflict between sex role and occupational role.

Attitudes and Perspectives

Although women may not have departed radically from earlier specialization preferences, many have asserted over the years that women bring a unique perspective to medicine. Has this changed? What is the evidence? Margolis, Greenwood and Heilbron (1983), in a recent large-scale study of 1100 residents in Obstetrics/Gynecology, found that male and female residents did differ on certain values and priorities. However, on many salient practice issues there were no differences. Motivational factors for entering the specialty were essentially similar. Where differences existed, the direction indicated greater commitment to global feminism and a critical stance toward paternalistic features of the specialty (e.g. not encouraging women to fully participate in choice of method of birth and contraception).

These researchers did find some sex differences in practice plans: Although the majority of both sexes desire private practice partnerships as career goals, men prefer it more than women (76 versus 62 per cent). Salaried practice with regular hours is a minority preference for both sexes although women prefer it more (35 per cent versus 13 per cent).

The study also found differences in views concerning controversial issues in the specialty. On eleven statements pertaining to controversial issues (e.g. abortion, contraception for minors, home births), there were four significant findings, all of which pointed to a more egalitarian attitude in the women. These findings match a trend toward liberal thinking in women in medicine as reported earlier by Lesserman (1981).

The most provocative result of the survey was that 17 per cent of the sample—both men and women—were interested in a part-time residency. The implications of this finding will be discussed in the last section of the chapter.

Power and Women Physicians

Power and authority within medical educational institutions resides in such academic roles as Chancellor, Dean, Department Chair, and Full Professor. In clinical practice, influence, power and decision-making capability come from being on hospital boards, holding office in local and national medical societies, having consultation status within government and third party groups, and being a member of a highly paid specialty such as the surgical sub-specialties.

Women continue to be poorly represented in all these leadership and prestigious positions. For example, in academia, for 1984 to 1985, there is only one woman Dean and 126 male Deans. As you go lower in the hierarchy, a larger percentage are female, approximately 9 per cent of the Associate Deans and 19 per cent of the Assistant Deans are women. Similarly, in respect to the faculty, 6 per cent of the medical school professors are female in comparison to 36 per cent of the instructors. There are only 64 female Department Chairs and 12 of these are serving in an acting or interim capacity (Turner, 1985). In general, women are promoted more slowly, are almost absent in top leadership roles, and hold positions lower on the status hierarchy in academia.

Scadron et al. (1982) studied attitudes toward women doctors in academia and they found that these women are regarded distinctly by different constituencies. Using a stratified sample of ten medical schools, attitudes toward female academicians were measured. Five groups were contrasted: male and female medical students, male and female faculty and top level administrators. There were some similarities, for example, the majority of all groups, approximately 80 per cent, saw women faculty as both inclined to do as much research as men and as bringing as much prestige to the institution.

On a number of issues, however, there were marked gender disparities and group disagreements. Generally, women medical students were the most supportive of women academicians, seeing them as needed to bring balance into academic medicine and as more sensitive to the health care needs of women. Three-quarters of the female students did not see women doctors who spend long hours at work as neglectful of family. Yet over 40 per cent of all three male groups (students, faculty, and administrators) saw long hours of women doctors as neglectful of household. Male medical students were least supportive of bringing more women into leadership roles. One can assume that when the advance of women potentially threatened male power or offered competition, there was skepticism about equalization.

Similarly, as in Slay and McDonald's (1981) study of men and women in academia, women faculty perceived themselves as less confident than male faculty (44 per cent) and less likely to get tenure (82 per cent).

The Consumer and Women Physicians

What are the effects on patient care of having more women doctors? If patients are motivated to seek out women doctors, career satisfactions and economic rewards for female doctors could be improved. This area is fairly unexplored. Engleman (1974) did early research which suggested patient negativity toward women doctors. However, Young (1979; 1980) found in experimental approaches using simulated situations that sex is not as important a factor as previously believed. In respect to patients' disclosures of symptoms, his research suggests that perceiving the doctor as technically competent and socially competent is more salient than sex in promoting trust in patients.

Considerable anecdotal information exists suggesting that women are more compassionate than men. Scott (1985) in recent research with 52 pediatric residents confirms this stereotype. He demonstrated that female physicians communicated at higher levels of empathy and respect in their examinations of children than male physicians. Interpersonal skills were assessed from videotaped medical interviews, using the Carkuff scales.

Lewis *et al.* (1985), in a related study, found higher levels of patient satisfaction with female Pediatricians. At least in Pediatrics, then, there is preliminary support for the view that women physicians communicate better than male peers and that this ability positively influences patient satisfaction.

Similarly, Roeske (1976) notes that in her review of various published personal accounts by women Psychiatrists that they are now more often sought out by female patients. These patients wish to clarify their feelings about being a woman and related beliefs of being second-rate and powerless. The empathy expressed in the relationship is highly valued. For some women patients it is the beginning of viewing other women as competent, caring and not as a sexual rival for a man's attention.

Changes in the Profession

Significant changes in the United States health care system have had considerable influence on the profession. Medicine no longer has the autonomy and prestige it had prior to the 1970s. Government regulations, third party payments and reviews, and bureaucratic controls have created problems which potentially diminish satisfactions. The entrance of profit organizations into health care has raised value conflict issues. At the same time, the doctor shortage of the 1960s and early 1970s has been alleviated so that, in many specialties, there are no shortages at all but rather oversupply.

Change and its Implications

What, then, has changed? Clearly entry has been eased. Problems arising from singularity and obvious minority status have been reduced with the increase in women in medical school classes. At the same time, significant issues relevant to the practice of medicine have not changed radically because these changes have many institutionalized resistances and take more time. The most salient area of slow change resided in female access to the highest echelons of power. This pattern is similar to Europe's where women have entered medicine in significantly larger numbers since the Second World War, yet they are not well represented in prestigious posts. Roeske (1984) comments that female physicians in England are not promoted as frequently as males since promotion is based on time spent in career and that almost a third of these doctors desire more work but are unable to move because of family commitments. She also notes that high taxation, problems with domestic help, and lack of child care centers further diminish career development for women.

Since women do not occupy top jobs, the kind of changes in the profession that could assist in their career/private life integrations are not likely to be supported through liberal program planning and policy changes. It is naive to believe that concerns of women physicians would be a high priority for the great majority of male decision-makers. Second, the role modeling and mentor relationships important to early and middle professional growth are likely to be diminished because so few models are available (Roeske and Lake, 1977). Third, the zest that comes from knowing no limits to professional competence is dampened by seeing so few women who have made it to the top and by sensing the disillusionment, lack of confidence and restricted freedom of some who have.

OCCUPATIONAL STRESS: GENDER ISSUES

Let us now return to the questions introduced at the beginning of the chapter. Are women doctors more stressed than men? This is a misleading and naive question on a number of counts: it assumes male doctors and female doctors are unitary groups and that stress is a constant over the career trajectory. The question also underestimates the amount of stress that is linked to the work itself—i.e., dealing with intense human emotions on a daily basis, professional responsibility, long hours, interruptions and emergencies. Notman, Salt, and Nadelson (1984) for example, found no significant differences between the sexes on amount of stress and number of perceived stressors in medical students from Harvard and Tufts.

It is more productive, then, to reformulate the inquiry and ask:

(1) Are some *sources* of stress different for men and women?
(2) Are the *times* at which stress is exacerbated different?
(3) Are the *coping* strategies distinctive?

Gender-linked Sources of Stress

Three sources of stress are reported to be more common in women: external prejudice, fragmentation, normative value conflicts (Cartwright, 1977; Ducker, 1974, 1980; Nadelson and Notman, 1983; Walsh, 1977). First, there is the stress that accompanies working in a prejudiced, non-supportive environment which does not accept women's place in the profession. We know from other studies that social support plays a mediating role in reducing the stress of life change (Antonovsky, 1979; Berkman and Syme, 1979; Cassel, 1976; Leavy, 1983). When this support is minimal or absent, physical illness and psychological impairment are more likely. Although there is more general social support than there used to be for women's entry into the profession, support is less in later career stages

(Lorber, 1981, 1983). The dearth of role models and sponsorship for post-doctoral élite fellowships as well as conventional views about the unsuitability of women for positions of power are examples of waning support during middle career years.

Although prejudice has been reduced on entry, it still can be a potent factor for minority women who suffer from double dosage. For example, Lovelace (1983) found in a study of young black women doctors that external prejudice was the most cited cause of stress. These black physicians had little or no difficulty with sex role conflict because the black culture expects women to be powerful, strong and oriented to work. Some, however, perceived the attitude of the general professional community to be judgmental and rejecting.

Cartwright's (1978) sample of women doctors educated in the late 1960s and early 1970s also revealed more stress in women of Japanese ancestry, particularly when these women left their native California environment and their families. The Japanese women, unlike the black women in Lovelace's sample, suffered from sex role stringency in their own culture which questioned assertiveness and dominance in women. When the profession expected such behaviors but offered little support, anxiety and career dissatisfactions were evident.

As more minority women enter medicine, Native Americans and Hispanic women for example, specific adaptations will develop which represent compromises between early sex role and later professional socialization expectations.

During the period of residency choice, Ducker (1987) viewed the attitude of male colleagues who see some specialties as unsuitable for women as a source of stress which promotes anxiety and constraint in females. Ducker's research suggested that external prejudice functions differentially in medicine so that a woman Pediatrician would be viewed by her male peers as doing what she should do—doing what comes naturally. At the same time, a woman Orthopedic surgeon would be seen as an anomaly since orthopedic surgery is thought of by male physicians as suitable for strong, athletic men. External prejudice probably functions unevenly across specialties, work settings, and geographic areas and is directed differentially to distinct target groups of women. Women will, in turn, respond differently to this stressor, depending on their early sex role socialization, personality, and inner and external resources.

The second major source of stress is fragmentation (Cartwright, 1978). This source is also termed role strain by Goode (1960) who states that strain is a result of the felt difficulty of meeting two or more significant role obligations. For women, this strain is a product of conflict and bargaining between occupational and traditional gender roles. Each physician's role obligations are unique. The woman who has chosen to be mother, spouse, as well as physician, will suffer more from fragmentation than one who has relinquished all obligations but physician.

On the simplest level there is not enough time to carry out all role requirements well. Juggling, fragmentation, compromise, and conflicts of allocation of allegiance and resources characterize a life where total role obligations are too demanding.

Time management problems alone, however, do not completely explain role strain. On a deeper level, discharging duties through instrumental behaviors (e.g. giving parties, cooking, finding appropriate schools for the children) are insufficient to meet role demands fully. Carrying out a woman's role in a satisfying and complete way requires expressive commitments as well (e.g. nurturance, empathic listening, support, and providing safe contexts for the maintenance and repair of human relationships). These emotional aspects of role cannot be carried out by a robot. The woman physician must be nurtured, rested, repaired if she is to serve as a conduit for family growth and development. Here is the rub. The private life of the woman professional shrinks because of the immensity of other role demands. Time for solitude, meditation, rest, play, appreciation of music, art and literature is rare, if there at all. This lack of time to replenish resources is generally not recognized in the literature, and it is a grave and fundamental omission. Equal pay for equal work is not an issue; however, equal play for equal work is.

In addition to prejudice and fragmentation, a third source of stress stems from internal normative value conflicts (Coser and Rokoff, 1971). Guilt and worry, as well as identity crises, can be emotional consequences of not feeling successful at both roles. Each role—role of woman and role of doctor—demands excellence in different ways and roles can clash on an unconscious level. In some women the relentless wish to satisfy both roles can lead to exhaustion and driven behavior.

Not every woman physician, however, suffers from intense role conflict. Cartwright (1979b) distinguished three role integrations—'superwoman', 'career of limited ambition', and 'medicine is my lust'. By far the most vulnerable to stress is the superwoman; it is she who reports the most stress (Cartwright, 1978). She is apt to select a prestigious, demanding specialty and work full time. She marries and has children and needs to see herself as examplary in this role. Also, she is zestful and adventuresome and often pushes herself to the limits of endurance. She demonstrates that stress is not synonymous with career or life dissatisfaction. Often, indeed, the superwoman is excited and challenged by life and would have it no other way.

The 'career of limited ambition' leads to less stress. In this pathway, the career is given a lower priority than the family. Women adopting this pattern are likely to have salaried jobs, work part-time and have non-continuous careers. This career track is not by definition dull since many women make the most of it by bringing their creativity to their position, but it can presage less career satisfaction because of lower income and limited opportunity for vertical advancement.

The third pattern, 'medicine is my lust', places medicine first. The woman may choose not to marry or, if married, will not have children. Nurturant and expressive needs are played out at work. Career satisfaction is very high and stress is not overwhelming. The negative side of this adaptation can be loneliness and the limitation of perceiving the world through one lens. Currently, since somewhere between 70–80 per cent of women doctors marry and the majority have children, this third adaptation is a minority position.

The Timing of Stress

Life stage is often slighted in the literature. Cartwright and Schmuckler (1982) contrasted a sample of older women college presidents, 62 per cent of the total populations of women college presidents in the United States, with a younger sample of women doctors. There was a significant difference in the effects of maternal responsibility on stress at these different ages. The fragmentation or juggling of early maternal responsibility with taxing work was significantly more for the doctors (mean age 32) than for the college presidents (mean age 51). The period of early career formation collides with the early stages of family formation and exacerbates stress. In contrast, for the college presidents, the family generally offered a safe harbor for difficult work. The source of stress for the presidents was in the work itself, rarely the family. These data demonstrate that sources of stress shift as the woman proceeds through her life cycle.

The comparison of women in these two élite occupations suggested a new metaphor of 'role montage' as a guide through the complexity, confusions and changes in lives over time. Role montage emphasizes the relatively and the changing balance in the parts of the self over time. A montage is patterned, complex, and multidemensional. It takes into account both rational and irrational shifts, overlapping of roles, and life-stage reorganizations. The montage will change over the lifespan so that a particular configuration dominates a specific life-stage which can be followed by another patterning. For example, in the just cited study, the sources of stress shift with life stage. The number of roles may be the same for women in their thirties as in their fifties, but the demands and emphasis of these roles change. In addition, a woman may adopt different integrations at different points in her life—a superwoman at one time and a career of limited ambition at another.

Figure 1 is the role montage of a 45-year-old physician who is married and has three children. She is practicing full-time and since her husband is also a physician, there is overlap between roles of wife and doctor. She was a professional artist before entering medical school. Although she still maintains some interest in the art world, it feels peripheral to the rest of her life. This montage is typical of a superwoman integration.

The concept of life stage is important but insufficient to portray the complexity of 'sense of self'. Role montage allows the contextual diversity

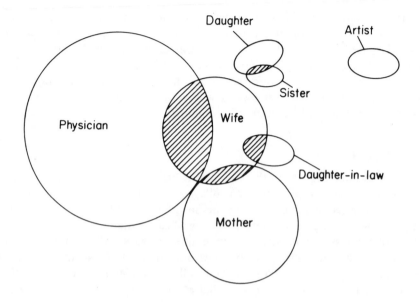

Figure 1 See text for explanation

provided by occupational setting to have saliency as well as simultaneously allowing for the contraction and expansion of other roles (family, community, private). The montage graphically portrays different timetables and choices and does not assume linear progression since the choices of professional women (marriage, children, changing positions, moving, divorce) are less rigid in following a social clock.

Other integrative concepts that view lives over time include Levinson's (1978) concept of the life structure. Since this theory relies heavily on male age norms, it may not be useful for female professionals. Helson, Mitchell and Moore (1984) developed the concept of 'social clock projects' to describe the lives of 132 college women who were studied longitudinally from young to middle adulthood. Adherence and non-adherence to expected patterns of marriage and motherhood ('feminine social clock pattern') or to upwardly mobile occupational goals were contrasted. The 'social clock project' emphasizes the integration of activities over time, but the authors themselves say that the concept does not do justice to the complex patterning of family and occupational and other roles.

Coping Strategies and Symptom Formation

Do women doctors adapt differently than men to the pressures of life? This provocative question can only be answered impressionistically. No adequate data base exists to permit a definitive answer. Concepts of career trajectory, adult life stage, and role montage assume careful attention to age, era of medical education, choice of medical school, specialty choice, personality, family formation, and social support. The literature is not systematic but anecdotal, cross-sectional, based on cohorts from selected schools, and uses demographic data which have flaws in method and definition of terms.

Impressionistically, then, women seem more than men to favor career dilution and dimunition as a way of keeping themselves balanced. This strategy is especially apparent in younger women in the early stages of career and family formation. They are more apt to work part-time and take salaried positions than men (Angell, 1981; Elliot, 1981; Heins *et al.*, 1977; Nadelson and Notman, 1983); they are also more apt to interrupt practice and training (Cartwright, 1977; Ducker, 1974; Mandelbaum, 1981). In a study of Detroit physicians, Heins (1979) found that significantly more women (34 per cent) than men (6 per cent) said they altered their career because of a relationship with the opposite sex. Weisman *et al.* (1986) investigated the work patterns of recently trained obstetrician-gynecologists and found that family role has an opposite effect on men and women, with married men with children working more hours than other family status groups and married women with children working the fewest hours.

Strategies that reduce or eliminate the demands of intimacy also are more common in women. They are less apt to marry (Heins and Braslow, 1981), utilize divorce more frequently (Lorber and Ecker, 1983; Rose and Rosow, 1972), and have fewer children (Heins and Braslow, 1981; Lorber and Ecker, 1983). These statistics reflect, in part, that the demands of intimacy are different for men and women. Women are culturally expected to perform more duties and services in the intimate relationship.

Although there is little direct evidence to support this assertion, disorders of untempered career ambition such as coronary heart disease and hypertension may be more common in males. Gerber (1983) asserts that a work-centered life is reinforced for males in medicine since it is linked to the attitudes of adventurous masculinity—toughness, boldness, and courage. The superwoman, described earlier, may also be more subject to these disorders than other women although no data are available to support this guess.

The literature on physician impairment is relevant to our inquiry since it focuses on severely maladjusted physicians who can do harm to themselves and their patients. The three most common problems reported are alcoholism, drug dependency, and depression. Currently, impaired physician programs are part of almost all of the State Medical Society programs. In 1980, 1608 impaired doctors were in contact with these programs. Drug and alcohol abuse problems appear more common in male doctors (*The Impaired Physician*, 1980).

On a national level, Gomberg (1979) reports there are approximately 4 to 5 male alcoholics for every female alcoholic. She notes that these figures vary with the criteria used to define a drinking problem, and the setting sampled. At the same time, women in the United States and cross-nationally use more licit drugs (prescribed drugs) than men (ratio of 2:1), while men utilize more illegal drugs. Doctors' easy access to drugs makes drug abuse a potential occupational hazard for both men and women. A study of alcoholics undergoing treatment at the Mayo Clinic points out that alcoholism also is a general occupational hazard of medicine because doctors were overly represented in their treatment groups (*The Impaired Physician*, 1980).

Depression, in contrast to substance abuse, may be more common in women doctors. Clearly, both nationally and in industrial European countries, women are more likely to be diagnosed as depressed. A 2:1 ratio is reported by Weisman and Klerman (19797 for the years 1936 to 1976. Suicide statistics for male physicians do not indicate that doctors take their lives any more than males in the general population. Some agree that the true extent of physician suicide is not known and others note that, because doctors undergo a stringent selection process, one should expect lower rates (Cartwright, 1979a).

Yet the suicide statistics for women physicians, specifically young women, are at least three times higher than for women in general (Steppacher and Mausner, 1974). Realize in interpreting these statistics that in general men are more likely to take their lives than women, while women are more apt to attempt the act but not carry it through. Women and men doctors do not differ in rates of 'successful' suicide if compared with each other. They do differ in age of suicide, with the women dying at an earlier age than the men.

Ducker (1987) does a thorough review of this literature on female suicide and depression and concludes that considerable controversy still exists, particularly in the area of inferring a high rate of affective disorders in women physicians on the basis of their suicide statistics. The issue of what constitutes an adequate comparison group for women physicians is raised.

A recent national study of law student suicides (Hamilton *et al.*, (1983) provides a good contrast group. Surprisingly, law student suicide rates were found to be very low, significantly lower than the average population for that age group. Women law students, despite being in a competitive, male dominated profession like women medical students, were not any more prone to suicide than their male peers. Furthermore, the female law student rate was lower than the general female population. Hamilton *et al.* speculates that medicine, in contrast to law, may be valuing individualism at the cost of community (cf. Cartwright, 1979a). That is, law students may be better integrated into the social order. It may also be the case that aggression is more freely expressed in law and thus is not turned inward. The adversarial process in law strongly contrasts with the care-taking of process of medicine.

A study of stress in 135 top female executives from the United Kingdom (Cooper and Davidson, 1982) offers yet another contrast group. Few physical symptoms were noted in these women with the exception of migraine headaches (24.4 per cent). However, psychological complaints were voiced with almost 70 per cent reporting tiredness and 60 per cent irritability. Depression was cited by almost one quarter of the sample. High incidence of smoking was apparent with 42 per cent smoking in contrast to 30 per cent of male managers. These investigators view women in high level management jobs as prone to type A behavior. Suicide was not cited as an occupational hazard, but substance abuse was.

RECOMMENDATIONS AND CONCLUSIONS

Current conditions lay the groundwork for more radical shifts in women's participation in the profession. Significant changes have occurred which make it possible for more women to enter medicine. Johnson (1983) states that 40 per cent of medical students will be female in 1990. Change has also occurred in the profession itself so that external controls on practice and payments have increased enormously. At the same time, Tarlov (1981) estimates that by 1990 the United States will have a surplus of 70000 physicians.

If women are to take advantage of their numbers and the transitional status of their profession, they would need to seek out leadership positions and see themselves as definers of situations rather than adjusters to the status quo. Power and authority must be perceived as desirable values and as not conflicting with sex roles. More women physicians would need to learn the skills and competencies of leadership, such as training in administration, politics, and conflict resolution; knowledge of short and long-range planning; fiscal management; networking, and the ability to identify resources and allocate them appropriately.

Although the above recommendations have merit, changes in these areas of leadership are likely to be slow because sex role stereotypes are tenacious. These attitudes are learned very early, some before the age of three. Radical changes in attitude toward the sexes have not occurred and are unlikely to in the near future. In their replication of a 1957 study of college students, Werner and La Russa (1985) found great persistence in sex role beliefs. These University of California students, who are known for their activism, still say men are more forceful, independent, stubborn and reckless, and women are more mannerly, giving, emotional and submissive. The only major difference over the decades is a greater inclination to view women more favorably.

The current climate of the profession could be a potentially powerful factor in promoting change in medical education and practice since a slower growth in numbers of doctors would be advantageous. Reorganization of medical specialties and residency training programs would offer women and some men more satisfactory and profitable careers and reduce role stress. Extended and de-accelerated curricula would be more consonant with today's national needs. Six-year medical school programs, an optional year off between medical school and residency, part-time residency programs, and a three-day practice week are examples of de-accelerated education and practice. This tempo shift would assist female doctors in their work/private life integrations as well as represent a sane and reasonable approach to supply–demand alterations in medical care.

Formal institutional accommodations to the private lives of women represent the most important needed change in the medical system if gender-linked stress is to be reduced. Systematic study of the profession's resistance to experiment with change in the time structure of training is needed as is investigation into an entrenched professional ethos which encourages complete commitment to the profession and disparages the well-rounded life. Although the tempo of learning medical facts would be slower, other things would be learned in the interim which complement and enhance the art and practice of medicine.

There is little need for turning out more and more physicians; slower pacing of medical training with greater emphasis on integrated, well-balanced living would be a positive direction for men and women in medicine. If women are to do more than just lament the current ethos of the profession, they need to consciously reappraise the values and activities that would empower them to make changes. Leadership, power, influence and money have been sex-linked for a long time; they need not be forever.

REFERENCES

Angell, M. (1981). Women in medicine: Beyond prejudice, *The New England Journal of the American Medical Women's Association,* **304,** (19), 1161–3.
Antonovsky, A. (1979). *Health, Stress and Coping.* Jossey-Bass, San Francisco.
Bauder-Nishita, J. (1980). Gender specific differentials of medical practice in California, *Women and Health,* **5,** 5–15.
Berkman, L. and Syme, L. (1979). Social networks, lost resistance and mortality: a 9-year follow-up study of Alameda County residents, *American Journal of Epidemiology,* **109,** 186–204.
Berquist, S. R., Duchac, B. W., Schalin, V. A., Zastrow, J. F., Barr, V. L. and Borowiecki, T. (1985). Perceptions of freshman medical students of gender differences in medical specialty choice, *Journal of Medical Education,* **60,** 379–83.
Bonar, J. W., Watson, J. A. and Koestler, L. S. (1982). Sex differences in career and family plans of medical students, *Journal of the American Medical Women's Association,* **37,** 300–308.
Cartwright, L. K. (1977). Continuity and noncontinuity in the careers of a sample of young women physicians, *Journal of the American Medical Women's Association,* **32,** (9), 316–21.
Cartwright, L. K. (1978). Career satisfaction and role harmony in a sample of young women physicians, *Journal of Vocational Behavior,* **12,** 184–96.
Cartwright, L. K. (1979a). Sources and effects of stress in health careers. In G. C. Stone, F. Cohen, and N. E. Adler (eds), *Health Psychology: A Handbook* (pp. 419–445). Jossey Bass, San Francisco.
Cartwright, L. K. (1979b). The integrative challenges of the young woman doctor: a step beyond the barriers. In *Proceedings of Eighteenth Annual Conferernce on Research in*

Medical Education. Association of American Medical Colleges. Washington, DC.
Cartwright, L. K. and Schmuckler, J. M. (1982). Women college presidents and women physicians: a comparison of two samples. Paper presented at American Psychological Association, Washington, DC.
Cassel, J. C. (1976). The contribution of the social environment to host resistance, *American Journal of Epidemiology*, **104**, 107–23.
Cooper, C. L. and Davidson, M. J. (1982). The highest stress on women managers, *Organizational Dynamics*, Spring, 44–53.
Coser, R. L. and Rokoff, G. (1971). Women in the occupational world: social disruption and conflicts, *Social Problems*, **18** 535–54.
Davidson, L. R. (1979). Choice by constraint: the selection and function of specialties among women physicians in training, *Journal Health Polit. Policy Law*, **4**, 200–20.
Ducker, D. G. (1974). The effects of two sources of role strain on women physicians. Unpublished dissertation, the City University of New York.
Ducker, D. G. (1978). Believed suitability of medical specialties for women physicians, *Journal of the American Medical Women's Association*, **33**, (1), 25–32.
Ducker, D. G. (1980). The effects of two sources of role strain on women physicians, *Sex Roles*, **6**, 549–59.
Ducker, D. G. (1987). Role conflict for women physicians. In C. D. Scott and J. E. Hawks (eds), *Heal Thyself: The Health of the Health Professional*, Brunner-Mazel, New York.
Eiler, M. A. (1983). *Physician Characteristics and Distribution in the U.S.* Survey and data resources. American Medical Association.
Elliot, C. M. (1981). Women physicians as workers, *Journal of American Medical Women's Association*, **36**, 105–8.
Engleman, E. G. (1974). Attitudes toward women physicians. A study of 500 clinic patients, *Western Journal of Medicine*, **120**, 95–100.
Ferner, B. M. and Woodward, C. A. (1982). Career choices, work patterns and perceptions of undergraduate education of McMaster medical graduates: comparison between men and women, *Canadian Medical Association Journal*, **126**, 1411–14.
Gerber, L. A. (1983). *Married to their Careers*, Tavistock Publications, New York.
Gomberg, E. S. (1979). Problems with alcohol and other drugs. In Gomberg, E. S. and Franks, V. (eds), *Gender and Disordered Behavior*, Brunner/Mazel, New York.
Goode, W. (1960). A theory of role strain, *American Sociological Review*, **25**, 483–96.
Hamilton, M. J., Pepitone-Arreola-Rockwell, F., Rockwell, D. and Whitlow, C. (1983). Thirty-five law student suicides, *The Journal of Psychiatry and Law*, Fall, 335–44.
Heins, M. (1979). Career and life pattern of women and men physicians. In Shapiro, E. C. and Lowenstein, L. M. (eds), *Becoming a Physician*, Ballinger Publishing Co., Cambridge.
Heins, M. and Braslow, J. (1981). Women doctors: productivity in Great Britain and the United States, *Medical Education*, **15**, 53–6.
Heins, M., Smock, S., Martindale, L., Jacobs, J. and Stein, M. (1977). Comparison of the productivity of women and men physicians, *Journal of American Medical Association*, **237**, (23), 2514–17.
Helson, R., Mitchell, V. and Moore, G. (1984). Personality and patterns of adherence and non adherence to the social clock, *Journal of Personality and Social Psychology*, **46**, 1079–96.
Johnson, D. G. (1983). *Physicians in the Making*, Jossey-Bass, San Francisco.
Kaplan, S. R. (1982). Medical school and women over 30, *Journal of the American Medical Women's Association*, 37 (2), 39–50.
Leavy, R. (1983). Social support and psychological disorders, *Journal of Community Psychology*, **11**, 3–21.

Leserman, J. (1981). *Men and Women in Medical School*, Praeger, New York.
Levinson, D., Darrow, C. N., Klein, E. B., Levinson, M. H. and McKee, B. (1978). *The Seasons of a Man's Life*, Knopf Books, New York.
Lewis, C. L., Scott, D. E., Wolf, M. H. and Pantell, R. H. (1985). Parent satisfaction with children's medical care and parent adherence intent: Development of two questionnaire measures. Unpublished manuscript, University of California, San Francisco, Department of General Pediatrics, San Francisco.
Lorber, J. A. (1981). The limits of sponsorship for women physicians, *Journal of the American Medical Women's Association*, **36**, 329–38.
Lorber, J. A. (1983). Career development of male and female physicians, *Journal of Medical Education*, **58**, 447–56.
Lorber, J. and Ecker, M. (1983). Career development of female and male physicians, *Journal of Medical Education*, **58**, 447–56.
Lovelace, J. C. (1983). Role conflict, role integration, and career satisfaction in Afro-American physicians. Unpublished dissertation, California School of Professional Psychology, Berkeley.
Mandelbaum, D. R. (1981). *Work, Marriage, and Motherhood: The Career Persistence of Female Physicians*, Praeger, New York.
Margolis, A. J., Greenwood, S. and Heilbron, D. (1983). Survey of men and women residents entering United States Obstetrics and Gynecology programs in 1981. *American Journal of Obstetrics and Gynecology*, **146**, 541–6.
McGrath, E. and Zimet, C. N. (1977). Female and male medical students: Differences in specialty choice selection and personality. *Journal of Medical Education*, **52**, 293–300.
Nadelson, C. C. and Notman, M. T. (1983). What is different for women physicians? In S. C. Scheiber and B. B. Doyle (eds), *The Impaired Physician*, Plenum, New York.
Notman, M. T., Salt, P. and Nadelson, C. C. (1984). Stress and adaptation in medical students: who is most vulnerable? *Comprehensive Psychiatry*, **25**, 335–66.
Roeske, N. A. (1976). Women in psychiatry: a review. *American Jounral of Psychiatry*, **133**, 365–72.
Roeske, N. C. A. and Lake, K. (1977). Role models for women medical students. *Journal of Medical Education*, **52**, 459–66.
Roeske, N. C. A. (1984). An International perspective on women as patients and as physicians. Paper presented at International Medical Women's Association Meeting, Vancouver, British Columbia, Canada.
Rose, K. D. and Rosow, I. (1972). Marital stability among physicians, *California Medicine*, **116**, 95–9.
Scadron, A., Witte, M. H., Axelrod, M., Greenberg, E. A., Arem, C. and Meitz, J. E. (1982). Attitudes toward women physicians in medical academia, *Journal of the American Medical Association*, **247**, (20). 2803–7.
Scott, D. E. (1985). Pediatrician's interpersonal skills and parents' satisfaction with the medical interview. Unpublished dissertation, California School of Professional Psychology, Berkeley.
Slay, T. and McDonald, A. (1981). Female professors/male professors career development: Attitudes, benefits, costs, *Psychological Reports*, **48**, 307–14.
Steppacher, R. C. and Mausner, J. S. (1974). Suicide in male and female physicians, *JAMA*, **228**, 323–8.
Tarlov, A. (1981). *A Summary Report of the Graduate Medical Education National Advisory Committee*. Vol. 1, DHHS Publication (Health Resources Administration) No. 81–651, US Government Printing Office, Washington DC.
The Impaired Physician: Building Well-being (1980). Proceedings of the Fourth AMA Conference on the Impaired Physician, Oct. 30–November 1, 1980, Baltimore, Maryland.

Turner, K. (1985). *Women in Medicine Statistics*, Association of American Medical Colleges, Washington DC.
US Bureau of the Census (1984). *Statistical Abstract of the United States: 1985* (105th edition). Washington, DC.
Walsh, M. R. (1977). *Doctors Wanted: No Women Need Apply*, Yale University Press, New Haven.
Weisman, M. M. and Klerman, G. L. (1979). Sex differences and the epidemiology of depression. In Gomberg, E. S. and Franka, V. (eds), *Gender and Disordered Behavior*, Brunner/Mazel, New York.
Weisman, C. S., Levine, D. M., Steinwachs, D. M. and Chase, G. A. (1980). Male and Female Physician Career Patterns: Specialty Choices and Graduate Training, *Journal of Medical Education*, **55**, 813–25.
Weisman, C. S., Teitelbaum, M. A., Nathanson, C. A., Chase, G. A. and King, T. M. (1986). Sex differences in the practice patterns of recently trained Obstetrician-Gynecologists, *Obstetrics and Gynecology*, **67**, 776–81.
Werner, P. D. and La Russe, G. W. (1985). Persistence and change in sex-role stereotypes, *Sex Roles*, **12**, 1089–1100.
Young, J. W. (1979). Symptom disclosure to male and female physicians: effects of sex, physical attractiveness, and symptom type. *Journal of Behavioral Medicine*, **2**, 159–69.
Young, J. W. (1980). The effects of perceived physician competence on patients' symptom disclosure to male and female physicians, *Journal of Behavioral Medicine*, **3**, 279–90.
Zimny, G. H. and Shelton, B. R. (1982). Sex differences in medical specialty preferences, *Journal of Medical Education*, **57**, 403–5.

Stress in Health Professionals
Edited by R. Payne and J. Firth-Cozens
© 1987 John Wiley & Sons Ltd.

Chapter 5

Stress in Surgeons

Roy Payne

Fatigue, pressing family problems, a long queue of patients waiting to be seen, a touch of the flu—all the excuses that individuals routinely use in everyday life, are inadmissible on a surgery service. Bosk (1979), p. 55.

In a very real way every time a surgeon operates, he is making book on himself. (p. 30)

These quotations from the excellent ethnographic study of surgeons conducted by Bosk convey the pressure of the demands surgery makes on the surgeon and his/her family. The heroic scale of these demands is almost mythical in our society, but one aim of the present chapter is to examine the evidence relating to the scale of these demands and to ask whether they are severe enough to create physical or psychological damage to those who practice the profession of surgery. There is not a huge amount of empirical evidence about surgeons but I shall present data on mortality, heart-rates, biochemical indicators, subjective reports of stress and strain, and observations from spouses about the effects of being a hospital surgeon. Before examining these, however, I shall describe the nature of surgery as a profession and indicate the rewards it brings as well as the costs. Finally, I shall consider how surgeons cope with their jobs and what might be done to facilitate their coping.

BECOMING AND BEING A SURGEON

Surgical training must be one of the lengthiest in the professions. Having completed five years in medical school the aspirant surgeon in the UK spends one year as a House Officer, two years as a Senior House Officer, three years as a Registrar, three to four years as a Senior Registrar and finally is accepted as an autonomous surgeon fully responsible for his/her own patients when the rank of Consultant is achieved. They are still taking formal exams up to the rank of Senior Registrar and studying for them, all this fitted into a working week which decreases from an average of perhaps 90 hours per week to 70. They will also be expected to carry out research if they are to succeed in getting a consultant post.

They will regularly be on duty overnight and at weekends. In his autobiographical account of, *The Making of a Surgeon* Nolen (1971) observes,

> eating and sleeping were luxuries for the intern. He ate and slept only as he deserved to eat and sleep; leisurely meals and long hours in bed were never for the intern, but if you hustled you could at least bolt 2 or 3 meals a day and find 5 hours for the sack (p. 17).

Between them Nolen and Bosk provide detailed persuasive accounts of the life of surgeons and trainee surgeons. Nolen's is based on his own experience and is described largely as his training affected him and his family though he does use illustrative examples from his colleagues. Bosk's account is based on observations of two teams of surgeons collected over several months and enriched by discussions with the surgeons. Bosk's book is also enriched by a theoretical focus, for Bosk is particularly concerned to understand how surgeons deal with errors and the theoretical implications this has for how professions control their members more generally.

I shall describe Bosk's conclusions because if surgery is stressful it is partly because of the real, or potential consequences of errors and failures. This is not only because of the potential seriousness of errors, but also because they are usually so public. Throughout their training and practice surgeons, and other medical specialists, are publicly interrogated by their seniors about the state of a patient, the treatment being given, the nature of the disease and other diseases the symptoms might indicate. Feedback on failure or ignorance is immediate, often humiliating and brooks no right of reply. As a Resident trainee surgeon in Bosk's study observed;

> You make one public enemy like this bastard (his attending, ie. immediate superior) and he can ruin your career.... It doesn't matter whether you're right or wrong or anything. You just have to take it (p. 94).

An informed reader of Bosk's book would be able to tell that the error committed by the above Resident would be what Bosk calls a 'moral error'. That is, it was not just a matter of having made a technical mistake or even an error of judgement such as misdiagnosing an illness. A moral error would involve not showing proper concern for the patient. This might even be because of what most of us would regard as a reasonable excuse such as having worked 30 hours non-stop, having the flu or whatever. It might be answering the Attending (Consultant) back or trying to defend a wrong decision. It might even be for failing to learn from a previous technical error, or at least failing to learn consistently. Such a failure would be assumed to arise, not from lack of ability, but lack of concern/motivation. Bosk's observations of surgeons led him to propose that technical errors are forgiven because everyone makes them, but they are only forgiven once.

There is a general reluctance to let a technical failure be a conspicuous occasion for social control since its sources are so variegated, since the decisions demanded are so subtle and so complex, since it happens to everyone, and since it is believed that the responsible physician will draw the proper lessons from the evidence. (p. 174)

Moral errors are not forgiven, not even once. They are punished sharply and immediately. Firstly, those who commit moral errors are shamed by their superiors, and only a highly visible show of genuine repentance and total conformity to the prevailing norms will persuade the superordinate that the slip was a once and for all error. If moral errors occur regularly and the individual is unable to extinguish immoral behaviour, then, 'the individual is extinguished from the group' (p. 180).

One of the reasons that a trainee surgeon's life may be stressful, as opposed to just demanding, is that the judgements about what is a moral failure are made by his/her superiors and the standards set may differ from one surgeon to another. Until the trainee is an Attending/Consultant, however, reality is defined for them by their superiors. A scientifically sound practice may be totally unacceptable to a particular superior and in the end clinical experience will be regarded as superior to scientific prediction unless the scientific results are overwhelmingly in favour of one particular solution.

These observations and accounts by Bosk and Nolen respectively convey sufficiently well the long hours, physical demands and pressures to avoid failure that are experienced by surgeons, and particularly by surgeons who have not become fully fledged members of the profession. And this is in the context of a job where 'Not some, not most, but all doctors, at one time or another, make errors' (Nolen, p. 57).

Such vivid descriptions of occupational life would lead many people to conclude that surgery is such a stressful occupation that it would eventually lead to a range of stress-related illnesses and ultimately to an early grave. What is the evidence for this?

Evidence from statistics on death rates does not support such a conclusion. The following short-list (Table 1) compares the Standardized Mortality Ratios for several groups of workers, all of whom were males of working age (15–64 years). The SMR for the whole population is 100 because it is the following ratio:

$$\frac{\text{Number of deaths observed}}{\text{Number of deaths expected}} \times 100$$

and for the whole population the number of expected deaths is defined as the number actually observed. If there are less deaths amongst a given group than you would expect to observe, given their prevalence in the population, then the SMR is less than 100. As can be seen in Table 1 medical practitioners have an

SMR well below 100, though higher than radiographers and considerably lower than male nurses. It must be borne in mind that there is a strong effect by social class on SMRs which get higher as social class gets lower (Fletcher and Payne, 1980). Unfortunately, there are not separate statistics for surgeons as they are a relatively small occupational group, but Doll and Peto (1977) compared SMRs for Hospital Specialists with those of General Practitioners and found that the Hospital Specialists actually had a somewhat lower SMR. There is no evidence here then that groups like surgeons die prematurely young.

Figures on morbidity and sickness absence are difficult to obtain for professional groups like these, but since sickness absence also varies by social class (Fletcher and Payne, 1980), with the professional groups having the lowest rates, it is likely that surgeons have no more than other professional groups. On the other hand, suicide is twice as high amongst the medical profession compared with the general population, and alcoholism is at least as high, whilst drug addiction is at least 30 times higher (Linn and Zeppa, 1984). These behaviours suggest that medicine is a stressful occupation for some of its practitioners, even though the majority live to a respectable age and are not unduly unhealthy during their careers. What might account for the relatively low level of illness amongst a group that does appear to have such a demanding job?

KARASEK'S MODEL OF JOB STRAIN

Karasek (1979) proposes four broad groups of occupational situations which are derived from two dimensions. The first is job demands which concerns the difficulty of tasks and how hard one has to work to complete them. The second is the amount of discretion a person has over his work. Karasek divides each of these two dimensions into two and thus produces the following four categories of jobs:

	Title	Example
High demand—Low discretion	= Strained job	Machine minding, Food Industry
High demand—High discretion	= Active job	Medical work, Management
Low demand—Low discretion	= Passive job	Office work
Low demand—High discretion	= Low strain job	Sales, Technical

Taken from Kauppinen-Toropainen, Kandolin and Mutanen (1983).

The job situation that produces high occupational stress leading to psychophysiological strain is the one where demands are high, but discretion/control is low. When demands are high but discretion is high this

Table 1 Standardized mortality ratios for males
(15–64) based on UK deaths, 1970–1972

	No. of deaths	SMR
Medical practitioners	665	81
Radiographers	24	69
Dentists	144	72
Nurses	671	112

produces what Karasek calls an 'active' job. Whilst I have tried to show that surgery is highly demanding intellectually, physically and emotionally it is also evident from the accounts by Bosk and Nolen that surgeons have considerable discretion and control over their subordinates and their patients. Since they are saving lives and doing a socially worthwhile job they are also open to receiving considerable rewards and support for what they do. In terms of Karasek's model then, surgeons would appear to be in an 'active' job rather than a 'strained' job.

Another point to bear in mind with surgeons in particular is that it is a job where many try to do it, and many fail. Competition is severe, so that only the very able tend to survive. There is thus a kind of natural selection where those who cannot cope with the rigours of the job are weeded out before they fully qualify.

Linn and Zeppa (1984) have actually shown that medical students who choose surgery as a speciality differ from other medical students. They studied 169 junior medical students just before they started a three-month surgical rotation, and at the end of this period. The students were asked to rate the stressfulness of 31 events during the previous four weeks and further asked to say whether the events were seen as favourable or unfavourable sorts of stress. Another part of the study asked the students to rate the stressfulness of different medical specialties and surgery was rated by 99 per cent of the students as being the most stressful before the surgical rotation. At the end of the surgical rotation 93 per cent rated it as the most stressful. Sixty-nine of these students still elected to pursue their most stressful speciality and for 71 per cent of these this was surgery.

Two points need emphasizing before further results are presented. Firstly, the second most stressful speciality was internal medicine, but only about 40 per cent described it that way, so there is high consensus that surgery is stressful. The reasons given for the stresses of surgery were: long hours, life and death decisions, consequences of judgements or lack of appropriate skills, amount of work and the time involved.

When these students were followed up after graduation, by which time they were training to be surgeons, it was found that they had not performed better than other students in exams, but those who had selected what they saw as stressful specialities (usually surgery) had (1) seen just as much stress in surgery as others, but had rated much less of it as unfavourable stress, (2) rated themselves as higher on self-esteem, (3) saw themselves as being more in control of things that happened to them (more internal as measured by locus of control (Rotter, 1966)). Various other studies reported by Linn and Zeppa have also found students who selected surgery to have a distinctive personality profile which is summarized by them as: 'extremely self-confident, authoritarian, intolerant of ambiguity, and fitting into a career that they saw as supplying status and economic rewards'.

In sum, medical students see surgery as very stressful, but those who choose to do it have particular qualities which enable them to cope with the stressors they see in a surgical career.

Since surgery is such a demanding training it is not only true that students who choose a surgical career cope with its stresses, it is also true that they enjoy what they do. At the end of a study to be reported later Payne *et al.* (1984) and Payne and Rick (1986a and 1986b) interviewed the surgeons about their jobs. Some of their comments reflect the positive experiences they obtained from the practice of their profession.

All comments refer to cardio-thoracic surgery:

> It is a great challenge, it has to be done well as you have much less room for making mistakes, you have to do things fast, and new things are continuously emerging in the discipline, so that you feel you are on the top of the wave. It's a superb intellectual challenge. You have to keep reading to keep on top.

> When you know you've got no room for mistakes it really does make you concentrate. It's not hard work for me. I enjoy it.

Nor does this satisfaction and challenge occur only during operating as is expressed in the following statement:

> I like getting complex problems. I like dealing with patients in Intensive Care who are acutely ill with multiple problems that are very challenging. Their multiple problems cut across a lot of medical boundaries, and dealing with the patients, and the other specialties that we call in to help us really stimulates me.

Similar comments can also be found throughout the books by Bosk (1979) and Nolen (1971).

Whilst the findings of Linn and Zeppa and the quotations from our work illustrate some reactions to being a surgeon these particular surgeons, and others, were part of a more systematic study which attempted to understand the experience of practising cardio-thoracic surgery. The study was designed to test some of the predictions made by Karasek, Russell and Theorell (1982) under the assumption that surgery is high on demand, but also high on discretion or control. The full details of the study can be found in Payne *et al.* (1984). Part of the 1984 study was replicated whilst carrying out a study of the anaesthetists who work with the same surgical team, and the results of these studies can be found in Payne and Rick (1986a and 1986b). The following draws on the more important findings of those studies.

A FIELD STUDY OF STRESS IN SURGEONS AND ANAESTHETISTS

In study 1 a team of eight surgeons ranging in rank from House Officer to Consultant was studied one day per week for twelve weeks. During each 24-hour period the following measures were taken.

(1) Self-reports of how demanding the job had been during the previous few hours. A range of potential demands were surveyed such as technical skills, demands from patients, demands from relatives, physical demands.
(2) Self-reports of whether the surgeon had felt stressed during the previous few hours, and if they had been stressed/strained, how severe they felt the stress was, and how long it had lasted.
(3) 24-hour urine samples were collected and assayed for VMA, which is a metabolite of the catecholamines adrenaline and noradrenaline, and cortisol.
(4) During each 24-hour period one of the surgeons wore an ambulatory heart-rate recorder. Observations of work activities were made so that changes in heart-rate could be related to changes in activities.

Study 2 followed the same design but concentrated mainly on the anaesthetists working with the surgeons. In study 2, however, it was possible to replicate part of study 1 by collecting 24-hour urine samples from the surgeons, and asking them again to answer the simple question on stress/strain outlined at point (2) above.

As indicated already, the theoretical framework guiding this work is that of Karasek, and in 1982 Karasek *et al.* boldly made predictions about the physiological consequences of working in strained versus active jobs. The relevant points are summarized below:

Strained job	Active job
High adrenaline and noradrenaline (VMA)	Low adrenaline and noradrenaline (VMA)
High cortisol	Low cortisol
Above average heart-rate and blood pressure	Below average heart-rate and blood pressure

Before testing these predictions on the data from the surgeons and anaesthetists it is also necessary to establish if they saw their jobs as high on demand and high on autonomy as our interpretations of the reports by Bosk and Nolen imply.

Table 2 shows the mean score for a range of demands for both surgeons and anaesthetists. The scale used is reproduced below to help interpret the mean scores:

	Score
Not applicable	0
Dealt with demand without help	1
Felt needed sometimes	2
Dealt with by getting help	3
Failed to deal even with help	4

Since the mean scores in Table 2 are just over 1 or below the data show that most of the time both groups are coping with demands from these different sources, but the surgeons rate their demands as significantly higher and it is worth noting that knowledge and physical demands are rated as highest of all. Since these measures were constructed for this particular study it is difficult to compare these results with other groups, but they have been used by the author with psychiatric nurses and this group rates their jobs as less demanding than either of these two groups of specialists.

Table 2 Mean scores for job demands of surgeons and anaesthetists

Item	Surgeons	Anaesthetists
Demands on knowledge	1.53	1.15
Physical demands	1.35	1.17
Colleagues demands	1.21	0.96
Demands on skills	1.19	1.11
Demands from other departments	1.19	0.92
Demands from patients	0.88	0.69
Demands from relatives of patients	0.82	0.15
	$n=108$	$n=89$

Furthermore, when asked if they had felt strained during the last few hours both surgeons and anaesthetists said 'yes' on half the occasions they were asked the question. The psychiatric nurses said 'yes' on only 25 per cent of the occasions they were asked. Relatively then, the surgeons report higher levels of demand, but like most well trained professionals they are usually able to cope

Table 3 Frequency distribution (percentages) of perceptions of authority, support and satisfaction

	Feeling you did not have necessary authority to make the decision needed				
	NA	Did not happen	Happened once	Happened twice	Happened more than twice
Surgeons (n=108)	4	81	13	2	
Anaesthetists (n=89)	6	85	8	1	
	Feelings about support from colleagues/coworkers				
	NA	Gave all support needed	Support good most of time	Support sometimes lacking	Support lacking lot of time
Surgeons (n=108)	3	83	11	2	
Anaesthetists (n=89)	9	76	12	3	
	Satisfaction with way things went				
	NA	Very satisfied	Quite satisfied	Slightly dissatisfied	Very dissatisfied
Surgeons (n=108)		47	40	9	3
Anaesthetists (n=89)		53	31	15	1

NA, not applicable. Reproduced by permission of Springer-Verlag from Payne and Rick (1986b)

with the demands, though the reports of frequent strain that both they and the anaesthetists report indicates there are psychological costs.

According to Karasek (1979) the effects of a highly demanding job may be mitigated by having high discretion or authority in the job, and many others have shown that support can alleviate job stress (Cohen and Wills, 1985). Table 3 shows ratings of authority/discretion, support from colleagues and satisfaction with the way the last few hours have gone.

As is evident both surgeons and anaesthetists report high levels of discretion, high levels of support and high satisfaction. On the whole, then, these data indicate that these doctors have an 'active' rather than a 'strained' job.

Evidence for the physical demands of these jobs is more readily available from the 24-hour recordings of heart-rate and the observations made with them. This is not because heart-rates are high, but because these records indicate the number of hours the surgeons and anaesthetists worked whilst wearing them. The mean number of hours was over 13 for the surgeons and over 11 for the anaesthetists. As shown in Table 2 physical demands were also ranked second as the most demanding aspects of the work by both surgeons and anaesthetists.

Whilst studies of stress amongst surgeons are rare there have been several which have used heart rate as an indicator of stress.

HEART-RATE AS AN INDICATOR OF STRESS

A brief summary of these studies and others on professional groups is listed below in Table 4 which includes the names of the authors.

As Table 4 shows there is some difference in the studies relating to surgeons though two of them agree highly that the mean is about 100 bpm, and given that trawlermen who are actually fishing only average 112 bpm the rate of 120 bpm quoted by Foster *et al.* does appear to be high. It is evident from this table that a major determinant of heart-rate is the level of physical activity involved. Indeed, the best controlled study amongst these is the one by Becker, Ellis and Goldsmith (1983) because they monitored oxygen consumption as well as heart-rate. Oxygen consumption is a good indication of the general metabolic demands being made by the body and much of the variation in heart-rate is due to changes in these demands. They concluded that there was little evidence to show that increases in heart-rate amongst surgeons whilst operating is due to psychological stress.

Table 4 Mean heart rates in different occupations

Surgeons whilst operating (Foster *et al.*)	120 bpm
Surgeons whilst operating (Becker *et al.*)	99 bpm
Surgeons whilst operating (present study)	100 bpm
Anaesthetists performing narcosis (Lazarus and Weiss)	90 bpm
Managers (Hennigan and Wortham)	80 bpm
Teachers whilst teaching (Leonard)	93 bpm
Trawlermen fishing (Rodahl and Vokac)	112 bpm

Reprinted with permission from Payne and Rick (1986a), copyright (1986) Pergamon Journals Ltd.

Perhaps the data from the study by Payne and Rick (1986a) can be used to illustrate this point. Table 5 compares the surgeons and the anaesthetists on four different activities. The only activity that produces a different mean heart-rate for the two groups is for 'operating' when the heart-rates for surgeons are higher. For most of the time spent in the operating theatre the anaesthetists are only a metre or so away from the surgeons, but they are usually sitting, and they are not directly under the heat produced by the operating lights. These differences in

Table 5 Comparison of mean heart rates of surgeons and anaesthetists across four types of work periods

	Anaesthetists	Surgeons
Period operating	78.3 ± 13.3 (10)	100.5 ± 15.1 (8)
Tea/coffee break	82.1 ± 13.9 (12)	88.8 ± 14.8 (10)
Driving car	80.9 ± 9.1 (7)	83.6 ± 8.6 (5)
PO intensive care	83.9 ± 15.9 (10)	88.3 ± 13.9 (10)

Reprinted with permission from Payne and Rick (1986a), copyright (1986) Pergamon Journals Ltd.

posture, activity and physical location will, according to Becker *et al.*, explain why the surgeons have higher heart-rates than the anaesthetists.

It would be misleading, however, to conclude that surgeons do not experience stress whilst operating, and that this experienced stress does not sometimes lead to increases in heart-rate. As mentioned earlier, whilst the surgeons studied by Payne and Rick (1986a) were wearing the heart-rate recorder their actual activities were observed and noted. These authors report several examples of surgeons doing difficult procedures during which they both reported feeling stressed, and their heart-rates increased considerably. Examples of these incidents were, inserting catheters into small children, and making difficult decisions about what to do during an operation where unanticipated difficulties had occurred. What was particularly interesting in some of these situations was that the heart-rate of less experienced surgeons would rise when faced with such decisions, but having consulted a senior colleague on the telephone, heart-rate would decrease once the responsibility of the decision, and the decision itself, had been clarified. These examples provide interesting physiological evidence for the effect of social support in dealing with stressful situations.

In summary, studies of heart-rate show that whilst operating surgeons' heart-rates are higher than those for other professionals such as managers and teachers, but that most of the increase can be explained by the physical demands of operating, and the high temperatures produced by the operating theatre lights. However, heart-rate can be shown to rise for several minutes at a time when difficult, stressful procedures are being performed, and these occur quite regularly for most surgeons.

In terms of the predictions made by Karasek, Russell and Theorell (1982) earlier these data are consistent with the claim that heart-rate (and blood pressure) are not unusually high in 'active jobs'. There is, at least, no evidence they are high as is predicted for 'strained jobs', though it must be re-emphasized that heart-rate is largely affected by the physical demands of the job, and most work on job stress implicitly assumes psychological as well as physical strain. Heart-rate is not, therefore, the most reliable indicator for testing these predictions, but since it has been used in several studies of surgeons it is data very relevant to the present discussion.

CATECHOLAMINES AND CORTISOL AS INDICATORS OF STRESS

Current theorizing about the role of the catecholamines and cortisol in stress is that in the early stages of stress both have a positive role to play in enabling the person to cope with stress. If the stress is chronic, however, there is evidence that chronically excessive amounts of both can cause damage to vital tissues and blood vessels increasing the risk of cardiovascular disease (Henry and Stephens, 1977). Furthermore, catecholamines and cortisol are believed to increase under different circumstances. The catecholamines are believed to increase in response to ongoing demands for increased physical and mental efforts, and cortisol to prolonged feelings of helplessness or distress (Frankenhaeuser and Johansson, 1986).

It is this sort of theorizing that led Karasek, Russell and Theorell (1982) to propose that 'active' jobs would lead to low cortisol levels since they are not distressing. Karasek *et al.* also proposed that active jobs would be associated with low catecholamines since they do not demand excessive effort, though it seems to the present author that some active jobs will demand great physical and mental effort, and the validity of this particular part of their theorizing may be in doubt. Fortunately, for surgeons and anaesthetists at least, we can put the theory to empirical test.

The 24-hour urine samples collected from the surgeons and anaesthetists were assayed for cortisol and VMA which is the common metabolite of the two catecholamines adrenaline and noradrenaline, and thus an index of the amounts of them that have been utilized by the body in the previous 24 hours. The results showed that both surgeons and anaesthetists produced amounts of VMA which are the same as those produced by a normal population of healthy people.

In a study of physicians carrying out cardiac catheterization, which is a procedure the physicians all described as stressful, Ira, Bogdonoff and Durham (1962) found that adrenaline increased during the procedure, but the absolute levels achieved were in most cases within normal limits. These findings are both consistent with Karasek *et al.*'s predictions about active jobs.

The one finding in the present studies that is clearly inconsistent with their predictions is that relating to cortisol. In Payne *et al.* (1984) it was shown that the urinary cortisol levels of surgeons were outside the normal levels on 72 per cent of the occasions for which data were collected. In this study a strong relationship between cortisol level and length of experience was also found, suggesting that longer exposure to the demands of surgery was associated with higher levels of cortisol. This was interpreted to mean that the high cortisol levels were a reflection of the high demands of a surgical career and an indication of chronic physiological strain. The relationship between cortisol and length of experience was not replicated in the follow-up study of surgeons and anaesthetists (Payne and Rick 1986b) but the high level of cortisol was replicated. It was also found that the anaesthetists had higher than normal cortisol levels, though they reported slightly lower levels of stress than the surgeons, and had slightly lower cortisol levels. These results tend to reflect that the stressfulness of surgery as a career reported by students (Linn and Zeppa, 1984), and by those in the speciality, is at least reflected in chronically raised levels of cortisol. Whether these levels are high enough to indicate a clinical risk is not known, but it is clear that the long hours and heavy responsibilities surgery carries do require the body to be ready for action on a continuing basis.

These cortisol results are inconsistent with the model proposed by Karasek *et al.*: jobs which are highly active have their physiological and psychological costs as well as their positive psychological and social benefits. The costs may be underestimated by the surgeons themselves. Bates (1982) asked different groups of medical doctors, including hospital specialists such as surgeons, to rate how often they arrived home feeling emotionally drained. About 20 per cent said this often happened, but when these answers were compared with those of the doctors' spouses there was a huge discrepancy. Over 80 per cent of the spouses said this often happened. As we have already seen from the studies reported by Linn and Zeppa surgeons are confident they can cope with stress, but this confidence may lead them to repress or deny it, and their spouses may have a better understanding of the costs their jobs make on them. The chronically high cortisol does suggest some long-term costs, though this evidence must be judged against the more macro evidence provided by the statistics on death rates and morbidity referred to earlier.

SUMMARY

The self-report data show that surgeons say they have experienced strain on 50 per cent of the occasions on which they were asked. Even though the degree of strain is usually moderately intense, and does not last longer than an hour or two, they are chronically exposed to this sort of experience. This chronicity of experienced strain combined with the long hours they work appears to result in abnormally high levels of cortisol which might indicate a long-term effect on health and well-being. Surgery is certainly seen as a stressful speciality by medical students and by the spouses of the surgeons (and other hospital specialists). What can be done to alleviate this job stress?

CHANGING JOB STRESS

If the data in Table 2 are to be believed the major demands that tax the coping capacity of surgeons are those made on their knowledge/skills and those made on their capacity to cope with fatigue. Both of these agree with the major stresses reported in the Linn and Zeppa study. The justification for having trainee surgeons (and other medical specialists) working very long days is usually that it enables them to gain experience quickly. There is obvious truth in this, but many of the hours spent by young doctors are actually spent on rather routine matters. By increasing manpower it would surely be possible for one doctor to be responsible for such routine work and for him/her to call out another trainee if something of interest happens. Since a major perceived demand is on skill and knowledge of current developments this might be one way of creating additional 'spare' time in which this skill and knowledge could actually be kept up to date. This small increase in manpower might provide a way of killing two birds with a

Table 6 Types and sources of social support

	Material	Social		
		Cognitive	Emotional	Behavioural
Formal organization (rules, regulations and specialists)	Providing: Money Tools People Good physical environment Inducements	Advice by experts: Doctors Counsellors Consultants Superiors	Support provided by experts: Counsellors Occupational health nurses Welfare officers Supervisors (rarely)	Take person off job or change job Find someone else to solve problem Give early retirement Take responsibility from person
		Person is largely a recipient		
Informal organization (mutual expectations and self-help)	Loaning to each other: Money Tools People Space	Pooling problem-solving resources by widening information network which may include 'experts' known personally to group members	Support spontaneously marshalled by the group. If given is more likely to be felt as genuine by the recipient	Help person to do the job or do it for him while he recovers Share responsibility with person
		Person is both giver and receiver		

Reproduced by permission of Wiley & Sons from Payne (1980).

single stone. Another reason that is given for the long hours worked by hospital specialists is that they take responsibility for 'their' patients so that they can provide continuity of care. Whilst this appears to have considerable advantages, in practice the care of the patient is regularly shifted from one specialist to another, and it must surely be possible to organize responsibility for patients on a delegated basis within a speciality, just as happens between specialities. Delegation of work occurs in other areas of hospital life, as well as in other organizations. Other professions manage to plan the range of experiences their young professionals need without working them day and night for years at a time. Reducing these demands then seems to be a question of resources and attitudes on the part of the professions themselves.

There may be forces/values/prejudices within the profession which make such changes very difficult to achieve. I referred earlier to Bosk's ethnographic study of surgeons and the distinction he drew between the control of technical errors and the control of moral errors. From Bosk's descriptions of how failure is dealt with it is clear that trainee surgeons build up their moral credits in the profession by the amount and quality of the commitment they show towards their patients. Thus 'busting your butt' and 'sweating blood' are ways in which trainees show they have been socialized into the moral, if not the technical norms, of the profession. These powerful ruling values of a training in surgery are succinctly captured by Bosk's reports about what senior surgeons look for in their juniors: they refer to them as the 3 A's, 'availability, affability and ability—in that order'. (p. 176.)

If these major demands (stressors) cannot be diminished, whether for political or practical reasons, then two broad strategies are suggested from the demands, supports-constraints model (Payne, 1979) which has guided the studies reported here, and which is outlined in the introduction. The most commonly prescribed strategy is to provide social support which enables surgeons to cope with their job demands.

There is a large literature on social support which has recently been reviewed comprehensively by Cohen and Wills (1985). Much of this literature focuses on support which is emotional in nature, though some aspects of it include advice and help with problem-solving. Considered more broadly, however, support includes many other things. Table 6 is taken from Payne (1980) and indicates two major things about support. Firstly, that it can be provided by the Formal Organization through the provision of specialist counsellors and standard management practices, and secondly by the Informal Organization. The development of the informal organization partly depends on the values and practices of senior managers in the organization, but it also depends much on the 'team spirit' that develops amongst people in their everyday relationships. The 'strong' personalities defined by Linn and Zeppa (1984) that are attracted to surgery makes the spontaneous development of such positive social climates more problematic than it might be amongst other professional groups. The second point that Table 6 makes is that support consists of providing material help by providing adequate resources (including extra people) as well as advice and emotional support.

In increasing or improving support, organizations are often reducing constraints. In terms of the demands, supports-constraints model, however, it is useful to consider what factors may be acting as constraints and preventing surgeons meeting their heavy demands as effectively, and as efficiently as they may wish to. In an empirical study of perceived supports and constraints it was shown by Payne (1980) that work colleagues are more often seen as supports than constraints. The things that are seen as constraints, however, are things which the hospital administration and senior consultants in their managerial roles, can do something about. The things most commonly reported as constraints on improving job performance are: management–trade union relationships, systems for giving feedback on performance, the lack of clear goals, relationships between departments and specialties, administrative bureaucracy, the ability to influence the rewards for junior staff, and issues about status. It would be unwise to underestimate the size of the task that faces organizations who do decide to tackle these fundamental organizational issues. The history of 'planned organizational change' shows a move from optimism in the 1960s to a more hard-headed realism in the 1980s (Golembiewski, 1986), but much has been learned about social engineering methods for facilitating change, and professional guidance is available to managers and consultants who do decide to remove some of these constraints, and/or build more supportive social systems (Huse and Cummings, 1985).

The demands, supports-constraints framework suggests ways of altering environmental stress, but it does not directly help the individual decrease their vulnerability to increasing stressors. There are, of course, the many psychological defence mechanisms such as rationalization, denial and projection, but in an interesting study of coping Pearlin and Schooler (1978) found that these were less effective in the work environment than they were in other life roles such as economic problems and family problems. They suggested that this may be because the work system is much more tightly controlled by others and that bosses and colleagues make it difficult to ignore the stresses that may exist. Changing the work environment to minimize stress does, therefore, seem to be a more useful strategy. Nevertheless, individuals can affect their stress resistance by adopting the appropriate life style, which is to avoid overeating, overdrinking and undersleeping. Reasonable amounts of exercise need to be taken regularly and a change is as good as a rest. These recommendations come, of course, from the medical profession themselves, but in training young doctors, and even in employing consultant surgeons the profession itself creates the very conditions that make these difficult to achieve. Sleep is often short and/or interrupted, it is difficult to fit exercise into a day which is largely unpredictable, and there is a culture developed in medical schools that alcohol, and other drugs (Norman, 1980) are appropriate means of dealing with emotional difficulties. Meals are taken when they can be managed, and the actual food eaten is frequently poor in its dietary content (Firth, 1986). Even recognizing that surgeons face a demanding career it does seem that for some of them, maybe even a majority of them, the advice, 'Physician heed thyself' might be better taken.

It is all too easy in the stress literature, however, to blame the person either for bringing stress upon themselves, or for their own weakness in being unable to deal with it. The evidence is that surgery is a demanding job and that for most surgeons at some time it is stressful. The provision of good staff, adequate resources, the time to acquire new knowledge and skills, and help in developing good social support systems could do much to diminish these potentially damaging experiences, both for surgeons and their patients.

REFERENCES

Bates, E. (1982). Doctors and their spouses speak: stress in medical practice, *Sociology of Health and Illness*, **4**, 1, 25–9.
Becker, W. G. E., Ellis, H. and Goldsmith, R. (1983). Heart-rates of surgeons in theatre, *Ergonomics*, **26**, 803–8.
Bosk, C. L. (1979). *Forgive and Remember: Managing Medical Failure*, University of Chicago Press, Chicago.
Cohen, S. and Wills, T. A. (1985). Stress, social support and the buffering hypothesis, *Psychological Bulletin*, **98**, 310–57.
Doll, R. and Peto, R. (1977). Mortality among doctors in different occupations, *British Medical Journal*, **1**, 1433–6.
Firth, J. (1986). Levels and sources of stress in medical students, *British Medical Journal*, **292**, 1177–80.
Fletcher, B. (C) and Payne, R. L. (1980). Stress and work: a review and theoretical framework, part I, *Personnel Review*, **9**, 1, 19–29.
Foster, G. E., Evans, D. F. and Hardcastle, J. (1978). Heart rates of surgeons during operations and other clinical activities, and their modification by oxprenolol, *Lancet, i*, 1323–25.
Frankenhaeuser, M. and Johansson, G. (1986). Stress at work: psychobiological and psychosocial aspects, *International Review of Applied Psychology*, **35**, 287–99.
Golembiewski, R. T. (1986). Organization Analysis and Praxis: Prominences of Progress and Stuckness. In C. L. Cooper and I. Robertson (eds), *International Review of Industrial and Organizational Psychology*, J. Wiley, Chichester.
Henry, J. P. and Stephens, P. M. (1977). *Stress, Health and the Social Environment*, Springer-Verlag, New York.
Huse, E. G. and Cummings, T. G. (1985). *Organization Development and Change*, West Publishing, St. Paul, MA.
Ira, G. H., Bogdonoff, M. D. and Durham, N. C. (1962). Application of radiotelemetry in man for continuous recording of heart-rate, *Journal of American Medical Association*, **180** (11), 976–7.
Kagan, A. and Levi, L. (1974). Health and environment—psychosocial stimuli: a review. *Social Science and Medicine*, **8**, 225–41.

Karasek, R. J. (1979). Job demands, job decision latitude and mental strain: implications for job redesign, *Administrative Science Quarterly*, **24**, 285–308.

Karasek, R. A., Russell, R. S. and Theorell, T. (1982). Physiology of stress and regeneration in job related cardiovascular illness, *Journal of Human Stress*, **8**, 29–42.

Kaupinnen-Toropainen, K., Kandolin, I. and Mutanen, P. (1983). Job dissatisfaction and work-related exhaustion in male and female work, *Journal of Occupational Behaviour*, **4**, 3, 193–207.

Lazarus, R. S. (1966). *Psychological Stress and the Coping Process*, McGraw-Hill, New York.

Linn, B. S. and Zeppa, R. (1984). Does surgery attract students who are more resistant to stress? *Annals of Surgery*, **200**, 5, 638–43.

Nolen, W. A. (1971). *The Making of a Surgeon*, Cassells, London.

Norman, J. C. (1980). Histrionics, vignettes and quartets: a syndrome of stress in heart surgeons, *Cardiovascular Diseases Bulletin of the Texas Heart Institute*, **7**, 4, 339–43.

Payne, R. L. (1979). Demands, supports, constraints and psychological health. In C. J. Mackay and T. Cox (eds), *Response to Stress: Occupational Aspects*, International Publishing Corporation, London.

Payne, R. (1980). Organizational stress and social support. In C. L. Cooper, and Payne, R. (eds), *Current Concerns in Occupational Stress*, J. Wiley, London.

Payne, R. L., Rick, J. T., Smith, G. H. and Cooper, R. G. (1984). Multiple indicators of stress in an 'Active Job'—cardiothoracic surgery, *Journal of Occupational Medicine*, **26**, 11, 805–8.

Payne, R. L. and Rick, J. T. (1986a). Heart-rate as an indicator of stress in surgeosn and anaesthetists, *Journal of Psychosomatic Research*, **30**, 4, 411–20.

Payne, R. L. and Rick. J. T. (1986b). Psychobiological Markers of Stress in Surgeons and Anaesthetists. In T. H. Schmidt, T. M. Dembrowski and M. Blumen (eds), *Biological and Psychological Factors in Coronary Heart Disease*, Springer-Verlag, Berlin.

Pearlin, L. I. and Schooler, C. (1978). The structure of coping, *Journal of Health and Social Behaviour*, **19**, 2–21.

Rotter, J. B. (1966). Generalized expectancies for internal vs. external control of reinforcement, *Psychological Monographs*, **1**, Whole No. 609.

Stress in Health Professionals
Edited by R. Payne and J. Firth-Cozens
© 1987 John Wiley & Sons Ltd

Chapter 6

Stress in Psychiatrists

Frank R. Margison

THE ROLE OF PSYCHIATRISTS

A psychiatrist in the UK spends five or six years at medical school, followed by a compulsory year practising hospital medicine before full registration. He or she may then spend some time in training posts for other branches of medicine followed by a period of specialized training which has two phases. The first takes at least three years, usually including specialist periods such as child psychiatry. After taking a professional examination involving evaluation of theory and clinical practice the trainee psychiatrist continues for a further three or more years in higher training posts with increasing clinical responsibility. At this point, in the early to mid-thirties typically, as in other branches of medicine the great divide is crossed and the psychiatrist takes up a consultant post (the only hospital post having full clinical autonomy). The consultant will have responsibility for the overall treatment of patients even when under the care of other professionals and other doctors still in training. This clear distinction between a psychiatrist in training and a consultant is linked to distinct patterns of workload and job stress.

Some psychiatrists specialize within their field—the main areas being child and adolescent psychiatry; forensic psychiatry; psychiatry of the mentally handicapped; psychiatry of the elderly; and psychotherapy. Lesser degrees of specialization in alcoholism, drug dependence, rehabilitation and social psychiatry are possible.

All psychiatrists are exposed in training to an eclectic approach but there is still considerable polarization between psychiatrists employing organic illness models and physical treatments and those emphasizing a social–psychological basis. It is still quite possible for psychiatrists to receive training heavily biased towards either the biological or the psychological pole.

PREVIOUS WORK ON STRESS

Most previous studies have been directed to the trainee psychiatrist. Some authors (e.g. Merklin and Little 1967) see initial problematic reactions as necessary to professional development. The 'Beginning Psychiatry Syndrome' title was coined to refer to transitory neurotic symptoms and psychosomatic disturbances—these were seen as distressing but necessary formative experiences in the development of a psychiatrist. Halleck and Woods (1962) noted that there were few psychiatry residents without moderate/severe anxiety or depressive symptoms at times. They also commented that most residents 'worry about loss of sanity'. Several other authors, Pasnau and Bayley (1971), Merklin and Little (1967), Book (1973), have pointed out that this can lead to the trainees overidentifying with the sick patient, and questioning their own development, maturity and defence mechanisms.

Several authors (Chessick, 1971; Merklin and Little, 1967; Ungerleider, 1965) have commented that trainees take on the most difficult patients but are then placed in an impossible bind. Halleck and Woods (1962) note that the psychiatry resident has the dilemma of becoming involved (when he tends to over-react and suffer along with his patients) or alternatively keeping a distance (when he feels himself to be, or is criticized by others as being, detached).

BURN-OUT: THE FANTASY OF THE PERFECT PROFESSIONAL

Freudenberger and Robbins (1979) pointed out that a therapist generally 'is full of feelings—feelings of hurt, anger, joy and sadness that he must share, but is often unable to share with or communicate to anyone, especially not his patients'. For the psychiatrist this position is held to an untenable degree under the guise of personal clinical responsibility—a laudable principle but prone to leave the psychiatrist increasingly vulnerable to the more serious consequences of job stress.

Of the many definitions of 'burn out' some refer to a syndrome indistinguishable from depressive neurosis (Pines and Aronson, 1981), while others refer to a particular dynamic constellation with 'fatigue or frustration brought about by devotion to a cause, way of life or relationship that failed to produce the expected reward' (Freudenberger and Richelson, 1980). Both of these states of disillusionment and depression are possible consequences of the stresses inherent in the psychiatrist role. Two alternative definitions refocus attention on work aspects and the consequences for patients. The first of these defines burn out as 'the progressive loss of idealism, purpose, and concern as a result of condition of work' (Edelwich and Brodsky, 1980). The second alternative definition examines the damaging consequences for the patient when the professionals 'lose all concern, all emotional feeling for the people they work with, and come to treat them in a detached or even dehumanised way' (Maslach, 1976).

RISKS TO PSYCHIATRISTS

The Registrar-General's figures (1978) showed three conditions where doctors have markedly raised levels of mortality: suicide, three times higher than the general population, and 1.5 times higher than socio-economically matched controls; cirrhosis which is again three times higher, and road traffic accidents, two times higher.

Conflicting views have been expressed about the accuracy of the suicide estimates. Rich and Pitts (1979) suggested that the rates were exaggerated whilst Rose and Rosow (1973) have shown an underestimation of physician suicide numbers. The latter view, of underestimation, was supported by the past-chairman of the American Psychiatric Association Task Force on Suicide Prevention (Ross, 1973).

Among doctors psychiatrists have the highest rates. Blachly, Disher and Roduner (1968) gave estimates of suicide rates for different medical specialties ranging from 61 per 100,000 for psychiatrists to 10 per 100,000 (about the general population rate) for paediatricians. The timing of suicide has been shown to be different among doctors, peaking in mid-life rather than showing a linear increase with age as in the rest of the population. The peak was shown to be between 45-64 by Steppacher and Mausner (1974).

The rate among female doctors is particularly worrying. Craig and Pitts (1968) reported a rate four times higher than the general population and Steppacher and Mausner (1974) reported a rate three times higher than the general population. These findings seem specific to female doctors as the rates were not elevated among other female professionals in nursing and teaching. Female medical students are particularly at risk accounting for a third of all suicides among young, single women (Rucinski and Cybulska, 1985).

Several attempts have been made to explain doctors' high suicide rates. Rose and Rosow (1973) found that other health workers with direct patient contact were twice as prone to suicide as controls, suggesting that this facet of doctors' lives may be an important part of aetiology. The ready availability of drugs may determine the mode of suicide amongst doctors who show a preference for drug overdosage as a method of suicide—but the absence of a raised rate among pharmacists suggests that it may not be a causal factor.

Prior vulnerability could account for the raised rates: certainly Bjorksten et al. (1983) found higher rates of perceived stress in medical students as opposed to other undergraduates. However, this may reflect a difference in roles rather than individual characteristics (Firth, 1986). Cramond (1969) showed that medical students were less anxious than other students, and in the same study, showed also that doctors with direct clinical contact with patients were more anxious than doctors without such contact, suggesting that the increased anxiety might be related to the job rather than prior vulnerability.

Suicide among doctors does seem to be associated with concurrent psychiatric morbidity as three-quarters of doctors who commit suicide are depressed at the time of suicide (Ross, 1973; Barraclough et al., 1974).

OTHER PYSCHIATRIC MORBIDITY

The problem of psychiatric disorders among doctors is reported elsewhere in this book (Scheiber). Rates are difficult to ascertain accurately because of biased reporting and altered patterns of obtaining health care. There are few studies which give differential rates between medical specialties although there are suggestions that depression, alcoholism, and drug addiction are common in the specialties with high suicide rates—particularly psychiatrists and anaesthetists (Vincent, Robinson and Latt, 1969).

Watterson (1976) carried out a postal questionnaire study between 1970 and 1974 of all 3575 doctors in British Columbia. He identified 214 who were psychiatrically ill representing an annual incidence of 1.3 per cent. Twenty-seven per cent of the patient-doctors had a primary or secondary diagnosis of alcoholism or drug dependence and 50 per cent had a diagnosis of affective disorder (depression and/or anxiety). The figure of 1.3 per cent probably underestimates the true level of illness, perhaps because of a high threshold for reporting symptoms in a postal questionnaire.

Murray (1977) in a controlled study of admissions of male doctors to psychiatric hospitals in Scotland between 1963-72 found higher rates of depression, alcoholism and drug dependence among the doctor-patients.

Doctors in general, then, seem to be particularly susceptible to certain disorders and there is evidence from suicide rates and the association of suicide with depression of particularly high rates among psychiatrists. The aetiology is uncertain but a combination of early susceptibility combined with particular stresses associated with a clinical load seems the most plausible explanation.

FAILURE TO COPE

The largest systematic survey of psychiatric trainees was from the Task Force of the American Association of Directors of Psychiatric Residency Training who studied emotional problems of residents in psychiatry in some detail using questionnaire methods (Russell, Pasnau and Traintor, 1975). They studied 91 per cent of the 4085 general psychiatry residents in post during the study period. Seven per cent of these 3737 residents did not complete the study year and 68 (26 per cent) of these terminated because of emotional illness. Of the group suffering from emotional illness the diagnosis was behaviour or character disorder in 29 (43 per cent), severe neurosis or depression in 24 (35 per cent), psychosis in 12 (18 per cent), and suicide in 4 (giving a crude rate of suicide of 106 per 100000). A further 6 per cent of the sample were reported to have finished the year despite marginal performances and/or emotional difficulties. There was no significant difference in rates for women psychiatry trainees nor foreign medical graduates. The report goes on to make a number of suggestions about prior screening, using staff and fellow trainee interviews. Greater availability of psychotherapy or sensitivity groups was also suggested. In support of these suggestions they note elsewhere in their review that they found that a large number of residents facing problems could complete their residency training programmes with reasonable success when adequate support was available.

Little comparable data is available on other post-graduate medical trainees but nevertheless several authors support the view that psychiatrists may be particularly vulnerable. The alternative explanations of psychiatric trainees being vulnerable at intake or that psychiatry is an inherently stressful profession each have their proponents.

It seems likely that the suggestion of Zilboorg (1967) that minor anxiety and depressive symptoms are part of early career development and represent the negotiation of developmental tasks, offers a useful explanation of minor difficulties but does not fully account for the serious psyschiatric disturbance which occurs in some practitioners.

SPECIFIC STRESSORS

Attitudes to Psychiatrists and Job Stress

The attitudes of three main groups powerfully influence the self-perception of psychiatrists.

Within medicine the status of psychiatry has improved considerably in the last two decades with the change from an asylum-based specialty to an acute hospital specialty but most psychiatrists are used to the comment in liaison work with other medical specialties that 'you are different from most psychiatrists—you must be the one psychiatrist who is not crazy'. Not surprisingly, while most psychiatrists learn to accept these stereotypes, there is a tendency to fight to maintain an identity as a credible physician, perhaps by suggesting a rare organic diagnosis to out-guess the physician.

Other staff attitudes

The minefield of the so-called multidisciplinary team is a source of considerable conflict and ambiguity. The Trethowan report, for example, on the Future of Psychological Services (1970) encapsulates this ambiguity by confirming the view that medical responsibility should be carried within the team by the doctor and with that an overall responsibility for the patient's treatment. At the same time the report acknowledges that other professionals have their own individual responsibilities and are answerable in certain areas to their own managers. The report reinforces this ambiguity by stating that clinical psychologists have 'independent' professional status signifying that they are not a profession ancillary to medicine but without specifying what this independent status entails in practice.

With these inherent role ambiguities and contradictory notions of responsibility it is not surprising that the psychiatrist's role is under constant structural tension. There is no possibility of resolution on the one hand to truly equal team member status (because of externally determined responsibilities from, for example, the General Medical Council) nor to an acknowledged team-leader status. In addition, the members of the team typically wish to resolve this ambiguity in opposing directions, some moving to a simpler hierarchical structure and some towards democratic or consensus decision-making.

Public attitudes

Fear of mental illness is linked to a fear of psychiatrists, perhaps through guilt by association. In social situations half-joking references to 'mind readers', 'shrinks' and 'trick cyclists' have a shadow-side of the threat of the psychiatrist's power of compulsory detention and the personal fears of madness. Although these fears may not be of great significance in a social setting they are reflected within clinical work by fear in the patient–doctor relationship.

The negative feelings towards the psychiatrist may be masked by denial and then only become manifest in later non-compliance with treatment, or they may be manifest in an exaggerated respect for the powerful physician who knows best. Overt hostility and denigration of the psychiatrist, however, is not uncommon, particularly in settings where the patient is intensely fearful.

Psychiatrists in training

In a pilot study carried out in north-west England by the author and Dr Liz Germany, trainees were asked about perceived stresses faced during training. The trainees were asked to respond to a simple question about what they found stressful in their jobs. They were asked to make a list of aspects of their jobs which they found stressful. The twelve trainees responded with 103 stresses (mean 8.6, range 5–16). We categorized this simple data *post hoc* and the main groupings are given below.

The most frequently rated stress was labelled *Overwork*—of 25 comments, 10 specifically mentioned the 'on-call' commitment (on average a trainee psychiatrist will work overnight three nights per fortnight and one full weekend in three or four in addition to 'normal' working hours of 45 hours per week).

This work pattern is not only demanding but is also difficult to regulate and often leads to a queue of patients awaiting assessment many of whom are obviously distressed and demanding immediate intervention. The pressure to meet internal deadlines while studying for exams was another common theme. These comments should be seen in conjunction with the well recognized trend for the least experienced trainee to see the most difficult and demanding patients (Chessick, 1971; Merklin and Little, 1967; Ungerleider, 1965).

'*Relationships with other staff*' was rated next most frequently with 20 responses, 16 relating to conflicts with senior staff (consultants) where the trainees reported a perceived lack of support, lack of feedback, conflicting ideology and fear of disapproval.

Most trainees also mentioned '*performance related*' stresses. Of 16 responses, most related to presentations at public meetings. The trainees mentioned fears of humiliation or exposure of professional inadequacy in public settings.

'*Organisation*' problems were reported on 13 occasions. Typical examples were the demands of having to respond urgently to a radio pager 'bleep', usually to trivial requests which could have waited. This demand for immediate response was seen as highly disruptive to the trainees' work and to their ability to relate to individual patients.

Many comments reflected a lack of thought in planning for even the simplest needs of the trainees. For example, trainees often missed meals and were subject to unavoidable timetable clashes of commitments which were not resolved by senior staff. The trainees were often subjected to impossible time/performance demands.

In a related area 12 responses reflected '*inadequate resources*' as a stress—most frequently the pressure to deal with acutely ill patients with insufficient support and/or supervision. Less frequently mentioned was the pressure to resolve clinical difficulties when the physical resources were inadequate, for example, a lack of admission beds.

A further group of 14 responses were difficult to classify but seemed to focus on '*threats to self-esteem*'. Five responses mentioned negative self-perceptions and fear of unknown aspects of self revealed in their clinical work. the inability to cope with distressed patients, direct attacks on self-esteem by some patients, and the negative self-image faced after experiencing dislike or even hatred of a patient were examples under this heading. Although infrequent, some stresses reported were extremely intense and involved '*personal threat*'. Typical examples involved the fear or actuality of physical violence; patients abusing the trainees home telephone number; working alone at night; and dealing with violent and emotionally disturbing incidents. For example, trainees in one hospital were expected to trace case notes alone at night in a deserted part of the building. Some trainees mentioned episodes of potential or actual violence towards themselves.

This preliminary study showed a wide range of perceived job stresses not dissimilar from many other 'service' professions. Most responders covered several categories from these main headings. In follow-up discussion the psychiatrists in training were clear about avenues which could resolve many of these stresses for them but felt themselves individually powerless to change an institutional system or that their complaints if articulated would be perceived as 'moaning' and might prejudice promotion chances.

The last two groups of stresses—threats to self-esteem and personal threats are worthy of further comment as the issues are more complex than simply being exposed to noxious stimuli. These personally threatening events are frequently associated with a sense of isolation and powerlessness. On some occasions a disproportionate level of personal distress is linked to intense identification with the other person which seems to reactivate earlier conflicts and echo early patterns of object relationships.

Example

One trainee who had been practising psychiatry for one year had been on call twice that week. He had admitted four patients that day, one of whom had been particularly ill and disturbed. The acute admission ward was closed and barely adequate levels of nursing care were available. The patient, a previously normal woman, had made two very serious attempts to kill herself by hanging herself with piano wire and running in front of a heavy lorry. She had intensely distressing delusions about having killed and eaten her baby. She was hallucinating the taste of the child's burning flesh. The psychiatrist had found the admission particularly disturbing for several reasons; he was aware of a strong identification with the patient and also with her husband; he was disturbed by her intense experiences and was concerned about providing adequate resources to care for her. He was also half aware of the disturbingly violent qualities of her fantasies—cannibalism, violent death, and mutilation—with which he felt preoccupied all day.

During the early hours he was called to an extreme emergency on the ward, the woman having made severe lacerations to her throat when the nurse left the room for a few seconds. The doctor was involved with the rest of the emergency medical team in the technicalities of saving her life which was made particularly difficult by her savage anger at them for their efforts. She felt she deserved to die and that their actions would lead to the death of her family. As the trainee was the only person in the medical team known to her, he was in the bizarre situation of trying to converse with her to gain her confidence and co-operation whilst the rest of the team were carrying out the emergency procedures, whilst at the same time she was expressing intense hatred for their interference with her suicide attempt.

This is, of course, a particularly traumatic event and perhaps not typical. However, the psychiatrist's later understanding of the event's significance for him are worthy of comment. He reported nightmares about the event and felt preoccupied by these memories for several weeks. Part of his difficulty was related to his non-involvement with continuing clinical care as the patient was the responsibility of a different clinical team. The nursing staff involved were also upset and shaken by the event and their sense of responsibility for its occurrence. However, the ward atmosphere and ethos precluded any full discussion except a technical review of the occurrence and specifically the nature of the underlying mental state. These issues were, of course, important as the discussion about the event led to a clearer nursing policy, and a discussion about the cause of her illness. However, on this occasion and typically for trainee psychiatrists there was no opportunity to talk about the personal impact of the distressing experience. It was only in subsequent years that the psychiatrist was able to make better sense of the events and their effects on him. He became more aware of his own fears of violent emotions in himself and others; aware of his need for, but fear of, intimacy; his sense of powerlessness and helplessness in the face of these events. He was also initially disturbed by the unexpected tangle of emotions which arose—feelings of intense identification, feelings of attraction to her in this inappropriate and bizarre setting, feelings of anger, and feelings of alienation and later exclusion.

Not all traumatic events evoke such disturbing resonances but the theme of the psychiatrist's initial shame and embarrassment at experiencing intense feelings in himself is common. One model for understanding the nature of these stress responses is based on an application of object relations theory. The trainee psychiatrist is made susceptible by the intense work pressures so that key events are able to reactivate highly defended areas based on his own early relationships (Firth, 1985). Normally defences associated with a professional role keep these experiences at bay but in settings of intense personal threat underlying themes of helplessness, exclusion, rage, impotence, sadistic and masochistic wishes and other responses which relate to early experiences are released. These intense feelings are experienced as shameful representing as they do 'un-owned' aspects of the self. The difficulty in accepting such feelings is compounded by their occurrence in a setting where a 'professional', competent persona is being maintained.

Consultant psychiatrists

No formal study has yet been carried out of the job stresses perceived in consultant psychiatrists but within a series of training events organized for them in the North Western Regional Health Authority and University of Manchester the main themes to emerge overlapped only to a limited extent with the above. A recurrent theme was the lonely position—'the buck stopping here' when things go wrong. Although consultants reported variable levels of personal support from colleagues (medical and non-medical), the sense of personal isolation within their professional role was a common theme. Linked with this was an almost universal sense that other professions expected omniscience whilst simultaneously attacking them for arrogance and élitism.

The second main area of stress involved the conflicting demands to work directly with patients whilst investing energy in fighting to maintain resources from an ever-diminishing pool. Most consultants spent a considerable amount of time on committees, many of which seemed only marginally relevant but were involved in the distribution of necessary resources.

A third recurrent theme was of a sense of external 'audit' and criticism from a variety of sources including the Mental Health Act Commission, the Health Advisory Service, local pressure groups, visits from training accreditation committees, and pressures from within their own management structure. Even when these external bodies were pursuing constructive goals there was often an atmosphere of external threat and the sense that those criticizing the work of the psychiatrist were out of touch with the clinical reality of dealing with severely disturbed patients. Many consultants used emotive words like 'embattled' and viewed themselves as trying to hold together services at considerable personal expense. Although the reported job stresses were different in the two groups— trainees and consultants—it was noticeable that both groups found the organizational and structural aspects of their jobs at least as stressful as the direct patient contact.

The *transitional phase* from training to career posts has been generally neglected in the literature but was a subject of one study of 263 psychiatrists (Looney et al., 1980). They reported a high prevalence of stress-related symptoms in this phase but also reported that most psychiatrists had effective coping mechanisms and perceived themselves as increasing in growth, mastery and confidence. They noted, however, that successful coping with this developmental career point was particularly related to the presence of effective support systems outside the work setting. Seventy-three per cent of the psychiatrists reported anxiety as a problem ranging from moderate to incapacitating; 58 per cent experienced depression to a similar extent. These figures cannot easily be compared with population norms because of the way the questions were asked. However, the authors give other data on concurrent stresses: 47 per cent experienced difficulties with patients; 45 per cent stress in marriage; 40 per cent stress about change of friends; 39 per cent stress about moving; 28 per cent sexual problems; 26 per cent health worries; 24 per cent significant sleep disturbance; 23 per cent major weight change; 15 per cent physical illness; and separation or divorce in 14 per cent.

Overall, however, these subjects, despite high reported levels of stress, rated high levels of personal mastery and confidence.

Ways of Coping

In the study described above, the following coping mechanisms for those at career transition points were stated in order of frequency:

(i)   Emotional support from spouse or other loved one.
(ii) Play and recreation.
(iii) Consultation with colleagues.
(iv) Relationships with professional peers.
(v)   Vacation or time off.
(vi) Reading, creative activities, hobbies and exercise.

In a further analysis the authors found that dimensions of attachment to loved ones and to professional colleagues were most important to the respondents.

Considering the coping styles of trainees, Ungerleider (1965) describes the first year of training in psychiatry as 'that most difficult year' and discusses the development of defences against helplessness and powerlessness, and issues of controlling and being controlled. In the different context of developing psychotherapeutic interviewing skills, Kagan (1980) points out in some detail how, in recalling problematic interviews with patients, the trainees use 'feigned ignorance' and other unhelpful modes of coping to keep at bay two basic fears: of seduction and aggression—both being the object and being the perpetrator. Sharaf and Levinson (1964) discuss early coping via a 'quest for omnipotence' and the use of intense and inappropriate identification when this quest fails. The inappropriateness of identification is difficult to assess—many trainees report considerable personal stress from close identification with the patient's suffering. However, in another guise as empathy (the main difference being the less intense and overwhelming sense of similarity) these feelings are encouraged as evidence of therapeutic skill.

The Cruciform Effect

In their paper on the cruciform effect Gowler and Parry (1978) described four classic ways of avoiding organizational and personal stresses. These four themes can be applied to most professions but are appropriate in the context of the psychiatric profession particularly to consultant psychiatrists.

Easing is a way of reducing stress by *'opting out' of direct patient contact*—this manoeuvre applies mainly to senior staff although many senior staff do describe satisfaction from some aspects of their clinical contact. Most typically 'easing' is shown by the 'servicing' of other professionals through providing supervision rather than working directly with patients.

Seizing is a way of *using technical procedures* to minimize the personal effects of dealing with distressed patients. Psychiatry offers particular opportunities for this strategy with powerful tendencies apparent within the profession as a whole to give priority to the classification of disorders, the use of an organic illness paradigm and the use of pharmacological interventions.

Freezing involves the *use of restriction* to minimize stress. It is used in two key ways by psychiatrists. First, the psychiatrist can limit available services to a restricted group of patients or conditions, and second, can resolve his or her conflicts by 'professionalization' with increasing emphasis on delineating clear professional boundaries and responsibilities. In its extreme form the psychiatrist adopts a rigid authoritrian role determining the overall service the patient receives within a restrictive hierarchical environment.

The fourth coping style, *melting*, is a complex hybrid, typically with the psychiatrist *'dissolving' professional affiliations* and allying him or herself to a radical ideology. This often involves the psychiatrist in working with an abstraction like 'the community' whilst maintaining an image of himself in an idealized working relationship.

For all of these coping styles there are positive aspects allowing the psychiatrist to resolve intolerable conflicts. However, in their extreme form they lead to a restricted professional repertoire with an emphasis on 'survival' rather than the development of good clinical practice.

Some of these coping strategies vary with seniority. As in most professions the senior psychiatrist tends to take on an increasing 'easing' role—reducing face-to-face contact with patients to take on a more administrative role. However, there are also considerable role differences between teaching hospital and other consultants. Personality variables are also important in determining the extent to which strategies such as 'seizing' and 'freezing' are used. The pressure is on to produce standardized patterns of working with little room for the patient who does not easily fit, some psychiatrists find this a comfortable pattern which reduces uncertainty and leads to standardized packages of treatment based on diagnosis.

'Melting' is a particularly seductive strategy as it allows the professional to maintain enthusiasm and optimism that constructive change can occur by avoiding two important sources of conflict. The recipient of interventions becomes an abstraction which cannot show personal distress and can be redefined according to whichever ideology is currently fashionable. Also, by embracing an apparently radical ideology and loosening affiliations with the specific professional role the psychiatrist can distance himself or herself from potential hostility based on higher earnings and power whilst at the same time keeping these benefits.

An example of other defensive mechanisms in action on a psychiatric ward is given by Aitken (1984) in an account of the admission of a patient seen by her for psychotherapy. The patient had been admitted after an episode of self-injury and the ward team used mechanisms of denigration and infantilization to keep the patient in the role of the wayward and manipulative child. The difficulty of functioning as an effective ward team is demonstrated clearly in her account of the usually affable and supportive psychiatrist showing reluctance to side with the therapist as this would risk disturbing the 'ward on whose domestic harmony his easy work relationship relied'. Aitken extends her account using a military metaphor—'the patient as enemy': 'Like an occupying army the staff members were surrounded by outward compliance, but felt under constant threat of attack from any direction'.

The psychiatrist is often at a centre of the web of complex interrelationships between staff members. The use of the strategies outline in the 'cruciform effect' minimize the role of stress inherent in being a 'team leader' without managerial responsibility for most of the staff team. At best a consensus can be reached, particularly in some specialized settings like a therapeutic community. Even here Hobson (1979) points out that leadership is needed to maintain secure boundaries in relation to the outside world embodied often in the complex management system of the National Health Service.

PREVENTION

Some of the sources of stress outlined above are clearly resolvable through simple means whilst others are complex and operate at a macroscopic, national level involving core attitudes to the role of the professional. This section deals briefly with three possible levels of prevention: first, with the selection and training of psychiatrists; second, with specific measures to reduce the psychiatric casualties amongst psychiatrists themselves; and third, addressing the structural problems inherent in the psychiatrist role.

SELECTION, TRAINING AND ASSESSMENT

Miller and Burstein (1969) in a sensitive paper on the professional development of psychiatric trainees discuss the interrelationship between assessment methods and the facilitation of learning. They reinforce the important distinction to be made between the consequences of dealing with developmental tasks and neurotic symptomatology.

They also note, however, that there are more and less adaptive ways of dealing with these developmental tasks and note the potential for fulfilling the role of the helpless child during training. These authors are acutely aware of how assessment can induce shame and are aware of the overriding need to move the trainee from pupil to collaborator. They differentiate four areas; traditional educational attainment and skills; stylistic variables; personality variables; and neurotic conflicts. Their assessment involves the trainee interviewing a patient with two teachers observing. The trainee then has a post-interview discussion with the teachers during which time his ability to conceptualize and communicate his understanding is assessed. They comment on the various ways that deficits in skills, stylistic differences, personality differences and neurotic conflicts can interfere with the trainee's development. In the work of Miller and Burstein the variety of defences used and the trainee's coping style are taken seriously in assessing change and indirectly the assessment can identify areas requiring attention which could ultimately protect the trainee from the stressful aspects of this job.

SPECIFIC MEASURES

There are some stresses in the working life of the trainee which are specific to particular settings. Cotton and Pruett (1975) comment on the disturbing feelings aroused within trainees in a community psychiatry training setting. Many of their points would also apply to other specialist settings, for example, in forensic psychiatry, alcoholism treatment units, and adolescent units, where the trainee works in relative isolation, alongside a well established team, in a setting which challenges the trainee's developing sense of authority and expertise. These authors comment on the feelings of anxiety, loneliness and anger experienced. They scheduled a formal weekly meeting to discuss aspects of the community psychiatry experience to maintain some continuity between their previous ward-based work and the community experience. The sense of disappointment on realizing their inability to achieve their fantasized roles was a common theme in these meetings. They reported that the meetings did alleviate the sense of alienation.

The need for personal therapy for psychiatrists, both in training and in career posts is controversial within the United Kingdom although much more widely accepted elsewhere in the world. Potentially, personal therapy could have a preventative role, but whilst there is good evidence of a positive impact from psychological therapies generally, there has been inadequate evaluation of these interventions in psychiatrists as the client group. It remains an open question whether the traditional psychodynamic form of personal therapy is the most advantageous in the specific area of reducing psychiatric morbidity amongst psychiatrists. There are other plausible contenders such as a problem-solving approach which would encourage the trainees in a group-setting to identify sources of stress, share the resulting feelings but then take responsibility for taking whatever steps are necessary to minimize such stresses.

Group-based strategies have been tried in several work settings involving health professionals with an emphasis on ventilation and catharsis at one extreme, or alternatively a problem-based approach emphasizing ways of modifying the stress at the other. Informal settings which provide the opportunity to share difficult clinical and work-related problems followed in some systematic way by the formulation of strategies to deal with identified difficulties, have been shown to be effective in groups of nurses facing highly stressful work settings (Scully, 1983). The author suggests ways in which such groups can be successfully focused on 'work-related' issues rather than becoming 'therapy' groups which have a different set of aims, related to insight, self-understanding and personal growth.

> In keeping with the consultation nature of the support group, content must be work-related. Discussion of personal issues would violate the goal of increasing the

staff's effectiveness because it would, in reality, increase their vulnerability.... Topics such as how to help families in crisis, how to ease the strain of death of patients, how to care for demanding patients, how to handle conflict between staff members, how to approach abrasive staff, how to offer each other support are all appropriate and can lead to useful suggestions for reducing stress levels at work. (p. 189).

With slight modification the above can be used in a multidisciplinary setting. The temptation always is for a support group to slide into becoming an ineffective therapy group: ineffective because there is no contract and no consensus about how much personal material can be expressed.

At times, more direct methods of offering help are needed when a psychiatrist becomes or is in danger of becoming ineffective as a consequence of psychiatric disorder. Many states in the United States now have 'sick doctor' statutes which use measures such as revoking the licence to practice as a way of pushing the physician into treatment and rehabilitation.

The General Medical Council in the UK has a similar statutory function but the Health Committee of the GMC which was brought into being in the Medical Act (1978) has taken an active role in minimizing the punishment aspect and maximizing the therapeutic aspect of their statutory functions.

Formal procedures exist in the NHS hospital service and in general practice to recommend suspension of sick doctors but these devices are poorly understood and applied inconsistently. Rawnsley (1985) has pointed out several factors which operate to reduce the chance of a sick doctor receiving help. Two of the common conditions—alcoholism and depression—may lead to a lack of insight, and in addition the sick doctor may well feel embarrassed at the thought of approaching local colleagues. Rawnsley was instrumental in setting up informal services in the UK through the Royal College of Psychiatrists with the Association of Anaesthetists and the Association of Surgeons. A more recent initiative by the British Medical Association supported by many professional bodies has led to the establishment of a National Counselling and Welfare Service for Sick Doctors from all branches of the profession. The scheme is specifically non-statutory and non-coercive. A doctor who is seriously worried about illness and its effects on the fitness to practice of a colleague may telephone a central contact point giving the specialty and geographical area of the sick doctor. A name and telephone number is given of a national adviser from a panel of senior doctors in the same branch of medicine. The colleague can then contact the national adviser who may contact the 'patient–doctor' or may arrange for another specialist within the service to do so. No permanent records are kept and the doctor may refuse the offer in which case the only action taken by the counselling service is to inform the original referring colleague (Rawnsley, 1985). This system provides a significant improvement on previous arrangements by offering a confidential yet organized service to professional colleagues in all specialties.

Running through all these discussions is the conceptual difficulty of separating the truly impaired physician from those encountering temporary difficulties in a highly stressful work setting. Indeed, even when these possible interventions are successful at the individual level, a simplistic model of 'therapeutic intervention' to deal with 'illness' is inadequate. An adequate model would take into account the relationship of the individual to the larger organization in the context of that individual's past.

STRUCTURAL ASPECTS

Altering the structural aspects of the psychiatrist's role is potentially the most effective way of reducing job stress. However, little work has been carried out on the differential impacts of the various elements of a psychiatrist's role. At the microscopic level it seems that most psychiatrists divide their time so that direct face-to-face patient contact amounts to less than a quarter of their working week, but during this time they have a sense of considerable time pressure and constant backlog. Many psychiatrists are surprised at the relative brevity of direct patient contact, but the realization of this is an almost inevitable consequence of the work patterns and additional administrative and supervisory responsibilities. They relieve the psychiatrist from some of the experience of being submerged in a limitless sea of clinical demands.

At a higher level of organization, groups of psychiatrists spend little time together and often work in a paradoxically isolated way. Although most of their work is spent with others—patients or colleagues—they are often responsible for patient care on several sites with poor administrative support for the running of a complex service. Improvements in administrative and secretarial support coupled with increased informal contact with colleagues would go some way to mitigating these effects.

As mentioned earlier, the structural role *vis-à-vis* other health service professionals is problematical. The psychiatrist is the highest salaried member of the multidisciplinary team and carries particular legal and organizational responsibilities as would an executive in other work settings. Nevertheless, the limits of authority and responsibilities delegated to the consultant are often passed on by folklore and are difficult to clarify. Useful suggestions clarifying the nature of medical responsibility and the function of the multidisciplinary team can be found in *Responsibility Issues in Clinical Psychology and Multidisciplinary Teamwork* (British Psychological Society Division of Clinical Psychology, 1986).

Future research could usefully attend to the factors which are protective against the severe stress-related responses. The previous research discussed here highlights the importance of stressful work-related events being seen in a developmental context. Work is also necessary to clarify further the structural stresses of the psychiatrist role and the optimum organization of that role to minimize unnecessary stress.

REFERENCES

a 'Brook, M. F., Hailstone, J. D. and McLaughlan, I. E. Y. (1967). *British J. Psychiatry*, **113**, 1013. Cited in Rucinski and Cybulska (1985).
Aitken, S. (1984). The patient as enemy, *Changes*, **2**, (2), 54–5.
Barraclough, B., Bunch, J., Nelson, B. and Sainsbury, P. (1974). *British J. Psychiatry*, **125**, 355. Cited in Rucinski and Cybulska (1985).
Bjorksten, O., Sutherland, S., Miller, C. and Stewart, T. (1983). Identification of medical student problems and comparison with those of other students, *J. Med. Education*, **58**, 759–67.
Blachly, P. H., Disher, W. and Roduner, G. (1968). Suicide by physicians, *Bull. of Suicidology*, Dec. 1–18.
Book, H. (1973). On becoming a psychotherapist, perhaps. *Canad. Psychiatric J.*, **18**, 487–93.
British Psychological Society Division of Clinical Psychology (1986). *Responsibility Issues in Clinical Psychology and Multidisciplinary Teamwork*, British Psychological Society, London.
Burton, A. (1972). Twelve therapists, Jossey-Bass, San Francisco.
Chessick, R. D. (1971). How the resident and superviser disappoint each other, *Am. J. psychother.*, **25**, 272–83.
Craig, A. G. and Pitts, F. N. (1968). *Diseases of the Nervous System*, **29**, 763. Cited in Rucinski and Cybulska (1985).
Cramond, W. A. (1969). *Aust. and NZ J. Psychiatry*, **3**, 324. Cited in Rucinski and Cybulska (1985).
Cotton, P. G. and Pruett, K. D. (1975). The affective experience of residency training in community psychiatry, *Am. J. Psychiatry*, **132** (3), 267.
Edelwich, J. and Brodsky, A. (1980). *Burnout: States of disillusionment in the Helping Professions*, Human Sciences Press, New York.
Evans, J. L. (1965). *Am. J. Psychiatry*, **122**, 159. Cited in Rucinski and Cybulska (1985). op cit.
Farber, B. A. (1983). *Stress and Burnout in the Human Service Professions*, Pergamon, New York.
Firth, J. (1985). Personal meanings of occupational stress: Cases from the clinic, *Journal of occupational Psychology*, **58**, 139–48.
Firth, J. (1986). Levels and sources of stress in Medical Students, *Br. Med. J.*, **292**, 1177–80.
Fisher, H. J. (1983). A psychoanalytic view of burnout. In B. A. Farber (ed.) *Stress and Burnout in the Human Service Profession*, Pergamon, London.
Freudenberger, H. J. and Richelson, G. (1980). Burnout: the high cost of high achievement, Anchor Press, Garden City, NY.
Freudenberger, H. J. and Robbins, A. (1979). The hazards of being a psychoanalyst, *Psychoanalytic Review*, **66** (2), 275–96.
Gowler, D. and Parry, G. (1978). Professionalism and its discontents, *New Forum*, **5**, 54–56.
Halleck, S. C. and Woods, S. M. (1962). Emotional problems of psychiatric residents, *Psychiatry*, **25**, 339–46.

Hobson, R. F. (1979). The Messianic Community'. In R. D. Hinshelwood and N. Manning (eds) *Therapeutic Communities: Reflections and Progress*, RKP, London.
Kagan, N. (1980). Influencing human interaction—eighteen years with IPR. In Allen K. Hess (ed.) *Psychotherapy Supervision*, Wiley, New York.
Looney, J. G., Harding, R. K., Blotcky, M. J. and Barnhart, F. D. (1980). Psychiatrists' transition from training to career: stress and Mastery, *Am. J. psychiatry*, **137**, (1), 32–6.
Maslach, C. C. (1976). Burned out, *Human Behaviour*, **5**, 16–22.
Mawardi, B. H. (1979). Satisfactions, dissatisfactions, and causes of stress in medical practice, *JAMA*, **241**, 1483–6.
Mawardi, B. H. (1983). Aspects of the impaired physician. In B. A. Farber (ed.) *Stress and Burnout in the Human Service Professions*, Pergamon, New York.
Merklin, L. and Little, R. B. (1967). Beginning psychiatry training syndrome, *Am. J. Psychiatry*, **124**, (2), 193–7.
Miller, A. A. and Burstein, A. G. (1969). Professional development in psychiatric residents, *Arch. Gen. Psychiatry*, **20**, 385–94.
Murray, R. M. (1977). *British J. Psychiatry*, **131**, 1. Cited in Rucinski and Cybulska (1985).
Pasnau, R. and Bayley, S. (1971). Personality changes in the first year of psychiatric redisdency, *Am. J. Psychiatry*, **128**, 79–84.
Pines, A. and Aronson, E. (1981). *Burnout: from tedium to personal growth*, Free Press, New York.
Rawnsley, K. (1985). Helping the sick doctor: a new service. *Br. M. J.*, **291**, 922.
Registrar-General (1978). Decennial Supplement, England and Wales 1959–63 on Occupational Mortality, HMSO, London.
Rich, C. L. and Pitts, F. N. (1979). Suicide by male physicians during a five year period, *Am. J. Psychiatry*, **136**, (8), 1089–90.
Rose, K. D. and Rosow, I. (1973). Physicians who kill themselves, *Arch. Gen. Psychiatry*, **29**, 800.
Ross, M. (1973). Suicide and the psychiatrist, *Am. J. Psychiatry*, **130**, 937.
Rucinski, J. and Cybulska, E. (1985). Mentally ill doctors, *Br. J. Hosp. Med.*, Feb. 90–94.
Russell, A. T., Pasnau, R. O. and Traintor, Z. C. (1975). Emotional problems of residents in psychiatry, *Am. J. Psychiatry*, **132**, (3), 263–7.
Scully, R. (1983). The work setting support group: a means of preventing burnout. In B. A. Farber (ed.) *Stress and Burnout in the Human Service Professions*, Pergamon, New York.
Searles, H. P. (1965). *Collected papers on schizophrenia and related subjects*, International Universities Press, New York.
Steppacher, R. C. and Mausner, J. S. (1974). *JAMA*, **228**, 323. Cited in Rucinski and Cybulska (1985).
Sharaf, M. F. and Levinson, D. J. (1964). The quest for omnipotence in professional training, *Psychiatry*, **27**, 135–49.
Shorrt, S. E. D. (1979). *Canadian Medical Association Journal*, **121**, 283. Cited in Rucinski and Cybulska (1985).
Trethowan Report (1970). *The Future of Psychological Services*, HMSO, London.
Ungerleider, J. T. (1965). That most difficult year, *Am. J. Psychiatry*, **122**, 542–5.
Vaillant, G. E., Sobowale, N. C. and McArthur, C. (1972). Some psychological vulnerabilities of physicians, *New England J. Med.*, **287**, 372–5.
Vincent, M. O., Robinson, E. A. and Latt, L. (1969). *Canadian Med. Assocn Journal*, **100**, 403. Cited in Rucinski and Cybulska (1985).
Watterson, D. J (1976). *Canadian Med. Assocn J.*, **155**, 311. Cited in Rucinski and Cybulska (1985).
Zilboorg (1967). Personal communication cited in Merklin and Little (1967).

PART II

Non-medical Health Professionals

Stress in Health Professionals
Edited by R. Paynes and J. Firth-Cozens
© 1987 John Wiley & Sons Ltd

Chapter 7

Stress Amongst Dentists

Gerry Kent

Dentistry has something of a reputation for being a stressful occupation, particularly amongst dentists themselves. For example, when O'Shea, Corah and Ayer (1984) asked their sample of practising dentists 'Compared with other professions, do you believe that dentistry is more stressful, less stressful or about the same?', 75 per cent replied that it was more stressful and only 5 per cent felt that it was less stressful. This perception might be encouraged by the generally negative image of dentistry held by the public, where there is widespread anxiety about visiting the dentist. In many respects it seems that this type of health care is stressful for everyone concerned.

This chapter reviews the research in this area, concentrating upon studies where data have been collected. While there are many papers in the literature based on anecdotal evidence or on the 'common knowledge' that the practice of dentistry is stressful, these are not included here. There are some indications that the stressors experienced by patients in their everyday lives can contribute to dental problems (e.g. gingivitis (Milgrom *et al.*, 1983, Schulger, 1949) and caries (Morse *et al.*, 1982)) but this research also falls outside the scope of the present review. There has been very little work on the stressors felt by staff employed by dentists, such as hygienists and dental assistants: in fact most of the work discussed here has been performed on white male dentists practising privately.

This chapter comprises three sections. The first is on the stressors experienced by dentists. Self-report questionnaires provide most of this information although some researchers have taken physiological measures of dentists at work. Possible health hazards associated with the use of chemicals are also included. The second section reviews the research on the reactions and symptoms associated with stress in dentistry. This includes epidemiological studies on medical and psychological illness amongst dentists. The final section examines possible methods for reducing stress.

SOURCES OF STRESS

Self-reports

The survey has been the most popular method for assessing the type and severity of stressors in dentistry. Typically, a sample of dentists have been asked to indicate which aspects of their practice cause them the most stress. Sometimes items have been offered and respondents asked to indicate the extent to which each affects them, while in other studies the questions have been open-ended and coded later. Most frequently, questionnaires have been sent through the post with between one-third and two-thirds of the sample replying.

The open-ended approach is typified by Godwin *et al.* (1981) who posted a questionnaire to 200 recent graduates, receiving a reply from 133 (66.5 per cent). When asked to identify 'the sources of greatest stress', 73 per cent mentioned patient management, which included some reference to patient fear and anxiety, late or missed appointments and patient dissatisfaction with their services, 50 per cent mentioned business management problems, such as collection of fees, cash flow problems, overhead and insurance, and 38 per cent indicated that their own perfectionism led to frustration with the discrepancy between their high ideals for care and the realities of day-to-day dentistry. Problems with staff management, particularly their relationship with incompetent staff, were cited by 33 per cent, and 26 per cent indicated that time pressures, particularly when treatment fell behind schedule, was a source of stress. The technical aspects of practice did not seem to be pertinent. Ingersoll *et al.* (1978) found similar results. When dentists who had been practising for some time were asked to identify problems with patients, 93 per cent of the sample identified at least one problem. Business management, patient compliance, fearful patients and patients who missed or cancelled or who were late for appointments headed the list. Problems with auxiliaries included staff training and turnover and lack of professionalism. These two studies used American samples, but Kent (1983) posted a questionnaire to a sample of 148 UK dentists, with a 38 per cent response rate. When they were asked which problems with patients they found the most troublesome, aspects of the dentist–patient relationship (where patients seemed rude or inconsiderate), patient anxiety and lack of preventive care were the most frequently cited problems.

A second approach has been to provide a list of possibilities and to ask the respondents to indicate the degree to which each is stressful. An advantage of this method is that it provides information about the conditions of practice which are seen as relatively stress-free. The largest survey of this kind has been reported by Dunlap and Stewart (1982a) where the readers of *Dental Economics* completed a questionnaire provided in a previous issue. The readers were asked to indicate if they 'always', 'frequently', 'occasionally', 'seldom' or 'never' experienced stress from a list of six possibilities. Clearly, the dentists ($N = 3700$)

felt themselves to be under stress and that many always or frequently had problems with perfectionism, with patients having pain, with fear in patients and with feeling under pressure to make money. Similar findings were reported in another journal-based survey by Stern (1979). Here over 1000 dentists replied, being asked to rank order 15 items. Patients' experience of pain, patient movement in the chair and waiting for late patients or those who don't show topped the ranking list. By contrast, concern with lack of skill was ranked 14th. Another selected sample, this time with dentists attending a conference, was studied by O'Shea, Corah and Ayer (1984). Again, falling behind schedule, striving for technical perfection and causing pain to patients were ranked highest, with too much of the same work and competition with other dentists being low in stressfulness. That this last factor was ranked low is interesting, because dentists' concern about their future practice is beginning to show up in other reports. A perceived reduction in the demand for dental services, due to a lessened need for restorative work, is becoming a worry for some practitioners (Abel et al., 1983).

Generally speaking, there is some agreement in these reports that dentists find anxious and unco-operative patients, the possibility of inflicting pain, and the pressure of keeping to a schedule considerable sources of stress. While striving for perfection is a stressor for many dentists, they tend to believe that they have the necessary technical skills for the job and do not find the routine work of dentistry stressful (see also Cooper, Mallinger and Kahn, 1978; Page and Slack, 1969; Eccles and Powell, 1967). While such results have much face validity (when they are presented to meetings of dentists there is much head-nodding all around), there are criticisms of the self-report approach. First, it is not clear that people are able to identify accurately those events which cause them the most distress. It may be that dentists are largely unaware of those situations which could have adverse consequences, especially in the long term. These could include chemical hazards to health as outlined below. A second criticism is that these studies give results for dentists as a group, and individual differences are not taken into consideration. Although a large proportion of dentists find keeping to a schedule stressful many do not and those events which are ranked low overall may be the most significant sources of stress for some dentists. In the O'Shea, Corah and Ayer (1984) study, for instance, every one of the items was rated at the most stressful end of the scale by someone, even the lowest ranked overall.

A somewhat more sophisticated approach was used by Corah, O'Shea and Skeels (1982). Dentists were asked not simply how stressful they found certain situations, but how frequently they occurred and how much they bothered the dentist when they did occur. For example, the patient grabbing the dentist's hand occurred only infrequently (once a week or less for 94 per cent of the sample), but this behaviour was ranked as most bothersome by the dentists overall. On the other hand, patients showing fear happened more often (more than twice a week for 75 per cent), but was ranked least bothersome of the 10 events. Some events, such as patients missing their appointment or being late and patients not paying their bills, were both very frequent and very bothersome.

All of the above research concerns the incidence of routine stressors in dentistry. There is remarkably little evidence about the incidence of major problems, such as the death of a patient under general anaesthetic or serious allergic reactions to drugs. Young (1975) surveyed dentists in England, asking about their experiences with such serious problems in the previous five years. With only a 20 per cent response rate, caution is required in extrapolating his results, but 43 per cent of the responding dentists had experienced at least one occasion when resuscitation of a patient was necessary. These were due to cardiac arrest (0.0187 cases/dentist/year), cardiovascular collapse (0.0280 cases/dentist/year), respiratory arrest (0.020) and allergic reactions (0.0037). While the incidence is thus quite low, the average practitioner may worry about his or her ability to cope with such situations because of the lack of experience with them. This was typified by one respondent who claimed that he had given some 50,000 general anaesthesias to patients over the past ten years without trouble, but added the rider 'so something has to happen soon'.

Physiological measures

A third criticism of self-reports is that these perceptions are not related to other correlates of stress, such as personality characteristics or physiological indices. There is much less research in this area. Roder, Lewis and Law (1961) noted that many dentists say that they dislike having the parents of a child patient in their operatories, but when the heart rate of six dentists during the administration of a local anaesthetic in the presence and the absence of a parent was monitored, no significant differences were found. Eccles (1969) recorded heart rate under three conditions: while reading a book, while carrying out conservation treatment with a patient (including a local anaesthetic, drilling and filling a tooth), and while carrying out identical treatment on a phantom head. Here, the dentists' heart rates were lowest while reading a book and similar while treating the phantom head, but only slightly higher when the real patient was confronted. GSR has also been monitored: Eccles (1970) found that the GSR of dentists tended to rise just before treatment was given and that after preparation of the tooth was completed and the placing of amalgam begun the GSRs of both dentists and patients decreased. The rise in the dentists' GSRs did not seem to be due to any apprehension on the part of the patients since simultaneous rises in both dentists and patients were very rare. Finally, Bilodeau *et al.* (1983) recorded ECGs from 28 male army dentists during a 24-hour period which included a full working day. The dentists were also asked to keep a diary of their activities and difficulties with patients. Only rarely could a change in ventricular rhythms be associated with an encounter with a difficult patient.

While these studies appear to be the only ones available on qualified dentists' physiological activity while treating patients, two other groups of researchers have related dentists' perceptions of stress to their physical health. Howard *et al.* (1976) examined 33 Canadian dentists, asking them about their patterns of work, taking a history of symptoms indicative of stress and assessing their physical fitness. They found that dentists who were always or usually ahead of schedule had a higher physical work capacity (cardiovascular fitness as measured by a bicycle ergometer), and an increase in stress symptomatology was associated with an increasing tendency to fall behind schedule. The dentists' job satisfaction was estimated by replies to the question 'How strongly do you feel it would benefit you to change jobs or your type of work activity?': the best predictors of job satisfaction were the job's perceived interference with the dentists' personal lives and the length of time in the same location. To a lesser extent, the number of stress symptoms was also related to low job satisfaction. Finally, Howard *et al.* classified the dentists in their sample as Type A or B, but this was not significantly related to whether or not they fell behind schedule.

The other study which included physiological measures of stress is reported by Cooper, Mallinger and Kahn (1978). They first asked dentists attending a conference to rate the stressfulness of 15 items associated with dentistry. In common with the studies discussed earlier, coping with difficult patients, trying to keep to a schedule and having too much work were ranked highest while coping with the routine and dull work associated with practice was ranked lowest. Several scales of a personality inventory (the Cattell 16PF) were also administered. In addition, Cooper *et al.* collected some physical health data, including sitting pulse rate, systolic and diastolic blood pressure and stress ECG results. Raised diastolic blood pressure was primarily associated with age, but high rankings of 'dentist as inflictor of pain', 'coping with administrative duties', 'having too little work' and the factor of anxiety on the 16PF were also associated with high DBP. Interestingly, elevated DBP was associated with dentists who did not rank 'coping with difficult patients' highly, leading Cooper *et al.* to suggest that those dentists who did not acknowledge this as a source of stress were at risk. Taken together, these factors accounted for 32 per cent of the total variance in blood pressure. Many of the same variables were associated with raised systolic blood pressure. That the denial of coping with difficult patients was associated with risk factors suggests that some dentists may not be fully aware of their stress and the causes of it. This points out the disadvantage of relying too heavily on dentists' perceptions of stressors.

Borderline or abnormal ECG readings had somewhat different correlates with ratings of stress. Here low patient appreciation, routine and dull work, as well as sustaining and building a practice were related to ECG readings. The personality characteristics of being 'controlled and socially precise', 'venturesome' and 'less emotionally stable' were also associated with stress ECG patterns.

Female dentists

As mentioned above, one problem with most studies on stress in dentistry is that the samples are not representative of the profession as a whole. The results are based on either selected samples (e.g. delegates at a conference) or questionnaires have been sent through the post (often with low response rates). It may be that dentists who have not participated in these surveys experience quite different stressors or, indeed, none at all. A group which is only marginally represented in the above research is women. Dental schools are only now recruiting a substantial proportion of females so that the particular problems faced by them have not been explored in any depth. There is the argument that women suffer from greater role strain and role conflict than men, but there appears to be no empirical data on these issues. In a survey of American women who graduated between 1975 and 1981, 77 per cent were involved in dental activities at least 30 hours per week, but only anecdotal evidence of the difficulties was provided (Tillman and Horowitz, 1983). Women may encounter some of the problems faced by other minority groups (in 1979 only 1.5 per cent of the practising dentists in the US were women) but it seems that for students at least, being black or of oriental background presents more of a problem than being female (Mesa et al., 1981). However, there is some evidence that being female has presented difficulties in the past. In a survey reported in 1973 (Austin, Maher and Lomonaco, 1973), many women reported that they were 'never quite accepted as dental students' by either faculty or fellow students. While 77 per cent felt that they had encountered no more difficulties than their male peers, some believed that both students and faculty viewed them with suspicion until they had proved themselves. Women's minority status is changing, though, and currently almost half of the new students entering dental schools are female. Eventually, this change may be reflected in the proportion of women holding academic positions in universities. In 1978 only 5 per cent of the academics in UK dental schools were women, but this had increased to 9 per cent by 1980 (Over and Spencer, 1983).

Students

Students form another group of people who experience particular stressors within the profession. While several studies (e.g. Eli and Shuval, 1982) have shown that dental students become less 'people-orientated' and more 'status-orientated' as they pass through the course, none have controlled for the possibility that any changes are due to increasing age, rather than socialization into dentistry. The stressors reported by students depend to some extent on their year of the course, but academic concerns having to do with the volume of material to be learned, rather than concerns with conceptual difficulty, are generally rated highly. Goldstein (1979) asked his first year students to rate 14 items on a four-point scale, finding that the use of time, mastery of the volume of material and inconsistent feedback from staff were rated highest. Sachs, Zullo and Close (1981) identified five factors, including a psychosocial dimension (items such as 'conflicts with classmates', 'being treated as though you were immature and irresponsible' and 'dealing with authoritarian, unsympathetic instructors'), academic concerns ('being unable to learn everything', 'preparing for and taking exams', and 'fear of making a mistake in your work'), time concerns ('lack of time for family or intimate friends', 'lack of time for recreation'), isolation concerns ('feeling lonely') and worries about finances ('running out of money for tuition and other expenses'). At least some of these stressors appear to be common to training in many health professions (medical students also complain about lack of time, for example) and can exacerbate the stresses of such life changes as leaving home for the first time or needing to make a new set of friends. Yablom et al. (1983) found that 49 per cent of their sample scored over 200 LCUs and 22 per cent over 300 on the Holmes and Rahe SRRS for the previous 12 months, indicating a relatively high level of life changes.

The concerns of senior dental students were canvassed by Simpson, Biller-Karlsson and Willard (1982). For them, finances, patient load and competition from peers were the main sources of stress. Students' concern about the latter factor may be increasing since they are not being enthusiastically welcomed by practising dentists at a time when patient need for restorations is decreasing and the output from dental schools is high. While academic concerns are generally rated highest for junior students, seniors appear to become increasingly concerned with issues of patients' management. Simpson, Biller-Karlsson and Willard (1982) found that seniors experienced more stress from patient complaints and anxiety than did practising dentists.

As in the case of qualified dentists, there has been relatively little research on the behaviour and physiological responses of students as they deal with patients. Wurster, Weinstein and Cohen (1979) asked students to rate their confidence in their ability to deal with difficult patients. The students were given a set of hypothetical situations, such as 'Four-year-old Donna attempts to leave the chair during placement of a rubber dam', and were asked to indicate their ability to cope with such situations on a 10-point scale. The students were then divided into high and low confidence groups and their actual behaviour with child patients noted. The patients of less confident students accounted for 87 per cent of the unco-operative behaviour shown by all the children in the study. Since the children were assigned to the students without knowledge of their confidence level, it seems unlikely that this over-representation was due to the children's personalities or pre-existing levels of anxiety. Rather, it would seem that the students' ability or inability to manage their patients was responsible. Kurz-Kummerle et al. (1983) used the Wurster, Weinstein and Cohen (1979) confidence scale in a similar study but added physiological and self-report measures of anxiety before and during two appointments, the first for prevention and the second for a restoration. The children's physiological activity and behaviour were also noted. Students who felt less confident in their skills at the restorative visit had children who were rated as more anxious than those of students who reported no change or an improvement in their confidence. The children of students who were very concerned about being evaluated by staff were more disruptive than children of students who were less concerned. Students' heart rate at the announcement that they were about to begin drilling was correlated with the children's anxiety and degree of disruptiveness. Overall, students' subjective reports of anxiety and physiological activity were related to the behaviour and physiological responses of their child patients. While it is not possible to establish cause and effect here, it is likely that there is some circularity, with anxiety in the student making management more difficult, resulting in increased patient disruptiveness and heightened student anxiety.

The general picture given by the above studies is that it is the interpersonal and financial sides of dentistry which are responsible for the greater proportion of stress experienced. Dentists feel well-prepared for the technical side of their work, but less well-prepared for the social aspects of practice. While women have reported some discrimination in the past, there are indications that society's attitude toward female practitioners in all health professions is changing, so that their problems may be due more to role strains and conflicts not peculiar to dentistry. Dental students' concerns appear to change over the years of their teaching, being concentrated upon academic problems (especially the volume of material to be learned) early on and upon patient management in the senior years. Whether heightened physiological activity in dentists is associated with patient management problems is unclear, with only a few reports of such research being available.

Health hazards

The above studies are concerned with the psychological and social sources of stress in dentistry, but there is another important area—the long-term exposure to noxious and toxic substances. The use of mercury in the mixing of amalgam is the most widely-publicised danger. Since dental practices are traditionally small concerns, they have not been covered in Britain by acts about health and safety at work, so that the handling of mercury has not been specified or monitored closely. However, some recent legislation has made practices liable to visitation by inspectors, so that tighter controls may be forthcoming. Mercury can be absorbed through the fingers during mixing or mercury vapour can be inhaled, particularly during the removal of old amalgam (Richards and Warren, 1985). There are some reports of serious illness and death which can be attributed to mercury poisoning (e.g. Merfield *et al.* 1976) and while most dentists now avoid direct contact, high levels of vapour have been reported in the dental environment. For example, Gronka et al. (1970) found that one in 10 of the offices they surveyed had vapour levels above that recommended. Mechanical amalgamators do not seem to provide the complete answer (Nixon and Rowbotham, 1971). The American Dental Association takes the position that some people are particularly sensitive to mercury poisoning and that it poses little threat for most dentists (Council on Dental Materials, 1983), but there is continuing concern (Rothwell, Frame and Shimmin, 1977) and a search for alternative materials.

Another aspect of the dental environment which may pose a health threat is the repeated exposure to gases, both nitrous oxide as a sedative and halothane as a general anaesthetic. Perhaps the most important study in this area was conducted by Cohen et al. (1980). With the co-operation of the American Dental Association, they surveyed 138 000 American dentists (98.5 per cent of whom were male), asking about their use of inhalation anaesthetics. They then contracted a sub-sample of 30 000 dentists, some of whom were non-users, some light users and some heavy users of anaesthetics. These dentists were asked about serious medical problems that earlier research had suggested were associated with exposure to anaesthetic gases; notably, liver, kidney and neurologic diseases, malignancies and pregnancy outcomes in the family. Cohen et al. (1980) were able to achieve a 73.6 per cent response rate. Although no relationship between the incidence of malignancies and the extent of halothane use was found, there was a higher incidence of liver diseases amongst heavy users (3.22 per 100 of population) than amongst non-users (1.87/100). Similar effects were found for the incidence of neurological diseases (3.58/100 versus 1.92/100) and renal lithiasis problems (2.44 versus 1.87). Generally speaking, the incidence of these problems for light users fell between the other two groups.

Earlier research had also suggested that exposure to anaesthetic gases was associated with a heightened risk of pregnancy complications in the wives of dentists, a suggestion given further support by Cohen, Brown and Wu (1980). The wives of non-user dentists had a spontaneous abortion rate of 6.7 per 100 pregnancies, those of light users 7.7/100, and of heavy users, 10.2/100. The argument was that the anaesthesia has an effect on either the sperm or semen of males. On the other hand, there was no relationship between the extent of exposure and the likelihood of congenital abnormalities in the children.

The direct effect of exposure to gases on female dentists is less clear, due to the small proportion of women in the profession. Nixon et al. (1979) attempted to overcome this problem by sending a questionnaire to all of the female dentists registered in the UK. Of the 2291 pregnancies reported, the female dentists had a higher rate of spontaneous abortion, very premature deliveries and perinatal mortality than would be expected for their social class. However, the reported pregnancies covered a period of almost fifty years, and the control groups used were not comparable with the dentists on many factors. Furthermore, there was only a 53 per cent response rate: this is important because it seems likely that women who had complications in their pregnancies were more likely to respond to the questionnaire, thus inflating the rate of problems. However, Cohen, Brown and Wu's (1980) study is again helpful here, because they surveyed 30 000 chairside assistants, 99 per cent of whom were female. The sample's heightened incidence of liver, kidney and neurological diseases were, like the dentists', related to the extent of exposure to anaesthetic gases, as was the rate of spontaneous abortions. Assistants working with non-users reported 8.1 abortions per 100 pregnancies, those working with light users 14.2, and those working with dentists who made heavy use of anaesthetics reported an incidence of 19.1/100. There was no relationship between extent of anaesthetic use and the incidence of congenital abnormalities.

There is a need for both further research in this area (particularly on women) and for better ventilation in dental surgeries (Jones and Greenfield, 1977). As the use of general anaesthesia declines, the use of nitrous oxide for relative analgesia has increased: future research might concentrate on the extensive use of RA (Allen, 1985).

There are several other potential health hazards. While the high-speed equipment has commonly been supposed to lead to hearing loss, this seems unlikely given the relatively low recorded noise levels in dental surgeries. Dentists do not suffer tinnitus or hearing difficulties with any greater frequency than do other profession-matched groups, and it has been argued that the greatest danger in this area is misdiagnosis, where hearing loss can be too readily attributed to noise (Coles and Hoare, 1985). The high-speed equipment may, on the other hand, lead to particles being ejected from the patient's mouth at high speed and to the formation of an aerosol of saliva and microorganisms (von Krammer, 1968; Djerssi, 1971). The availability of drugs may make dentists susceptible to their abuse (Barnes, 1974) and there is concern about the use of ultra violet light for the polymerization of some materials (Rock, 1974).

Finally, there is the hazard of exposure to diseases carried by patients. Until recently, most concern has centred around hepatitis, and several studies have found a higher than would be expected incidence of hepatitis in dentists (Czaja, 1984), such as one report of a questionnaire survey of American dentists (Feldman and Schiff, 1975) and another based on blood samples of UK dentists (Glenwright et al., 1974). Now, however, there is more concern about AIDS, particularly since dentists have been defined as a high risk group. This concern is reflected in recent articles informing dentists how to identify patients with AIDS and how to protect themselves from infection (e.g. Silverman et al., 1986; Jakush, 1986).

RESPONSES TO STRESS

The second main area of research into the stress of dentistry concerns the effect of stressors on morbidity (both organic and psychological) and mortality. As

Stress amongst dentists

was the case for research on stressors, a popular approach has been to canvass dentists, requesting information on the incidence of their illnesses. To begin with, it is clear that many dentists believe that their job causes symptoms of stress. Briller (1946) received 2400 replies to a questionnaire asking dentists if they felt certain conditions were due to their work: 88 per cent considered eyestrain, 67 per cent neurocirculatory defects and 66 per cent pain in the back to be occupational diseases. As part of their survey of *Dental Economics* readers, Dunlap and Stewart (1982a) asked dentists how frequently they experienced symptoms of stress. Thirty-four per cent said that they always or frequently felt physically or emotionally exhausted, 38 per cent always or frequently worried or anxious, and 26 per cent that they always or frequently had headaches or backaches.

However, it is not clear if these rates are very different from those of the general population. If, in fact, dentists are particularly vulnerable to such symptomatology, then it can be argued that dentists who consult a physician will be more likely to show these symptoms than other groups of medical patients. Two rather old studies have looked at this possibility. Austin and Kruger (1947), working in a mid-Western clinic in the US, found that the incidence of gastrointestinal, rheumatic and cardiovascular disorders were no higher in the dentists they treated than for the rest of their patient population, but Bernstein and Balk (1953) found a much higher incidence of psychological problems associated with anxiety states. While they found that the rate of cardiovascular problems was higher than for their other patients, it was no higher than for other professional groups.

Bilodeau *et al.* (1983), in their above-mentioned study of the ECG patterns of army dentists, argued that since cardiac arrhythmias have been induced in both animals and man subjected to stress, dentists should show a higher incidence of arrhythmias than people in the 'normal' population if they work under conditions of great stress. However, they found no evidence of such a higher incidence.

Another approach has been to rely upon epidemiological data. The Bureau of Economic Research and Statistics (1975) examined the death certificates of 4190 dentists for the period 1968–72. The percentage of dentists dying from a wide variety of specific diseases was very similar to the white male population of similar age. In fact, dentists lived an average of about three years longer than the general population of white males. The incidence of stress symptoms can also be compared with surveys of members of the general population. Horwitz (1982), for example, reviews epidemiological research in which people were asked whether they had experienced thoughts and feelings or had engaged in behaviour which psychiatrists consider symptomatic of mental disorders. On average, about 20 per cent of the general population can be considered to have been 'severely' psychiatrically impaired by these criteria, with an additional 50 per cent having had symptoms indicative of mild to moderate impairment. Depending on the study, between 4 and 15 per cent of males have been found to be depressed (Goldberg and Huxley, 1980). Similarly, physical illnesses are often encountered in epidemiological surveys. When a sample of healthy hospital workers not taking medication at the time were asked to keep a diary of their feelings, 25 per cent reported an inability to concentrate, 23 per cent reported excessive sleepiness and 40 per cent fatigue in the previous three days (Reidenberg and Lowenthal, 1968). Had these people been dentists, such difficulties may have been attributed to the job and called occupational hazards.

Low back pain is an often-reported complaint made by dentists. About one-third to one-half report a degree of back trouble, a proportion which increases with age (Fauchard Academy Poll, 1965). This rate is higher than for the general population, where less than one in five report persistent difficulties (Nagi, Riley and Newby, 1973; Crook, Rideout and Browne, 1984). Back pain has been attributed to the rather awkward posture taken by dentists as they work, but it does not appear to be related to whether the dentist stands or sits (Cline et al., 1983; Paul, 1969). It may be due to the precise work a dentist performs where there is prolonged hypertonicity of the arm, shoulder and back muscles. A study of EMG recordings of dentists at work would be useful here. Another possible cause is more mundane: a dentist may wash his or her hands 50 to 60 times a day, so that unless the washbasin is at a comfortable height, this could aggravate any existing back strain. Low back pain may also be associated with the high incidence of anxiety states noted above. In their study of people with low back pain, Nagi, Riley and Newby (1973) asked their sample about experience with anxiety: people suffering back pain reported a significantly higher level of anxiety symptoms than people with no pain.

Another issue has to do with the relative stressfulness of various specialities within dentistry. In an often-quoted study, Russek (1962) surveyed general dental practitioners, oral surgeons, orthodontists and periodontists, inquiring about their experience of coronary heart disease and hypertension: 8.4 per cent of the general practitioners, 6.1 per cent of the oral surgeons, 4.7 per cent of the orthodontists and 2.9 per cent of the periodontists had CHD. No effect was found for hypertension, but this is often a symptomless condition found only at a medical screening (see Cutright et al., 1977). The interesting result was that the ranking of CHD incidence was the same as the specialities' stressfulness as judged by a panel of seven dentists. While this finding can be interpreted as an indication that the job requirements of the specialities were in some way responsible for the varying incidence of CHD, the possibility that dentists who are most vulnerable to CHD are self-selecting into some areas of dentistry more than others cannot be ignored. Of course, this point about self-selection applies to all of the comparisons between dentists and other groups. Vaillant, Sobovale and McArthur (1972) work suggests that something of the sort happens in medicine, where physicians were found to be more vulnerable than other members of a university population and people who chose general practice, in particular, seemed the most vulnerable.

A Bureau of Economic Research and Statistics report (1977) speaks to the controversy mentioned earlier concerning the possible health hazards in the dental office. It can be argued that if working as a dentist poses a serious threat to health then dentists could be expected to die earlier or to die of specific diseases more frequently than people in the general population. That the Bureau found no such differences suggests that these hazards have little obvious effect. On the other hand, the Bureau cite only mortality figures and this is a rather crude measure of health. The incidence of many chronic or disabling but not fatal diseases is not known. For example, the Bureau's statistics do not show how many pregnancies end in miscarriage or how many handicapped children are born into dentists' families. More detailed information is required to answer these kinds of questions.

Burn-out

Dentists would appear to be prime candidates for burn-out, a syndrome of emotional exhaustion and cynicism which is frequently found amongst professionals who work directly with people. Such groups as physicians, nurses, policemen and lawyers have been studied, and dentists have much in common with them. Low appreciation from clients, a large number of clients dealt with and an often cramped and noisy environment are some factors which have been found in these other professions to be associated with burn-out (Pines, Aronson and Kafry, 1981; Maslach and Jackson, 1981). Maslach and Jackson (1982) found that amongst physicians the greater the proportion of time they spent in direct contact with patients, the higher their scores on the emotional exhaustion scale on the MBI. Since the income of private dental practitioners is wholly based on their amount of patient contact, they tend to work to a tight schedule. The kinds of activities which serve to counteract burn-out—time taken for administrative duties, teaching and interpersonal contact of a social sort with colleagues—do not contribute to income. Whereas Maslach and Jackson (1982) found in their study of physicians that those scoring low in emotional exhaustion often sought the advice of others and talked with their co-workers about any difficulties they were having, many dentists work alone in single practices where such opportunities are restricted. Unrealistic expectations and perfectionism, which may be encouraged in dental training (Waldman, 1981), may also make dentists particularly vulnerable to burn-out.

Edelwich and Brodsky (1980) suggest that dentists can undergo five stages on a road to burn-out: (1) the Practice Honeymoon, where the recent graduate enjoys the challenge of dentistry, voluntarily overworking and becoming over-involved with his or her patients, (2) the Drill and Fill Blahs, where the job becomes boring and the gap between expectations and reality widens, (3) the Operatory Blues, when depression sets in and where the dentist perceives something is wrong but cannot see what to do about it, and (4) Crisis, where the situation becomes critical and the dentist becomes frustrated and full of doubt. If no positive changes take place, the fifth stage—Pulping Out—occurs, when an emotional breakdown is inevitable.

Unfortunately, there is no evidence to support or refute such an unhappy progression for individuals, nor are there data on the incidence of burn-out in dentistry as a whole. It is by no means clear that dentists do burn out to any greater degree than other helping professionals. Set against the aspects of dentistry which can lead to burn-out, dentists do not experience other important factors. There is relatively low uncertainty about their role *vis-à-vis* patients and other professionals, and they have a relatively high degree of control over their activities with patients. In what appears to be the only study in which a recognized burn-out inventory (the MBI) has been given to dentists, Klausner and Green (1984) found that staff at dental schools scored lower on emotional exhaustion and depersonalization and higher on personal accomplishment than the normative group. This finding cannot be extrapolated with much confidence to private dental practitioners, however, since the conditions of work for academic staff are so different from full-time practitioners. To some extent, job satisfaction can be used as an alternative measure, though, and here the evidence suggests that about one dentist in five is very dissatisfied. Powell and Eccles (1970) reported that 19 per cent of their UK sample said that they 'disliked' or 'disliked very much' their job, and amongst Howard *et al.*'s (1976) Canadian dentists, 20 per cent were considered to be dissatisfied (as measured by the question 'How strongly do you feel it would benefit you to change jobs or your type of work activity?'). Even though those rates are similar to other occupations, job dissatisfaction has been linked with poor performance in other professions (e.g. incautious prescribing in physicians, Melville, 1980), so is there some reason for concern here and further research is needed.

Suicide

Of all the reactions to the stress of dental practice, the incidence of suicide within the profession has received the most publicity. It is based on a few reports where the suicide rate in dentists was found to be two or three times higher than the rate for the general population. However, since the proportion of dentists who actually commit suicide and the proportion of dentists in the population are both small, these studies are based on tiny numbers. In the earliest report (Blachly, Osterud and Josslin, 1963), the suicide rate was found to be twice as high as for males older than 19 (62/100000 versus 32/100000) and higher than for the next most vulnerable group (attorneys at 53/100000). The data consisted of a sample of 2674 suicides over a three-year period, but only nine dentists were actually involved. Similarly, Simpson *et al.* (1983) examined the death certificates of Iowa residents from 1968 to 1980. Eight dentists were identified as suicides, giving a risk of about 1.6 times that for comparable age and sex groups in the US. In another study (Rose and Rosow, 1973) the death certificates of all the people who died in California from 1959 to 1961 were examined. Of the 7471 suicides, 20 were dentists, giving a rate of 63/100000, as compared with 28/100000 for the adult male population. This study is useful because the rate for all health professionals was also calculated. When a number of other groups was included (physicians, pharmacists, etc.), the overall rate was 74/100000, a figure similar to the dentists. This suggests that it is being a member of the health profession which predisposes to suicide, rather than being a dentist. Perhaps it is the giving of direct care to patients or self-selection into the health professions which is associated with suicide. It has also been said that comparisons between health professionals and the general population are not valid because doctors, dentists, pharmacists and so forth have a greater knowledge about effective methods and would therefore have a higher rate of successful attempts. Perhaps a measure which included unsuccessful as well as successful attempts would give a more accurate picture of the situation.

What must also be set against the studies which have found a higher suicide rate amongst dentists are those which have found little difference. Amongst South African dentists, Dean (1969) found only five suicides, against an expected rate of 17.65 for the total white male populations. A lower than expected rate has also been found in the UK (Hill and Harvey, 1972) and the Bureau of Economics Research and Statistics report (1977) indicates that American dentists die from suicide at almost the same rate as the general white male population. Thus, although there is some evidence that dentists are more prone to commit suicide, it is based on small numbers and it is about equally likely that research will find a lower or similar incidence than a higher one. What must be remembered about any finding in this area is the general reluctance for coroners to bring down a suicide verdict, with the remote possibility that this reluctance is greater for dentists than for other professional groups.

In summary, most dentists believe that their profession is more stressful than most. However, where mortality statistics have been collected, there is little evidence that dentists die any younger or from specific diseases any more frequently than other health professionals and the well-publicised findings that dentists commit suicide more frequently should be viewed with some scepticism due to the small numbers involved. On the other hand, high levels of anxiety seem relatively prevalent and this could be associated with low back pain and, possibly, with burnout. More research on the effect of potential health hazards is clearly required, especially on women who practice while pregnant.

ALLEVIATION OF STRESS

There are several routes which could be taken when considering the reduction of stress experienced by practitioners. Some of these would involve a wider sociological analysis. The commonly held view in the general population that a visit to the dentist will necessarily entail pain seems to be based less on experience than on cultural beliefs. Since this anxiety about pain contributes to dentists' difficulties, a change in society's attitudes about dentistry would be very helpful. Another social factor is fluoridation of the water supply. Although this measure has clear benefits in reducing caries (and thus reducing the need for anxiety-provoking restorations), many areas are not fluoridated. The activities of local dental associations are instrumental in local government decisions in this area, so that one way in which dentists might be able to reduce stress arising from patients' anxiety would be to press for fluoridation.

Given existing social circumstances, though, there are other steps which can be taken. In order to discover which methods might be effective in reducing stress, perhaps the most obvious approach is to ask dentists themselves about the methods they use. O'Shea, Corah and Ayer (1984), for example, asked an open-ended question about how their sample dealt with stress. The replies ranged from exercise (34 per cent), through to time off (10 per cent) and hobbies (6 per cent). Similarly, Godwin et al. (1981) found that recent graduates cited sports activities most frequently. Although such methods may be effective in the short term and exercise will increase fitness, what is most notable about these studies is that most dentists tend to avoid, rather than attempt to change, the situation. Simple avoidance was typified by one dentist who claimed that he would 'not continue to treat a patient who is a problem to me. As a result I have only patients I like and they like me' (Corah, O'Shea and Skeels, 1982).

Another body of literature describes the advice given by dentists to other practitioners. The quality of this advice varies considerably, from Morse (1983), who when discussing the problem that female dentists are often expected to move with their husbands, suggests that the 'solution to this potential problem should be worked out by husband and wife before it arises', to more thoughtful and sensitive suggestions. The approach taken by Bosmajian and Bosmajian (1983) provides an ideal first step. They argue that stress can only be reduced if an individual is aware of those situations which cause stress for him or herself. As noted earlier, different dentists have difficulties with different situations. To this end, they provide a 'stresslog'. The individual is encouraged to note the situations where stress occurs, what the events imply, and what responses were made. The completion of such a diary allows the dentist to see repeating patterns in both events and responses.

Once this detailed record has been made, further steps could be taken to change the situation. Dunlap and Stewart (1982b) make several suggestions about how to tackle stress, including careful attention to diet, taking enough exercise to keep fit, developing a social support system, learning relaxation techniques and setting attainable goals. Their advice is valuable because they encourage the dentist to specify the sources of stress and to make specific plans. The results of the stresslog may indicate that the dentist is frequently frustrated by the quality of his or her work. Here, Ireland's (1983) approach may be useful. He borrows ideas from Ellis's Rational Emotive Therapy. Ellis (see Sagarin, 1973) suggests that an individual's assumptions about situations can lead to difficulties if they lead to faulty or unhelpful perceptions. If these assumptions are pointed out and questioned, more effective ways of viewing situations can be worked out. Ireland (1983) suggests that many dentists hold such erroneous assumptions as:

(1) One should be appreciated by all of one's patients.
(2) To be worthwhile, one must be thoroughly competent and successful in his field.
(3) One should become emotionally involved with one's patients.
(4) There is always a right, precise and perfect solution to a patient's problems, and this solution must always be found.

For another dentist, it may be patients' anxiety which often results in stress. Dental anxiety is very resistant to extinction, so that a patient may remain anxious despite many pain-free visits (Kent, 1984a). Fortunately, there is much help available from psychologists. They have had success in relieving anxiety through a variety of techniques such as relaxation, systematic desensitization, role or behaviour modelling and hypnosis (Kent, 1984b). Some of these techniques can be used by dentists themselves while clinical psychologists can also be approached for assistance. Since missed and late appointment keeping has also been associated with anxiety, this other source of stress might also be alleviated with the use of these psychological techniques.

Alternatively, the stresslog may reveal that it is actual interactions with patients which cause most stress. No matter what he or she tries, a dentist may find that many patients do not co-operate in the chair during treatment or in the long-term planning of preventive care. The way in which dentists react to their patients affects the degree of disruptive behaviour and co-operation shown by patients. It will be remembered, for example, that Wurster, Weinstein and Cohen (1979) found that students' confidence in their ability to cope with anxious and disruptive child patients was related to the amount of disruptiveness shown by the children. Coercion (attempting to overcome disruption by threatening, ridiculing or using physical restraint) was strongly related to subsequent non-co-operation, while direction and guidance (e.g. providing a straightforward statement of instruction while encouraging the patient) was strongly related to subsequent co-operation. Similar results have been found with qualified dentists and adult patients (Weinstein et al., 1982). These findings suggest that training in interpersonal and communication skills may be of much value in reducing dentists' difficulties in this respect (Furnham, 1983; Proceedings of the National Conference on Applied Behaviour Science, 1983). Examples of programmes which attempt to help students in this way can be found in Jackson (1975), Levy,

Domoto and Olson (1980) and Gershen et al., (1980). Such training may also increase patients' satisfaction with the social aspects of their care, a factor which is associated with attendance patterns (Kent, 1984c): perhaps the increasing concern over falling patient numbers could be reduced if more patients were satisfied with their dentist's interpersonal skills.

Some dentists may find that the stressful situations often involve relationships with assistants rather than with patients: for example, anger at a receptionist who does not keep the appointment book straight or frustration with a hygienist who seems to alienate patients. The acquisition of effective management skills are important here (Emling, 1980). Dental students may identify a completely different set of stressors. For some it could be a lack of confidence in dealing with patients while for others it could be their workload and test anxiety. Some dental schools provide workshops on study skills and encourage small group discussions amongst students where problems can be aired, strategies for studying shared and emotional support given (Schwartz, Elgenbrode and Cantor, 1984).

Given that there is a wide variety of potentially useful stress reduction techniques, there is surprisingly little experimental evaluation of these amongst dentists. While altering their perceptions of stressful situations, increasing their communication skills, and reducing patients' anxieties can be expected to alleviate the stress of dentistry, there would be more confidence in their effectiveness if more research had been conducted. In what seems to be the only experiment in this area, Tisdelle et al. (1984) randomly allocated dental students who signed up for a stress management programme to either a treatment group or to a waiting list control group. The treatment group were given six seminars where the psychology of stress was taught didactically by psychologists and various techniques for reducing stress (deep muscle relaxation, cognitive modification techniques and the usefulness of leisure activities) were discussed and practised. The scores of the students who received this training improved on a stress awareness questionnaire (which indicated how much they knew about stress and its effects and strategies for managing it). Their systolic blood pressure was also reduced when the pre- and post-programme measures were compared. By contrast, there were no changes for the waiting list control group. When the treatment group was assessed again three months later, there were further improvements on the stress awareness questionnaire and a reduction in both trait anxiety and the number of situations which were reported to cause stress. It appeared that the students needed additional time, after the completion of the course, to practice the techniques and assimilate what they had learned.

CONCLUSIONS

This chapter began with O'Shea, Corah and Ayer's (1984) finding that 75 per cent of dentists believed their profession to be more stressful than others. It would seem from this review that many dentists do consider themselves to be under much stress. When questionnaires have been posted to dentists asking them about sources of stress, some have volunteered such comments as 'Please help us', 'I hope that you can do something about this situation' and 'You left out the most important question—have you ever considered suicide?'. Such comments speak to a high level of distress amongst some practitioners.

Whether this distress is due to the occupation, though, is another question altogether. While O'Shea, Corah and Ayer (1984) found that most dentists believed their occupation to be very stressful, 77 per cent reported that they were under much less or somewhat less stress compared with other dentists. It may be that 'everyone knows' dentistry is stressful but that this is based on expectations rather than experience. To say that the stress of dentistry is a myth may be too strong a conclusion, but it does not seem to be substantially greater than that of other health professions. In general, psychological and medical indices of health do not support the view that the practice of dentistry leads to ill-health or suicide with any greater frequency. The one health problem that has turned up is low back pain, and this could be associated with anxiety.

This general conclusion is not meant to imply that further research is unnecessary. The effect of potential health hazards, in particular, requires further work. Nor is it meant to imply that nothing should be done to relieve the stress that dentists do experience. What is needed here is more research on the day-to-day stressors of practice, with physiological and behavioural measures supplementing self-reports of stress. These self-reports are better collected through the use of diaries and stresslogs than through the kinds of global ratings commonly used. The use of micro-analysis techniques, where both dentists and their patients are monitored over a series of appointments would provide a more detailed picture of the stress of practice. While such studies would assist in the understanding of situations which contribute to stress for dentists in general, the problems felt by individuals are equally important. It is usual in psychological therapies for a therapist to adapt a technique to the individual patient, so that assistance can be given for a particular difficulty. Similarly, it would be important to monitor individual dentists' working styles and stressors and provide feedback on a one-to-one basis.

Such research would represent the kind of collaborative work which would be fruitful for both psychologists and dentists. On the one hand it would provide an opportunity for psychologists to test the effectiveness of their approaches, developed in clinical or analogue settings, with subjects who do not show signs of psychopathology but who nevertheless have real life difficulties. On the other hand, such research may be of practical benefit to dentists in their day-to-day work and, possibly, their long-term health and psychological well-being.

REFERENCES

Abel, S., Bakdash, M. B., Born, D. O. and Loupe, M. J. (1983). Occupational stress and coping mechanisms as reported by dentists, *J. Dent. Res. AADR Abstracts*, **62**, 175, Number 52.
Allen, W. (1985). Nitrous oxide in the surgery: pollution and scavenging, *Br. Dent. J.*, **159**, 222–30.
Austin, G. B., Maher, N. M. and Lomonaco, C. J. (1973). Women in dentistry and medicine: attitudinal survey of education experience, *J. Dent. Ed.*, **37**, 11–17.
Austin, L. J. and Kruger, G. O. (1947). Common ailments of dentists. A statistical study, *J. Am. Dent. Assoc.*, **35**, 797–805.
Barnes, R. (1974). Hazards in the dental office, *Aust. Dent. J.*, **19**, 4–6.
Bernstein, A. and Balk, J. L. (1953). The common diseases of practicing dentists, *J. Am. Dent. Assoc.*, **46**, 525–9.
Bilodeau, L. P., Moody, J. M., Rathburn, J. D. and Krant, R. A. (1983). Evaluation of ECG changes in dentists treating awake patients, *Anaes. Prog.*, **30**, 193–6.
Blanchy, P. H., Osterud, H. T. and Josslin, R. (1963). Suicide in professional groups, *New Eng. J. Med.*, **268**, 1278–82.
Bosmajian, C. P. and Bosmajian, L. S. (1983). *Personalised Guide to Stress Evaluation*, Mosby, London.
Briller, F. E. (1946). Occupational hazards in dental practice, *Oral Hygiene*, **36**, 1194–7.
Bureau of Economic Research and Statistics (1975). Mortality of dentists, *J. Am. Dent. Assoc.*, **90**, 195–8.
Bureau of Economic Research and Statistics (1977). The occupation of dentistry: its relation to illness and death, *J. Am. Dent. Assoc.*, **95**, 606–613.
Cline, J. S., Shugars, D. A., Fishburne, C. D. and Williams, D. (1983). Survey of musculoskeletal pain among South Carolina dentists, *J. Dent. Res. AADR Abstracts*, **62**, 175, Number 53.
Cohen, E. N. (1974). Occupational disease among operating room personnel, *Anaesthesiology*, **41**, 321–40.
Cohen, E. N., Brown, B. W. and Wu, M. C. (1980). Occupational disease in dentistry and chronic exposure to trace anaesthetic gases, *J. Am. Dent. Assoc.*, **101**, 21–31.
Coles, R. and Hoare, N. (1985). Noise-induced hearing loss and the dentist, *Br. Dent. J.*, **159**, 209–218.
Cooper, C. L., Mallinger, M. and Kahn, R. (1978). Identifying sources of occupational stress among dentists, *J. Occu. Psychol.*, **51**, 227–34.
Corah, N. L., O'Shea, R. M. and Skeels, D. K. (1982). Dentists' perceptions of problem behaviors in patients, *J. Am. Dent. Assoc.*, **104**, 829–33.
Council on Dental Materials (1983). Safety of dental amalgam, *J. Am. Dent. Assoc.*, **106**, 519–20.
Crook, J., Rideout, E. and Browne, G. (1984). The prevalence of pain complaints in a general population, *Pain*, **18**, 299–314.
Cutright, D. E., Carpenter, W. A., Tsaknis, P. B. and Lyon, T. Q. (1977). Survey of blood pressure of 856 dentists, *J. Am. Dent. Assoc.*, **94**, 918–19.
Czaja, A. J. (1984). Hepatitis and the dentist, *J. Am. Dent. Assoc.*, **108**, 286–7.

Dean, G. (1969). The causes of death of South African doctors and dentists, *S. Af. Med. J.*, **43**, 495–500.
Djerssi, E. (1971). Some problems of the occupational diseases of dentists, *Int. Dent. J.*, **21**, 252–69.
Dunlap, J. E. and Stewart, J. D. (1982a). Survey suggests less stress in group offices, *Dent. Econ.*, **72**, 46–56.
Dunlap, J. E. and Stewart, D. (1982b). Suggestions to alleviate dental stress, *Dent. Econ.*, **72**, 58–64.
Eccles, J. D. (1969). The heart rate of dentists at work, *Br. Dent, J.*, **126**, 216–20.
Eccles, J. D. (1970). Skin conductance change in dentists and patients during conservation treatment, *Dent. Prac. Dent. Rec.*, **21**, 43–8.
Eccles, J. D. and Powell, M. (1967). The health of dentists: a survey in South Wales. 1965–1966, *Br. Dent. J.*, **123**, 379–89.
Edelwich, J. and Brodsky, A. (1980). *Burnout*, Human Sciences Press, NY.
Eli, I. and Shuval, J. T. (1982). Professional socialisation in dentistry, *Soc. Sci. Med.*, **16**, 951–5.
Emling, R. C. (1980). Employee and patient management in times of stress, *Compend. Cont. Educ. Dent.*, **1**, 351–5.
Fauchard Academy Poll (1965). One of every three practitioners affected with back trouble, *Dent. Surv.*, **41**, 69–70.
Feldman, R. E. and Schiff, E. R. (1975). Hepatitis in dental professionals, *J. Am. Dent. Assoc.*, **232**, 1228–30.
Furnham, A. (1983). Social skills and dentistry, *Br. Dent. J.*, **154**, 404–8.
Gershen, J. A., Marcus, M. and Strolein, A. (1980). An application of interpersonal process recall for teaching behavioral science in dentistry, *J. Dent. Educ.*, **44**, 268–9.
Glenwright, H. D., Edmondson, H. D., Whitehead, F. and Flewett, T. H. (1974). Serum hepatitis in dental surgeons, *Br. Dent. J.*, **136**, 409–13.
Godwin, W. C., Starks, D. D., Green, T. G. and Koran, A. (1981). Identification of sources of stress in practice by recent dental graduates, *J. Dent. Educ.*, **45**, 220–21.
Goldberg, D. and Huxley, P. (1980). *Mental Illness in the Community*, Tavistock, London.
Goldstein, M. B. (1979). Sources of stress and interpersonal support among first year dental students, *J. Dent. Educ.*, **43**, 625–9.
Gronka, P. A., Bobkoskie, R. L., Tomchick, G. J., Bach, F. and Rakow, A. B. (1970). Mercury vapor exposure in dental offices, *J. Am. Dent. Assoc.*, **81**, 923–5.
Hill, G. B. and Harvey, W. (1972). Mortality of dentists, *Br. Dent. J.*, **132**, 179–82.
Horwitz, A. (1982). *Social Control of Mental Illness*, Academic Press, NY.
Howard, J. H., Cunningham, D. A., Rechnitzer, P. A. and Goode, R. C. (1976). Stress on the job and career of a dentist, *J. Am. Dent. Assoc.*, **93**, 630–36.
Ingersoll, T. G., Ingersoll, B. D., Seime, R. J. and McCutcheon, A. B. (1978). A survey of patient and auxiliary problems as they relate to behavioral dentistry curricula, *J. Dent. Educ.*, **42**, 260–63.
Ireland, E. J. (1983). Dental practice burnout, *Compend. Cont. Educ. Dent.*, **4**, 367–9.
Jackson, E. (1975). Establishing rapport, 1. Verbal interaction, *J. Oral Med.*, **30**, 105–10.
Jakush, J. (1986). Infection control in the dental office: a realistic approach, *J. Am. Dent. Assoc.*, **112**, 458–68.
Jones, T. W. and Greenfield, W. (1977). Position paper of the ADA Ad Hoc committee on trace anaesthetics as a potential health hazard, *J. Am. Dent. Assoc.*, **95**, 751–6.
Kent, G. (1983). Psychology in the dental curriculum, *Br. Dent. J.*, **154**, 106–9.
Kent, G. (1984a). Anxiety, pain and type of dental procedure, *Behav. Res. Ther.*, **22**, 465–9.

Kent, G. (1984b). *The Psychology of Dental Care*, Wright & Sons, Bristol.
Kent, G. (1984c). Satisfaction with dental care, *Med. Care*, **22**, 583-5.
Klausner, L. H. and Green, T. G. (1984). What does professional burnout mean to the dental educator?, *J. Dent. Educ.*, **48**, 91-4.
Kurz-Kummerle, S., Melamed, B. G., Kaplan, L. R. and Ronk, S. (1983). Dental students' anxiety as it influences child patients' fear behaviours. In R. Moretti and W. A. Ayer (eds) *The President's Conference on the Dentist-Patient Relationship and the Management of Fear, Anxiety and Pain*, American Dental Association, Chicago.
Levy, R. L., Domoto, P. K. and Olson, D. G. (1980). Evaluation of one-to-one behavioral training, *J. Dent. Educ.*, **44**, 221-2.
Maslach, C. and Jackson, S. E. (1981). The measurement of experienced burnout, *J. Occup. Behav.*, **2**, 99-113.
Maslach, C. and Jackson, S. E. (1982). Burnout in health professions: a social psychological analysis. In G. S. Sanders and J. Suls (eds) *Social Psychology of Health and Illness*, pp. 227-57, Erlbaum, Hillsdale.
Melville, A. (1980). Job satisfaction in general practice: implications for prescribing, *Soc. Sci. Med.*, **14A**, 495-9.
Merfield, D. P., Taylor, A., Gemmel, D. M. and Parrish, J. A. (1976). Mercury intoxication in a dental surgery following unreported spillage, *Br. Dent. J.*, **141**, 179-86.
Mesa, M. L., Clark, M., Austin, G. and Barden, M. (1981). Ethnic and cultural determinants of the perceptions of female dental students, *J. Dent. Educ.*, **45**, 576-80.
Milgrom, P., Marder, M., Williams, B., Beaton, R. and Weinstein, P. (1983). Stress and gingivitis: changes over 15 weeks, *J. Dent. Res. AADR Abstracts*, **62**, 187, Number 154.
Morse, D. R. (1983). Choices to cut professional stress, *Dent. Manag.*, **23**, 25-9.
Morse, D. R., Schacterle, G. R., Furst, L., Goldberg, J., Greenspan, B., Swielinski, D. and Susek, J. (1982). The effect of stress and meditation on a salivary protein and bacteria: a review and pilot study, *J. Hum. Stress*, **8**, 31-9.
Nagi, S. Z., Riley, L. E. and Newby, L. G. (1973). A social epidemiology of back pain in a general population, *J. Chron. Dis.*, **26**, 769-79.
Nixon, G. S. and Rowbotham, T. C. (1971). Mercury hazards associated with high speed mechanical amalgamators, *Br. Dent. J.*, **131**, 308-11.
Nixon, G. S., Helsby, C. A., Gordon, H., Hytten, I. E. and Renson, C. E. (1979). Pregnancy outcome in female dentists, *Br. Dent. J.*, **146**, 39-42.
O'Shea, R. M., Corah, N. L. and Ayer, W. A. (1984). Sources of dentists' stress, *J. Am. Dent. Assoc.*, **109**, 48-51.
Over, R. and Spencer, J. (1983). Sex ratio of academics in the dental schools of U.K. universities, *Br. Dent. J.*, **154**, 259-60.
Page, C. M. and Slack, G. L. (1969). A contented profession? A survey of old London dentists, *Br. Dent. J.*, **127**, 220-25.
Paul, E. (1969). The elimination of stress and fatigue in operative dentistry, *Br. Dent. J.*, **127**, 37-41.
Pines, A., Aronson, E. and Kafry, D. (1981). *Burnout: From Tedium to Personal Growth*, Free Press, NY.
Powell, M. and Eccles, J. D. (1970). The health and work of two professional groups: dentists and pharmacists, *Dent. Practitioner*, **20**, 373-8.
Proceedings of the National Conference on Applied Behavioral Science (1983). *J. Dent. Educ.*, **47**, 66-106.
Reidenberg, M. and Lowenthal, D. (1968). Adverse non drug reactions, *New Eng. J. Med.*, **279**, 678-9.

Richards, J. and Warren, P. (1985). Mercury vapour released during the removal of old amalgam restorations, *Br. Dent. J.*, **159**, 231-2.
Rock, W. P. (1974). The use of ultra-violet radiation in dentistry, *Br. Dent. J.*, **136**, 455-8.
Roder, R. E., Lewis, T. M. and Law, D. B. (1961). Physiological responses of dentists to the presence of a parent in the operatory, *J. Dent. Child*, **28**, 263-70.
Rose, K. D. and Rosow, I. (1973). Physicians who kill themselves, *Arch. Gen. Psych.*, **29**, 800-5.
Rothwell, P. S., Frame, J. W. and Shimmin, C. V. (1977). Mercury vapour hazards from hot air sterilizers in dental practice, *Br. Dent. J.*, **142**, 359-65.
Russek, H. I. (1962). Emotional stress and coronary heart disease in American physicians, dentists and lawyers, *Am. J. Med. Sci.*, **243**, 716-25.
Sachs, R. H., Zullo, T. G. and Close, J. M. (1981). Concerns of entering dental students, *J. Dent. Educ.*, **45**, 133-6.
Sagarin, E. (ed.) (1973). *Humanistic Psychotherapy: The Rational-Emotive Approach*, Julian Press, New York.
Schluger, S. (1949). Necrotizing ulcerative gingivitis in the Army: incidence, communicability and treatment, *J. Am. Dent. Assoc.*, **38**, 174-7.
Schwartz, R. M., Elgenbrode, C. R. and Cantor, O. (1984). A comprehensive stress reduction program for dental students, *J. Dent. Educ.*, **48**, 203-7.
Silverman, S., Migliorati, C. A., Lozadn-Nun, F., Greenspan, D. and Conant, M. A. (1986). Oral findings in people with or at high risk for AIDS: a study of 375 homosexual males, *J. Am. Dent. Assoc.*, **112**, 187-92.
Simpson, R., Biller-Karlsson, I. and Willard, D. (1982). Stress in dentistry: a comparison of dentists, hygienists and students, *J. Dent. Res., AADR Abstracts*, **61**, Number 771, 264.
Simpson, R., Jakobsen, J., Beck, J. and Simpson, J. (1983). Suicide statistics of dentists in Iowa, 1968-1980, *J. Am. Dent. Assoc.*, **107**, 441-3.
Stern, F. M. (1979). A workshop on stress, *Dent. Econ.*, **69**, 60-2.
Tillman, R. S. and Horowitz, S. L. (1983). Practice patterns of recent female dental graduates, *J. Am. Dent. Assoc.*, **107**, 32-5.
Tisdelle, D. A., Hansen, D. J., St. Lawrence, J. S. and Brown, J. C. (1984). Stress management training for dental students, *J. Dent. Educ.*, **48**, 196-201.
Vaillant, G. E., Sobovale, N. C. and McArthur, C. (1972). Some psychologic vulnerabilities of physicians, *New Eng. J. Med.*, **287**, 372-5.
von Krammer, R. (1968). High speed equipment and dentists' health, *J. pros. Dent.*, **19**, 46-50.
Waldman, H. B. (1981). The turmoil of the dental practitioner, *Prof. Psychol.*, **12**, 461-9.
Weinstein, P., Getz, T., Ratener, P. and Domoto, P. (1982). The effect of dentists' behaviors on fear-related behaviors in children, *J. Am. Dent. Assoc.*, **104**, 32-8.
Wurster, C. A., Weinstein, P. and Cohen, A. J. (1979). Communication patterns in pedodontics, *Percept. Mot. Skill.*, **48**, 159-66.
Yablom, P., Maykow, K. P., Rosner, J. F. and Levy, A. I. (1983). Dental student stress as measured by life event change, *J. New Jersey Dent. Assoc.*, **54**, 20-27.
Young, T. M. (1975). Questionnaire on the need for resuscitation in the dental surgery, *Anaesthesia*, **30**, 391-401.

Chapter 8
Stress in Staff Working with Mentally Handicapped People

Sophie Thomson

INTRODUCTION

Working in the field of mental handicap has changed drastically over the past thirty years. The pressure for change came partly from the realization in the 1950s that mentally handicapped people can benefit from education and training, and partly from the general social aim of moving provisions for people with mental disorders from institutions into the community.

These major changes in the philosophy of care and means of providing services have produced considerable disorganization, uncertainties and conflicts within the organizational structures and within the individuals trying to provide a service.

The traditional model of a doctor acting as medical superintendent, leading a group of other professionals in a well defined hierarchy to provide long-term care for people who are presumed to be unable to take responsibility for themselves in any real way, is now giving way to more liberal approaches. However, at the interface between the old model and the new ones the staff and recipients of the service are struggling to adjust and acquire the necessary skills and training to attempt to 'normalize' mentally handicapped people for the community. It is now realized that most mentally handicapped people are not mentally ill. Although the incidence of mental illness in mental handicap is higher than the general population, the figures vary considerably between different surveys (Reid, 1983).

However, the potential for development, whether educational, social or psychological, remains very difficult to assess accurately, and therefore to set realistic goals. This adds to the lack of clarity in defining appropriate training for both staff and clients and developing suitable resources.

With the growing public interest in the welfare of mentally handicapped people comes greater and much needed money and support. However, it also means public scrutiny in the form of media coverage and public enquiries that can be demoralizing and destructive for staff, already stretched in coping with large numbers of people. Most staff have been trained in the custodial model of care and are often unclear about what their new role entails, let alone receiving any specific training.

Working in mental handicap has traditionally been an unpopular speciality, especially amongst doctors. This paucity of interest is mirrored in the paucity of research on staff working in this area. Workers in mental handicap are sometimes mentioned in literature on mental health professionals, but whether or what particular difference there might be has rarely been investigated. In Chernis and Egnaties' (1978) study on community mental health programmes it was found that clients who tend to be less successful (including mentally retarded, after-care clients, drug addicts or individuals with severe characters disorders) created more stress in their care and service providers. Sarota (1974) found in institutions for the mentally retarded that greater client contract was associated with more job satisfaction. However, there are important 'within-group' differences.

Consequently the author conducted a questionnaire survey of professionals working with mentally handicapped people working in one London region, to try and identify

(i) How stressful these people perceived their jobs to be;
(ii) What they found stressful, and in particular what aspects of working with mentally handicapped clients distressed them;
(iii) How they knew when they were stressed;
(iv) Their coping strategies.

The questions were adapted from those used in the literature used to assess stress in other mental health professionals, except for the items specifically related to mental handicap which were suggested by various professionals in the field.

A full account of the questionnaire and results is available at the end of the chapter. However, the outstanding results are:

(1) Fifty three per cent of people find working with mentally handicapped people is moderately stressful. This did not vary between sex, hospital or community base, profession or whether or not there was a relative with mental handicap.

(Whether or not people working in mental handicap are more stressed by their work than others in the mental health field is clearly not part of this preliminary study.)

(2) The general items concerning precipitators of stress show that 'too much to do' was rated highly by 44 per cent of subjects, and 'feel the job is never

done' was rated highly by 38 per cent of subjects. The relatively small number of people who rated highly 'not sure what's expected' (8.6 per cent of subjects) would suggest that it is the volume of work that is critical and not so much the ambiguity and role conflict cited as important by other researchers (Chernis, 1980).
(3) Items relating particularly to mentally handicapped clients rated as less important as stressors than colleagues' 'attitudes and habits' (37.1 per cent), 'problems with clients' families' (28 per cent) and 'the policies of the institution or agency' (49 per cent).

It is also salutary that in this sample, hospital workers rated as significantly more stressful than community workers the two factors of 'colleagues' attitudes and habits' and 'the institutional policies'.

Whether this reflects concern over philosophy of care or day-to-day bureaucratic frustrations is not clear, but is exemplified by one of the additional comments on my questionnaire:

I often feel attempts at improving care are stifled by the sheer weight of organisation that is needed to implement the simplest things such as shopping or outings.

STRESSES IN MENTAL HANDICAP

Mentally handicapped people are very intimately related to their context because of their dependence and the responsibility that therefore needs to be taken (or not taken) by society in general and the welfare services in particular. Therefore it seems pertinent to understand the relevant stressors in (1) the social settings and environment, as well as (2) the interpersonal factors and (3) intrapersonal factors that may stress the people who care for them.

Environmental stresses

The physical environment of many institutions for mentally handicapped people is probably similar to that of many large institutions, at least in Britain. However, the clientele left behind after the more able people move into the community will necessarily be the more physically dependent and the more disturbed people. This means that the enclosed, somewhat self-sufficient unit of the older institution where the more able residents helped practically and socially with the more dependent clients will become less common. Behaviourally disturbed individuals can create damage to property and more severely handicapped people require attention to their physical needs that can limit the aesthetic appeal of a large ward. However, in the author's survey it was the community workers who found the physical environment more distressing. It has now become clear that community care is a lot more expensive than was initially envisaged. Physical resources in the community for mentally handicapped people rarely existed (outside family homes) until very recently. Inadequate or inappropriate resources may have to be used. Mentally handicapped people have not been allowed (or taught) to stand up for their rights and demand facilities, and can easily be placed in unsuitable accommodation.

Society's attitudes

Society's changing attitude to mentally handicapped people is reflected in a plethora of media coverage exploring and expressing the realities within the lives of mentally handicapped people. In the nineteenth century mental handicap was confused with moral handicap, and people were sent off to institutions far away from society. Ideas of their innate perculiarity ranged from seeing them as capable of strange behaviour, including sexual and aggressive misdemeanours, to being spiritually gifted (the word 'cretin' comes through the French from the Latin 'christianus', meaning christian). It would appear that the myths, fears and fantasies surrounding mental handicap are being exposed and explored now and hopefully with will result in a more sympathetic view of the people who suffer from handicap. Jung (1953) wrote about the 'shadow' side of individuals and groups as the unacknowledged darker side that is hidden from conscious view. Perhaps the collective shadow side of mental handicap is the unacknowledged fear, hate and anger about the damaged intellect which our society holds in such high esteem. Also the image of the village idiot, sometimes even seen as the 'sin eater' in previous centuries, suggests how easy it can be to project our darker side onto these unfortunate people and then try to dispose of them.

Only in the past few years, during the move into the community, have people been faced with their feelings and responses to mentally handicapped people as they are asked to integrate them into the community. The staff working against these fears, myths and prejudices on behalf of mentally handicapped people can find themselves bewildered and hurt by responses from society.

Television and media coverage of mental handicap institutions has recently exposed the staff to public scrutiny and criticism. For example, the BBC film 'The Silent Minority' portrays mentally handicapped patients as forgotten, abused, and betrayed by staff (and society) and the staff as uncaring, overworked and indifferent.

Public enquiries such as the Normansfield Enquiry (1978) fuel staff anxieties about not living up to expectations, with fears of litigation and poor staff morale. In this report, staff were accused of less than adequate treatment of residents. Reports in the literature indicate that handicapped children are abused more frequently than other children. The question of why staff might behave in such an unacceptable manner remains unanswered. But it seems logical to assume that these abuses occur when the coping resources of their carers are exceeded.

In the present climate of unemployment it may be that people enter or stay in jobs they do not really like for fear of not getting another. There are still job opportunities in mental handicap, unlike the more glamorous medical specialities.

It may also be that mental handicap attracts people who do not want the challenges and competition in other areas of the health service and move into a system where the recipients of care cannot or will not make criticisms or demands they cannot deal with. This group may exacerbate the problems of the institutional framework, making it more like the inflexible custodial model that is so often caricatured.

Organizational

In the later 1970s a number of government committees of enquiry reported on subjects related to, or specifically focused on, mental handicap. These culminated in the 'Care in the Community' (DHSS, 1981) initiative which endorsed the plan to provide community-based alternatives to institutional provision. The organizational structure needed to deal with more modern approaches to the care of mentally handicapped people has not really taken shape in most places. Notwithstanding the stressors involved in transferring to a different pattern of service provision, the present system also has its difficulties. In Maslach and Pines' (1978) study of staff in various mental health facilities in San Francisco they found several important factors in organizational structure that contributed to staff stress.

One was that the larger the ratio of patients to staff the less staff members liked their jobs. Shortage of staff is an almost universal problem in mental hospitals and hostels, many of which see themselves as functioning 'below minimum safety levels'. Added to this staff shortage is that the training requirements for the role of a hospital nurse and community worker remain unclear. It is becoming obvious that a broader training for residential staff (hospital or community) is needed to work alongside the traditional nurse, teacher, care staff and social worker. Another finding in the Maslach and Pines study was that the higher the percentage of schizophrenics in the patient population the less job satisfaction staff members expressed. Since the transfer of more able mentally handicapped people into the community, during the past five to ten years, it is the more disruptive and disturbed people left behind, increasing the percentage of people who are either psychiatrically ill or too dependent and disabled to leave an institution. This makes greater demands on the staff who previously received at least some practical help and social stimulation from the less handicapped patients.

A third important finding by Maslach and Pines was that 'Staff who could afford to take time out to withdraw temporarily to other work activities when they did not feel like working directly with patients showed more favourable attitudes to patients.' It is more difficult to take time out from direct contact with mentally handicapped patients than the mentally ill, especially if the door is locked and there are few other staff to take over the duties of caring for a highly dependent group of residents.

The issue of responsibility remains unclear. Psychiatric patients are usually considered responsible for themselves but mentally handicapped people are often considered unable to be responsible for themselves. The issue is further confused by the fact that most mentally handicapped inpatients are informal admissions and the dilemma of who has ultimate responsibility can give rise to controversy between staff or sometimes between staff and families.

For example, John is a 29-year-old moderately mentally handicapped man who was admitted to a mental handicap hospital informally (i.e. not under a Mental Health Act Section) because he was damaging property in a hostel. He says he wants to leave hospital and find his own accommodation. His elderly parents say he should come home with them, although they find it very difficult to cope with his violent outbursts. The hospital staff are aware that the chances of John finding any accommodation or occupation are extremely slim and that his history suggests he may well get into trouble with the law (again). There is a meeting with John, his family and the staff to try and make some plans. No decision can be reached. Who makes the ultimate decision and takes responsibility when an agreement cannot be reached? The ambiguity and potential conflicts within this complex dilemma seem a recipe for distress all round!

In my study, policies of the institution were more often rated as highly stressful than any other suggested stresses, and this was especially true amongst hospital workers. It was also noted by Sarota (1974) in his survey (Employee Satisfaction in Agencies Serving Retarded Persons) involving 542 staff, that 'satisfaction with the agency is the crucial component of overall satisfaction amongst individuals working with mentally retarded persons'. More investigation is needed to clarify what these figures really indicate.

Interpersonal factors

Relationships with clients

> I was seized with a tearful rejection of all that ugliness. How could they live in such distorted bodies and without mind for this complex world of ours! I couldn't go and join them then. I was overwhelmed and pained at their condition. Was that because they were anonymous—not people to me?

This quotation is by someone who has worked for seventeen years with mentally handicapped people. Some people in the field confess that they occasionally have this sort of experience amidst the background of enthusiasm, care and commitment in which they normally work. Perhaps this 'window' into another view is important to acknowledge for the health of both the care-giver and the clients. In my study, difficulties with the mentally handicapped clients themselves were rated relatively low compared with other stresses. The slow pace of change, which can feel like no change, stands over, however.

Slow pace of change was rated by 21.9 per cent of people as highly stressful. This is in keeping with Sarota's (1974) finding that 28 per cent of all respondents and 41 per cent of these with high contact with mentally retarded people cited slow pace of change or lack of client progress as a source of dissatisfaction. Moreover, has data 'suggest the manner in which the employee deals with this issue significantly affects his level of satisfaction'. The satisfaction of seeing results from work done is clearly an important factor.

Feedback from clients was rated highly by 48 per cent of workers in the study as helping the staff to cope with stress. The more able clients who can respond verbally may well account for this, but this has not yet been investigated.

One of the difficulties in working with mentally handicapped people is knowing what goals to set and how to balance reality with hope and optimism. Mentally handicapped people vary greatly in their skills and potential, and it can only be an experienced guess at how much progress an individual can make. For example, it would be very easy to under- or over-estimate Steve's potential. He speaks about three words only but takes great delight in outsmarting the medical students on a Rubik cube! Who knows how much he might achieve in time?

The current thrust of Normalization (Wolfensberg, 1972) for mentally handicapped people may compound the difficulty of setting realistic goals, allowing staff, especially inexperienced members, to aim for inappropriate targets and providing possible confusion and conflict in goal-setting.

Of staff in my study, 20 per cent had a relative who was handicapped. The stress they experienced and their ways of coping did not vary significantly from others, except they they found 'working as part of a team' more difficult. It is not known whether this figure of 20 per cent is representative of workers in mental handicap elsewhere, but it makes sense of what is anecdotally written about the effects of having a mentally handicapped member in the family. For example, Carr (1985) has found that having a mentally handicapped relative can motivate an interest in working in this discipline.

As mentioned above, mentally handicapped children have been reported to be physically abused more frequently than other children. Various postulates have been made to explain this—such as their unattractive appearance, poor responsiveness and the exhaustion of the parents' coping resources (Oliver, 1975). It is more common when parents are unsupported by a family or social network. By analogy, it seems possible that when staff caring for mentally handicapped people are unsupported, the danger of maltreatment may arise. This makes the issue of relationships between staff, and mutual supports, very important.

Relationships between staff

Team structures vary throughout Britain. In many places there are no teams at all in a functional sense, either because the medical superintendent model and his hierarchy remain or because teams have not yet been built up. Where teams are operating, there may be different philosophies of care and different professional disciplines meeting at the multidisciplinary team meeting. Different salary structures are also evident—a potential source of rivalry—with the psychiatrist on a consultant's salary and others with variable rates of pay down to the nurses and other care staff who often do most of the face-to-face work on a wage that barely supports one person alone.

Colleagues' attitudes and habits rated very highly as a stressful factor in my study. However, 'informal support of colleagues' rated very highly as helping to deal with stress. This demonstrates the central importance of relationships with colleagues in either exacerbating or mitigating the stresses of this type of work. Good relationships can be enormously helpful in developing coping strategies; but bad relationships can themselves become a major stress. This latter comment may of course apply to many types of work in the human services. It is worth noting that stressful work relationships were reported significantly more often amongst hospital than community-based staff. Several respondents to the questionnaire also remarked on how stressful supporting their colleagues could be.

Psychiatrists, trained on a medical model, have to adjust to the different responsibilities and roles amongst team members. It is not necessarily the doctor who is the team-leader or chairperson any longer.

Psychologists, social workers, nurses and occupational therapists likewise have to accommodate their loyalties to their own profession and to the team at the same time. It may seem easier to by loyal to one's own professional hierarchy than to the team unless care is taken to deal with the tensions within the team. Hollins (1985) proposed a model for teamwork with suggestions for the specific and overlapping roles of team members, such as key workers for clients, link persons to agencies, and family forums for decision-making. These ideas would hopefully reduce tensions and role conflicts, ambiguity and overlap.

Relationships with families

In this study, problems and clients' families rated in 59 per cent as very or extremely stressful. Why should this be so? Perhaps one important factor here is the issue of reponsibility again. Parents normally feel responsible for their children until they are able to take care of themselves and that day is rarely reached with mentally handicapped people. 'Handing over' or sharing the responsibility of care can be a relief to some families but provoke anxieties and guilt in others, which means that 'letting' go can be very difficult. The experience of previous difficult relationships with professionals, often dating back to the time of diagnosis of the handicap, can colour the attitude of families to professionals. Likewise, professionals have their own histories, fears and anxieties about handicapped people and their families to deal with.

Intrapersonal

'Some work encounters echo personal tragedy'—social worker in mental handicap.

A striking number of those working with mentally handicapped people (20 per cent in this survey) have, or have had, relatives who were mentally handicapped. These staff have experience to draw on in understanding and dealing with the stresses they encounter. Whether they actually cope better than other staff has not been demonstrated, but obviously they have resources which *may* be valuable, both to themselves and to their fellow workers, as well as their clients, in dealing with the stresses of their work.

But what of the others? Why do they go into such a traditionally unpopular field?

Perhaps some people enjoy caring for dependent child-like people and manage to cope to a greater or lesser extent with the stresses that long-term parenting entails.

Winnicott (1958) spoke of 'primary maternal preoccupation' as the intense interaction that occurs between a newborn baby and its mother. This places a great many demands on the mother who is biologically prepared for this in normal circumstances. However, this may be disturbed if there is something abnormal with the baby, the maternal preoccupation with the baby becoming distorted and unable therefore to move into the next, healthy, stage, especially if the child remains infant-like. Likewise staff caring for dependent child-like mentally handicapped people can be inducted into a type of prolonged and pathological 'maternal preoccupation' as they replace the parents (usually mother) in their role as primary care-giver. However, staff members are not biologically prepared in the same physiological and psychological ways as the mothers, and excessive demands can be experienced (as well as guilt for not providing the utmost in care) and made worse by the prospect of their long-term nature.

Another way to understand why caring for mentally handicapped people may have its particular stresses is to view caring for other people's handicaps as an attempt to care for one's own inner handicapped side. The more energy and effort expended in caring for another person and their handicaps, the less energy is available for one's own needs. Hence, becoming exhausted would be an obvious sequel. If this is happening then perhaps it may also explain why colleagues find each other stressful, as they 'pick up' each other's unmet needs.

Freudenberger in his book (Freundenberger and Richelson, 1980) proposes that higher inner expectations drive people on towards attempting to reach unreachable (often poorly defined) goals. Many young enthusiastic people seem to enter the mental handicap field with very high hopes and ideals. How many then leave after a period of disillusionment is unknown. The current fashion of normalization can foster some very unrealistic expectations of what mentally handicapped people may be able to do.

Using a transactional analysis model, Zigmund (1984) suggests that health workers get caught in a 'malignant symbiosis' whereby their 'Parent' aspect gets locked into their client's 'Child' aspect, with the result that the care-giver's childlike part remains stifled and the care-receiver's adult and parent capacites remain unused. As mentally handicapped people are often seen as being like children then this model of the 'Me-care-giver: You-care-receiver' may be an unfortunate trap that limits the fullest life and growth of both parties.

Another psychodynamic view would be to postulate that working in the mental handicap field is a way of dealing with the personal or collective shadow of mental handicap (Jung, 1953, mentioned above). To deal with the futility and helplessness experienced in the face of the despair, anger and hatred about handicap, a person may use their energy working to provide a service to the people who suffer these handicaps. This could be a fruitful and enjoyable task but may also be never-ending, requiring a great deal of energy, because handicap can never be cured.

It could also be said that some of the emotional reactions experienced in working in mental handicap are about loss: loss of status professionally, and other practical losses (especially income for many who are not doctors). Perhaps loss of the ability to cure has to be faced in mental handicap more directly than in other branches of medicine. The denial of handicap, the anger towards families and other professionals, the bargaining and difficulty in accepting that although the person may grow in many ways the handicap will always stay, are responses not often faced fully during a professional training. To grasp this intellectually seems a lot easier than living and working with the reality daily and trying to adjust one's aims and satisfactions appropriately.

SYMPTOMS OF STRESS AND COPING STRATEGIES

Symptoms

The symptoms of stress reported in the author's questionnaire survey are in keeping with findings of other workers in the mental health field. Fatigue rated very high (33 per cent respondents reported this as always happening when they are stressed) with irritability, feeling shattered, feeling fed-up, and working less efficiently also rating high. However, 52.6 per cent subjects reported that they felt they were actually coping well at the time of the survey.

Coping Strategies

Of the suggested items that enabled people to cope with stress in this survey, 'informal support of colleagues' was rated by 93.9 per cent of subjects as moderately (13.4 per cent) or extremely (80.5 per cent) helpful. Feedback from the clients themselves was also rated as extremely helpful by 48.8 per cent respondents.

At present, not many staff working with mental handicap have the opportunity to be part of a staff support group, and this may be a useful avenue to investigate in an effort to capitalize on the importance of staff relationships in provoking and relieving stress.

CONCLUSION

The paucity of research on staff working with mentally handicapped people perhaps reflects the unpopularity of this discipline, which in turn may reflect society's disinterest in the topic.

The author's small pilot study shows that many of the stressors may be similar to those experienced by those working in other aspects of mental health, but that mental handicap has some particular stressors, especially at this time of great changes in methods of service provision. Further studies will need to investigate these specific factors, so that appropriate strategies of coping can keep pace with modern clinical practice.

APPENDIX: QUESTIONNAIRE RESULTS ON STRESS IN STAFF WORKING WITH MENTALLY HANDICAPPED PEOPLE

Method

One hundred and ten questionnaires were distributed to psychiatrists and paramedical stafff working with mentally handicapped people in hospitals and/or the community in one London regional service. All staff members attending community and hospital team meetings and academic meetings in one month were asked to complete the questionnaire.

Respondents rated their answers to proposed statements on a 1–5 point scale with 1 as 'not at all' and 5 as 'extremely' or 'always'. Results were condensed to make three categories by adding 1 and 2 together and 4 and 5 together, leaving 3 as a 'middle' category.

Results

A total of 82 questionnaires were returned by 47 female and 34 male staff (+ 1 not stated) of whom

The Questionnaire results

	Not at all stressful				Extremely stressful	Difference across groups (sex, clinical base, profession, w/without m/h relative)
	1	2	3	4	5	
1 How stressful do you find working with mentally handicapped people?	38%	53%			9%	
2 Things that make it stressful:						
Too much to do	37.8	18.3			43.9	
Too many different things to do	47.6	22.0			30.4	
Not sure what's expected	64.2	27.2			8.6	
Feel the job is never done	35.6	25.9			38.3	
Difference between what I can do and what I want to do	22.2	37.0			41.8	
Keeping work and home separate	59.8	18.3			21.9	
Difficulty in communication with clients	64.6	24.4			11.0	
Antisocial habits and appearance	83.8	12.5			3.8	
Clients not able to take responsibility for themselves	68.3	19.5			12.2	
Lack of gratitude from clients	89.0	6.1			4.8	
Physical attack (or threat of attack)	67.9	17.3			14.8	females > males, $p \leq 0.05$
Physical work-load	57.9	27.6			14.4	
Clients' difficulty in caring for themselves	72.0	17.1			10.9	
Slowness of change (or no change)	51.2	26.8			21.9	females > males, $p \leq 0.05$
Colleagues' attitudes and habits	29.6	33.3			37.1	hospital based > community, $p \leq 0.01$
Problems with clients' families	39.0	32.9			28.0	
Physical environment (smell, noise, &c.)	51.2	20.7			28.1	community > hospital based, $p \leq 0.01$
Policies of the institution/agency	28.4	22.2			49.4	hospital based > community, $p \leq 0.05$
Working as part of a team	85.4	12.2			2.4	

Stress in staff working with mentally handicapped people

How do you know when you are stressed?

	Not at all				Always or extremely
	1	2	3	4	5
Physical illness		31.5	12.3		6.2
Fatigue		23.5	43.2		33.4
Need days off		59.3	33.3		7.4
Work less efficiently		31.7	50.0		18.3
Feel fed-up		37.8	43.9		18.3
Feel bored		84.0	11.1		4.9
Feel scattered		41.0	35.9		23.0
Feel irritable		37.8	35.4		26.8
Feel hopeless		63.8	26.3		10.1
Stop caring		81.7	15.9		2.4
Feel depressed		59.8	25.6		14.7
Get indecisive		65.9	28.0		6.1
Want to resign		73.2	17.1		9.7

4 How are you coping now?

Not at all				Very well
8.5		39.0		52.6

5 Coping strategies

These help me to cope:

Informal support of colleagues		6.1	13.4		80.5
Support group meetings		21.0	35.8		43.2
Individual supervision/counselling		21.0	32.1		46.9
Feedback from clients		15.0	36.3		48.8
Drinking (alcohol)		71.6	21.0		7.4
Having a good laugh		12.3	30.9		56.8
Relaxation in sport or other activities		14.8	29.6		55.6
Religious faith		68.3	17.1		14.6
Medication		91.3	5.0		3.8
Feeling a piece of work is done		14.6	26.6		58.6
Others (please explain)					

6 Other comments:

21 (25.6 per cent) were psychiatrists
11 (13.4 per cent) were nurses
12 (14.6 per cent) social workers
38 (46.3 per cent) others, which included psychologists, occupational therapists ('trainers'), physiotherapists

The length of time spent working with mentally handicapped people ranged from 0.2 to 28 years, with a mean of 5.95 years.
The clinical bases were

14 (17.3 per cent) hospital based.
47 (58.0 per cent) community based.
20 (24.7 per cent) both hospital and community based.
1 not stated.

There were 16 (20 per cent) out of 80 who had a mentally handicapped relative. The word 'relative' was left unqualified on the questionnaire, so it is not known how close the relationship was.

REFERENCES

Carr, J. (1985). The effect of the severely abnormal on their families. In A. M. Clarke, A. D. B. Clarke (eds) *Mental Deficiency: The Changing Outlook,* 4th ed., Methuen, London.
Chernis, C. (1980). *Staff Burnout: Job Stress in the Human Services,* Sage, Beverly Hills.
Chernis, C. and Egnatios, E. (1978). Is there job satisfaction in the community? *Mental Health Journal,* **14**, 309–18.
DHSS (1981). *Care in the Community,* Department of Health & Social Security, London.
Freudenberger, H. and Richelson, G. (1980). *Burnout,* Arrow Books, London.
Hollins, S. (1985). The dynamics of teamwork. Chapter 24. In M. Craft, J. Bicknell and S. Hollins (eds), *Mental Handicap. A Multidisciplinary Approach,* Baillier Tindall, London.
Jung, C. G. (1953). Volume 7, *Collected Works,* p. 94, etc. Routledge and Kegan Paul, London.
Normansfield Enquiry (1978). DHSS Document.
Maslach, C. and Pines, A. (1978). Characteristics of staff burnout in mental health settings, *Hospital & Community Psychiatry,* **29**, 4, April.
O'Brien, J. and Tyne, A. (1981) *The Principle of Normalisation: A Foundation for Effective Service,* Campaign for Mentally Handicapped People, London.
Oliver, J. (1975). Epidemiology and family characteristics of severely abused children, *British Journal of Social and Preventative Medicine,* **29**, 205–21.
Reid, A. H. (1983). Psychiatry of mental handicap: a review, *J. Royal Society of Medicine,* **76**, July, p. 587.
Sarota, B. P. V. (1974). Employee satisfaction in agencies serving retarded persons, *Amer. J. Mental Deficiency,* **79**, 434–42.

Winnicott, D. W. (1958). *Collected Papers through Paediatrics to Psychoanalysis*, Tavistock, London.
Wolfensberg, W. (1972). *The Principles of Normalisation in Human Services*. National Institute of Mental Retardation, Toronto.
Zigmund, D. (1984). Physician heal thyself: the paradox of the wounded healer, *Brit. J. Holistic Medicine*, April.

Stress in Health Professionals
Edited by R. Payne and J. Firth-Cozens
© 1987 John Wiley & Sons Ltd

Chapter 9

Stress Amongst Social Workers

Andrée Rushton

INTRODUCTION

At a recent conference on stress, attended by over one hundred social workers, not a voice was raised in disagreement with the belief that social work is a highly stressful occupation. Most writers and researchers on the subject have taken a similar view, giving weight to the preceptions of social workers in the absence of more objective evidence. However, it is necessary to ask whether or not social work is highly stressful and to bear the question in mind as this chapter proceeds.

It is commonly assumed that social workers in health settings, who are the main focus of this chapter, lead more sheltered working lives than their colleagues in mainstream local authority social work. Whether or not this is true, or merely the product of envy or misconception, is another question the chapter will consider. In the process, it should not be forgotten that all social workers need to collaborate with health professionals and that the clients of local authority social workers in area teams have high rates of sickness, evidence of a need for a collaborative approach to caring. Although some comparison between social work in different settings is useful, it would be a mistake to make too strong a contrast.

Social work has come increasingly to the attention of the public in the course of this century, although what social workers actually do remains something of a mystery to outsiders. Such uncertainty reflects confusion about roles and tasks within social work itself. Debate within social work has centred on effectiveness, but reliable measures of effectiveness are hard to find. Social workers have also expressed a great deal of concern about the extent to which they are members of a profession. In the absence of an exclusive knowledge base or definable set of skills unique to social work, it has not proved possible to argue successfully for professional status. Thus it has been difficult for social work to justify itself.

In the present era of high unemployment and public expenditure cuts, social workers lack the resources and staffing to do the job required. New legislation is constantly heaping further responsibilities onto them and little control can be exercised over the actions of other authorities, even if special pleading manages to win a few battles.

However, society has high expectations of social workers. They are expected to prevent child abuse, cope with mental illness, care for elderly people at risk and generally enable the public to get on with life unhindered by uncomfortable thoughts about the more vulnerable members of society. If they are seen to fail, public criticism is harsh.

In the wake of the tragic deaths of children in local authority care at the hands of their parents, following the death of Maria Colwell in 1974, social workers have been subjected to unprecedented media hostility. Such a death is every social worker's nightmare and the attendant publicity is unwelcome and often unjust. The social workers' strike for local bargaining rights in 1979 was not entirely self-interested, because it was fuelled by dissatisfaction over cuts in services, but it provoked hostility from the media and undermined relationships with other professions.

In recent years, the relationship between social workers and local councillors has been marked by sharp conflict in the inner city areas. The prime example is found in the London Borough of Lambeth where in 1985 social workers walked out on strike, following criticisms from the chair of the social services committee after the death of a child in care. Social workers resent being criticized by elected members, who they feel know little about the job and are responding to ill-informed public pressure and to increased conflict between central and local government. Councillors on the other hand claim to know more about the needs of the local community than social workers. This dispute has lowered morale amongst social workers. It is symptomatic of a change in society whereby consumers and their representatives are challenging professional power.

The position occupied by social workers in society is far from comfortable or well understood. Doctors by sharp contrast are well established and much respected, which must compensate them to some extent for the stress encountered in their work.

The question now arises as to whether it is the nature of social work that causes stress, or the context in which social workers are placed, or whether it is a matter of personality or personal circumstances.

THE NATURE OF SOCIAL WORK

The broad purpose of social work is to improve social functioning by the provision of practical and psychological help to people in need. Thus the work is problem centred and often involves choosing between unsatisfactory alternatives. Some situations are potentially much more explosive than others, although given optimum conditions many crises could be prevented. Lack of adequate resources to meet the needs presented by clients is a constant factor, frustrating but familiar to all social workers. Much emphasis is placed during training on the relationship between client and worker and on developing professional standards of conduct based on social work values, for example, client self-determination and the avoidance of judging clients. Social workers are taught to show empathy, warmth and genuineness and to treat clients as people who are valid products of their social context. In the light of recent child abuse cases, however, the value of non-judgmentalism is being questioned.

Social workers experience both role conflict and role ambiguity in the nature of their work. Both these aspects of role structure have been correlated with stress reactions in studies of the caring professions (Cherniss and Egnatios, 1978; Weinburg, Edwards and Garove, 1979).

Role Conflict

In terms of role conflict, social workers are torn between the desire to care for people and act as their advocates and the duty to control, through undertaking statutory responsibilities. Should a child be removed from abusing parents with the consequent trauma of loss and disturbance, or left at home in familiar, but potentially threatening surroundings? Should a mentally ill client be deprived of liberty, when there is some doubt that he or she is dangerous or suicidal? Should a confused elderly person by supported riskily at home or go into residential care? Apart from the conflict inherent in carrying out statutory responsibilities, the social worker may have to balance the conflicting needs of family members and conflict between the requirements of the authority for an efficient service and the needs of clients. The social worker is often forced into taking risks, a situation which causes anxiety because the outcome is unknown. An expert on child abuse has suggested that social workers caught in a potentially violent situation react initially like a rabbit caught in the headlights and become petrified (Moore, 1984, p.18). All these aspects of role conflict are faced at some time or another by social workers in health settings, even if they undertake fewer statutory duties than their area team colleagues. Social workers on paediatric wards take part in child abuse conferences and take on such cases, as do social workers in primary health settings. The role of advocate or counsellor are less characterized by conflict and are experienced as less stressful in some ways.

Role Ambiguity

Role ambiguity increased for social workers with the formation of local authority Social Service Departments (SSDs) and the introduction of generic social work because the question of what social workers actually do became pressing. Apart from carrying out increasing amounts of statutory work, they give advice and information (a task for which they are often poorly equipped), act as advocates in helping clients obtain services and benefits, undertake a co-ordinating role where many services are involved with one family, offer counselling and may, if circumstances permit, practise therapy. Statutory duties are given the highest priority, but social workers who lack a theoretical orientation, or who have not formulated an approach to their work, may feel cast adrift when deciding which methods of work to choose or how far to take them. Good training should prevent this happening, but social workers are critical of their training because it can fail to teach the skills needed in the workplace (Davies, 1984, p.12). Experience of role ambiguity can easily force the social worker into taking on the roles of other agencies, for example, the Department of Health & Social Security (DHSS), local housing department and so forth. Social workers in health settings may find their skills poorly used if they lack a clear sense of purpose.

Role Autonomy

The degree of autonomy permitted the individual is a source of continuing debate in social work and is discussed in more detail below, in considering the context of social work. Autonomy is highly valued by the medical profession and perhaps it is because of this influence that social workers in health settings enjoy greater autonomy than those in area teams, who by contrast are permitted less freedom in decision-making, use of resources or contribution to policy-making and planning. The authors of one study comment that hospital based social workers had more responsibility for receiving referrals and could accept or reject work without reference to senior staff, especially in psychiatric hospitals. They also sought out referrals. Considerable freedom was observed in terms of caseload management (Parsloe and Stevenson, 1978, p. 227). Another study refers to the greater degree of control over working conditions enjoyed by social workers in hospitals. They saw clients by appointment in the hospital rather than at home, had more opportunity for casework, were less pressured by administrative tasks and not expected to provide practical resources. They could formulate objectives and had the freedom to carry them out (Satyamurti, 1981, p. 100).

Collaboration

Working in a hospital, primary health setting or child guidance clinic requires social workers to explain their roles and practice to members of different health professions and to understand the priorities and goals of the health services. Little priority may be given to social work activities in such a setting. This requires confidence and a secure identity of the social worker, without which the temptation to fall back on demonstrating the practical aspects of social work, those most readily understood and valued by health service staff, becomes too great. A dismissive or indifferent attitude to the social worker's counselling role may be hard to counteract if doctors are accustomed to deference or want beds cleared quickly. The social worker may then hesitate to challenge the views of doctors or nurses or not know how to cope with criticisms of social work plans or goals.

Other difficulties in collaboration between social workers and health service staff stem from status differences. The social worker is often in a junior position and will normally be accorded less status than doctors. Collaboration in such circumstances is less likely to be effective. Overlapping roles can be a source of support and shared endeavour or may engender rivalry and distance. Such overlap is particularly likely in psychiatric hospitals or between health visitors and social workers in primary health settings. Practical differences, like style of working, or use of time, can inhibit or encourage collaboration and opportunities for informal contact are particularly valued by social workers.

Differences in training and attitude need to be taken into account in collaboration between social workers and health service staff. Social workers are widely critical of doctors for displaying professional arrogance and for ignoring the social and emotional factors in illness. Doctors on the other hand dismiss social workers for being indecisive and for lacking interest in priority care groups of patients.

It is not known whether effective collaboration is stress reducing, but as a contributory factor in providing a successful service, it may reduce stress. Without such collaboration, social workers would effect little change in the lives of others.

Certain circumstances require area team social workers to collaborate with health professionals, for example, child abuse case conferences and the formal admission of patients to psychiatric hospitals. Doctors and social workers have for years disagreed over psychiatric admissions. The 1983 Mental Health Act designates the Approved Social Worker as the person who applies for compulsory admission of a patient to hospital on the recommendation of two doctors. This is to enable the social worker to act in the best interests of the patient and counteract the social disadvantages of many patients. Doctors are currently campaigning to have what they consider to be the social worker's veto removed so that the diagnosis and treatment of mental illness are entirely a medical matter.

Recent health service cuts have tended to sharpen conflict between doctors and social workers. Scare resources like beds have become the focus of dispute, with social workers trying to get patients admitted or delay discharge and doctors anxious to increase patient throughput.

Clients

The core of social work lies in relationships with clients, a source of stress even for very experienced social workers. The complaint is often heard that social workers have to carry the anxieties of clients; they may find clients intransigent and unwilling to change. Differences of perception intrude, clients' behaviour can seem difficult or incomprehensible and their expectations of social workers inappropriate. Like health professionals, social workers can encounter evidence of rape, incest, child abuse, serious psychiatric disorder, drug addiction, alcoholism and the effects of serious and terminal illness, although obviously the responsibilities of social workers are different. Because social workers are taught to be non-judgmental in their relationship with clients, they may find it hard to admit that the personalities and circumstances of clients cause stress in this way as it may seem like an admission of failure. It is necessary to cope with the anxieties and problems of others and to develop a high degree of self-awareness in the process. A more collaborative relationship could develop with the client, if this is appropriate, facilitated by client access to social workers' records.

However, there is no clear evidence to support such speculations. The parents of mentally handicapped children have noticed discomfort and avoidance in social workers (Browne, 1982, pp. 26–28). On the other hand, Fineman (1985, p.57) found that social workers were concerned to achieve the right emotional distance and sometimes delayed closing the case because of the relationship with the client. Some expressed protective feelings for children or other vulnerable clients or anguish and discomfort over controlling clients' lives. In a large-scale field study of social workers' views (Parsloe and Stevenson, 1978, p.300), the vulnerability of clients was felt to be a source of stress. The study also reported that social workers have high expectations of clients. Satyamurti (1981, p.124) found social workers showed little understanding of the community and spoke disparagingly of clients. Strategies to reduce stress included creating emotional distance and dealing with feelings of inadequacy and frustration by making jocular remarks about clients. These studies indicate the adoption of some defensive strategies as coping mechanisms in dealing with role problems.

The growing number of incidents of violence to social workers by clients is a matter of great concern. No research has yet been undertaken on this trend, which means that no firm figures are available. Two British social workers were murdered by clients in 1985 and in the London Borough of Camden, the same year saw four serious assaults on social workers (Murray, 1985, p.14). Growing unemployment, increasing poverty and cuts in benefits and services are forcing clients in the direction of violence. Closer study needs to be made of the events surrounding individual incidents, in order that guidelines can be drawn up for the protection of social workers. The best long-term solution is a positive commitment to the policy of community care and the provision of reasonable services and benefits.

THE CONTEXT OF SOCIAL WORK

Social workers in cities who are constantly faced with the tensions of urban life no doubt experience greater levels of stress than social workers in small towns and rural areas where the pace of life is slower. Social workers in Northern Ireland are working in a sensitive and risky political situation; some of the social workers interviewed there by Parsloe and Stevenson (1978, p.325) stated that they were accustomed to these circumstances. Others were wary of certain clients and took care to keep the troubles in mind in the course of their work.

The organizational context of social work is attracting increasing attention as a possible cause of job stress now that the administrative reform that led to the creation of large social services departments is some years in the past and its permanent effects are being assessed. Most social workers in Britain are employees of these local authority social services departments and work in area teams. They face a conflict between the demands made on them as employees of large organizations and their expectations of some professional autonomy (Glastonbury, Cooper and Hawkins, 1982; Gammack, 1985, p.13; Bamford, 1982, p.17). In recent years, this has been intensified by the development of more procedures, especially in child abuse cases, by lack of practical resources and by threats of disciplinary procedures. Most basic grade social workers carry a generic caseload but the boundary between generic and specialist work is not well defined and generic workers often feel that they are expected to have specialist knowledge. Heavy workloads are the norm and it is still not uncommon for social workers to carry 40 complex cases.

Social workers on different rungs of the bureaucratic ladder are subject to different stresses. If basic grade social workers complain about being expected to take on the work of specialists and of being poorly equipped for the task, senior practitioners, who do have specialist knowledge, are not sufficiently involved in policy making and their knowledge is often not well used within the department. Middle managers feel torn between the demands of those above and those below them, with little control over resources and poor support from senior management. Senior managers are themselves vulnerable because their departments are subect to rate-capping; they have to deal with strikes and have increasingly problematic relationships with councillors.

Social workers in health settings in Britain are not only SSD employees, but must relate to National Health Service (NHS) administrative and professional hierarchies as well. Performing this double act could mean that they experience more stress than their area team colleagues or alternatively that they somehow manage to elude the constraints of both by belonging fully to neither.

In recent years, hospital based social workers have drawn closer to the mainstream. Firstly, since 1974, they have been employed by SSDs, instead of by the NHS. Fears of extra duties have proved largely unfounded, although some statutory duties are undertaken and there are extra meetings for senior staff. However, they are vulnerable to local authority budget cuts (Parsloe and Stevenson, 1978, p.228). Secondly, all social workers now receive common basic training, whereas medical and psychiatric social workers used to be trained separately. Thirdly, perhaps as a result of common basic training, many hospital based social workers have had experience of working in area teams. Finally, the shift from institutional to community care now underway will bring many social workers out of the hospital and into the community for an increasing proportion of their time. This is already more true of social workers in psychiatric hospitals than of those in general hospitals. However, there is little evidence yet of hospital based social workers transferring cases to area teams, either from lack of trust or fear of overloading busy staff, or because hospital patients, who tend to be sick, elderly, disabled or mentally ill, would be given low priority to SSDs (Parsloe and Stevenson, 1978, p. 293).

The hospital setting presents a challenge to social workers. Hospitals have a distinct culture, with their own priorities, activities, language, dress and rituals, which are very different from those of social work. Social workers may feel that their priorities, the social and emotional problems of patients, receive little attention, partcularly in a large general hospital. In psychiatric and mental handicap hospitals, where the emphasis on medical care is much reduced, it may be easier to achieve priority for social work goals. However, social workers will have to withstand the well known effects of long-stay institutions, large old buildings, isolation from the community, perhaps inflexible routines. Much depends on the ability of those concerned to be articulate and convincing about their work and on the capacity of social work management to create a strong presence within the hospital.

Certain features of hospital based social work suggest that its challenges are stimulating rather than stressful to social workers. Senior staff carry a caseload as well as supervisory and management responsibilities, thereby continuing to provide a direct service and keeping in touch with social work practice in a way that reveals the influence of the medical profession. Some social workers are involved in the teaching of medical students, nurses and other NHS staff and in making case presentations to multidisciplinary teams (Law, 1982, p. 24; Rushton and Davies, 1984, p. 39). Both these practices are likely to increase job satisfaction and indicate that skills are being well used.

There are basically two ways of organizing social work in hospitals. The first, unit attachment, is the more common and is closely patterned on the medical specialisms. Chronic psychiatric wards in one study received little social work help because they were a low priority for medical care (Parsloe and Stevenson, 1978, p. 281). The term unit attachment refers to the attachment of a social worker to one or more units or wards and is more suited to burns or renal units or district acute units, where some knowledge of the process of treatment or recovery is essential, than to general medical, surgical or psychiatric wards. A dilemma exists for social workers attached to a unit in deciding how close to become to the intense culture of the unit. Supervision may be difficult because the supervisor may not know enough about the unit to be effective. The team on the ward or in the unit can provide support, but could alternatively be hostile or indifferent to the social worker (Addison, 1980, p. 352). Many social workers find support as the members of a multidisciplinary team, but problems arise if the social worker is prevented from carrying out appropriate roles or if the value of social work is denied.

The second way of organizing social work in hospitals is referred to as the social work team approach. Here a more centralised team provides a service to a number of wards through regular liaison. Skills can be used appropriately, allowing opportunities for specialization in method. The social work team in hospital can narrow the gap between the hospital department and the area team and enable SSD policies and resources to be better understood. It may therefore give more protection to social workers than unit attachment, but possibly limit their autonomy. The social work team can establish its own priorities instead of being strongly influenced by the multidisciplinary team. It can respond quickly to referrals and liaise with the community outside the hospital. It would be worth exploring whether the social work team in hospital reduces stress for its members. It is likely to prove a better form of support than unit attachment (Rushton and Davies, 1984, ch. 6).

The attachment of social workers to primary health settings is much more recent. Two factors gave impetus to the growth of this form of social work in Britain during the 1970s. One was the need to provide a service to deal with the high incidence of psycho-social problems in general practice (Shepherd et al., 1966; Cooper et al., 1975). The other factor was the importance of improving the poor relationship between SSDs and primary health teams. Collaborative schemes were viewed favourably by the Seebohm Committee (1968) and the British Medical Association. The reorganization of the NHS in 1974 and the transfer of social work support to the health service of the local authority which had been recommended by the Otton Report (1974) divided health and social services more than ever before. Collaboration between the services at all levels was considered vital although fraught with problems. On the whole, collaborative schemes have received very favourable reports, perhaps because they are limited to those group practices and health centres converted to a more social model of health care provision.

High levels of job satisfaction are recorded by studies of social workers in primary health settings. A study of the views of four social workers dealing with 168 clients during a six month period in 1977 stated that the social workers welcomed the opportunity to use their casework skills to a greater extent than would be possible in an SSD and saw their intervention as helpful and their clients largely satisfied (Rushton and Briscoe, 1981, p.61). The attachment of a social worker to a group practice in north London resulted in a detailed study of the work undertaken, with generally positive findings. The attachment was studied over a four-year period, involving 1000 cases and a range of methods of intervention (Goldberg and Neill, 1972). Both these studies, in common with most of the literature on social work in general practice, are based on social work records—the collection of standardized data.

A comparison of liaison schemes, where the social worker calls at a surgery or group practice to collect referrals, with attachment schemes where a service is provided from the health centre or group practice concerned, found liaison schemes failed to educate health service staff about social work, produced few referrals and did not improve relationships (Corney and Briscoe, 1977).

The work of the four attachment social workers referred to above (Rushton and Briscoe, 1981) was compared over a three-month period with that of three intake team workers in the local SSD area office (Corney, 1979, p.15). Workloads in the two groups were similar in terms of size of case load and hours worked. Results showed that the attachment social workers held more interviews, maintained contact with clients longer, had more contact with other agencies and considered that they were able to solve or alleviate more problems than the intake workers.

From these and other studies, it emerges that attachment schemes improve collaboration with GPs, health visitors, district nurses and other health service staff, allow a better mutual understanding to develop, produce social work of a higher standard, allow easier access to the service for the client than provided by the SSD, enable the social worker to use new skills and methods and make better use of the skills acquired in training. They also provide an opportunity to undertake research and permit the social worker greater independence, within the overall framework of accountability to the SSD.

Keys to the success of social work in primary health settings have been identified as careful preparation, an agreement about confidentiality, proper links with the SSD, the goodwill of NHS staff and a social worker who is confident and experienced. If these conditions are met, social workers would be expected to report high levels of job satisfaction and severe stress in their absence. It should be added that this is not a luxury service to which social workers can escape from the rigours of area team-work, because the literature reveals high referral rates of severe and difficult problems. Social workers in primary health settings may feel additional stress because they often carry both area team and NHS caseloads, offering a part-time service to both organizations. It should be realized as well that although 50 per cent of local authorities in Britain have arranged social work attachments to primary care settings, only a small minority of the total number of social workers in the country are actually involved (Gilchrist et al., 1978).

EVIDENCE OF STRESS IN SOCIAL WORK IN HEALTH SETTINGS

The term stress presents difficulties to researchers because it has a wide range of popular and specialized meanings (Rutter, 1981), but Selye's definition is generally accepted as a starting point: 'the non-specific (that is, common) result of any demand upon the body' (Selye, 1982, p. 7). A certain amount of the right kind of stress is stimulating and has a positive effect. The harmful effects of stress fall into three groups; somatic, psychological and behavioural. The concept of stress is thus broader than job satisfaction or dissatisfaction, but the two concepts are often referred to synonymously in the literature. Burnout is the last stage of stress and is defined as a state of total exhaustion caused by working with people in emotionally demanding situations. It is correlated with poor physical health, sleeplessness, increased consumption of alcohol, headaches, backaches, stomach-aches, nervousness, hopelessness and loss of idealism (Pines, 1982). This concept has attracted the enthusiastic attention of American researchers, but has scarcely begun to be felt in English social work literature, even if its existence is widespread amongst practising social workers. In examining evidence of stress amongst social workers at this relatively early stage of study of the subject, it is more useful to try and identify evidence of the whole range of stress reactions than to focus attention particularly on the phenomenon of burnout, the nature of which is a matter of debate.

The theoretical model expounded by Lazarus and Folkman (1984) can be applied to the analysis of stress amongst social workers. They argue that stress arises from individual or environmental factors or the interaction of the two and is evaluated by the individual concerned (cognitive appraisal). There follows an attempt at coping by adaptation, which may, if not successful, lead to burn-out. The emphasis in this model on both individual and environmental factors makes it particularly relevant to social work with its concern for the interaction of people with their environment. External pressures will not necessarily cause stress as individual responses vary widely, but the fact that they commonly cause stress retrieves the individual from the label of inadequacy and focuses attention instead upon the interaction between the individual and the environment. It is useful to examine social work with this model in mind because the attention of social workers is focused far more than is the case with other caring professions on the behavior of the individual or group in the environment and an interactionist approach to stress will be therefore most readily understood by social workers. Arguing along similar lines, Parry and Gowler have proposed the existence of a cruciform effect, that is, a set of demands which pull in opposing directions, leading to stress in the worker. They examine the tension between altruism and expertise on the one hand and organizational constraints and innovation on the other. The range of coping mechanisms which they identify shows how psychologists (or other caring professionals) flee from encounters with the client or patient after a period of stressful experiences into teaching, research or administrative roles. This model is applicable to social work, but is not extended to show how those who remain in direct service posts may possibly adapt successfully to their role and not seek escape from it. People who enter social work from a wish to care for others may choose to remain in contact with clients (Parry and Gowler, 1983).

The findings of occupational stress research have been reviewed in a recent book on the theoretical and clinical aspects of stress (Holt, 1982). Job dissatisfaction and work stress are related to exclusion from decision-making, role ambiguity and role conflict, poor use of skills and abilities and demands the worker cannot meet. Stressful events in the worker's personal life lower resistance to occupational stress. It is therefore to be expected that social workers experiencing these problems will be under stress. Research into stress in the caring professions has been mainly a North American concern to date, concentrating on the phenomenon of burn-out and showing, although not always conclusively, that professional carers experience high levels of stress (see Freudenberger, 1974; Cherniss, 1980; Maslach, 1982; Maslach and Pines, 1977). However, very little work has yet appeared on stress amongst social workers and still less is concerned with social workers in health settings. This makes it necessary to turn to more general studies of stress amongst social workers and to adopt a more discursive approach to the subject.

The evidence of stress amongst social workers is based largely on qualitative studies using self reports. Such an approach presents fewer methodological problems than measurements of physical reaction to stress or studies of behavioural observation and has intrinsic validity because a major focus of interest is on the response of the individual to the environment. The disadvantage of this approach lies in the lack of objective correlates. Studies of stress amongst social workers are not directly comparable with each other and this is a major failing.

North American social work research in this field, following stress research in the caring professions generally, has concentrated on the phenomenon of burn-out, with particular reference to child-care workers. British social work research has focused on area team social workers, whose highest priority is statutory child-care work.

Some attempt was made to assess the experience of social workers as a whole in North America by a study of 1173 social workers, randomly selected from the National Association of Social Workers' directory. A postal questionnaire was used to measure seven job facets as well as the subjects' likelihood of changing jobs in the near future as measures of job satisfaction and burn-out. (Jayaratne and Chess, 1983). Results show the social workers to have high levels of satisfaction. The study concludes that stress does not necessarily lead social workers to become dissatisfied or to change their jobs. This finding is at variance with the results of research on burn-out and further research is recommended. The most important predictors of job satisfaction and intent to change jobs were found to be challenge, promotion prospects and salary levels. The same data were used as the basis for another paper examining whether the emotional support provided by supervisors and colleagues moderates stress (Jayaratne, Tripodi and Chess, 1983). Results indicated a negative relationship between support and stress but no positive relationship was found, which is consistent with the results of general occupational stress literature quoted above.

A search of the literature has revealed only one article on stress amongst North American social workers in health settings. After a disappointingly brief literature review (no doubt brief because the field is so unexplored), it presents typologies of stress for application to social work in health settings. The article includes a stress assessment scale for social workers to rate personal, interpersonal and organizational stressors (Taylor-Brown et al., 1981, p. 91). The authors refer to the low status of social work in hospitals, conflicts with other professionals, the exclusion of social workers from decision-making and the newness and insecurity of health related professions, including social work. The inclusion of malpractice suits in the typologies gives them a distinctly North American appearance, but perhaps the equivalent source of stress in Britain would be child abuse enquiries, which exact a great toll of those involved.

A noted feature of British social work is the weak link between research and practice. In studying stress amongst local authority social workers and managers, one researcher bridged the gap between research and practice by offering a counselling service to the subjects, thus ensuring that the research offered a direct benefit instead of being seen as a burden (Fineman, 1985 p. 113). Social workers are encouraged by the structure of their occupation to leave practice and move early into management. This process has a dampening effect on interest in research, teaching and writing. Even so, the demands of practice leave little energy for reading and reflection. Social workers therefore often display indifference to research or are suspicious of becoming involved because it fails to offer them anything. Researchers have yet to prove that they have a serious influence on policy-making in this field.

There is a widespread belief among area team social workers, which seems to be shared by their hospital based colleagues, that hospital based social work is less stressful than area team-work. The dearth of research on social work in health settings is perhaps evidence of this belief, although not of the truth of it. Consequently, evidence of stress amongst social workers in health settings has to be teased out of the literature. In the case of hospital based social work, the literature is surprisingly scanty for one of the oldest established branches of social work and only one British journal article deals specifically with stress in this context, as quoted above (Addison, 1980, p. 341).

The literature on social work in primary health settings is more plentiful but the growth of this form of social work has been severely constrained by the low priority it has been accorded by SSDs in a climate of budget cuts. Although problems with collaboration are acknowledged, social workers in this setting do not seem to be subject to high stress levels. High levels of job satisfaction are recorded, as detailed earlier.

In a study of one urban children's department in process of transformation to a social services department, following the recommendations of the 1968 Seebohm report, a vivid portrayal is given of social workers in a period of uncertainty and chaos. The material is somewhat dated as it was collected in the early 1970s, although the book was not published until 1981 (Satyamurti, 1981). The author undertook two years part-time participant observation of the workings of the department, as well as holding structured interviews with social workers, their seniors and staff of other local organizations with related functions. She identified defences against stress in the staff and found that they chose sick leave, applying for promotion and resignation as paths of flight in the face of heavy workloads and organizational change. This pattern is commensurate with the behaviour described by Parry and Gowler (1983). For example, the average length of stay in the job was eighteen months. At the time, doctors were frequently critical of the high rates of job mobility amongst social workers. This situation has since changed, both because there are fewer jobs available and because that period of organizational change, and its attendant pressures, is over. Parsloe and Stevenson (1978, ch.13) were impressed by the number of social workers who had been in post for several years.

Satyamurti divides defences against stress into two groups: individual defences, which include using the system to the advantage of particular clients, low take-up of in-service training opportunities (presumably arising from a need to be on the spot all the time), little attempt to influence policy, non-compliance with regulations, avoidance of difficulties, being unavailable (taking sick leave and changing jobs), avoiding administrative and bureaucratic tasks, reluctance to take on new work or create initiatives. She found that collective defences included the use of team support, sanctions for labelling clients, denial of the value of senior management and antagonism to administrative staff based outside the team. The division of social work teams into intake and long term was a device designed to share the work more equally and reduce unpredictability of the work flow for the long-term teams. This is a revealing study of social work in a local authority setting at a point of change but its findings do not have general validity for social work because circumstances have changed. Caseloads are smaller, there is less confusion within social work departments and in some ways social workers have less autonomy because priorities are more clearly defined and there are more procedures to follow.

Considerable light was thrown on social workers' views, and therefore on their experiences of stressful situations, by a large scale descriptive study of social work teams, based on a combination of qualitiative and quantitative data. Eight fieldwork studies of area teams in England and their equivalent in Scotland and Northern Ireland were undertaken as well as studies of two psychiatric hospitals and five general hospitals (Parsloe and Stevenson, 1978). The purpose of the study was to examine social workers' activities and consider the implications for social work training. Several hundred interviews were undertaken and the respondents were asked to comment on pressures and satisfactions of their work. The cautious conclusion is reached that 'our studies, especially those in area teams, do suggest that social workers, in the country as a whole may be experiencing certain pressures, both of a kind and of a degree which may be counterproductive to effect work'. Less stress was reported by hospital based social workers than by those in area teams.

The authors of this study are of the opinion that social work is by nature stressful because it is problem oriented. Unpredictable events, rather than simple volume of work, emerge as the main source of stress. Fluctuations in urgent demand interrupt work plans and erode vital breathing space. Social workers in the study felt their situation was tolerable if they knew that they would get a chance to keep abreast of it. Seasonal fluctuations in the work flow, for example, winter crises with elderly people, were also felt to be a source of stress.

A qualitative analysis of stress in five teams of social workers in an urban social services department shows social workers, seniors and team leaders reporting a wide range of stress responses, in an articulate manner (Fineman, 1985). As the author points out, the language of social work is close to the language of stress and the concepts involved are very similar. Fineman examines four areas of the experience of 40 subjects, using taped interviews which he then analysed: characteristics of the self, job features, home circumstances and quality and quantity of support, showing how they interacted. His findings reflect those of the occupational stress literature generally: the subjects reported tension, anxiety, depression, panic, feelings of pressure, frustration, inability to relax, loss of confidence and an equally wide range of behavioural and physical symptoms of stress. Half the social workers in the study reported symptoms of psychological stress and a small minority had either reached the stage of burn-out or were nearly there. Stress came in phases rather than as a continuous flow for many of the social workers. Some reported elements of job satisfaction in their work, especially in working with elderly people and in short-term work. The support received by social workers, seniors and team leaders in the study was not enough, in their view, to protect them from the effects of stress, a finding comparable with the main literature on occupational stress. There was some suggestion that the effects of stress were mitigated by experience.

The advantage of the largely qualitative approach used in the foregoing studies is that it allows the researcher to probe in some depth and to make new discoveries along the way. However, innumerable questions are raised which the study method cannot answer, but which indicate the need for empirical studies to complement existing work. This was the approach taken in a Bradford study of 144 SSD social workers, middle management staff and administrators, plus small samples of probation officers and social workers from voluntary organizations (Mawby, 1979). The results showed the respondents in a state of low morale. General background factors, like age and sex, were only weakly related to types of problem raised, but qualifications and experience were significantly related. Over two-thirds of the respondents mentioned the economic problems of clients as a source of pressure on them in their work. Almost two-thirds cited problems with social work management. Nearly a third had problems in collaborating with outside agencies and only just over a quarter referred to difficulties with the job itself, that is, with their roles, contact with clients and relationships with collegues.

Only one other empirical study in the British social work literature directly concerns stress. Scheduled interviews were conducted with 603 social workers and managers in nine SSDs to ascertain the relationship between job satisfaction and organizational structure. The results showed that organizational constraints, like increased control, consciousness of hierarchy and more rule making, did not contribute to the fulfilment of the primary work role and became a source of job dissatisfaction. However, fulfilment of primary work role was correlated with professional activities undertaken outside the SSD; these activities were related to job satisfaction. Such findings are the norm in studies of large bureaucracies such as SSDs have undoubtedly become (Kakabadse and Worral, 1978, p. 51).

Apart from the research evidence and the journal articles referred to above, social work literature generally testifies to the view held by social workers that they experience high levels of stress. One writer (Baker, 1984) declared in a public lecture that he has held workshops for 1100 social workers about stress management and that, in his view, social workers are suffering from high levels of stress. He has met social workers for whom the stress of work has resulted in resignation, or a pretence of hard work, the reduction of contact with clients and colleagues, the denial that there is something wrong, a pretence of caring which shields cynicism, physical sickness, anxiety and even suicide attempts and psychotic episodes.

Despite the shortcomings of a lack of comparable, quantitative data, the literature on stress amongst social workers indicates that the vulnerability of clients, the lack of resources and the organizational constraints encountered by social workers are perceived by those in the field to be major causes of stress.

FACTORS MODERATING STRESSORS

Although there is no clear evidence in the literature on occupational stress that the support of colleagues and supervisors reduces stress, high support was correlated with lack of conflict, lack of role ambiguity, job security, use of skills and participation in decision-making (Pinneau, 1975). The strongest predictor of burn-out was lack of leadership in a study of child abuse projects (Armstrong, 1979). Lack of support and structure related to burn-out in new professionals in a public service agency (Cherniss, 1980). Lack of feedback was associated with burn-out (Maslach and Jackson, 1978) and excessive supervision concerned with line management rather than staff development resulted in job dissatisfaction in studies by Cherniss (1980) and Hall and Schneider (1973).

Support can be defined more broadly than supervision and the help of colleagues in that it can come from good training, values and beliefs, knowledge and acquired skills. However, the formal expression of support in social work is supervision, usually defined as a regular, uninterrupted weekly one-to-one session with the dual purpose of achieving accountability and furthering professional development. It is very highly valued in the social work literature (Bamford, 1982; Pettes, 1979). The textbook ideal is not upheld in practice. Half the subjects in one study referred to supervision as a critical factor, in positive or negative terms, in relation to their ability to cope with stress, but a third were not satisfied with the supervision. It was not of a high enough standard, or was too irregular and there was a fear that supervisors would judge social workers in a way that might affect their careers adversely. Seniors and team leaders were under stress because their communication with senior management was poor. In such situations, people turned to a network of informal support, at home or at work, to help them cope with the demands of the job (Fineman, 1985). Social workers in hospitals may receive less supervision because there are more senior staff who are considered not to need it. The emphasis seems to be more on improving professional practice than on line management.

The provision of informal support is usually thought to be a function of the social work team. It may not be possible to generalize from Fineman's study, but he does pierce the myth to some extent by showing how little team support existed in four of the five teams involved. Despite their position as members of a team, social workers had developed a privatized style in some cases and did not give the impression of being engaged in a common enterprise. The function of the team is not primarily to provide support, but to enable the work to be performed most effectively. However, a valued member of a trusted group will function better than someone who feels isolated and whose contribution is not valued.

A stimulating environment of the kind found in the larger child guidance clinics and some teaching hospitals would be expected to reduce stress. Competition for jobs in the London child guidance clinics is fierce for this reason and because the work is thought not to be stressful.

PERSONAL CHARACTERISTICS OF SOCIAL WORKERS

Stress amongst social workers could be caused by personality factors or personal circumstances, although it is likely that these sources of stress are only significant in a very small number of cases. However, it is possible that social work attracts certain personality types. A survey of 345 social work students, using a personality test, showed that they scored highly for warmth and sympathy, but did badly when it came to decisive thought and action (Rutherford, 1977). This is unfortunate because it is precisely these qualities of decisiveness that appear to have been lacking in social workers involved in child abuse enquiries. Another survey of social workers' personalities was based on tests with eight men and 26 women, using personality deviance scales and a personal disturbance scale. The results showed that the subjects were unlikely to attribute blame to others, were slightly submissive and had a low prevalence of personal disturbance (Bedford and Bedford, 1985, p. 87). However, the finding that social workers tend to be submissive might indicate learned female personality traits as three-quarters of the subjects were women. If these findings can be generalized from such a small sample and social workers are unlikely to be disturbed personalities, it follows that the cause of stress needs to be sought elsewhere.

One writer, drawing from personal experiences, claims that social workers are prone to depression (Charles, 1983). This claim has not been substantiated, but needs to be examined in the light of the fact that most social workers are women and women report more depression than men. It is also possible that people who are vulnerable to depression choose social work rather than another occupation because, unconsciously or otherwise, they wish to work through personal problems by helping others.

Little is known about the personal circumstances of social workers and their effect on working life. The Barclay Report (1982, p. 25) states that 65 per cent of field social workers in Britain are aged between 25 and 45. Most of them are women and of those in this age bracket, many are likely to have children, for whom they will no doubt have assumed the main responsibility. A third of the subjects of Fineman's study of stress amongst social workers (1985, p. 84) reported vulnerability to stress at work because of home circumstances. Some were carers of dependant relatives and others were lonely. Strangely, this study makes no reference to the child care responsibilities of the subjects.

Social workers who are carers may be able to find part-time work or a job-shared post, especially in hospital based social work departments. More flexibility is needed in this direction. However, it cannot be said that social work is free of institutional sexism. Men outnumber women by four to one in senior posts in social work, despite the fact that two-thirds of field social workers are women (Neill *et al.*, 1976).

This situation must be a source of stress for women, who have to work harder than men to succeed in social work as in other fields of endeavour. Nothing is yet known of black social workers' experiences of stress.

A collection of mental health workers' experiences of depression includes personal accounts by two social workers. In both cases, personal circumstances were at the root of the crisis, but there is evidence from the accounts of the authors that the demands of the workplace played a part (Rippere and Williams, 1985).

FUTURE DIRECTIONS

It is clear from the limited evidence available that some social workers consider that they are experiencing high stress levels and others have been observed to behave as if under stress. It seems likely that social workers in health settings are more protected from high stress levels than their area team colleagues. Further research would be likely to reveal that area team social work, particularly in cities, is highly stressful and lacking many of the known attributes of job satisfaction. However, although this chapter has been forced into a comparison between area team and health service social work, it should not be assumed that the latter is not stressful. Social workers in health settings are working in the shadow of a dominant medical profession and handling sensitive and difficult problems concerning illness, serious disability and death.

Considering first the future of research, social work in primary health settings is beginning to establish a credible research base, although more empirical studies are needed. With notable exceptions, hospital based social work has been largely ignored by researchers and writers. Hospital social work departments could follow the example already set in one area and research their own practice, aiming for comparable data. Stress research in any health setting should show awarenes of new developments like Community Mental Handicap Teams and community based mental health services and of budget cuts and restrictions in employment prospects.

Turning to social work practice, some changes in recent years, notably an increase in the proportion of trained social workers, should moderate the effects of stress. Training programmes need to address themselves to the management of stress so that students on all kinds of social work courses can learn to manage stress in themselves and others. The experience of high stress levels will lead to the use of coping mechanisms of a helpful or unhelpful kind and training in the management of stress is crucial to a constructive response. The bureaucratic response to problems is more rule making and therefore employing organizations may not be the best vehicle for stress reduction. There may be no obvious or easy answer: supervision is perhaps too management focused or even too cosy to be successful in reducing stress; peer group supervision relies on supportive team relationships which may not exist. Every solution has potential drawbacks, but if the problem exists in any given social work setting, it needs to be taken seriously and decisions made about how to approach it. Some critics have argued that decentralization, or 'going local' will restrict the opportunities to specialize and result in a fragmented service with little support given to small isolated social work outposts. Others are enthusiastic and hope for a service which is more responsive to community needs while still allowing social workers the chance to specialize. Although it is now recognized that specialization is necessary in social work and senior casework posts are common, no social worker should be expected to specialize only in child abuse, as this would place an intolerable burden on the worker.

The organizations employing social workers are clearly seen to be a source of stress in the studies discussed above. Stress management should not therefore merely be confined to counselling individual social workers, but should also focus on organizational change and on the maintenance of adequate staffing levels, so that social workers are not overloaded.

Although further research should be undertaken, it is not necessary to await the results before tackling the problem. At least one counselling service has been set up for social workers and others exist on a multidisciplinary basis. Employers, training courses and training departments, professional groups and union branches could create opportunities for social workers and their managers to examine stressful aspects of their work and identify necessary and feasible changes. Expensive stress management programmes in the North American style would not be needed (Cooper, 1985, p. 335). An article by Zastrow (1984, 141) examines organizational and individual strategies for the reduction of stress. Organizational strategies range from caseload reduction, to time away from pressure, limiting hours of work, increased training, a pleasant working environment, the development of social supports amongst staff and greater variety of work, Individual strategies include goal setting, time management, learning how to deal with stress, positive thinking, relaxation, exercise, outside activities, treats and the development of a sense of humour.

Reading this list, social workers may think of many reasons why these strategies are impossible to implement. Perhaps the first step towards change is to develop an awareness of the problem and its manifestations, a task in which both researchers and practitioners can join. Opportunities for social workers not only to reduce the workload and its pressures, but also to teach, specialize, undertake research and participate in policy-making are crucial to the maintenance of high standards and the creation of high morale.

REFERENCES

Addison, C. (1980). Tolerating stress in social work practice: the example of a burns units, *British Journal of Social Work*, **10**, 341–56.
Armstrong, K. L. (1979). How to avoid burnout: a study of the relationship between burnout and worker; organisational and management characteristics in 11 Child Abuse and neglect projects, *Child Abuse and Neglect*, **3**.
Baker, R. (1984). *Stress in Welfare Work*. National Children's Home, Occasional Papers, no 5, 1–24.
Bamford, T. (1982). *Managing Social Work*, Tavistock, pp. 49–69, 171.
Barclay, P. M. (1982). *Social Workers: Their Role and Tasks*, Bedford Square Press, p.25.
Bedford, A. and Bedford, J. (1985). Personality and personal disturbance in social workers, *British Journal of Social Work*, **15**, 87–90.

Browne, E. (1982). *Mental Handicap: The Role for Social Workers*. University of Sheffield: Joint Unit for Social Services Research, pp. 26-8.
Charles, J. (1983). When carers crash, *Social Work Today*, **15**, 12, 18-20.
Cherniss, C. (1980). *Staff Burnout—Job Stress in the Human Services*, Sage.
Cherniss, C. and Egnatios, E. (1978). Is There Satisfaction in Community Mental Health? *Community Mental Health Journal*, **14**.
Cooper, B. et al. (1975). Mental health care in the community: an evaluative study, *Psychological Medicine*, 372-80.
Cooper, C. (1985). The road to health in American firms, *New Society*, 6 Sept., 335-6.
Corney, R. and Briscoe, M. (1977). Investigation into two different types of attachment schemes, *Social Work Today*, **9**, 15, 10-14.
Corney, R. (1979). Different styles of intervention, *Social Work Today*, **11**, 1, 15-17.
Davies, M. (1984). Training: what we think of it now, *Social Work Today*, 24 Jan., 12-17.
Fineman, S. (1985). *Social Work Stress and Intervention*, Gower, pp. 57, 84, 113.
Freudenberger, H. (1974). Staff burnout, *Journal of Social Issues*, **30**.
Gammack, G. (1985). Split personality, *Social Work Today*, 26 Aug., 13-15.
Gilchrist, C. et al. (1978). Social work in general practice, *J. of the Royal College of General Practitioners*, **28**, 675-86.
Glastonbury, B., Cooper, D. and Hawkins, P. (1982). *Social Work in Conflict*, British Association of Social Workers.
Goldberg, E. and Neill, J. (1972). *Social Work in General Practice*, Allen & Unwin.
Hall, D. and Schneider, B. (1973). *Organisational Climates and Careers*, Seminar Press.
Holt, R. (1982). Occupational stress. In L. Goldberger and S. Breznitz (eds) *Handbook of Stress: Theoretical & Clinical Aspects*, Free Press, pp. 419-44.
Jayaratne, S. and Chess, W. A. (1983). Job satisfaction and burnout in social workers. In B. A. Farber (ed.) *Stress and Burnout in the Human Service Professions*.
Jayaratne, S., Tripodi, T. and Chess, W. A. (1983). Perceptions of emotional support; stress and strain in male and female social workers, *Social Work Research and Abstracts*, **19** (2), 19-27.
Kakabadse, A. P. and Worral, R. (1978). Job satisfaction and organisational structure: a comparative study of nine social services departments, *British Journal of Social Work*, **8**, 51-70.
Law, E. (1982). Light on hospital social work: a major study in Manchester, *Social Work Service*, **29**, 24.
Lazarus, R. S. and Folkman, S. (1984). *Stress, Appraisal and Coping*, Springer.
Maslach, C. (1982). *Burnout—The Cost of Caring*, Prentice-Hall.
Maslach, C. and Pines, A. (1977). The burnout syndrome in the day care setting, *Child Care Quarterly*, **6**.
Maslach, C. and Jackson, S. E. (1978). A Scale Measure to Assess Experienced Burnout: The Maslach Burnout Inventory. Paper presented to the Convention of the Western Psychological Association, San Francisco.
Mawby, R. I. (1979). Social work under pressure, *International Social Work*, **22**, 47-57.
Moore, J. (1984). Like a rabbit caught in headlights, *Community Care*, 4 Nov., 18-19.
Murray, N. (1985). Occupational Hazards, *Community Care*, 5 Sept., 14-15.
Neill, J. et al. (1976). Post Seebohm social services (1): the social worker's viewpoint, *Social Work Today*, **8**, 5.
Otton, (1974). *Social Work Support for the Health Service*, HMSO.
Parsloe, P. and Stevenson, O. (1978). *Social Service Teams: The Practitioner's View*, HMSO, pp. 227, 281, 288, 293, 300, 325.
Pettes, D. (1979). *Staff and Student Supervision*, Allen & Unwin.
Parry, G. and Gowler, D. (1983) Career stresses on psychological therapists. In D.

Pilgrim, (ed.) *Psychology and Psychotherapy: Current Trends and Issues*, Routledge & Kegan Paul.
Pines, A. M. (1982). Changing organisations. In W. S. Paine (ed.) *Job Stress and Burnout Research Theory and Intervention Perspectives*, Sage Publications.
Pinneau, S. R. (1975). Effects of social support on psychological and physiological strains. PhD thesis, University of Michigan, Ann Arbor.
Rippere, V. and Williams, R. (1985). *Wounded Healers: Mental Health Workers Experiences of Depression*, Wiley.
Rushton, A. and Briscoe, M. (1981). Social work as an aspect of primary health care: the social worker's view, *British Journal of Social Work*, **11**, 61–76.
Rushton, A. and Davies, P. (1984). *Social Work and Health Care*, Gower, p. 39 and Ch. 6.
Rutherford, D. (1977). Personality in social work students, *Social Work Today*, **8**, 9–10.
Rutter, M. (1981). Stress, coping and development: some issues and some questions, *J. Child Psychology and Psychiatry*, **22**, 4, 323–56.
Satyamurti, C. (1981). *Occupational Survival*, Blackwell, pp. 100, 124.
Shepherd, M., Cooper, B., Brown, A. and Kalton, G. W. (1966). *Psychiatric Illness in General Practice*, Oxford University Press.
Seebohm, F. (1968). *Report of the Committee on the Local Authority and Allied Personal Services*, HMSO.
Selye, H. (1982). History and present status of the stress concept. In L. Goldberger and S. Bresnitz (eds) *Handbook of Stress: Theoretical and Clinical Aspects*, Free Press, p. 7.
Taylor Brown, S., Johnson, K. H., Hunter, K. and Rockowitz, R. J. (1981). Stress identification for social workers in health care: a preventive approach to burnout, *Social Work in Health Care*, **7**, 91–101.
Weinburg, S., Edwards, G. and Garove, W. E. (1979). *Burnout Among Employees of Residential Facilities Serving Developmentally Disabled Persons*, University of Alabama.
Zastrow, C. (1984). Understanding and preventing burnout, *British Journal of Social Work*, **14**, 141–55.

Stress in Health Professionals
Edited by R. Payne and J. Firth-Cozens
© 1987 John Wiley & Sons Ltd

Chapter 10

Stress in Psychiatric Nursing*

J. Graham Jones

INTRODUCTION

Marshall (1980) notes that 'most writers start by taking the existence of stress among nurses for granted' (p. 20). This is perhaps not surprising when one considers that, among all professional groups, nursing has one of the highest rates of suicide and nurses top the list of psychiatric out-patient referrals (Gillespie and Gillespie, 1986). Bailey (1985) lists nurses as among a group of health professionals who may be regarded as 'the casualties of caring' as there is a growing amount of evidence to suggest that the nursing profession can indeed be a stressful one (Bailey, 1981; Claus and Bailey, 1980; Marshall, 1980).

Stress among nurses is a much researched area of interest. Several studies have identified dimensions of work demand experienced by nurses (e.g. Gray-Toft and Anderson, 1981; Ivancevich and Smith, 1981) while others have examined relationships between work demand and the affective and behavioural responses of nurses such as job satisfaction, job tension and performance (e.g. Bateman and Strasser, 1983; Ivancevich and Smith, 1982; Vredenburgh and Trinkaus, 1983). Furthermore, comparative studies of stress among nurses in different units (e.g. Gray-Toft and Anderson, 1981; Nichols, Springford and Searle, 1981; Parkes, 1982), among nurses with different levels of experience (e.g. Ivancevich and Smith, 1982), and among nurses with different types of qualifications (e.g. Gray-Toft and Anderson, 1981) have been carried out.

Whilst referring to nursing in general as a potentially stressful profession it is important to emphasize that nurses cannot be regarded as a homogeneous category. Marshall (1980) points out that stressors may be different for different types of nurse, for different types of ward and for different types of hospital. For example, Miller (1976) examined three contrasting types of general hospital in the United States and reported large differences in organizational structure and climate, staff attitudes, and type of patient which he then related to different causes of stress. Thus, it is clear that to make a statement to the effect that

---

* This work was carried out whilst the author was a Research Fellow at the MRC/ESRC Social and Applied Unit, Sheffield University.

nursing in general is a stressful profession is very much an over-generalization. This chapter discusses stress in a particular specialty area which has been sorely neglected, psychiatric nursing. Powell (1982) argues that psychiatric nursing is not just another specialty but is 'the other half of nursing' (p. 85) in that the role of the psychiatric nurse is quite different from that of the general nurse. The basis of their activities, he argues, rests on quite separate beliefs and traditions which are largely incompatible with one another. Powell believes that there is no similarity, except that both types of nurse are responsible for the care of patients, and that even so, the care that the psychiatric patient requires is fundamentally different from that required by a patient with a physical illness. It follows, therefore, that the intensity and sources of stress experienced by psychiatric nurses may differ from that experienced in other specialty nursing areas.

A computerized literature search of nursing stress revealed a paucity of studies which have examined stress in psychiatric nurses. Most of these studies have focused on nurses who work in physical health settings, such as intensive care units. However, as Dawkins *et al.* (1985) remark, 'since it is reasonable to assume that nurses who work in mental health settings are as susceptible to stress as other nurses, it is surprising that research has not yet systematically identified the sources of stress for this group' (p. 9). This chapter attempts to throw some light on this issue. However, it is first of all important to gain some knowledge and understanding of the environment in which the psychiatric nurse works, the role that the psychiatric nurse plays within that environment, and the nature of the psychiatric patient.

THE ROLE AND ENVIRONMENT OF THE PSYCHIATRIC NURSE

Traditionally, psychiatric nursing has been regarded as a lower status activity than general nursing and has attracted fewer highly educated recruits (Brooking, 1985). Brooking argues that this stems largely from the low status of nineteenth-century asylum attendants which has been passed down to late twentieth-century psychiatric nurses. Victorian asylums were large, usually isolated institutions where 'certified' undesirables were housed and in which the role of the asylum attendants was essentially custodial. Powell (1982) cites several studies carried out in the 1950s and 1960s which portray a similar function of mid-twentieth-century mental hospitals. Investigations carried out in American state mental hospitals (Belknap, 1956; Caudill, 1958; Cumming and Cumming, 1964) characterized the environment as being custodial in nature and in which the patients were regarded as irrational, irresponsible, without hope and requiring ordered and regulated care. This environment, accompanied by strict role differentiation of status levels, served to produce an atmosphere of impersonality, suspicion and distrust in attitudes and relationships. Martin (1959), referring to a syndrome of 'institutionalization', and Barton (1959), describing the situation as one of 'institutional neurosis', identified a similar system in operation in Britain. They described an environment in which the patients were apathetic and submissive and in which the ward staff were isolated and entrenched, carrying out their functions in an impersonal, task-orientated manner.

Out of these studies arose the belief that the role of the psychiatric nurse should not be merely a custodial one but that the nurse could also provide social stimulation and foster an atmosphere conducive to recovery. Consequently, the modern notion of the psychiatric nurse that has emerged is that their role is a multidimensional one. Cormack (1983) identifies the very diverse nature of the psychiatric nurse's prescriptive roles, comprising those of a doctor's assistant, sociotherapeutic, psychotherapeutic, behavioural and administrative roles. However, Cormack is extremely wary of such a diverse and seemingly demanding prescriptive role: 'the new role prescriptions, which supersede those of the nurse as a custodian and follower of "doctors orders" have undoubtedly confused, rather than clarified, the psychiatric nurse's role' (p. 18). In addition, the fact that the nurse's role also varies according to the nature of the work setting, e.g. acute versus psychogeriatric wards, further complicates the matter.

Patients are admitted into psychiatric hospitals for a variety of reasons but generally because they need treatment and are having difficulty in coping with life in the outside world. The large majority of these are short-stay patients, reflecting the recent trend towards discharging patients into the care of community services as soon as possible. In some cases 'dangerous patients', who pose a physical threat to themselves and others, are admitted into Special Hospitals in which there is a high security element which instils a prison-like atmosphere and environment. Bickerton, Sampson and Boylan (1979) have identified six general categories of conditions which psychiatric nurses may encounter amongst patients: organic conditions, including dementia and Huntington's chorea; psychotic conditions, including mania, schizophrenia and depression; neurotic conditions, including anxiety, phobias and obsessions; personality disorders, including psychopathic disorders; drug and alcohol dependence; and other disorders, such as anorexia nervosa.

The various wards in a typical psychiatric hospital catering for long-stay patients will provide accommodation for eating and sleeping and there will be workshops where patients can learn a trade or develop a hobby. Many hospitals have integrated wards in which male and female patients are cared for by a mixed staff of male and female nurses. The typical activities of the patients and staff on a continuing care psychiatric ward are well documented by Armitage (1986) who carried out an observational study of a twenty-bed ward in a large psychiatric hospital. This particular environment was characterized by a 'scruffy decor and well-worn soft furnishing as well as an overriding feeling of lack of space' (Armitage, 1986; p. 114). The patients on this ward spent most of the day in the occupational therapy or industrial therapy departments. The twenty patients were all male and the large majority had been diagnosed as schizophrenic. The average patient was in his mid-forties, having spent nearly half of his life in a psychiatric hospital. The staff on duty for these twenty patients varied from a relatively generous complement in the context of this particular hospital, such as a charge nurse, a state enrolled nurse (SEN), a student nurse and a nursing assistant, to a barely adequate complement of a staff nurse and two nursing assistants. The most frequently observed patient behaviour on the ward was sitting in the day room smoking, sleeping, or watching television. The nurse behaviour which was most frequent related to administrative and maintenance activities. Administrative duties included: keeping records; answering the telephone; reporting to other health care professionals, etc. Maintenance duties fell into three categories: maintenance of (1) patients' nutrition; (2) patients' personal hygiene; and (3) ward environment. Armitage emphasizes that surprisingly little nurse/patient interaction took place. Nurses tended to sit together talking to each other, playing board games with each other or watching television.

Fraser and Cormack (1975) report similar findings from a study in which nine patients were observed in a long-stay psychiatric ward. These authors also report an extremely low level of social activity on the ward and little interaction between the nurses and patients. Again the patients spent the majority of their time (at least 75 per cent) seated and the rest of it standing, looking out of the window or engaged in some ritualistic behaviour. The role of the nurse in this environment was, therefore, mainly one of observation and carrying out routine maintenance duties.

To characterize the activities observed by Armitage (1986) and Fraser and Cormack (1975) as typical of psychiatric nursing is, of course, very much an over-generalization. Towell's (1975) study of the roles of nursing assistants, pupil nurses and student nurses on three different types of psychiatric ward in the same hospital demonstrates that such a generalization is not possible. On the admissions ward, containing short-stay acutely-ill patients, nurses played a key linking role between the patients and most aspects of hospital arrangements. Nurses were concerned with acting as adjuncts to the medical staff in somatic treatment, with social interaction forming a significant component of their work. On the geriatric ward the nurses' dominant concern was with the administration of the basic physical necessitites for the patients, spending little time in verbal interaction with them. On the therapeutic community ward physical treatment was de-emphasized and nurses were mainly involved in interaction with patients. Towell concluded that the label 'psychiatric nurse' in fact encompasses a cluster of different roles, varying according to the setting in which they are performed.

Whilst it is clear that the role of the psychiatric nurse is dependent on the specific setting it is also apparent that in some circumstances there is a gulf between the role which is prescribed for nurses and their actual role (Cormack, 1976, 1983; Towell, 1975). Cormack (1983) states that the prescriptive and descriptive literatures relating to the role of the psychiatric nurse do not coincide in that nurses do not appear to be doing what they ought to be doing. The findings of Armitage (1986) and Fraser and Cormack (1975) in which the nurse's role was observed as comprising mainly observation and routine maintenance duties at the expense of providing a therapeutic milieu seems to support Cormack's claim.

POTENTIAL SOURCES OF STRESS IN PSYCHIATRIC NURSING

Patient Contact

The general attitude of nurses towards psychiatric patients is reflected in a study carried out by Wilkinson (1982). This was designed to examine whether brief training in a general hospital psychiatric unit affected the attitudes of a group of general nursing students towards psychiatric patients. The trainee nurses were asked to rate descriptions of twelve patients in terms of what they would expect it to be like to nurse such cases if they arrived as acute admissions to a general hospital. The case summaries comprised six patients with mainly medical problems, such as a burst duodenal ulcer or a broken leg, and six matched patients with mainly psychiatric problems, including severe depression, alcohol dependency and obsessive-compulsive neurosis. The findings demonstrated that both before and after a nine week period of psychiatric training the main component in the nurses' ratings was a factor of fear or threat accompanied by disgust which was most closely associated with the psychiatric patients described. Wilkinson reported that the nurses overwhelmingly regarded the psychiatrically labelled patients as more frightening, less likely to co-operate with treatments, and more likely to be violent and dangerous.

Taylor (1983) characterizes the 'plight' of some psychiatric nurses as follows:

> Left alone to cope at night in a ward of thirty or more patients, many of them doubly incontinent and violent, she may have to reach for unknown depths within herself in order to survive.... Nurses spend long hours, sometimes a working lifetime, in desolate wards, absorbing despair and hopelessness. The effect of such exposure has never been calculated. (p. 17).

Wallis (1986) describes a series of studies of nurses working in the psychogeriatric wards of several urban and rural psychiatric hospitals. Despite expressing a relatively high level of general satisfaction with their jobs the nurses identified a range of sources of dissatisfaction and frustration, of which patient contact was prominent. It was apparent that the nursing staff saw themselves as dealing with an intractable problem. They were responsible for caring for as many as thirty elderly patients in a ward, among whom diagnoses included dementia and psychosis. Many of them had been there for more than a decade and few would leave before their deaths. The nurses had to deal with behaviour which ranged from unpredictable violent outbursts to virtual withdrawal, and incontinence was endemic. Furthermore, nurses' hours of work were often long and the physical surroundings often drab and sparsely equipped. As Wallis (1986) notes, 'these are not high among the conditions one might wish to offer anyone as a recipe for high quality of working life'.

A dominant potential source of stress through patient contact involves violent behaviour from patients. Campbell and Mawson (1978) have described the problems and anxieties created by violence within a psychiatric unit. The particular unit referred to by these authors admits patients from a catchment area. This necessarily means that each ward within the unit contains a wide mixture of patients in terms of age, sex and diagnosis. From this patient mix Campbell and Mawson identify those patients who are unpredictably violent as presenting the biggest problem. All of them are middle-aged, diagnosed as psychotic with evidence of paranoid traits, of below average intelligence, and have caused serious injuries either to themselves or others. Three examples of such cases described by Campbell and Mawson are presented below:

Case No.1:
A 45-year-old man who was admitted only two days after being precipitately discharged from Rampton Maximum Security Hospital by a Mental Health Tribunal. He came with a very violent reputation and 23 years of institutionalization behind him, including convictions for grievous bodily harm. Whilst in hospital he attacked one female patient and caused immense anxiety to staff and other patients, with his threats of violence and aggressive behaviour. His stay in hospital lasted two and a half months and it culminated with him beating up a charge nurse following which he was removed by police and then transferred to Rampton.

Case No. 2:
Is a 39-year-old woman who had spent most of her life in mental hospitals and prisons. She attacked staff and patients, all of whom were women. She appeared to choose her victims carefully and caused a great deal of anxiety. After six admissions, lasting 2-3 months at a time, she was finally transferred to Broadmoor.

Case No. 3:
Is a 52-year-old man, diagnosed as schizophrenic. He is currently a patient within the unit and has been for the last 3 years. All in all he has had 17 admissions to the unit. His behaviour is characterized by unpredictable periods of aggression and violence towards himself and others, especially women. It is common for him to attempt to strangle people suddenly and without warning. Seventy such incidents have been recorded to date, the most serious of these are once when he viciously attacked a nurse with a zimmer aid, and another when he threw himself from a top storey window sustaining multiple injuries. Periodically he is nursed in one of the side-rooms, sometimes at his own request. It has not been possible for him to be placed in another hospital.

Extreme cases of this sort are usually dealt with in Special Hospitals. Since these represent very secure insitutions it is possible to compare the nursing staff in Special Hospitals to other custodial staff such as prison officers. There is some evidence to suggest that the job of a prison officer is a relatively stressful one. According to the Occupational Mortality Statistics (published by the Office of Population Census and Surveys, 1979), the number of deaths due to ischaemic heart disease was significantly higher in prison officers than in the general population. Smith (1984) reports evidence from North America that psychosomatic disorders such as incidences of back or skin trouble, hypertension and stomach complaints in prison officers are considerably higher than in the general population. Smith provides further North American statistics to show that prison officers have been found to have low psychological well-being as seen in complaints over their quality and quantity of sleep, nightmares, and excessive ruminations about work. A study by Smith (1985) further shows that prison officers score higher on feelings of fatigue, tiredness and cognitive confusion when compared with a normal working population. If one accepts that the job of a psychiatric nurse working in a Special Hospital is partly akin to that of a prison officer then the evidence does suggest that the job is a relatively stressful one.

Administrative and Organizational Factors

Brooking (1985) states that advancement in psychiatric nursing appears to be occurring at a slower pace than in general nursing, a factor to which she attributes a 'vicious circle' as being the main cause (see Figure 1). The underlying assumption of this cycle is that psychiatric nursing offers a low level of patient care. The resulting low level of morale and loss of prestige has, in turn, led to a lack of effective leaders because the profession has attracted less well educated recruits. This, accompanied by inadequate psychiatric training provision and lack of research, has resulted in poorly educated nurses. According to Brooking, this lack of educational provision has adversely affected nurses at all levels and has contributed to the largely negative public image of the psychiatric nurse. Wallis (1986) and Cope and Cox (1980) offer empirical support for Brooking's claims in studies in which nurses expressed unhappiness with their training at all levels.

Brooking also views the 'vicious circle' as being largely responsible for the 'role erosion' of psychiatric nursing. She states that the lack of a clearly defined role has meant that psychiatric nurses have failed to break away from medical domination: 'the excessive identification with general nurses has resulted in failure to develop an effective therapeutic function' (p. 464). This presents problems for psychiatric nurses who are trapped in the gulf between the role which is prescribed for nurses and the role which they actually perform in practice, a predicament evident in the studies of Armitage (1986) and Fraser and

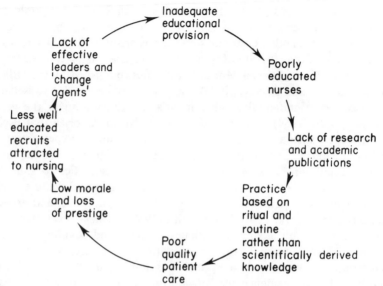

Figure 1 The 'vicious circle' in psychiatric nursing. Reproduced by permission of Blackwell Scientific Publications Ltd from Brooking (1985)

Cormack (1975) reported in the previous section. Wallis (1986) reports findings from Cope (1981) which support the contention that nurses have too little time available, largely due to staff shortages, for interpersonal, direct, patient care at a psychological level. Cope and Cox (1980) similarly report that the nurses in their study of a 400-bed rural mental hospital claimed that they were prevented from spending enough time with the patients so that, again, patient care was seen mainly in custodial terms and with little emphasis on practising the social and psychological skills in which they had been trained. A cross-section of staff in this study also reported lack of clarity about the general goals and objectives of the hospital. No one was clear what the hospital as a whole, or the wards in particular, were really trying to achieve. Vague goals were sometimes suggested by the nurses but none showed awareness of specific concrete goals which could act as a guide for the day to day functioning of staff. Wallis (1986) similarly reports nurses on psychogeriatric wards as displaying elements of confusion and anxiety, of being unsure 'where they were going', and uncertain about what the goals of a psychogeriatric unit could or should be.

Another potentially stressful factor for psychiatric nurses is poor communication. The nurses studied by Cope and Cox (1980) were particularly dissatisfied with communication between management and ward staff. The ward staff had little idea about what senior management did. They were seen as remote and out of touch with problems on wards and overall communication from the top downwards was seen as poor. Nurses also stated that it was sometimes unclear where responsibility and authority lay. Secker (1983) views this as a major problem:

> Psychiatric nursing is good work but I am saddened by the growth of bureaucracy which has taken away decision-making from the first-line managers, the charge nurses. Unless the men and women who hold these key positions are stimulated and encouraged to take a lot more responsibility I cannot see psychiatry attracting and keeping the calibre of nurse it needs. (p. 64).

Wallis (1986) similarly identifies inadequate consultation and communication both within wards and with managers resulting in non-involvement in decision-making as a major problem. This factor has been shown to be strongly related to the size of the psychiatric hospital. Rump (1979) studied a number of psychiatric hospitals in Australia and found that satisfaction amongst nurses in most ranks is negatively related to size, defined in terms of the number of staff, and he identified one of the major factors as communication between nurses and the psychiatric and medical staff. In a large institution the social distance between the professions appears to be accentuated. Futhermore, the types of demands inherent in the psychiatric hospital environment are common to what Goffman (1961) calls 'total institutions'. These demands include administrative and bureaucratic problems which may be attributed to strict accountability, lack of communication, and of standardization of policies. There are also specific and unique factors affecting the way nurses perceive their jobs, such as fear of assault and accusations of malpractice.

The last factor mentioned, accusations of malpractice, presents a problem in itself to the psychiatric nurse and serves to demonstrate another potential threat to the nurse, that is, lack of support from management. Considerable media attention has recently been given to alleged cruelty and violence towards patients by staff in some psychiatric hospitals, and particularly in Special Hospitals. Taylor (1983) severely criticizes the attitude and behaviour of the senior management in such circumstances:

> When a nurse strikes a patient in a mental hospital, the authorities and the press are usually very quick, if not eager, to react and to demonstrate their concern and moral outrage. The implication is that the nurse alone is to blame. The hospital completely dissociates itself from the act and the nurse often takes full responsibility for the inadequacies of the system. (p. 72).

Taylor feels that this is partly due to ignorance on the part of the administration who are unaware of the difficulties or 'emotional overloading' that the nurses experience: 'administrators in any capacity deal with words and figures and the implementation of proposals. The people they deal with do not usually break windows, defecate on the floor or mutilate themselves and others' (p. 72).

An additional problem facing the psychiatric nurse, which is closely related to accusations of malpractice, concerns that of legal responsibility. The helping professions are under increasing pressure to protect themselves from law suits brought privately by dissatisfied clients. Gomersall (1987) describes a situation in which legal protection takes precedence over the welfare of the client. The trend is for workers to safeguard themselves by rigidly following formalized and established policies and procedures. Gomersall describes this as 'defensive caring'. He cites as an example the close observation, or 'specialling' of patients in psychiatric units:

> at present the legal responsibility of the person performing the 'specialling' task is not always defined, but the very process of labelling an aspect of care in this way means that such legal responsibility is implicit and when harm does ensue then the member of staff will be likely to be held responsible (Gomersall, 1987).

In summary, this brief discussion suggests that psychiatric nursing is a potentially stressful occupation. The evidence suggests that nurses experience a variety of situtational variables which Cooper and Payne (1978) have identified as related to affective, behavioural and health measures of strain. These include role overload (caused mainly by staff shortages), role conflict and ambiguity (caused by lack of a clearly defined role), lack of communication, lack of participation in decisions, low autonomy, and lack of support from the management. The following section discusses the small number of empirical studies of the determinants and/or levels of stress in psychiatric nursing, some of which address these types of issues.

EMPIRICAL EVIDENCE

The very few empirical studies of stress in psychiatric nursing (to this author's knowledge there are only six studies which relate specifically to psychiatric nursing) which will be discussed here supports the statement made earlier in this chapter that this is a sorely neglected area of research. Of this small number, half are considered to be ill-designed with respect to general methodology and sample sizes so that they are not able to contribute to our present knowledge and, therefore, are not discussed here. Consequently, three studies remain which are considered in some detail.

The first of these studies is that reported by Cronin-Stubbs and Brophy (1984). This study is not necessarily concerned with stress as such but with a concept which is becoming increasingly popular, particularly in the North American literature—'burnout'. Maslach and Jackson (1981) define burnout as '... a syndrome of emotional exhaustion and cynicism that occurs frequently among individuals who do "people-work" of some kind' (p. 99). Thus, burnout is characterized by emotional exhaustion and negative, cynical attitudes and feelings about one's clients and one's self. This view of burnout sees the problem as a response to excessive stress (Bailey, 1985). Cronin-Stubbs and Brophy's study was primarily designed to examine burnout, measured by the Staff Burnout Scale for Health Professionals (Jones, 1980), and the moderating effects of social support, measured by the Norbeck Social Support Questionnaire (Norbeck, Lindsey and Carrieri, 1981). Two hundred and ninety-six staff nurses were involved in the study. The nurses were all female and worked in one of four specialty areas at one of the three large (900 to 1100 beds) American metropolitan medical centre hospitals. Psychiatric nurses ($n = 66$), were compared with nurses working in the operating room ($n = 65$), intensive care ($n = 74$) and medical ($n = 91$) specialty areas. The nurses were typically single, aged between 21 and 30 years old, and employed as nurses for between two and ten years.

Consistent with previous research (Pines and Kanner, 1982), social support was negatively associated and predictive of burnout. The findings from semi-structured interviews indicated that differences existed, not only in the nursing tasks performed, but also in the estimated amounts of interpersonal involvement and conflict experienced by the nurses. Psychiatric nurses reported experiencing greater intense interpersonal involvement and frequent conflicts with patients, families and colleagues than the other three categories of nurses. The psychiatric nurses also reported experiencing less on-the-job and off-the-job affirmation or feedback from others than intensive care nurses, and this variable was predictive of burnout. Cronin-Stubbs and Brophy suggest that this is due to the fact that most of their care occurs as interactions within the nurse–patient relationship so that psychiatric nurses' interventions are less observable and outcomes less concrete than are intensive care nurses'. They further suggest that in the case of their domestic lives psychiatric nurses may withdraw from intense relationships or find it difficult to step out of their roles as helpers to engage in mutually validating relationships. The results also seem to indicate that psychiatric nurses receive less aid or direct assistance than operating room nurses. The authors suggest that this may be due to the fact that members of a surgical team are dependent upon one another for the performance of their functions, whilst interdependence is not essential in the psychiatric nurses' work. These results suggest, therefore, that when compared with some other specialty nursing areas, psychiatric nurses are relatively low in both emotional and material support, making them potentially more prone to burnout. Unfortunately, the authors do not present mean burnout scores so that it is not possible to determine what proportion of the sample experience burnout and to what degree.

The second study is one which attempted to identify and quantify the stresses that occur in the lives of nurses working in a typical, large psychiatric hospital in the United States (Dawkins, Depp and Selzer, 1985). The sample in this study comprised 43 nurses, 41 of whom were females. Twenty-nine held supervisory positions and 14 were staff nurses, with an age range from 26 to 68 and a mean of 43. The average length of employment at the hospital amongst this sample was 10 years.

The study required nurses to rate the degree of stressfulness of each of 78 items or events that comprised the Psychiatric Nurses' Occuptional Stress Scale (PNOSS). The methodology adopted by Dawkins *et al.* is very similar to the Holmes and Rahe (1967) Social Readjustment Rating Scale technique. This procedure involves respondents comparing each event with a commonly experienced anchor event that has been assigned an arbitrary value of 500. Respondents are instructed to assign a proportionately higher number than 500 if they think that the event requires more adjustment than the anchor, and a proportionately lower number than 500 if it requires less adjustment. The geometric mean of the respondents' stress estimates for each event is then calculated and divided by ten. Finally, each event is rank ordered from most to least stressful. The anchor event used in Dawkins *et al.*'s PNOSS was 'a physical threat by a patient' and was chosen because '... it is an event that occurs frequently enough to be experienced by all clinical staff and its stressfulness is consensually acknowledged' (p. 10). The authors arbitrarily labelled items ranked 1 to 26 as 'high stressors', items ranked 27 to 52 as 'moderate stressors', and items ranked 53 to 78 as 'low stressors'. Those items which ranked as high stressors are presented in Table 1. Notice that individual items are also categorized as being attributable to six factors which were independently grouped by two of the investigators (interrater agreement was 0.90): negative characteristics of patients; administrative/organizational issues; limited resources; staff performance; staff conflicts; and scheduling issues.

Table 1   Psychiatric nurses' occupational stress scale items ranked as 'high stressors' (based on Dawkins, Depp and Selzer, 1985)

Items	Geometric mean	Rank	Category*
Not being notified of changes before they occur	125	1	A
Dealing with people in key management positions who are unable to make decisions	95	2	A
Lack of support from administration	88	3	A
Having excessive paperwork	84	4	A
Working for administration that believes in change for the sake of change	81	5	A
Being responsible for too many widely divergent things	72	6	A
Not having suggestions acted on in a timely fashion	65	7	A
Trying to do the job in spite of no one listening or caring	65	8	A

Stress in psychiatric nursing

Items	Geometric mean	Rank	Category*
Receiving no recognition for a job well done	64	9	A
Having adminstrative work interfere with patient care	61	10	A
The 'system' that never listens to suggestions from peers	60	11	A
Lack of adequate staffing in potentially dangerous environments	57	12	R
Working with hostile patients on an inadequately staffed ward	54	13	R
Having a shortage of patient's clothing	51	14	R
A physical threat by a patient	50	15	N
Having an employee reassigned to other units against his wishes	47	16	SC
Working with unskilled, non-professionals who resent new ideas	45	18	SC
Working with poorly motivated staff	45	18	SC
Lack of communication between disciplines	45	19	A
Having a doctor fail to notify staff of changes in patient's order and being held responsible	44	20	SC
Convincing doctors to order adequate medication	43	21	SC
Dealing with the hassle that occurs when you try to take action against incompetent staff	39	22	SP
Finding out what warehouse does not have ward supplies	39	23	R
Having another take credit for an idea or project that I initiated and worked hard on	38	24	SC
Receiving no response from complaints to chief Nurse after going through channels	36	25	A
Covering other wards because of unscheduled absences of other RNs	36	26	S

	No. of items in PNOSS	No. of high stress items
*N = Negative characteristics of patients	7	1
A = Administrative/organizational issues	25	13
R = Limited resources	17	4
SP = Staff performance	5	1
SC = Staff conflicts	16	6
S = Scheduling issues	8	1
Total	78	26

Thirteen of the high stress items, including the first eleven, are classified as arising from administrative/organizational issues. These thirteen items can be summarized as dealing with issues related to working in an 'unresponsive, unappreciative, uncommunicative work environment that makes changes for the sake of change, and that makes too many widely divergent demands on nurses (Dawkins, Depp and Selzer, 1985; p. 11). Staff conflicts may be viewed as a second major determinant of stress as it accounts for six of the high stress items, including 'having an employee assigned to other units against his wishes' and 'working with poorly motivated staff'. Limited resources follows in third place with four items which deal with such issues as working with hostile patients on an independently staffed ward, or finding out that the warehouse does not have ward supplies or clothing for patients. Negative patient characteristics ('a physical threat by a patient'), staff performance ('dealing with the hassle that occurs when you try to take action against incompetent staff') and scheduling issues ('covering other wards because of unscheduled absences of other RNs') are each represented by one item.

The authors conclude that psychiatric nurses view administrative and organizational shortcomings as the most stressful. Rather surprisingly, the findings suggest that negative patient characteristics are viewed as relatively unstressful. However, these results should be viewed with some caution. Firstly, the sample is a rather small one for this type of study. Furthermore, this sample does not constitute a cross-section of psychiatric nurses as it mainly comprises nurses in supervisory roles. Thus, they may have more involvement in administration than with patients as such. Secondly, as the authors emphasize, only 11 of the 78 items (i.e. those dealing with seclusion, convalescent leave and working with hostile patients) on the scale are specific to psychiatric hospitals. Of these 11 items, only four are perceived as generating high levels of stress. The remaining 67 items, representing the vast majority, refer to events that are experienced in general hospitals and by other speciality areas of nursing. Nevertheless, this study does provide a more detailed insight into aspects of the job which may be stressful to psychiatric nurses.

The final study reported in this section is that reported by Jones *et al.* (1987) and is an examination of stress levels in a sample of 349 nurses working in a large Special Hospital in England. This sample is rather unusual in nursing in that 73 per cent were males but this reflects the fact that the patients in this type of environment can be extremely dangerous. The sample was also rather unusual compared with some other psychiatric nursing samples in that 46 per cent had spouses working in the same hospital. This reflects the fact that this hospital is situated in a small, rural, closely-knit community in which it is a major source of employment. The independent measures in this study were nursing rank, sex, and whether a nurse had a spouse working in the hospital. Dependent health and well-being measures were general psychological distress, measured through the 12-item version of the General Health Questionnaire (GHQ) (Goldberg, 1972; Goldberg and Hillier, 1979), supplemented by the 7-item anxiety and depression scales (Goldberg and Hillier, 1979). Other dependent measures included perceived level of job demands and job supports/constraints. These were included in accordance with Payne's (1979) proposal that the wide range of situational variables that have been found to relate to strain can be parsimoniously encompassed by a model of occupational stress which involves the balance between these three factors.

The 30-item job demands scale and the 37-item job supports/constraints scale were generated by a combination of visits to wards and discussions with individuals from all levels of the nursing hierarchy. Principal components analysis of the job demands scale demonstrated the multidimensional nature of the nurse's role. Three types of demand emerged: 'administration', including such factors as 'contribute to conference meetings' and 'report patients' progress to medical staff'; 'patient supervision', comprising items such as 'continually observe patients'; and 'aversive' demands, including items such as 'undertake work I consider unnecessary' and 'work with patients I am afraid of'. Five types of support/constraint emerged: 'communication', including items which asked about the quality of communication between wards, between nursing staff and medical officers, and between shifts; 'administration', including items relating to administrative practice in the hospital and the clarity and speed with which management decisions are conveyed to nursing staff; 'social attitudes', focusing on the view of the hospital created by the media and the image or reputation of the service that the hospital provides; 'union influences', centring around the policies of, and protection offered by, the nursing staff's union; and 'help with patient care', including items concerning the competence of, and information received from, other colleagues when dealing with patients. Note that each of these factors could be reported as either a support or constraint, with high scores signifying a support.

The mean levels of reported general psychological distress, anxiety and depression are presented in Table 2. Considering distress first, when compared with some other employed samples, in which the mean score is usually somewhere around 8 to 9, the score of 10.24 for this nursing sample appears to be relatively high. Indeed, this score is higher than that of an employed sample (8.02) studied by Payne and Jones (1987) and both male (8.80) and female (8.53) employees in an engineering plant (Banks et al., 1980). This suggests that this sample of psychiatric nurses are relatively strained when compared with these other employed groups. On the other hand, when compared with some other samples in the health professions, the GHQ-12 score for this nursing sample is relatively low. Firth (1986), for example, reports a mean score of 11.66 for medical students whilst West and Savage (1987) report a mean score of 13.30 for health care workers. However, to provide some sort of general perspective, all of these scores are low when compared with the mean scores of unemployed samples, which are usually around 15 (e.g. Banks et al., 1980; Payne, Warr and Hartley, 1984; Payne and Jones, 1987). The mean scores on anxiety and depression were similar to other employed samples.

Table 2 Means of health and well-being scores. Reprinted with permission from Jones et al. (1987) Copyright (1987) Pergamon Journals Ltd

	Whole sample	Rank					Sex		Spouses works in same hospital?	
		Nursing Officer and above	Charge Nurse/ Sister	Staff Nurse	State Enrolled Nurse	Nursing Assistant	Male	Female	Yes	No
General psychological distress	10.24	10.33	11.04	10.38	9.63	9.63	9.89	10.98*	11.48	9.58***
Anxiety	4.80	4.67	5.74	4.90	4.25	4.23	4.61	5.23	5.43	4.44*
Depression	1.16	0.00	1.31	1.23	1.01	1.00	1.02	1.38	1.24	1.06
N	349	6	51	145	69	66	245	97	108	235

***p<0.001
**p<0.01
*p<0.05

As may be seen in Table 2, no significant differences emerged in health and well-being between the five nursing ranks. However, the respondents with a spouse working at the hospital reported higher levels of anxiety and distress than their counterparts. This is perhaps not surprising in the light of Cronin-Stubbs and Brophy's (1984) findings that the lives of psychiatric nurses, particularly in terms of engaging and sustaining mutually validating relationships, may in some cases be adversely affected by their jobs. Obviously, if both partners are encountering such problems then these difficulties are likely to be accentuated, possibly resulting in tension and anxiety. Furthermore, a marginal difference was revealed between male and female staff, with female nurses scoring slightly higher on psychological distress than male nurses. The authors to not claim, however, that this finding is exclusive to psychiatric nursing as it has been replicated in numerous community surveys (e.g. Bebbington *et al.*, 1981; Henderson, Byrne and Duncan-Jones, 1981).

Jones *et al.* attempted to relate the reported levels of health and well-being to reported levels of job demands and supports/constraints. Turning firstly to demands, the sample as a whole reported patient supervisory demands as being relatively high, administrative demands as moderate, and aversive demands as low. It is interesting to note from the correlations presented in Table 3 that although patient supervisory demands were high they were not related to health and well-being. Secondly, a moderate level of administrative demands correlated moderately and positively with distress and anxiety. Finally, aversive demands, perceived as relatively low, correlated strongly and positively with all three measures of health and well-being. The authors conclude that patient supervisory demands, although high, were presumably unrelated to stress because they represent the major function of the nurses and are expected to be high. Administrative demands, they argue, are probably considered as a subsidiary function of the job by many nurses, particularly those lower in the hierarchy, and may be an unwanted apsect of the job for many of them. Aversive demands, although relatively low, were strongly related to stress for those who experienced them.

The correlations in Table 3 relating types of support/constraint to health and well-being show that 'union influences' was the only type unrelated to any of the three measures. The relevant significant correlations were all negative, demonstrating, not surprisingly, that lower scores on the supports/constraints scale were associated with higher levels of distress. This relationship was particularly evident in the case of 'help with patient care', whilst the relationship was moderate in the case of 'communication' and 'administration'.

Whilst it is important to emphasize that this sample is a highly specialized and rather unusual one within psychiatric nursing, the findings of Jones *et al.*'s study suggest a group of people who accept and effectively cope with the demands and pressures of the core task of their job (i.e. patient care) but who find frustration and dissatisfaction within a large, highly structured organization in which this

Table 3 Correlations between health and well-being and job demands, supports/constraints. Reprinted with permission from Jones et al. (1987). Copyright (1987) Pergamon Journals Ltd

	Job Demands				Supports/Constraints			
	Administrative demands	Patient supervisory	Aversive demands	Communication	Administration	Social attitudes	Union influences	Help with patient care
Psychological								
Distress	0.09*	0.08	0.29***	-0.15**	-0.17**	-0.11**	-0.06	-0.25***
Anxiety	0.13*	0.05	0.24***	-0.12*	-0.13**	-0.08	-0.06	-0.25***
Depression	0.03	0.08	0.16**	-0.11*	-0.06	-0.06	-0.01	-0.07

***p<0.001
**p<0.01
*p<0.05

care takes place. This picture is similar to that already described in the first part of this chapter.

SUMMARY AND CONCLUSIONS

The nature of this chapter has dictated that only the negative aspects of psychiatric nursing have been discussed. It should be emphasized that this can be an extremely rewarding occupation. Nevertheless, the evidence suggests that certain aspects of the job are potential sources of stress to the psychiatric nurse. Two major factors emerge from the descriptive literature: patient contact, and administrative and organizational factors. In the case of patient contact, nurses' experiences may vary greatly according to the nature of the patient group and the specific setting in which the care is delivered. Administrative and organizational issues are seen as the other source of stress. The descriptive literature suggests that psychiatric nurses' training is generally poor and insufficient and that nurses experience a wide variety of negative influences, including: role overload (caused mainly by staff shortages); role conflict and ambiguity (caused by lack of a clearly defined role); poor communication, particularly between management and ward staff; lack of participation in decisions; low autonomy, and low levels of support from the management.

The empirical evidence in this area is extremely sparse. Furthermore, the findings from these studies somewhat contradict the descriptive literature. The descriptive literature tends to focus on the stress of nursing *per se*, but the empirical evidence suggests that stress in psychiatric nursing stems largely from organizational factors. A major weakness in two of the three empirical studies discussed (i.e. Cronin-Stubbs and Brophy, 1984; Dawkins, Depp and Selzer, 1985) is that they did not consider levels of burnout and stress in psychiatric nursing. Rather, they concentrated on factors which were related to burnout and stress. Jones *et al.* (1987), on the other hand, compared stress levels in their sample of psychiatric nurses with other samples. The nurses in this study scored higher on general psychological distress than other employed samples but their scores were well below those of unemployed samples.

It is clear that this area of research suffers from a severe lack of well-designed empirical studies. There is a need for studies examining stress levels and their determinants in large numbers of nurses from a wide variety of psychiatric settings. Only then can we attempt to successfully address some of the issues raised in this discussion.

ACKNOWLEDGEMENT

The author wishes to acknowledge the helpful comments of Moria Leahy, a Ward Sister at the Northern General Hospital, Sheffield, during the early drafts of this chapter.

REFERENCES

Armitage, P. (1986). The rehabilitation and nursing care of severely disabled psychiatric patients, *International Journal of Nursing Studies*, 23, 113–23.
Bailey, R. D. (1981). Counselling services for nurses—a forgotten responsibility, *Journal of the British Institute of Mental Handicap*, 9, 45–7.
Bailey, R. D. (1985). *Coping With Stress in Caring*, Blackwell, London.
Banks, M. H., Clegg, C. W., Jackson, P. R., Kemp, N. J., Stafford, E. M. and Wall, T. D. (1980). The use of the General Health Questionnaire as an indicator of mental health in occupational studies, *Journal of Occupational Psychology*, 53, 187–94.
Barton, R. (1959). *Institutional Neurosis*, Wright, Bristol.
Bateman, T. S. and Strasser, S. (1983). A cross-lagged regression test of the relationships between job tension and employee satisfaction, *Journal of Applied Psychology*, 68, 439–45.
Bebbington, P., Hurry, J., Tennant, C., Sturt, E. and Wing, J. K. (1981). Epidemiology of mental disorders in Camberwell, *Psychological Medicine*, 11, 561–79.
Belknap, I. (1956). *Human Problems in a State Mental Hospital*, MacGraw-Hill, New York.
Bickerton, J., Sampson, A. C. M. and Boylan, A. (1979). *Nursing Theory and Practice*, McGraw-Hill, London.
Brooking, J. I. (1985). Advance psychiatric nursing education in Britain, *Journal of Advanced Nursing*, 10, 455–68.
Campbell, W. and Mawson, D. (1978). Violence in a psychiatric unit, *Journal of Advanced Nursing*, 3, 55–64.
Caudill (1958). *The Psychiatric Hospital as a Small Society*, Harvard University Press, Cambridge, USA.
Claus, K. and Bailey, J. (Eds.) (1980). *Living with Stress and Promoting Well-Being*, Mosby, St Louis.
Cooper, C. L. and Payne, R. L. (1978). *Stress at Work*, Wiley, New York.
Cope, D. (1981). *Organization Development and Action Research in Hospitals*, Gower Press, Aldershot.
Cope, D. and Cox, S. (1980). Organization development in a psychiatric hospital: creating desirable changes, *Journal of Advanced Nursing*, 5, 371–80.
Cormack, D. (1976). *Psychiatric Nursing Observed: a Descriptive Study of the Work of the Charge Nurse in Acute Admission Wards of Psychiatric Hospitals*, Royal College of Nursing, London.
Cormack, D. (1983). *Psychiatric Nursing Described*, Churchill Livingstone, London.
Cronin-Stubbs, D. and Brophy, E. B. (1984). Burnout: can social support save the psychiatric nurse? *Journal of Psychosocial Nursing and Mental Health Services*, 23, 8–13.
Cumming, J. and Cumming, E. (1964). *Ego and Milieu: Theory and Practise of Environmental Therapy*, Tavistock Publications, London.
Dawkins, J. E., Depp, F. C. and Selzer, N. E. (1985). Stress and the psychiatric nurse, *Journal of Psychosocial Nursing and Mental Health Services*, 23, 9–15.
Firth, J. (1986). Levels and sources of stress in medical students, *British Medical Journal*, 292, 1177–80.
Fraser, D. and Cormack, D. (1975). The nurses' role in psychiatric institutions, *Nursing Times*, 18 and 25 December, 125–32.
Gillespie, C. and Gillespie, V. (1986). Reading the danger signs, *Nursing Times*, 30 July, 24–7.

Goffman, E. (1961). *Asylums*, Doubleday, New York.
Goldberg, D. P. (1972). *The Detection of Psychiatric Illness By Questionnaire*, Oxford University Press, Oxford.
Goldberg, D. P. and Hillier, V. F. (1979). A scaled version of the General Health Questionnaire, *Psychological Medicine*, **9**, 139–45.
Gomersall, J. (1987). Defensive caring, *Changes*. In press.
Gray-Toft, P. and Anderson, J. G. (1981). Stress among hospital nursing staff: its causes and effects, *Social Science and Medicine*, **15**, 639–47.
Henderson, S., Byrne, D. G. and Duncan-Jones, P. (1981). *Neurosis and the Social Environment*, Academic Press, London.
Holmes, T. H. and Rahe, R. H. (1967). The social readjustment rating scale, *Journal of Psychosomatic Research*, **11**, 213–18.
Ivancevich, J. M. and Smith, S. V. (1981). Identification and analyses of job difficulty dimensions: an empirical study, *Ergonomics*, **24**, 351–63.
Ivancevich, J. M. and Smith, S. V. (1982). Job difficulty as interpreted by incumbents: a study of nurses and engineers, *Human Relations*, **35**, 391–412.
Jones, J. G., Janman, K., Payne, R. L. and Rick, J. T. (1987). Some determinants of stress in psychiatric nurses, *International Journal of Nursing Studies*, **24**, 129–44.
Jones, J. W. (1980). *Preliminary Manual: The Staff Burnout Scale for Health Professionals (SBS-HP)*, London House Management Consultants, Park Ridge, Illinois.
Marshall, J. (1980). Stress amongst nurses. In C. L. Cooper and J. Marshall (eds) *White Collar and Professional Stress*, Wiley, Chichester.
Martin, D. V. (1959). Institutionalization, *Lancet*, **ii**, 1188.
Maslach, C. and Jackson, S. E. (1981). The measurement of experienced burnout, *Journal of Occupational Behaviour*, **2**, 99–113.
Miller, G. A. (1976). Patient knowledge and nurse role strain in three hospital settings, *Medical Care*, **14**, 8, 662–73.
Nichols, K., Springford, V. and Searle, J. (1981). An investigation of distress and discontent in various types of nursing, *Journal of Advanced Nursing*, **6**, 311–16.
Norbeck, J. S., Lindsey, A. M. and Carrieri, V. L. (1981). The development of an instrument to measure social support, *Nursing Research*, **30**, 264–69.
Parkes, K. R. (1982). Occupational stress among student nurses: a natural experiment, *Journal of Applied Psychology*, **67**, 784–96.
Payne, R. L. (1979). Demands, supports, constraints and psychological health. In C. J. MacKay and T. Cox (eds) *Response To Stress: Occupational Aspects*, International Publishing Company, London.
Payne, R. L. and Jones, J. G. (1987). Social class and re-employment: changes in health and perceived financial circumstances, *Journal of Occupational Behaviour*. In press.
Payne, R. L., Warr, P. W. and Hartley, J. (1984). Social class and psychological ill-health during unemployment, *Sociology of Health and Illness*, **6**, 152–74.
Pines, A. and Kanner, A. D. (1982). Nurses' burnout: lack of positive conditions and presence of negative conditions as two independent sources of stress, *Journal of Psychosocial Nursing and Mental Health Services*, **20**, 30–35.
Powell, D. (1982). *Learning to Relate? A Study of Student Psychiatric Nurses' Views of Their Preparation and Training*, Royal College of Nursing, London.
Rump, E. E. (1979). Size of psychiatric hospitals and nurses' job satisfaction, *Journal of Occupational Psychology*, **52**, 255–65.
Secker, J. (1983). Caring for the carers, *Nursing Times*, 9 March, 64.
Smith, T. (1984). Stress in the prison service, *Prison Service Journal*, October, 1984, 10–11.

Smith, T. (1985). Stress in prison officers: possible implications for the work of psychologists. A paper presented at the Biannual Conference for Prison Psychologists. Windermere Hydro Hotel, October 1985.

Taylor, J. B. (1983). The tip of the lash, *Nursing Times*, 30 October, 72.

Towell, D. (1975). *Understanding Psychiatric Nursing*, Royal College of Nursing, London.

Vredenburgh, D. J. and Trinkaus, R. J. (1983). An analysis of role stress among hospital nurses, *Journal of Vocational Behaviour*, 22, 82–95.

Wallis, D. (1986). Satisfaction, stress and performance: issues for occupational psychology in the 'caring professions'. Keynote address to the BPS Occupational Psychology Conference, University of Nottingham, January, 1986.

West, M. A. and Savage, Y. (1987). Stress, coping and innovation among health care workers. Paper presented to the BPS Occupational Psychology Conference, University of Hull, January, 1987.

Wilkinson, D. (1982). The effects of brief psychiatric training on the attitudes of general nursing students to psychiatric patients, *Journal of Advanced Nursing*, 7, 239–53.

Stress in Health Professionals
Edited by R. Payne and J. Firth-Cozens
© 1987 John Wiley & Sons Ltd

Chapter 11
The Impact of New Technology on Nurses and Patients*

Mike Fitter

INTRODUCTION

Many people expect the introduction of new technology to be an inherently stressful experience for those who work in the organization (Oborne, 1985). Why should this be the case? Is it no more than apprehension about the 'unknown' and personal doubts about whether one can manage to use the technology? Since there is a common assumption that new technology 'saves work' is there concern for the future of one's job? Previous studies have indicated that these concerns exist (Breakwell *et al.*, 1986; Hepworth and Fitter, 1981), but that, at least in primary health care, they are largely unfounded. Staff cope well with the use of the technology and the new possibilities opened up actually create extra work (Fitter *et al.*, 1986).

The introduction of new technology may result in organizational change, which is itself likely to be inherently stressful. However, in this case the stressful period is likely to be transitory. But it may also be the case that the new technology is introduced to achieve objectives which do not directly address the needs of its users. For example, an experimental system designed to improve the information available to General Practitioners during consultations with patients was described by the users as mildly stressful over an extended period (Herzmark *et al.*, 1984). This was because use of the system acutally increased the length of the consultation and put the doctors under greater time pressure. This was particularly undesirable since time pressure is a major source of stress for GPs (see Chapter 3).

This chapter focuses on the use of new technology by nurses in intensive care units. This occupational group is known to have many stressors in their work

---

This chapter is based on 'The impact of new technology on workers and patients in the health service: physical are psychological stress'. European Foundation for the Improvement of Living and Working Conditions, 1987. ISBN 92-825-6798-2. £8.00. Available from Official Sales Agents for European Communities publications. (Also published in French and German.)

environment (Hay and Oken, 1972). Moreover, intensive care has some of the most sophisticated equipment that health care providers use.

To what extent is new technology a source of stress for nurses and for their patients? And what possibilities exist to use technology in a way that reduces stress?

New Technology in Hospitals

Medical technology has a long history of use in hospitals. Some of the earliest technology was concerned directly with patient monitoring and treatment, and it is out of this that the advanced systems to be found in Intensive Care Units have been developed.

Intensive patient monitoring involves some of the most sophisticated equipment currently in use by nurses. A typical feature of these systems is that patients are monitored continuously with the aid of technology attached with electrodes. Data on the patient's heart rate etc. is monitored and analysed so that warning signals can be given if irregularities occur. The data and analyses are usually available at the patient's bedside, and in some installations are also monitored in a central 'control room'.

The technology is therefore constantly vigilant of the patient's condition and alerts the nursing staff when necessary. This should offer a feeling of security to patients that they are being 'looked after', but may also create feelings of anxiety and alienation in relation to the 'technological' and strange environment, to having electrodes attached, the TV screens, alarms, etc.

In addition to traditional nursing, the nurses' work consists of monitoring the equipment and responding to alarms. This requires new skills in order to be able to interpret and use the information coming from the monitoring equipment.

The increased use of technology has generally required more specialized skills and this has been a contributory factor in the reorganization of hospitals into specialized health care units. Much of the advanced monitoring and treatment technology is now found in such units, which have also led to increased specialization within the medical and nursing professions. Specialist units have also been created for carrying out clinical test procedures, for dispensing medication, and for domestic services.

This has resulted in a fragmentation of the hospital services and created a need to 'integrate' them in order to provide an effective overall service. Again the service of technology has been sought and there are currently pilot systems aimed at developing an integrated Hospital Information System, which will provide the necessary information and communication links to co-ordinate the specialized units and central services.

Computer-based data processing systems were first developed in hospitals for general administrative purposes—accounts, wages, statistics, etc. The next area to be developed was the central service units—for pharmacy management etc. The nursing sector is now beginning to come into contact with computer-based information systems, though so far with little direct contact for nursing staff. The nursing process has yet to be computerized.

The Impact of New Technology on Nurses and Patients

The introduction of new technology is often accompained by the reorganization of work, for example, through increased division of labour and specialization of skills. Changes in organizational structure and work organization also have an impact on staff and patients and thus the analysis of new technology must examine both the indirect impact through organizational change, and the impact as experienced directly.

There is now a substantial amount of research on the social and psychological effects of new technology (Oborne, 1985). Much of this is concerned with the ergonomic aspects of design—creating a match between the person and the machine. The earlier research focused on perceptual-motor skills, but more recently attention has turned to more complex 'cognitive' skills. Some researchers have emphasized the need to design technology to suit the physical, mental and social needs and abilities of its users. Others have concentrated on the needs for high quality training in the use of equipment so that users are in a position to work with it competently and confidently. Clearly both good design and training are important, the alternative being ineffective use and stress for the users.

Working with new technology has brought a qualitative change in the content of work for many people, particularly in those jobs characterized by a high level of skills, for example nursing. Compared with 'traditional' work, working with new technology may be characterized by:

(1) A shift from manual to intellectual skills.
(2) A growing distance between the users and the product or process they are working on.
(3) A shift from concrete, visible targets to more abstract ones.
(4) Representation of the work process as a mental model that is acted on through intervention and regulation, without the work process necessarily being accessible or directly observable to the user.
(5) Increasing skill requirements and the need to regularly update skills (Agervold and Kristensen, 1985).

These conclusions are general, and to date there has been little specific research of the impact on health care providers. It seems likely though, that the above factors will apply in particular to nurses using advanced monitoring technology.

There is a danger that if nurses come to rely on the monitoring technology, their role could become more passive and this could lead to an atrophy (or de-learning) of conventional powers of observation and nursing skill. If there is an increasing tendency to rely on monitoring equipment to decide when the patient's condition is moving in a dangerous direction, this may in time become the only means of assessment, and the nurse will be dependent on the technology. This 'de-skilling', if it occurred, would have particularly stressful consequences in the event of machine unreliability or breakdown, when a nurse might have difficulty switching from a passive role to active responsibility for patients. Stress itself can have a debilitating effect and make nurses less confident and effective in their intervention and treatment in relation to patients. Alternatively, however, the beneficial effects of the technology may *relieve* stress for the nurses by supporting them in the provision of patient care.

For the patient, who is the 'object' on which the process control technology is operating, there is a potential danger of becoming more distanced from the nursing staff. Thus any reassurance provided by the technology may be more than offset by the alienating effects of reduced contact with nurses. The environment of an Intensive Care Unit is likely to be stressful for patients (constant light and noise etc.) which might compound their anxious state, inevitably induced by the seriousness of their illness. There is some evidence that Intensive Care Units can be disorientating for conscious patients after a few days, and they can suffer from amnesia (Jones, 1979; Kornfeld, 1969).

Previous research has found that nurses new to intensive care technologies tend to react in one of two ways. They either concentrate on the machines to the exclusion of the patient, or alternatively disregard the machine completely and concentrate on the patient (Yates, 1983).

To avoid some of the difficulties experienced by nurses it seems important that they should be actively involved in the introduction of new technology, and that continued development should take into consideration the experience nurses posses in patient care and the use of the technology (Zielstorff and Birckhead, 1978).

A number of studies have examined nurses and patients attitudes to new technology in medical settings (Cruickshank, 1982, 1984; Hepworth and Fitter, 1981; Potter, 1981; Pringle, Robins and Brown, 1984; Reznikoff *et al.*, 1967; Rosenberg *et al.*, 1967; Startsman and Robinson, 1972). Generally the results indicate that although nurses tend to have more negative attitudes than doctors, direct experience of new technology results in more positive attitudes. Senior nursing staff (management) tend to be more positive than basic grades. Specialist nurses, for example those in Intensive Care Units, are also more positive than nurses on general wards. This may be a consequence of more direct experience of technology generally. There may also be a degree of self-selection, nurses inclined towards technology being more likely to work in specialist units.

Similarly patients who have had experience of computer technology, either through personal use or because they had experienced their doctor using one during a consultation, have more positive attitudes to their use in medicine. Also younger and male patients tend to have more positive attitudes.

However, previous studies have not examined directly patients' experience of hospital technology and this is one of the aims of the studies reported in this chapter.

Stressors in Intensive Care Units

The rapidly increasing costs of secondary (hospital) health care has placed greater strains on hospital resources. This has constrained, and in some instances reduced, the number of nursing staff available. The consequence of these factors is greater pressure on nursing staff and a feeling of being 'overworked'. It is against this background that the impact of new technology is being assessed.

A number of studies have been carried out in the past on stress in nursing work generally (Dohrenwend and Dohrenwend, 1974; Eden, 1982; Gray-Toft and Anderson, 1981; Jokinen and Poyhonen, 1980; Tabor, 1982; Vredenberg and Trinkous, 1983). The results point repeatedly to certain factors which must be considered as highly relevant and typical causes of stress. These factors are briefly described, with a view to identifying whether they lie in working conditions which could be affected and changed by the introduction of new technology.

(1) Nurses feel a high level of responsibility for the well-being of patients who are sick, and perhaps dying. They must also deal with the emotional aspects of relating to patients and their relatives, frequently under considerable time pressure.
(2) Generally nurses have a high workload with exceptional peaks, when for example new admissions occur. These events can create acute overload and possible stress reactions.
(3) The work can be physically arduous involving lifting of patients and other heavy objects.
(4) Shiftwork is the norm, and this is made more arduous by frequent overtime and the need to substitute for absent colleagues at short notice.
(5) Conflict can occur with other professional groups, and with doctors in particular. Because doctors have authority for medical decisions nurses may have to seek permission for their actions, e.g. whether they can give a piece of medical information to an anxious patient.
(6) Nurses can have responsibility for instructing trainees and supervising

junior staff. This can create stress, particularly when a shift is short of trained staff and is dependent substantially on inexperienced trainees.
(7) The unpredictability of the work and of the patient's condition can create uncertainty as to the appropriate course of action or treatment. If doctors are not immediately available this can be particularly stressful.
(8) Medical knowledge and technology changes fairly rapidly, and thus nurses need regular training to keep up to date. Research has shown training often to be inadequate in the circumstances and this can be a source of stress.

Many of these factors are more stressful as a consequence of the increased throughput of patients resulting from the policy of reducing the time that patients spend in hospital.

The main factor which has been found to compensate nurses for this lengthy list of stressors in their working lives is that the job is usually regarded as highly meaningful, and valued by patients and society generally. The work has many of the qualities regarded as good job characteristics, namely responsibility, meaningfulness, skill, variety, etc. Also important for dealing with stressful situations is support from colleagues and from superiors. Whether this is available will depend on structural characteristics of the organization (Gray-Toft and Anderson, 1981). In a positive climate nurses will perceive it to be possible to influence events and avoid or minimize the impact of some of the stressors. The evidence suggests that for the individual this is a better way of dealing with a stressful environment than by individual 'coping' responses.

Some research has studied intensive care nursing specifically (for example, Bishop 1983; Claus, Bailey and Selye, 1980; Farmer, 1978; Huckaby and Jagla, 1979; Jacobsen, 1978; Reichle, 1975). The general finding is that the above stressors also apply in intensive care but some are experienced more intensely. For example, patients are more likely to die, and the work can be particularly demanding, physically and mentally. Additional stress factors specific to intensive care are:

(1) The ward environment is usually unrelenting. Bright lights are commonly on for 24 hours a day and are accompanied by regular noise of the equipment in operation.
(2) Working with the technology creates additional pressures and requires additional knowledge and skills not part of a nurse's vocational training.
(3) There can be a need for rapid and complex decision-making if a crisis develops through a patient's sudden deterioration or by an equipment failure.
(4) There is a substantial risk of accidents in intensive care.
(5) When patients begin to recover they are usually removed to a less intensive

ward, thus cutting off the potential for a nurse to relate to the patient at the point when it would be more easily possible.

However, Bishop (1983) has observed that 'the emotional consequences experienced by nurses working in these units are barely mentioned' (p. 181).

Although the evidence shows that these additional stressors exist in intensive care environments they are to some extent compensated for because the positive aspects of the work are also experienced more intensely. That is the job is regarded as especially prestigious and meaningful.

CASE STUDIES IN INTENSIVE CARE

As part of its 1984/85 programme of work, the European Foundation for the Improvement of Living and Working Conditions undertook research into the impact of new technology on workers and patients in the health services. The terms of reference focused in particular on physical and psychological stress, as experienced by nurses and patients in a hospital environment. Case studies were carried out by researchers in Denmark, Ireland, Italy, the United Kingdom, the Netherlands, and the Federal Republic of Germany. To illustrate the overall findings, some of the results from these studies are summarized below. For a fuller account see Fitter (1987).

The Irish Study

The Irish study used a range of questionnaires and other techniques to examine nurses' views of their work, stressors, and new technology in five hospitals in the Dublin area. A major stressor perceived by nursing staff was the way that their work was organized, which resulted in a high pace of work and time pressure, and a lack of staff with the necessary skills. The work environment was not seen as supportive and there was a reported lack of teamwork. The main means of coping with stress was to 'unwind' after work, since nurses perceived only limited opportunity to influence the sources of stress in the workplace. Although they regarded their work as meaningful and important, they felt they did not get sufficient recognition for it.

A number of questionnaire items directly assessed the impact of new technology. The picture emerged that the majority of nurses viewed new technology as helpful in their Units, enabling them to do a good job. However, more specific questions indicated nurses' concern about their using the technology, and the extent to which it took their attention away from the patient.

A 15-item questionnaire scale was used to examine nurses' perceptions of stress created by the technology. The items focused on:

(a) Machine demands and anxiety.
(b) Combining machine monitoring with patient monitoring.
(c) Cognitive aspects of machine handling.

The items were rated on a four point scale (1 = no stress to 4 = considerable stress). Table 1 shows the five items which were reported as causing the greatest stress, each having a score of more than 2.0.

It is apparent that equipment reliability was a major source of stress for the nurses. This is indicated by items 1 (poor maintenance) and 4 (breakdowns) in Table 1. This finding is similar to a finding of the Danish study in which false alarms with the equipment were a major stressor. Nurses reported that not everyone had the same understanding of the functions and uses of the equipment and this could lead to mistakes. Equipment sometimes appears to break down because of the large number of staff handling it.

Table 1   The top five technology stressors reported by 52 nurses, the mean score for the item (four point scale) and the percentage of nurses reporting 'considerable stress'

Item	Mean Score	Percentage 'considerable stress'
1 Poor maintenance of machines	2.69	35
2 Not having sufficient understanding of how key pieces of equipment work	2.72	21
3 Spending too much time and energy with the technology and not giving enough time to talking to and supporting the patient	2.68	14
4 Breakdown of machine	2.58	21
5 Handling all the technology and life-support machines effectively for each patient	2.27	12

Problems were seen to arise because of inadequate consultation with nursing staff over the acquisition of equipment even though they were the principal users. This varied from hospital to hospital. In Hospital A the advice of nurses was not sought when equipment was installed. The nurses found this frustrating since they felt many simple problems with the technology could be overcome or avoided if use was made of their knowledge and expertise. Hospitals B and C had a policy of involving senior nursing staff in decisions about technology, and the level of satisfaction with it was higher in these hospitals.

Although the new technology was seen as enhancing nurses' skills the demands placed on nurses by its use were a major source of stress (items 2 and 5). Forty-five per cent of nurses indicated they were dissatisfied with the training they received. Training provided by the hospitals was mainly on the job, consisting of either special training in the Unit, or learning by experience. Only a quarter of nurses attending off-the-job courses. Nurses indicated that they had difficulty getting leave of absence to attend recognized courses, since the Department of Health did not make any provision for such training or recognize it as in-service training. It was agreed that training provided by equipment suppliers, whether through demonstrations or through instruction manuals, was inadequate for the specialist work nurses in intensive care have to perform. Moreover, nurses had insufficient time to learn from suppliers' demonstrations. The supplier's primary goal is to sell the equipment to the hospitals, though it does have responsibility to ensure that the users of new equipment have become skilled in its use. However, it is the hospital organization that needs to recognize that learning and training takes time, and that in the long run such training is likely to reduce stress arising from inadequate knowledge, and from working with colleagues who are inexperienced in the use of new technology. With no specialist training provided, trainee nurses learned about the technology informally, and indicated that they felt fearful of using the equipment. These concerns were very real and frightening when nurses were dealing with seriously ill patients. Because of the inadequate training there was a concern that through insufficient understanding of the detailed functioning of the technology nurses may become too dependent on it. A principal fear behind the criticisms of the training appeared to be the serious consequences that lack of understanding of life sustaining equipment could have on the patient, and on the erosion of traditional nursing skills.

The third major source of stress was that involvement with the technology took time away from relating to the patient (Table 1, item 3). Moreover 77 per cent of nurses perceived their work as becoming more impersonal because of new technology, and 69 per cent agreed that 'they have become a technician because of new technology rather than a carer'.

More specific probing of nurses' views suggested that nurses saw the technology as having a mediating effect between themselves and the patient (71 per cent indicating that the technology had distanced them from the patient). However, 79 per cent of nurses also agreed that 'you cannot differentiate between technical and non-technical aspects of the job—they both serve to care for the patient'. It seems that rather than usurping their role, technology is seen as *part* of that caring role.

It was striking from observational work in one of the Units that nurses appeared to compensate for a reduction in personal contact by continually talking to patients who were apparently unconscious. Nurses viewed the new technology as potentially intrusive and liable to cause patients considerable distress and anxiety. Once patients demonstrated that they could resume physiological functioning without the aid of machines they were disconnected. Nurses based their observation of patient distress on the physiological and emotional cues which patients displayed while attached to the equipment. In the view of some nurses, equipment was used in some cases for no clear reason, particularly in the case of equipment which was not life sustaining. When its use cannot be justified on medical grounds they felt it should be abandoned in favour of the patient's psychological welfare.

New technology highlights some ethical dilemmas for nurses. It creates the possibility of prolonging the patient's life but perhaps at a cost of a lower quality life since more patients are surviving who would have previously died. This was particularly the case for babies in the neonatal unit who may have sustained brain damage. These concerns raised questions for the nurses about the desirability of maintaining a patient on a machine if there were little chance of recovery. They were also concerned about when to turn a machine off, particularly if there was another patient who could perhaps be better helped by the availability of a scarce resource. These dilemmas were an additional source of stress for staff in high technology units.

Patients' views were assessed through a questionnaire administered to a sample of 18 who had received coronary care. For 89 per cent of them their general level of anxiety regarding the technology was low. More detailed probing revealed an overall positive perception of new technology used in their diagnosis or treatment while in hospital. They expressed a high degree of confidence in the nurses' abilities and use of technology. They did not generally experience any feelings of alienation from the nurses because of the technology, although they did see the technology as placing an additional burden on the nurses, whom they saw as insufficiently rewarded for their specialist work. While 50 per cent reported a feeling of dependency on the technology, 93 per cent indicated they were grateful it was available for coronary treatment.

The Danish Study

The Danish study focused on the impact of a computer-based patient monitoring system in a coronary care unit. The study combined interview data and established questionnaires to assess nurses' psychological and psychosomatic stress reactions. Nurses also kept daily work descriptions and recorded their stress reactions at the end of each shift. The data was used to categorize the 32 nurses into three sub-groups (low, medium and high functioning) based on their level of reported stress.

The study confirmed the presence of many of the work environment stressors that have been found in previous hospital studies, in particular the high pace of work, complex cognitive demands, dealing with seriously ill patients and their relatives, shiftwork, and working with unreliable technology. Job factors which compensated for these stressors were the importance of the work combined with a high degree of responsibility, and job variety, and opportuntiy to use skills. There was also a high level of support from colleagues and superiors, and a

Table 2 Distribution of personal variables between low, medium and high functioning groups

	Sex: Number of		Age (yrs)	Experience in the ward (yrs)	Worked previously with new technology
	Women	Men			
Low functioning group	8	0	29.4	1.7	38%
Medium functioning group	14	3	30.9	2.9	47%
High functioning group	5	2	31.9	4.4	71%
Average	27	5	30.7	3.0	50%

Table 3 Distribution of psychological stress variables between low, medium and high functioning groups. Scale variations from −2 to +2

	N	Perceived social support	Action and coping strategies	Burn-out	Mental fatigue	Psychological stress	Psychosomatic stress
Low functioning group	8	0.75	−1.00	−0.75	−1.63	−1.25	−0.88
Medium functioning group	17	1.47	−0.24	0.24	−0.82	−0.35	0.24
High functioning group	7	1.71	0.57	0.57	0.14	0.57	1.43
Average	32	1.31	−0.22	0.02	−0.77	−0.34	0.26

climate of co-operation. The low functioning group of nurses contained a predominance of younger nurses with little previous experience of working with new technology (see Table 2). These nurses reported less social support at work (Table 3) and were more likely to report *individual* strategies for coping with stress (such as unwinding after work), though such strategies were seen as less effective then dealing with the source of stress by attempting to influence the work environment. The 'assigned' method of nursing, which paired patient and nurse for a shift, was also seen as reducing the need for contact between nurses and contributing to the isolation experienced by some of the nurses in this group.

Almost all the nurses regarded the monitoring technology as an aid to their work—a safety net that gave them a certain amount of freedom. However, some nurses also saw it as straining their relationship with the patients because of its tendency to distract them from direct communication. Training in use of the technology was mainly carried out by the nurses themselves passing on their skills. It was estimated that it took at least a year to feel adequately qualified, and over half the nurses felt dissatisfied with the training programme.

As well as helping them, the nurses saw the technology also as a stressor, and views fell into three main categories:

(1) The interpretation and assessment of information provided by the equipment was a cognitive stress. This was particularly the case when sitting in the control room monitoring several screens simultaneously.
(2) The alarm system was an important element of the monitoring installation, and it was also the one part of the monitoring system that all nurses said was seriously stressful because of the frequent and inaccurate alarms. But although everyone perceived frequent alarms as a stress, the justification for their existence was not contested. The supportive function of the alarms was acknowledged by 80 per cent of nurses. Assessment of whether an alarm were true or false, and thus whether it demanded action, was obviously a matter of experience. For example, only the youngest nurses said that they found this assessment stressful, whereas the great majority—more than two-thirds—found that with experience it was relatively uncomplicated. Nevertheless the over-stimulation caused by the frequent alarms led to a cognitive 'switching off'. This defensive coping strategy was reported to have possible damaging longer-term consequences for the nurses' self-image and professional pride.
(3) The monitoring technology 'demanded' a response. The availability of resuscitation equipment made it possible to deal with a cardiac arrest. The nurses therefore felt *obliged* to respond in all circumstances. This could at times conflict with their own views on the ethical desirability of resuscitation. There were frequent discussions amongst nurses and with doctors who had the responsibility for the decision. Even though it was the doctors' decision, the considerations were prominent in the nurses' thinking and promoted feeling of stress.

A severe stress factor in working with the monitoring equipment was when it broke down. Two-thirds of the nurses reported it as stressful. The extent of the stress varied, experienced nurses could take it in their stride whereas inexperienced nurses could be very concerned, for example:

> I've experienced a breakdown and it was dreadful. The alarm kept on going and it spat out paper. It howled along the whole corridor, and people are fully aware that when it howls something is *really* wrong. Of course it also affected us—and we couldn't make it stop. Also, it takes a frightful time to connect up all the alarms again, and if you have to do this at a time when you're really busy it's very stressful. It's also hectic and confusing when suddenly no patients are being monitored any more—you feel helpless; how are the patients? You have to think for yourself...

The majority of nurses reported that the technology had no overall effect on the quality of their work, or on job satisfaction because the positive effects of the aid were cancelled by the stress of false alarms, and the tendency to become preoccupied with the monitors.

All patients had positive views about the ward and its staff. They tended to have contradictory views about the technology, in part seeing it as necessary and reassuring, but also finding it a bit frightening and alienating. There is a policy on the ward of promoting the active participation of patients in their recovery. There was concern that some patients either became pre-occupied with the monitors measuring their own vital functions, or felt they should adopt a completely passive role in the hands of the staff and the technology.

Stressors Identified in the Case Studies

The following stress factors were identified as relating directly to the use of new technology:

(1) *Enhanced cognitive demands.* Although monitoring technology may remove some of the burden of constant vigilance, the equipment was complex and frequently required sophisticated interpretations.

(2) *Poor design and equipment failures.* Several of the studies reported that the monitoring equipment produced frequent 'false alarms'. These were particularly stressful to nursing staff, especially when, as a result of poor design, it was difficult to decide immediately whether the alarm was in fact false.

(3) *Lack of adequate training.* This was the most commonly reported problem and stressor—and perhaps the most serious. As a consequence of insufficient training in the use of the equipment (frequently no more than the supplier's introduction, or learning on the job from partially knowledgeable colleagues) the other problems were magnified. That is, the cognitive demands on staff were increased and false alarms made more difficult to diagnose.

(4) *Ethical questions.* The technology made it more possible to sustain life. Several nurses commented that this could raise difficult questions in their own minds. Although the doctors had the formal responsibility, the nurses were faced with the question of, in what circumstances, a patient's life should be sustained if it was likely to result in only partial recovery and a future 'low grade' life. Also, since the technology was sometimes a scarce resource, questions arose about priorities for its use when no equipment was immediately available for a patient who could benefit from it.

The problem of high workload was reported in all the case studies. It served to magnify the effects of many of the other stress factors. There appear to be a number of causes for this common finding:

(a) There appeared to be a general shortage of nursing staff in hospital units. The Netherlands study suggested that shortages do not just occur in high technology units. In fact they can be worse in low technology units because, in a situation of fixed overall health budgets, increased resources for high technology units have the effect of 'draining' resources from other units.
(b) Advances in medicine and technology make possible *more* diagnostic and therapeutic procedures. These usually involve nurses in extra work, for example, carrying out the procedure or keeping administrative records of tests performed outside the unit. Since some of these procedures are invasive to patients, more time is required providing psychosocial support.
(c) Over recent years a policy has been widely introduced that leads to patients spending less time in hospital, and less time in the intensive care unit. The consequence is that the same number (or more) administrative, diagnostic and therapeutic procedures have to be carried out during a shorter stay. This intensifies the nurses' work.

This catalogue of stressors is, to some extent at least, offset by some positive job characteristics and environmental supports. These are:

(1) *High job quality*. Nurses, particularly in intensive care, experience a high degree of meaningfulness, responsibility, independence, variety and scope for development in their work. The other side of the 'pressure' coin is a responsible job held in high esteem by society, and by patients who are usually very grateful.
(2) *Opportunities*. Intensive care in particular provides opportunites for nurses to enhance their skills, and achieve promotion and increased pay.
(3) *Social supports*. This factor can be either positive or negative, depending on the 'climate' in the unit or hospital. For example, the Danish study found good relations within the unit between colleagues and with superiors. The atmosphere was seen as supportive and non-hierarchical. On the other hand, the Irish study found a bureaucratic climate and lack of recognition for nurses. 'Team work' was seen as poor and unsupportive. The Italian study commented that relations between nurses in the intensive care unit were good, but that the introduction of computer-based monitoring equipment has reduced the need—and opportunity—for communication between nurses, particularly at the point where one shift handed over to the next. Thus the study reported a lack of support amongst staff.

Stress Reactions and Coping

The Danish, Italian and Netherlands studies assessed nurses' stress reactions to their work environment. Overall, intensive care nurses did not appear to exhibit serious stress symptoms. The Danish report found indications of fatigue and psychological stress but few psychosomatic symptoms. Nurses who exhibited more symptoms tended to be young, relatively inexperienced, and without prior work experience of new technology. The Italian report found stress levels in the intensive care unit similar to levels experienced by other groups of workers. However, because of the shift system, fatigue did accumulate over several shifts, and was only relieved by the two-day break. The Netherlands report found a slight tendency for nurses in the lower technology units to experience greater stress.

Thus the extensive environmental stressors resulted in relatively mild stress symptoms. This may, in part, be due to the compensating positive qualities of the nurses' job. It may also indicate that nurses who experienced more stress transferred to a less demanding work environment. Some of the studies examined the ways that the nurses said they coped with stress. In the Irish study many nurses found it necessary to 'unwind' in their own time after work. They experienced little opportunity to influence their working environment which they reported as bureaucratic and unsupportive. The Danish study found that the nurses experienced most stress also tended to resort to *individual* coping strategies. It may be that the more experienced nurses felt more able to influence the sources of stress since the environment was seen as generally supportive. This appeared to be the more effective strategy for dealing with stressors if circumstances permitted it. However, all studies reported the time pressure that nurses work under. The Netherlands study concluded that, under such circumstances, there was not enough time or opportunity to participate in planning or other decisions which might have made it possible to influence the work environment.

The majority of nurses saw the benefits of using new technology, and in particular its life sustaining potential. However, they also experienced serious problems with its use, which fell into two broad categories—problems with design and reliability, and problems resulting from inadequate training. False alarms from monitoring equipment were a major source of anxiety and were focused on by the Danish, Italian and UK reports. All the studies concluded the training was insufficient.

Patients' Responses to New Technology

The Danish, Irish and Italian studies interviewed patients who had direct experience of intensive care. Generally patients had very positive views of the service they had received and were particularly grateful to the nurses. There did not appear to be any evidence that patients felt 'distanced' from nursing staff as a result of the technology.

However the Irish, Italian and Netherlands studies reported that the technology and the physical environment could be intrusive and invoke anxiety.

The Italian study reported that patients' relatives would have liked more information about the equipment in use. Invasive procedures also reduced patient mobility and brought a greater risk of infection. The UK study pointed out that the policy of shortest possible stay in a unit could create a 'conveyor-belt' environment.

The environment could be stressful for patients, and this seemed to depend on what support was provided by nursing staff to compensate, and on the environment itself. In some units, several patients were in a single ward and therefore shared the same environment. The Italian study highlighted a phenomenon referred to as the 'Intensive Care Syndrome' in which patients experienced temporal–spatial disorientation and almost total amnesia of the period in the unit. This may be attributed to a 'sensory deprivation effect', induced by no windows and constant lighting, and lack of routines and other cues to differentiate day and night in the unit. It may also be a mechanism which patients used to 'switch off' from the distress of other patients being experienced around them. There own invasive treatment may also have been a cause, and the study found a tendency for patients to tear off monitoring or treatment equipment. Since this endangered the patient's life, doctors administered a massive sedation. This may have been a cause of amnesia.

Individual rooms may provide a more positive environment, adaptable to the needs of the individual patient. However, there may be negative consequences for the nurses, who derive support from being with their colleagues and simultaneously being able to observe patients from a central point. Remote computer-based monitoring allowed the nurses to monitor from a central point even when the patients were in single rooms, but made it difficult to directly observe the patients. However, it may contribute to the positive team-work within the unit.

NEW TECHNOLOGY AND THE DEVELOPMENT OF THE NURSES' ROLE

The case studies identified a trend towards independent functions which may result in the nursing profession, in its classic form, ceasing to exist. New professions could be created, and patient care would then be provided by separate occupations for:

(1) Physical care and domestic work: tasks requiring minimal training in patient care.
(2) Psychosocial care: tasks involving psychologists, social workers, sick visitors, etc.
(3) Curing activities: tasks performed by paramedical workers trained in technical procedures.
(4) Medical advice: decisions made by medical consultants.

Were this degree of fragmentation and specialization to take place, a likely consequence would be isolation of workers within each branch of health care and greater problems of co-ordination. Nursing provides a valuable contribution which would be lost if the above trends continue extensively. This is the opportunity and ability to provide integrated support to patients, to respond to their physical and emotional needs, by providing information, care, guidance and organization.

A recurring theme in the case studies is the lack of involvement that nursing staff have had in the introduction of new technology, even though they were its main users. It is common for new equipment to 'arrive' for almost immediate use. Sometimes nurses are involved at a fairly advanced stage of installation when most of the technical and organizational decisions have been made, and the technology must be 'adapted' to the local environment and work situation.

Many of the nurses commented that they felt the technology could be of greater benefit to patient care, and less stressful to them, if they were more involved in its development, and the plans for its use. However, there appear to be at least four major pre-conditions for effective participation to take place.

(1) There must be a willingness on the part of hospital management for such involvement to take place. This might result from a recognition that more *effective* use of the technology could be a consequence.
(2) Nursing staff must *want* to participate in planning the development in their work. The evidence suggests that they do, but
(3) The high workload results in insufficient time and opportunity to get involved in organizational activities. Therefore more time needs to be made available.
(4) To make a useful contribution to technical developments nurses need sufficient practical experience of the potential and likely consequences of using new technology. This requires concrete training and practice *prior* to the installation of equipment.

The introduction of new technology into the work environment, like any other significant development, will stimulate change and uncertainty. This will almost inevitably be a source of stress for people working in that environment. Yet it is clear from the case studies reported in this chapter that that major sources of stress endure, well beyond the 'settling in' period. Despite the need to improve the work environment, the reasons behind the introduction of new technology rarely seem explicitly to address the problems faced by nursing staff.

There is too little consideration of the nurses' role as professional workers in the design of hospital information systems. If computer applications are to *benefit* the nursing process and assist nurses, either by reducing the workload or providing useful information, they are going to need the participation of nurses in their development.

REFERENCES

Agervold, M. and Kristensen, O. S. (1985). *The Impact of New Technology on Experienced Workers*. European Foundation for the Improvement of Living and Working Conditions, Dublin.
Bernhard, P. (1983). Psychological aids for the personnel of intensive care units. In H. J. Hannick, M. Wendt and P. Lawin (eds) *Psychosomatics of Intensive Medicine*, Stuttgart, New York.
Bishop, V. (1983). Stress in intensive care unit, *Occupational Health*, **35** (12), 537–43.
Caplan, R. D. *et al.* (1975). *Job Demands and Work Health: Main Effects and Occupational Differences*, US Government Printing Office, Washington DC.
Claus, K. Bailey, J. and Selye, H. (1980). *Living with Stress and Promoting Well-Being*, The CU Mosby Company, London, Toronto.
Cruickshank, P. J. (1982). Patient stress and the computer in the consulting room, *Social Science Medicine*, **16** (14), 1371–6.
Cruickshank, P.J. (1984). Computers in medicine: patients' attitudes, *Journal of the Royal College of General Practitioners*, **34**, 77–80.
Dohrenwend, B. S. and Dohrenwend, B. P. (eds) (1974). *Stressful Life Events: Their Nature and Effects*, John Wiley, New York.
Eden, D. (1982). Critical job events, acute stress and strain, *Organizational Behaviour and Human Performance*, **30**, 312–29.
Farmer, F. S. (1978). The impact of technology on nursing, *Nursing Mirror*, 28 September, 17–20.
Fitter, M. J. (1987). *The Impact of New Technology on Workers and Patients in the Health Service: (Physical and Psychological Stress) Consolidated Report*. European Foundation for the Improvement of Living and Working Conditions, Dublin.
Fitter, M. J., Garber, J. R., Herzmark, G. A., Robinson, D. and Jones, R. V. H. (1986). *A Prescription for Change: The Longer Term Use and Development of Computers in General Practice*, HMSO, London.
Gray-Toft, P. and Anderson, J. C. (1981). Stress among hospital nursing staff: its causes and effects, *Social Science Medicine*, **15**, 639–47.
Hannich, H. J., Wendt, M. and Lawin, P. (eds) (1983). *Psychosomatics of Intensive Medicine*, Stuttgart, New York.
Hay, D. H. and Oken, D. (1972). The psychological stresses of intensive care unit nursing, *Psychosomatic Medicine*, **34**, 2, 109–18.
Hepworth, S. and Fitter, M. J. (1981). Nurses' attitudes to computers in hospitals. Memo No. 419, MRC/ESCR Social and applied Psychology Unit, University of Sheffield.
Herzmark, G., Brownbridge, G., Fitter, M. and Evans, A. (1984). Consultation use of computers by General Practitioners, *Journal of the Royal College of General Practitioners*, **34**, 649–54.
Huckaby, L. M. D. and Jagla, B. (1979). Nurse's stress factors in the intensive care unit, *Journal of Nursing Administration*, **9** (2), 21.
Jacobsen, S. F. (1978). Nurses' stress in intensive and non-intensive care units. In S. F. Jacobsen and H. M. McGrath (eds) *Nurses Under Stress*, John Wiley, New York.
Jokinen, M. and Poyhonen, T. (1980). *Stress and Other Occupational Health Problems Afflicting Practical Nurses*, Institute of Occupational Health, Helsinki.
Jones, J. *et al.* (1979). What the patients say: a study of reactions to an ICU, *Intensive Care Medicine*, **5** (2), 89–92.
Karasek, R. A. (1979). Job demands, job decision latitude and mental strain: Implications for job redesign, *Administrative Science Quarterly*, **24**, 285–308.

Kornfeld, D. S. (1969). Psychiatric view of the ICU, *British Medical Journal*, **1**, 108.
Lazarus, R. S., Cohen, J. B. and Folman, S. (1980). Psychological stress and adaption—some unresolved issues. In M. Selye (ed.) *Guide to Stress Research*, Von Nostrand, New York.
Oborne, D. (1985). *Computers at Work: A Behaviour Approach*, John Wiley and Sons, Chichester.*
Parkers, K. R. (1982). Occupational stress among student nurses: a natural experiment, *Journal of Applied Psychology*, **67** (6), 784–96.
Potter, A. R. (1981). Computers in general practice: the patient's voice, *Journal of the Royal College of General Practitioners*, **31**, 83–5.
Pringle, M., Robins, S. and Brown, G. (1984). The patient's view, *British Medical Journal*, **228**, 28 January.
Redfern, S. J. (1979). The charge nurse: job attitudes and occupational stability. PhD thesis, University of Aston, Birmingham.
Reichle, M. J. (1975). Psychological stress in the intensive care unit, *Nurses Digest*, **3**, 12–15.
Reznikoff, M. *et al.* (1967). Attitudes towards computers among employees of a psychiatric hospital, *Mental Hygiene*, **51**, 419–25.
Rosenberg, M. *et al.* (1967). Attitudes of nursing students towards computers, *Nursing Outlook*, **15**, 44–6.
Selye, H. (1976). *The Stress of Life*, McGraw-Hill, New York.
Startsman, T. S. and Robinson, R. E. (1972). The attitudes of medical and paramedical personnel towards computers, *Computers and Biomedical Research*, **5**, 218–27.
Tabor, M. (1982). Health care job stresses, *Occupational Health and Safety*, **51** (12), 20–25.
Vredenberg, D. J. and Trinkous, R. J. (1983). An analysis of role stress among nurses, *Journal of Vocational Behaviour*, **22** (1), 82–95.
Yates, L. J. (1983). Technology in nursing, *Nurses Focus*, **5** (2), 8.
Zielstorff, R. D. and Birckhead, L. M. (1978). Automation in nursing, *Nursing Administration*, March, 49–53.

Stress in Health Professionals
Edited by R. Payne and J. Firth-Cozens
© 1987 John Wiley & Sons Ltd

Chapter 12

Medical Technologists and Laboratory Technicians: Sources of Stress and Coping Strategies

John M. Ivancevich

and

Michael T. Matteson

Medical technologists and laboratory technicians frequently refer to themselves as the unseen members of the health care team. This is not an altogether inapt description since most users of medical service have had little or no contact with these health care personnel and virtually none see them in their usual work environment, the clinical or medical laboratory.

Frequently referred to as clinical laboratory scientists by their professional associations, these are the trained personnel who as members of the health care team are responsible for assuring reliable test results which contribute to the prevention, diagnosis, prognosis, and treatment of physiological and pathological conditions. This includes producing accurate test results, correlating and interpreting test data, assessing and improving existing laboratory test methods, and designing, evaluating, and implementing new testing methods and procedures (ASMT, 1980).

Additional responsibilities include obtaining and processing specimens of blood, urine, sputum, feces, spinal fluid, and body tissue utilizing appropriate techniques and maintaining the integrity of the specimen in relation to the tests to be performed; establishing and maintaining systems for the identification, transportation, storage and disposal of specimens adhering to relevant policies and regulations including medico-legal custodial responsibilities; calibrations and operation of instruments and equipment using the appropriate materials and following established protocols; developing and monitoring quality assurance systems to insure adequate quality control of services provided and competence of laboratory personnel; and promoting an awareness and understanding of the services they render to the consumer and public and other health care professionals (ASMT, 1981).

PURPOSE OF THIS CHAPTER

In this chapter, we will examine the occupational stress experienced by medical technologists and laboratory technicians. Every occupation has a unique set of environmental events and circumstances that some job incumbents interpret as being stressful. Although medical technologists and laboratory technicians are important parts of the health team they are perhaps the least studied in terms of job stress and how to cope with dysfunctional stress.

The literature on occupational stress and the coping strategies used by medical technologists and laboratory technicians is ill-defined, unfocused, and somewhat limited. The purpose of this chapter is to describe the nature, sources, and available research regarding medical technologist and laboratory technician stress. We also examine coping processes that have been and are used to deal with occupational stress. Coping is examined since stress on the job is inevitable and may even be desirable within manageable limits. When possible, and if available, empirical results documenting these descriptions will be used. Also, a general framework to guide needed research will be highlighted.

Recently, theorists and researchers have proposed that occupational stress can be better understood and addressed if a multidisciplinary approach is used (Jamal, 1984; Revicki and May, 1985). That is, by using biomedical, behavioral science, and occupational theories, research, and applications a clearer perspective will emerge. Unfortunately, the called for multidisciplinary approach has not been applied in studies of medical technologists, laboratory technicians or, for that matter, most occupations.

Historically, interest in studying stress in occupations evolved because of its potential role in causing illness and health problems. Consequently, most definitions and frameworks used to examine stress exclude any discussion of positive effects. Stress formulations have pointed to consequences in a manner that frankly has converted the neutral concept of stress into a value laden construct. Therefore, although we will not turn this knowledge base around and broaden the perspective, it is important to recognize that some amount of stress in the work of medical technologists and laboratory technicians is vital to their growth, development, and motivation.

THE MEDICAL TECHNOLOGIST AND LABORATORY TECHNICIAN: JOB DESCRIPTIONS

Before proceeding with an examination of stress among medical technologists and laboratory technicians, we need to clearly examine the similarities and differences in the work of these professions. A major difference between a medical technologist and laboratory technician is primarily one of skill and responsibility level, which in turn is directly a function of educational requirements. Laboratory technicians can be certified after completing a two-year associate degree program beyond high school. The program focuses on clinical training curriculum which includes areas of medical ethics and conduct, medical terminology, basic chemical solutions, manipulation of specimens and an introduction to basic hematology, urinalysis, and blood banking. Technicians perform routine uncomplicated procedures which involve single-step processes where discrimination is clear, errors are few and easily corrected and results of the test can be confirmed with a reference test or source within the working area.

Most medical technologists, on the other hand, are college graduates (three years of college is the minimum requirement) with heavy emphasis in biological and chemical sciences, in addition to a twelve-month clinical training program. Medical technologists perform complex analyses and error correction, and must have the knowledge of physiological conditions affecting test results in order to confirm results and develop data which may be used by physicians in determining the presence and extent of disease. Graduate work at the masters and even doctoral level is frequently undertaken by technologists as part of a career advancement strategy. Some states require medical technologists to be licensed; virtually all career technologists complete an examination to become certified as professional technologists by one or several certification boards.

Medical technologists and laboratory technicians work in any setting that deals with analyses of biological processes and products. Approximately two-thirds work in hospital laboratories. The remaining work in labs in clinics of physicians' offices or work for pharmaceutical companies, public health departments, public and private research institutions, and medical departments of industrial firms (Chronical Occupational Brief, 1979).

From a historical perspective, medical technology is a relatively recent addition to the allied health care profession. Whether in fact it is a 'profession' or an occupation is a question which has been debated for numerous years. The American Society of Medical Technology, which is the professional association for technologists in the United States, takes the position that technologists are practicing scientists and that the body of knowledge with which they deal, the skill they must demonstrate, and the code of conduct to which they must adhere qualifies what they do as a profession (Price, 1978; ASMT, 1981). The question is more than one of semantics or of self-enhancement in that it has implications for such issues as certification and licensure and whether union representation is appropriate.

Regardless of how one views the 'professional' issue, the advent of medical technology in the United States is, for all practical purposes, post-First World War. While medical laboratories began appearing around the turn of the century, the first medical technology training programs were not established until the 1920s (Williams, 1976). At that time, there were approximately 3500 workers classified as medical technicians, but that figure did not differentiate between what today we designate as medical or laboratory technologists and technicians, and it also included some dental and industrial workers. Then, as now, medical technology was a female dominated profession, with some 2000 of those 3500 being female. Today, the American Society for Medical Technology has a membership of about 100,000, with an even greater concentration of females.

The laboratory is an exacting work environment. It demands extremely high levels of accuracy in performance, frequently under severe time pressures, and with the consequences of an error almost always being serious and sometimes even fatal. Because of the context and requirements of work in a laboratory it can be suggested that job stress may be a major concern among some medical technologists and laboratory technicians. The nature of the people drawn to the laboratory, coupled with certain attributes inherent in the work environment, combine to produce a relatively high degree of career frustration, disillusionment, and burnout. In any occupational setting, if stress is excessive, the potential negative consequences to both the individuals experiencing the stress and the organizations that employ them are many and may be expressed in a variety of different ways. As we shall see, the laboratory is no exception to this general rule.

A CONCEPTUAL MODEL

Even a cursory review of the occupational stress literature results in a series of definitions, jargonese, and frameworks. We prefer to not add to the already unmanageable series of lists. Instead we prefer to use a simple framework referred to here as the Activator-Reaction-Consequence (A-R-C) model (Elliott and Eisdorfer, 1982). Activators are designated as those internal and external environmental events or conditions that change a person's present state. There are actual and potential activators. These actual and potential activators are called stressors.

A person has a *reaction* to activators in terms of a physical or psychological response. Over a period of time the reaction may change. For example, a medical technologist may initially fear losing her job after being reprimanded by a supervisor. However, this initial reaction may change to anger because the supervisor is perceived to be so unfair.

Consequences are the sequellae to reactions. Sometimes, consequences occur long after a reaction or closely follow a reaction. One possible consequence of the activator-reaction linkage can be changes in physical and/or mental health.

The sequence of activator to reaction to consequence can be predictable in some circumstances. Usually, however, a degree of predictability can only be achieved in experimentally controlled conditions. Typically, sequences are much

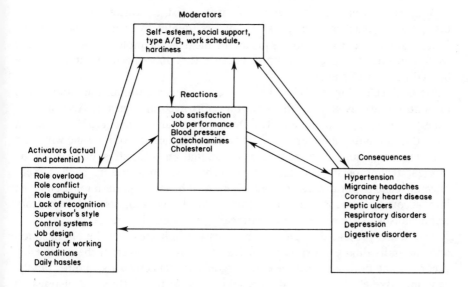

Figure 1 Stress framework for studying medical technologists and laboratory technicians

more complex and are influenced by mediators or moderators. These are the modifiers that act on each stage in the A–R–C sequence to produce individual variations. An understanding of the role of moderators can help explain why medical technologists or laboratory technicians experience similar work situations differently.

Figure 1 presents the activator–reaction–consequence–moderator framework used to guide our examination of occupational stress among medical technologists and laboratory technicians.

The activator catergory includes a number of role factors. The medical technologist and laboratory technician must deal with requests from different individuals (conflict) for work and analysis, a large number of requests (overload), and occasionally, ambiguous requests. In addition, there is the supervisor's style or how a person in charge attempts to influence and direct subordinates. A supervisory style that is incompatible with a subordinate's preferred style or needs can result in excessive stress and eventually a negative reaction such as a cutback in performance or anxiety that contributes to changes in physical conditions.

The organizationally sanctioned controls used to oversee the work of the medical technolgist or laboratory technician can be restrictive, arbitrary, or coercive. Orders to file reports, conduct work as the supervisor desires, or work specific shifts can be stressful. The working conditions, lighting, space, and colors, can also be stress producers.

A set of activators or sources of stress exist to various degress of all occupations—teachers, accountants, lawyers, dental hygienists, stockbrokers. Their nature, intensity, and frequency in medical technology and laboratory work can only be speculated upon because they have been investigated in a limited number of studies.

Medical technologists and laboratory technicians are unique individuals who respond in various ways to the activators portrayed in Figure 1. According to experts such as Appley and Trumbull (1967) and Selye (1976), it is an individual's unique make-up which provides an indication of how she will react to certain conditions. Therefore, in any examination of the stress experienced by medical technologists and laboratory technicians, moderators such as self-esteem, social support networks, and Type A/B behavior pattern must be taken into account. Perhaps there are some medical technologists and laboratory technicians who are more characterisitically predisposed to stress.

The model presented to guide our discussion indicates that the organization and the individual are primary sources of stress. However, to be completely accurate, one must also include extra-organizational activators—home, family, economy. We elected to not discuss or include at this early stage of research development this important part of each of our lives. Instead we will emphasize only research that examines work-related stress, reactions, and consequences. Our decision to exclude extra-organizational activators is based on the fact that to date very few theorists and researchers have even attempted to integrate work and extra-organizational activators.

Occupational Stress Research

The health care field is a highly stressful environment. There is undoubtedly a variety of contributing factors, including the nature of the individuals attracted to these professions, the life and death nature of the health care business, the physical and psychic demands made on health care providers, and simply the fact that health services is a labor intensive industry. By far the greatest amount of research in the area of occupational stress among health care providers has focused on physicians. Numerous studies and conferences have documented and addressed the stress problems of physicians (see, for example, Steppacker and Mausner, 1974; Frederick, 1979; American Medical Association, 1982). Few of the numerous other members of the health care profession have been identified as experiencing high levels of occupational stress. Including nurses, dentists, physical therapists, hospital administrators, paramedics, and laboratory personnel.

While the research which addresses work stress among laboratory personnel in general, and medical technologists and laboratory technicians especially, is not numerous, it can none the less be categorized in one of two ways: research which has focused on relating stress with occupations in general and which consequently has highlighted medical laboratory personnel as falling into the high stress group, or research directed specifically toward obtaining information dealing with the role, extent, and causes of stress among laboratory personnel.

As an example of the former, Terborg (1985) cites a National Institute for Occupational Safety and Health study which, by focusing upon death rates and admission records to hospitals and mental health facilities, ranked various occupations by reasonably objective measures of stress. Included in the seven highest rated occupations was that of laboratory technician, the only health-related occupation mentioned in the high stress group.

In a related and methodologically similar study, Colligan, Smith and Hurrell (1977) report even more striking results. These investigators examined admission records of community mental health centers in one state to determine the incidence rate of diagnosed mental health disorders for the 130 occupations with the largest number of workers in the state. Computing admission rates per 1000 workers to control for variations in the total number of individuals employed in an occupation, six were health related, with four of those in the top ten. Medical technologists and laboratory technicians both were included among those in the top ten ('You Can Cope', 1977).

These studies were intended to provide a basis for defining certain occupations as posing mental health problems due to the stressful demands made up job holders. It should be noted, however, that there are a number of potentially serious limitations (acknowledged by the authors) with these kind of data. First, professional and managerial workers are probably under-represented due to the greater likelihood these individuals would seek treatment at private, rather than public, facilities. Second, occupational differences in mental health admissions are not necessarily a function of work-related stress rather than other life stresses which may be related to occupation, such as education or socioeconomic level. Third, causality cannot be assumed here, even if the occupation-admission rate link is one of cause and effect, which is not entirely clear.

Because medical technology is a female dominated occupation, a comment regarding sex differences is appropriate here. In Colligan, Smith and Hurrell's (1977) study, 39 per cent of the workers were female, but females constituted 53 per cent of mental health admissions. Is this because women are disproportionately represented in high stress occupations? Or does it perhaps suggest that some occupations are ranked high because they are female dominated? Makosky (1980) concludes that women have higher depression scores and higher levels of psychophysiological symptoms that do men. Is that a true sex difference or is it perhaps a sex role difference? Or is it simply an indication that women are more open about admitting problems and seeking help than are men? On the other hand, Warr and Parry (1982) found in reviewing the literature on employment status and psychological well-being that women are similar to men when occupational involvement, the quality of non-work relationships, and the quality of the job role are similar for males and females. Clearly there are important questions that need to be asked and empirically investigated among medical technologists and laboratory technicians.

The second categorization of laboratory-focused stress research includes those studies which have focused specifically upon medical technologists and/or laboratory technicians. Once again, the literature is sparse, although at least one comprehensive study involving a large number of laboratory workers in numerous locations in the United States has been completed and will be described in detail subsequently.

The first attempt to address the question of stress in the laboratory came about directly as a result of the previously cited Colligan *et al.* (1977) study. Interested in why the job of medical technologist received such a high ranking, Woolley (1978) interviewed a small number of technologists in selected hospitals. Attempting to learn the causes of stress, Woolley identified such factors as the constant pressure for accuracy in performing tests, physicians and their failure to understand the constraints under which technologists work, the inadequate monetary and human rewards, lack of recognition from nurses of the critical role playing by the technologists, and exposure to disease and disease-bearing organisms. No attempt was made to distinguish between major and minor stress sources or between differences in frequency versus intensity. While the Woolley (1978) data are anecdotal in nature from a very small sample, the study does represent the first attempt to identify stress sources in the laboratory. Elving (1978) in a similar anectodal manner, identified similar stressors in an article for general consumption in the popular press.

A more scientific investigation of the cause of stress among medical technologists and technicians was undertaken by Griffin and Klun (1981). These investigators, associated with a medical technology teaching program, complied a test of potential stressors based upon talking with technologists, reviewing the literature, and their own personal experiences. This list was pretested with both practicing technologists and medical technology graduate students. After revisions, through the addition, deletion, and combination of items, 22 stressors were included for the study. Table 1 shows these stressors in descending order of most to least stressful as ranked by *all respondents in the study.*

Questionnaires, asking the respondent to rank order the items on the basis of how much stress each was responsible for causing, were mailed to 150 hospital laboratories. Three labs in each state, one of which was part of a hospital with fewer than 100 beds, and two which were associated with hospitals of over 100 beds, were randomly selected. Ninety-four surveys were returned (64 per cent response rate) completed by technologists, technicians, and certified laboratory assistants.

As can be seen from an inspection of Table 1, many stressors are not unique to the laboratory, but may be present in virtually any organizational setting. Lack of communication (4), being overworked (7), meeting deadlines (8), lack of support from a supervisor (9), lack of recognition (10), lack of authority (14),

Table 1 Rank Order of Stressors from Griffin and Klun (1981)

1. Doctors: Their failure to understand the laboratory situation and/or standing over you waiting for test results.
2. Stats.
3. The need for accuracy.
4. Lack of communication: Between lab shifts; between lab and doctors and staff.
5. Fear of making an error: Clerical error, test error, instrument error, identification error of patient or specimen.
6. Fearing a patient may die because of your mistake.
7. Being overworked.
8. Meeting deadlines.
9. Lack of support from pathologist and/or supervisor.
10. Lack of recognition and/or appreciation by physicians and other hospital staff.
11. Taking home the fear of a mistake.
12. Performing back-up methods to which you are no longer accustomed when the usual method is unavailable.
13. Knowing the patient you are working on may die.
14. Lack of authority to make decisions.
15. Low wages.
16. Working conditions: too hot, too cold, lack of space.
17. Job evaluations.
18. Exposure to contagious diseases.
19. Being uncertain of your job responsibilities.
20. Working with fellow employees.
21. Being unqualified for the work you are doing.
22. Working with caustic or toxic chemicals.

low wages (15), working conditions (16), performance evaluations (17), uncertainty about job responsibilities (19), fellow employees (20), and being unqualified for the job (21) fall into this category. Other stressors represent conditions or concerns that are unique to the laboratory setting. Included in this category are doctors (1); stats (2), which are emergency orders for tests requiring that all other work be stopped, fearing a patient may die because of mistake (6); taking home the fear of a mistake (11); knowledge that a patient may die (13); exposure to contagious diseases (18); and working with caustic or toxic chemicals.

Among the higher ranked stressors, not a great deal of difference was found in the ordering between small (less than 100 beds) and large (more than 100 beds) hospitals. The most significant differences involved the two stressors of fear of making an error and meeting deadlines were ranked fourth and ninth respectively by technologists in small hospitals and reversed (ninth and fourth) by those in larger ones. Comparisons between supervisory and non-supervisory technologists were also made among the higher ranked stressors. Again there was not a great deal of difference with the largest rank changes occurring with the three stressors of being overworked, lack of support, and lack of recognition. Supervisors ranked these items fourth, seventh, and eleventh, respectively, while non-supervisors rated them eighth, eleventh, and seventh.

One stressor which was not included in the Griffin and Klun (1981) questionnaire, was none the less mentioned by a number of respondents as being an important cause of stress. This was the lack of professional identity. As one respondent states, 'Few people know who we are, what we do, what kind of training we've had. This is true not only of the general public (who in jest call us vampires) but also of other professions in the medical field'. This comment tends to validate the opening sentences of this chapter.

THE NATIONAL MEDICAL TECHNOLOGIST STUDY

In 1979, the authors of this chapter began a comprehensive study of medical technologists and laboratory technicians designed to identify the extent and cause of job-related stress and coping mechanisms employed in dealing with perceived stress. With the co-operation of the leading professional medical technology journal in the United States, a brief description of the proposed research project was published (Matteson, 1979), along with a form for those technologists interested in participating to complete and return to the study investigators. A total of 904 individuals initially agreed to participate. Several volunteers were eliminated either because they were not technologists or technicians or because they were not employed on a full-time basis. This reduced the initial sample to 822.

A 468-item questionnaire was prepared specifically for this project. A number of dimensions were assessed, including: overall stress, work-related stress, nonwork-related stress, and specific stressors (e.g. role conflict, politics, rewards, communication problems, and responsibility pressure); personality characteristics (e.g. tolerance for ambiguity, coronary-prone behavior patterns, locus of control, and tension discharge characteristics); health issues (including number, duration, and severity of health complaints, work missed for health reasons, rate at which health affected work performance, and psychosomatic symptoms); and possible stress-related behaviors (alcohol consumption, tranquilizer use, asprin use, coffee consumption, and smoking behavior). Additionally, participants were asked to complete an open-ended form describing: (1) a work incident they found particularly stressful; (2) the most significant sources of work stress for them; and (3) what they did to try and deal with stress in their lives. Of the 822 individuals receiving the questionnaire, usable reponses were received from 682 for a response rate of 83 per cent. In view of the fact that the average time required for the participants to complete the materials was two hours and 45 minutes, the rate of return was considered excellent. Because of the sheer size of the study, only highly significant findings will be summarized here.

Overall work stress. Of the various stress measures used, one was an indication of overall work related stress to which the participant was asked to

Table 2 Summary of significant work-related variables

*** 1. *Goal direction.* The extent to which the organization is perceived to lack direction and have poorly understood plans and objectives.
*** 2. *Politics.* The extent to which politics rather than performance affect organizational decisions.
*** 3. *Supervisory style.* The extent to which the quality of supervision is felt to be lacking.
*** 4. *Organizational practices.* The extent to which administrative policies and practices hinder rather than facilitate performance.
*** 5. *Communication.* The extent to which the flow of information is neither timely nor sufficient.
*** 6. *Participation.* The extent to which management is receptive to input from employees.
*** 7. *Underutilization.* The extent to which job assignments are not challenging and do not require full use of skills and abilities.
*** 8. *Dissatisfaction.* The extent to which there is general dissatisfaction with the job and/or the organization.
*** 9. *Role ambiguity.* The extent to which people do not clearly understand what is expected of them.
*** 10. *Role conflict.* The extent to which people are presented with conflicting demands or an unclear chain of command.
*** 11. *Quantitative overload.* The extent to which there is too great a volume of work to accomplish in the allotted time.
*** 12. *Qualitative overload.* The extent to which job requirements exceed the ability or skill level of the person performing the job.
*** 13. *Career progress.* The extent to which there are few opportunities to advance and/or learn new skills and techniques.
*** 14. *Time pressures.* The extent to which unreasonable deadlines and time demands are imposed.
*** 15. *Responsibility pressure.* Feeling an overwhelming responsibility to do the job correctly and quickly despite any problems or inadequacies of equipment or assistance.
*** 16. *Quality concern.* Feeling concerned about being able to adhere to quality standards in the face of other demands.
*** 17. *Job vs. nonjob conflict.* Extent to which job demands interfere with family and/or leisure activities.
*** 18. *Intrinsic rewards.* The extent to which the job provides a feeling of internal satisfaction, challenge and accomplishment.
*** 19. *Extrinsic rewards.* The extent to which the job provides security, good working conditions, and acceptable pay and fringe benefits.
*** 20. *Importance rewards.* The extent to which the job has status and prestige and is viewed as important relative to other jobs in the organization.
** 21. *Control rewards.* The extent to which the job occupant can control work rate and effort and attention necessary to do the job.
*** 22. *Occupatonal self-esteem.* The extent to which the job-holder views herself or himself to be successful, important, and doing a good job.
*** 23. *Job satisfaction.* The degree of overall satisfaction experienced from the job.

**Significant at $p < 0.001$, F-test between high and low stress groups.
***Significant of $p < 0.0001$, F-test between high and low stress groups.
High stress group = 243; low stress group = 179.

respond regarding how frequently the situation described was a source of stress. Reponses could range from 'never' through 'always', using a seven-point scale. In one analysis the sample was divided into a low work stress group (average per-item response of 3 or less) and a high work stress group (average per-item response of 5 or more). Table 2 summarizes those work-related variables measured which showed significant differences between low and high stress groups. The first fourteen were measures developed primarily for this study (see Appendix for scale); variables 15–23 were modified from those used in previous research (House, McMichael and Wells, 1979).

Variables 1–14 in Table 2 were all four-item measures in which the respondent was asked to indicate how often the condition or situation described was a source of stress. Note that this is different from indicating the frequency of the condition. Thus, for example, in the case of goal direction, a respondent could perceive a definite and chronic lack of goal direction on the part of the organization but might not experience any degree of personal stress as a consequence. In each case the difference in these first fourteen measures was in the expected direction. That is, the high work stress group reported higher levels of stress on these measures than did the low work stress group.

Variables 15–17 were three-item measures. Once again, the differences were significant in the expected direction. This high stress group indicated they felt more responsibility pressure, more quality concern and more job versus nonjob conflict than the low stress group. Variables 18–21 were four-to-eight item measures, all reflecting some aspect of the potential rewards associated with the job. For these items respondents were asked simply to indicate how true a series of positively worded statements were with respect to the four reward categories, with the low stress groups agreeing more strongly with the positive statements than did the high stress group.

Variable 22 were a three-item measure designed to assess the extent to which the respondents felt that the work of a medical technologist was important and that they were a success in their chosen occupation, with the high stress group reporting lower occupational self-esteem. The final variable in Table 2 was a five-item measure of overall job satisfaction. Not surprisingly, the low stress group reported higher levels of satisfaction than the high stress group. This finding of a relationship between stress and satisfaction is consistent with the data on medical technologist's job satisfaction ratings reported by Broski, Manuselis and Noga (1982).

In addition to the measures in Table 2, a number of nonwork-related or job-independent variables were significantly related to overall work stress. This high work stress group was younger and comprised of a disproportionately large number of females. Similarly, number of years in the profession was associated with overall stress, with fewer years working as a medical technologist correlating with high stress. Clearly, years in the profession and age are highly correlated and, consequently, the former may be what accounts for the latter's significant difference between the two groups.

Not surprisingly, Type A behavior (Friedman and Rosenman, 1974) was related to stress among laboratory personnel, with more Type A respondents in the high stress group and more of their Type B counterparts in the low stress group. The differences in stress levels between As and Bs become even greater in Type As in Type A organizations as compared with Type B technologists working in Type B organizations. (For a complete treatment of the notion of Type A and B organizations and how this is related to stress among medical technologists, see Matteson and Ivancevich, 1982b).

Other job-independent variables which showed significant differences between high and low work stress groups included scores on a screening scale for psychiatric symptoms (depression, restlessness, worry, general nervousness, etc.); the frequency, severity and total number of incidences of 28 specific psychosomatic health complaints reported experienced during the most recent six months; the extent to which ill health had affected job performance; frequency of prescription tranquilizer use; reported feelings of impending nervous breakdown; and the extent of experiencing a decrement in job performance because of feeling below par. With all these variables the most recent six-month period was used as the time frame, and in all cases the differences between the high and low stress groups were in the expected direction.

While the variables included in the questionnaire used in this study provided a great deal of information about stress among medical technologists, the questionnaire did not directly address specific causes or sources of stress, nor did it directly provide information regarding stress coping strategies and mechanisms. To address these issues, a second questionnaire was prepared, using the responses to the three open-ended questions from the first questionnaire as a basis for identifying specific sources of stress and coping mechanisms.

The second round of data collection in the study was accomplished using a 318-item questionnaire constructed, in part, from the open-ended responses received in the first round. Part I consisted of 22 job factors derived from the first round and which described potentially stressful job occurrences (e.g. pressure for immediate results, lack of advancement opportunities, need for accuracy, etc.). Respondents were asked to rank these potential stressors twice, first in terms of how *frequently* the event was distressing and then in terms of how *upsetting* or *distressing* the event was. Similarly, Part II consisted of 28 ways a respondents might deal with stress. These, like Part I, were derived from open-ended responses received in round one of the study (e.g. confide in a spouse, meditate, confront the person or situation causing the distress, etc.). Respondents were first asked to rank these in terms of how they would *prefer* to deal with their stress, and then rerank them in terms of how they *actually* dealt with stress. Subsequent parts of the questionnaire repeated items that were included in the first round of data collection. Tables 3 and 4 summarize the findings from the first two parts of the questionnaire.

Table 3 shows the rank order of stress sources in terms of both frequency and intensity. Thus, for example, pressure for immediate results is the highest rated stressor in terms of the frequency with which it causes stress, while lack of communications is the highest ranked with respect to the intensity of the stress experience. As can be seen in Table 3, the ordering by intensity follows closely the ordering by frequency. Only three items deviate by five places or more between the two sets of ranks: equipment failures, poor physical working conditions, and fear of making an error. These differences indicate that the first two of these are not, in terms of their impact on people, particularly serious stressors, while the third (fear of making an error) is a particularly potent stressor when it occurs. The relative rankings shown in Table 3 are similar to those reported by Griffin and Klun (1981), although there are some fairly large differences in specific items (e.g. need for accuracy was second in the Griffin and Klun study, twenty-first in Matteson and Ivancevich).

Although not shown in the table, there were some differences in rankings when respondents were divided in the high and low stress groups discussed earlier. With respect to frequency, the low stress group indicated a far higher frequency with respect to equipment failures, patient test selection, and physicians. The high stress group, on the other hand, ranked significantly higher in lack of advancement, lack of support from supervisor/pathologist and poor quality of supervision. It appears that the low stress group reports a higher frequency of events which tend to upset the flow of specific tasks, while the high stress group focuses on larger, more pervasive issues.

Even greater differences between the low and high stress groups exist among the intensity rankings. The number one item, for example, for the low stress group was pressure for immediate results, which ranked thirteenth for the high stress technologists. Similarly, lack of advancement opportunities was second for the high stress group and fifteenth among the low stress group. In general, the differences between high and low stress technologists with respect to intensity is one of emphasis. Career progress and achievement stressors received high rankings from high stress respondents, while stressors related to interactions with people rated high among low stress respondents. The data suggests that the high stress technologists tend to be individuals who are career oriented and who are experiencing frustration in satisfying that orientation.

Overall there is nothing particularly surprising in the rankings for either frequency or intensity. Some stress sources appear to be a function of laboratory management (e.g. lack of communications, lack of supervisor support, poor supervision quality, job and role ambiguity). Increased management awareness and skill training may offer a partial solution to these problems. Others (e.g. poor financial rewards, lack of recognition, lack of advancement, and physicians) may be related to an undervaluing of the medical technologist's job by others. For most people, feeling that what they do is neither appreciated nor understood by others is a source of distress. Medical technologists are no different in this regard. Some of these stressors can be reduced by educating people as to the real worth and contribution of the medical technologist.

Table 3 Rank Order of Stress Sources in Terms of Frequency and Intensity

Stress source	Total sample-frequency ($N = 462$)	Total sample-intensity ($N = 462$)
1. Pressure for immediate results	1	2
2. Lack of communications	2	1
3. Constant interruptions	3	5
4. Scheduling and workload problems	4	4
5. Interpersonal conflicts	5	3
6. Equipment failures	6	11
7. Patient test selection	7	6
8. Physicians	8	8
9. Lack of advancement opportunity	9	10
10. Lack of support from supervisor and/or pathologist	10	7
11. Poor quality of supervision	11	13
12. Lack of recognition	12	9
13. Apathy of peers and supervisors	13	15
14. Poor financial rewards	14	14
15. Poor physical working conditions	15	20
16. Favoritism	16	17
17. Lack of professionalism among staff	17	18
18. Fear of making an error	18	12
19. Being blamed unjustifiably for errors	19	16
20. Job and role ambiguity	20	19
21. Constant need for accuracy	21	21
22. Exposure to contagious disease	22	22

The National Medical Technologist Study, besides examining stress, also investigated the coping processes used by medical technologists. Table 4 displays the rankings for the 27 coping mechanisms included in the questionnaire. They are shown in terms of *preferences* for handling stress and by actual *frequency* of use. In general, the two rank orders are very positive in that the order corresponds very well with what is known about positive and negative ways of dealing with stress. Thus, confrontation, exercise, confiding in a spouse, talking with friends are high in both ranks, while less positive approaches such as prescription medicine, illegal drug use, and smoking were low. The most significant difference between the preference and frequency rankings had to do with suppression of feelings, which ranked 26th as a preference and ninth in terms of actual frequency. It no doubt owes its higher frequency rating to the fact that it represents a socially desirable reaction. Frequently, we are taught it isn't nice to show anger and that polite people keep 'bad' feelings to themselves. Thus to vent negative feelings goes against how many people were taught to behave. The same explanation may partially account for the much higher position of rationalization in the frequency rankings compared with preferences.

Table 4 Rank Order of Coping Mechanisms in Terms of Preferences and Frequency

Stress solution	Total sample-preference (N = 462)	Total sample-frequency of use (N = 462)
1. Confront stressor (person or situation)	1	2
2. Engage in exercise or sports activity	2	7
3. Confide in spouse	3	3
4. Visit and/or talk with friends	4	5
5. Seek solitude	5	4
6. Complain to someone	6	1
7. Engross yourself in a hobby	7	25
8. Have a drink (alcoholic)	8	12
9. Physically express frustration	9	11
10. Cry	10	15
11. Sleep	11	6
12. Listen to music	12	26
13. Pray	13	14
14. Go out (to a movie, take a drive, etc.)	14	20
15. Read	15	16
16. Use marijuana or similar drugs	16	18
17. Eat	17	10
18. Rationalize your feelings	18	8
19. Take prescription medicine (tranquilizers, etc.)	19	21
20. Smoke a cigarette	20	17
21. Yell	21	24
22. Do household chores	22	19
23. Watch TV	23	13
24. Shop	24	27
25. Take a break	25	22
26. Suppress your feelings	26	9
27. Meditate	27	23

Effective coping is certainly important to mental (and physical) health, but a work environment which minimizes stressors also minimizes the need to cope. For most laboratory personnel, work represents a time commitment exceeded by no other single activity in their lives. Ideally, this time should be satisfying, should contributive positively to the quality of life, should respect health, and should leave adequate time for rest and leisure pursuits. Unfortunately, this is not the case for many technologists. For them the work environment contains numerous sources of tension, anxiety, frustration, and conflict. Rather than providing satisfaction, it is often a source of dissatisfaction. Rather than contributing to growth, it inhibits it. Rather than respecting health, it often serves as a catalyst for physical and mental health problems. And rather than allowing planned for leisure time, it may become a central time commitment that detracts from the development of offwork pursuits.

COPING: FURTHER CLARIFICATION

Lazarus and Folkman (1984) define coping as constantly changing cognitive and behavioral efforts to manage specific external and/or internal demands that are appraised as taxing or exceeding the resources of the person. It is important to note their use of the word *manage*. By using the word manage Lazarus and Folkman suggest that employees such as medical technologists and laboratory technicians can minimize, avoid, tolerate, and accept the stressful conditions as well as attempts to master the environment.

Effective coping with job stress can serve numerous functions for employees. Mechanic (1974) cites three important coping functions: dealing with social and environmental demands, creating the motivation to meet those demands, and maintaining a state of psychological equilibrium in order to direct energy and skill toward external demands.

An important part of the coping process is the way an individual appraises the environment (e.g. pressure for immediate results, lack of communications, constant interruptions). The first appraisal made is asking: What is at stake? Coping efforts are made in response to stressful appraisals that signal harm, loss, threat or challenge. Harm or loss refers to damage that has already occurred, threat refers to harm or loss that has not yet occurred but is anticipated, and challenge refers to an anticipated opportunity for mastery or gain. If a medical technologist attempts to cope with the pressure for immediate results she is, in effect, attempting to change the relationship between herself and the person applying the pressure or change her feelings about job pressures. Thus, coping is a dynamic process that involves a relational circumstance: person (medical technologist) and environment (physician making a request). The idea that stress is determined by a relationship between the person and the environment has been expressed by numerous writers (McGrath, 1970; Van Harrison, 1978; Withey, 1962).

Research on Coping

Folkman and Lazarus (1980) conducted an empirical study on the ways 100 adults coped with the stressful events of daily living. Seven monthly interviews were conducted. At the conclusion of the interviews participants indicated on a 68-item 'Ways of Coping' checklist those strategies used to cope. The items included defense coping (e.g. avoidance, suppression), information seeking, problem-solving, and direct action coping methods. In general, the researchers found that emotion-focused forms of coping are likely to be used when there has been an appraisal that nothing can be done to modify harmful or challenging environmental conditions. Problem-focused forms of coping were used when the participants felt that conditions were amenable to change.

Billings and Moos (1981) used a random selection of families within specific census tracts in the San Francisco Bay area to study coping responses to stressful life events. The researchers found that participants relied more on active attempts to deal with an event and less on avoidance or indirect coping methods. The active steps included cognitive (e.g. tried to see the positive side) and behavioral (e.g. talked with spouse, talked with professional person).

The National Medical Technologist coping results displayed in Tables 3 and 4 suggest that emotion-focused forms of coping are the type most used. This finding, coupled with the coping research results reported in the literature, suggest that medical technologists (1) used active methods to deal with job stress; (2) relied on emotion-focused coping activities; and (3) may have reached the point of concluding that they must engage in emotional coping practices because there is little they can do to modify (problem-based coping) their working situation.

RESEARCH AGENDA: STRESS AND COPING

As indicated in the chapter, the rigor and depth of research involving medical technologists and laboratory technicians' occupational stress and coping activities is limited. There is little agreement among researchers on what work events are even disruptive. This is a common problem among stress researchers and it needs to be thoroughly addressed so that a body of knowledge on the job-related stressors among medical technologists and laboratory technicians begins to emerge, so that research can become more focused.

Stress

The lack of clarity on what constitutes stress among medical technologists and technicians can be improved with focused, systematic research studies that employ a multimodal approach to studying stress. Researchers should describe and define the stressors they are studying, identify the reactions and consequences, and identify the moderators of the stress–reactions–consequences link. The data gathered on stressors, reactions, consequences, and moderators should be collected using self-report, interview, historical, and personal observation modes of data collection. That is, reliance on a single approach for studying these factors should be avoided and discouraged. Single mode approaches take less time, but they may miss important information on how medical technologists and laboratory technicians became stressed and react to such stress.

There is a pressing research need to examine work conditions, events, and situations faced by medical technologists and laboratory technicians so that we learn why they become stressful. Many researchers have preselected stressors on the basis of familiarity and convenience and pay little attention to whether they are really stressful for job incumbents. Research on a job incumbent-generated set of stressors could produce more accurate information on what makes an event or situation stressful to medical technologists or laboratory technicians. Such research would permit the compilation of lists of potential stressors that have a reasonable probability of being stressors in specific settings among specific individuals.

We are simply raising the issue of whether researcher-generated lists of stressors are a better and more precise picture of the stress experienced by medical technologists and laboratory technicians than what the job incumbents themselves could develop. At this point there can only be speculation about which list is more accurate. There is a possibility that the researcher and job incumbent lists would be quite different because of perceptual, experience, and observation variances.

Research efforts to identify health changes among medical technologists and laboratory technicians that are associated with exposure to stressors should be increased. The manner in which a medical technologist or technician deals with stress may affect health, attitudes, or overall social functioning. Identification of patterns of consequences associated with a stressor or a group of stressors might offer a better understanding of the cumulative effects of stressors and what are the most effective coping procedures.

Another important unanswered research question centers on moderators. Researchers need to study various types of moderators and determine which individuals they affect. Such research may identify medical technologists and technicians who are most likely to have a particular reaction or consequence to a specific stressor. This information could be used for counseling and intervention purposes. In order for this line of research to yield relevant results more attention must be paid to isolating crucial mediators and developing accurate measures for their assessment.

There is a need to address the reaction-to-consequence sequence in Figure 1 more closely. Whether or not there is a stress effect on the immune system of medical technologists and technicians has not been studied or reported in the literature. Researchers studying other occupational groups suggest that stressors are risk factors for many types of infections, rheumatoid arthritis, and for some forms of cancer (Ader, 1981; Keicolt-Glaser, *et al.*, 1984; Laudenslager *et al.*, 1983). They further suggest that a reduced immune system capability is a major problem in these health disorders. Studies using medical technologists and technicians have, at this point, failed to address the immune system. The effects of stress on the immune system is a relatively new area of research. For many years, most researchers have believed that immunological function was independent of psychosocial factors. However, recent research suggest that this assumption is no longer tenable. The immune system appears to be integrated with other physiological processes and to be subject to some regulation by the brain (Ader, 1981).

There is a clear need for interdisciplinary studies of the entire sequence of activator–reactions–consequences. In order to fully comprehend the connections between stress, health, psychological, sociological, and work behaviors a wide range of research expertise must be focused on the entire sequence. Few researchers possess such a range of expertise. Therefore, in order to advance our understanding of medical technologist and technician stress, reaction, and consequences, an interdisciplinary team approach is needed.

Coping

The brief review of the empirical research on coping in general, and coping among medical technologists and laboratory technicians specifically, indicates that there have been few systematic investigations of the cost and benefits of coping processes in terms of health, stress reduction, and quality of life. There is an obvious need in the empirically-based literature for some order in assessing coping. Asking medical technologists or laboratory technicians 'How did you cope with _____?' is apt to result in various interpretations. What would happen if we asked a medical technologist how she coped with a stat request? Perhaps the technologist does not view the stat request as really urgent; or perhaps she views it as a serious situation; or are we asking about dealing with a disliked physician who harasses technologists with stat requests?

The 'How did you cope with _____?' question is too broad and general. A more specific, focused approach to assessing coping is needed. Studying and researching a critical incident methodology may be the way to assess specific coping processes. First researchers would need to identify critical job incidents. Then the medical technologist or laboratory technician could report how she behaved, felt, and handled the critical incident. This method needs to be studied to determine if it more accurately portrays coping processes in everyday workplace situations. There are, of course, problems with this type of assessment, such as inadequate memory, that need to be addressed by researchers.

Subjective reports have been the primary type of coping data collected by researchers. Despite the inherent problems associated with subjective reports, they are likely to be used in the future to assess stress and coping. One research suggestion that seems worthwhile is to continue efforts to use multiple methods of assessment. That is, researchers should continue to analyze subjective, behavioral, and physiological coping and stress data simultaneously. Although research indicates that studies using multiple measures are difficult to interpret because results produced from one method are uncorrelated with findings from another method, useful information can be gathered. We need to know how coping affects behavior, perceptions, and physiology. Until more comprehensive assessments are conducted, the picture of the role coping plays in behavioral, emotional, and physiological responses will be ambigious and rather incomplete.

The brief sample of empirical data on coping processes in this chapter reveals some interesting gaps in understanding coping with stress among medical technologists and laboratory technicians. First, relatively little is known about the specific processes used by medical technologists and laboratory technicians to cope with job and/or life stresses. What are the major coping responses being used and for what type of stress are they used? Second, we know little about how effective, problem-focused, emotion-focused, or avoidance strategies are among medical technologists and laboratory technicians. Third, there is the unresearched issue of cost versus benefits of alternative coping strategies. Research on the cost versus benefits of various coping strategies among medical technologist and laboratory technicians would be an interesting avenue to take, especially during this era of skyrocketing health care expenditures.

FINAL THOUGHTS ON RESEARCH STRATEGIES

In general, occupational stress research has for the most part been retrospective. The currently available stress and coping research using medical technologists and technicians have followed the same traditional retrospective approach. Such studies have methodological limitations, including potential biases about which subjects are studied, imprecise measurement techniques, and problems with subject recall. The selection of a research strategy to use when investigating medical technologists and technicians depends on the type of explanation one is seeking. Bullock and Stallybrass (1977) propose that there are seven different kinds of explanations: (1) deductive, (2) probabilistic, (3) causal, (4) functional, (5) purposive, (6) teleological, and (7) genetic. They further collapse these seven into two broad categories. 1-3 are designated as causal/predictive and 4-7 are designated as descriptive/purposive. Both categories of research apply to conducting additional research on medical technologists and technicians.

Researchers are most likely to be interested in causal/predictive research whereas practitioners are more likely interested in descriptive and purposive explanations. A combination of research methods called methodological triangulation can potentially maximize both categories of explanation. Developing a research strategy that incorporates cross-sectional surveys, interviews, archival materials, and unobtrusive observations is what triangulation entails (Jick, 1979). As already suggested in the chapter, use of multiple methods can uncover some unique variance which otherwise would have been ignored by any single method. Given the complexity of medical technologist and technician stress, progress in understanding seems more likely through the use of multiple methods.

The selection of subjects, samples, and settings for future research of medical technologists and laboratory technicians is another issue that requires developing an innovative research strategy. Fletcher and Payne (1980) found that only 10 per cent of the working population report strain at any one time. Thus, studies which sample randomly from such a population would include 90 per cent who do not suffer strain. This could lead to establishment of a conclusion that stress among medical technologists and technicians is not a major problem. The conclusion could be partially correct. However, the 10 per cent of the population may be having significant problems that can affect the entire work-force. Methods must be considered and used that include the 10 per cent of the work population who are strained and the methods need to determine whether this group is acutely or chronically strained. In order to select out a higher proportion of the strained group a procedure other than randomization must be incorporated. It is important to learn as much as possible about the stress, reactions, and consequences sequence from the strained segment of the work population because they need the most help, are the most costly in terms of absenteeism, turnover, insurance premiums, and are often the least productive. Of course, the cost versus benefits of using a non-randomized sample must be carefully evaluated in selecting out the strained portion of a work population.

Long-term, longitudinal research strategies applied to medical technologists and technicians in different size organizations and in different countries could provide important data. Baseline information could permit comparisons across countries and in different settings. Follow-up studies of the same subjects would greatly enhance our understanding of the sequential activator, reaction, consequence effects. Who gets stressed? How? What physical health problems are and remain the most pervasive? What interventions have positive effects?

Our understanding of occupational stress and coping among medical technologists and laboratory technicians is likely to proceed in a non-focused manner unless researchers and practitioners join forces to take systematic action. Unless further integration of research expertise, conceptual frameworks, and research strategies occurs, little improvement in our understanding will occur. We propose that prospective studies, methodological triangulation, and longitudinal designs are steps in the right direction. These steps certainly will require the use of rigorous and innovative procedures.

REFERENCES

Ader, R. (ed.) (1981). *Psychoneuroimmunology*, Academic Press, New York.
American Medical Association (1982, Fall). Fifth conference on the impaired physician. Portland, Oregon.
American Society for Medical Technology Body of Knowledge Task Force (1980). *Clinical Laboratory Sciences Body of Knowledge: Content Outline*. Houston, Texas.
American Society for Medical Technology (1981). *Statement of Competence for Practitioners in the Clinical Laboratory Sciences*. Houston, Texas.
Appley, M. H. and Trumbull, R. (1967). On the concept of psychological stress. In M. H.

Appley and R. Trumbull (eds) *Psychological Stress*, Appleton-Century-Crofts, New York.
Billings, A. G. and Moos, R. H. (1981). The role of coping responses and social resources in attenuating the stress of life events, *Journal of Behavioral Medicine*, 4, 139–59.
Broski, D. C., Manuselis, G. and Noga, J. (1982). A comparative study of job satisfaction in medical technology, *American Journal of Medical Technology*, **48**, 207–11.
Bullock, A. and Stallybrass, O. (1977). *Fontana Dictionary of Modern Thought*, Fontana Books, London.
Chronicle Occupational Brief (1979). *Medical Technologists*, Chronical Guidance Publications, Inc., Moravia, NY.
Colligan, M. J., Smith, M. J. and Hurrell, J. J. (1977). Occupational incidence rates of mental health disorders, *Journal of Human Stress*, 3, 34–9.
Elliott, G. R. and Eisdorfer, C. (1982). *Stress and Health*, Springer, New York.
Elving, R. (1978). Their jobs test limits of stress. *The Milwaukee Journal*, 21 May.
Fletcher, B. and Payne, R. (1980). Stress and work: a review and theoretical framework, *Personnel Review*, 20–28.
Folkman, S. and Lazarus, R. S. (1980). An analysis of coping in a middle-aged community sample, *Journal of Health and Social Behavior*, 21, 219–39.
Frederick, C. J. (1979). Being a doctor may be hazardous to your health, *Medical World News*, 20 Aug., 68–78.
Friedman, M. and Rosenman, R. H. (1974). *Type A behavior and your heart*, Knopf, New York.
Griffin, P. and Klun, C. L. (1981). Laboratory stress: what causes it? *American Journal of Medical Technology*, **46**, 490–94.
House, J. S., McMichael, A. J. and Wells, J. A. (1979). Occupational stress and health among factory workers, *Journal of Health and Social Behavior*, 20, 139–60.
Jick, T. D. (1979). Mixing qualitative and quantitative methods: triangulation in action, *Administrative Science Quarterly*, 24, 602–11.
Jamal, M. (1984). Job stress and job performance controversy: an empirical assessment, *Organizational Behavior and Human Performance*, 33, 1–21.
Keicolt-Glaser, J. K., Garner, W., Speicher, C., Penn, G. M., Holliday, J. and Glaser, R. (1984). Psychosocial modifiers of immunocompetence in medical students, *Psychosomatic Medicine*, **46**, 7–14.
Laudenslager, M. L., Ryan, S. M., Drugan, R. C., Hyson, R. L. and Maier, S. F. (1983). Coping and immunosuppression: inescapable but not escapable shock suppresses lymphocyte proliferation, *Science*, 221, 568–70.
Lazarus, R. S. and Folkman, S. (1984). *Stress, appraisal, and coping*, Springer, New York.
Makosky, V. P. (1980). Stress and the mental health of women. In M. Guggentag, S. Salasin and D. Belle (eds) *The Mental Health of Women*, Academic Press, New York.
Matteson, M. T. (1979). An invitation to participate in a longitudinal study of stress among medical technologists, *American Journal of Medicial Technology*, **45**, 381–2.
Matteson, M. T. and Ivancevich, J. M. (1982a). Stress and the medical technologist: I. A. general overview, *American Journal of Medical Technology*, **48**, 163–8.
Matteson, M. T. and Ivancevich, J. M. (1982b). Stress and the medical technologist: II. Sources and coping mechanisms, *American Journal of Medical Technology*, **48**, 169–76.
Matteson, M. T. and Ivancevich, J. M. (1982c). Type A and B behavior patterns and self-reported health symptoms and stress: examining individual and organizational fit, *Journal of Occupational Medicine*, **24**, 585–9.
McGrath, J. E. (1970). *Social and psychological factors in stress*, Holt, Rinehart & Winston, New York.

Mechanic, D. (1974). Social structure and personal adaptation: some neglected dimensions. In G. V. Coelho, D. A. Hamburg and J. E. Adams (eds) *Coping and Adaptation*, Basic Books, New York.
Price, G. D. (1978). Competence equals professionalism, *American Journal of Medical Technology*, **44**, 416–18.
Revicki, D. A. and May, H. J. (1985). Occupational stress, social support, and depression, *Health Psychology*, **4**, 61–77.
Selye, H. (1976). *The Stress of Life*, McGraw-Hill, New York.
Steppacher, R. C. and Mausner, J. S. (1974). Suicide in male and female physicians, *Journal of the American Medical Association*, **228**, 323–8.
Terborg, J. R. (1985). Working women and stress. In T. A. Beehr and R. S. Bhagat (eds) *Human Stress and Cognitions in Organizations*, pp. 245–86, John Wiley, New York.
Van Harrison, R. (1978). Person–environment fit and job stress. In C. L. Cooper and R. Payne (eds) *Stress at Work*, John Wiley, New York.
Warr, P. and Parry, G. (1982). Paid employment and women's psychological well-being, *Psychological Bulletin*, **91**, 498–516.
Williams, M. R. (1976). *An Introduction to the Profession of Medical Technology*, Lea & Febiger, Philadelphia.
Withey, S. B. (1962). Reactions to uncertain threat. In G. W. Baker and D. W. Champman (eds) *Man and Society in Disaster*, Basic Books, New York.
Woolley, A. E. (1978). High rating in job-stress report is low blow to lab workers, *Lab World*, **29**, 20–28.
You can cope with stress. (1977). *Clinical Laboratorian*, Fall, 5–7.

APPENDIX: VARIABLES TO MEASURE FIRST FOURTEEN CATEGORIES IN TABLE 2

INSTRUCTIONS: For each item indicate how often the condition described has been a source of distress to you *during the last six months*. Some items may describe conditions which are not a source of distress; others may describe conditions which are constant sources of distress in your organizations; still other items will describe conditions which vary as sources of distress. For each item record the number (1 through 7) which best describes how often the condition described has been a source of distress for you during the last six months.

Mark 1 if the condition is NEVER a source of distress.
Mark 2 if the condition is RARELY a source of distress.
Mark 3 if the condition is OCCASIONALLY a source of distress.
Mark 4 if the condition is SOMETIMES a source of distress.
Mark 5 if the condition is OFTEN a source of distress.
Mark 6 if the condition is USUALLY a source of distress.
Mark 7 if the condition is ALWAYS a source of distress.

1. People do not understand the mission and goals of the organization.
2. Supervisors do not go to bat for their subordinates with their bosses.
3. People tend to take credit for someone else's work achievements.
4. Career success is not based on job performance.
5. There is no upward flow of communications.

6. People are not allowed to participate in making significant decisions.
7. People are not able to use their full range of skills on the job.
8. I look outside the organization to find satisfaction.
9. The overall strategy of the organization is not clearly understood.
10. Supervisors are not concerned about the personal welfare of their subordinates.
11. There is a tendency to exchange favors with people of higher rank in the organization.
12. The performance appraisal criteria used in the organization are ambiguous.
13. The communication flow in the organization is inaccurate.
14. Management doesn't seek the opinions of knowledgeable people about job matters.
15. Job assignments lack challenge and stimulation.
16. The level of satisfaction I derive from being part of this organization is less than I want it to be.
17. The organization has no important goals and consequently lacks direction.
18. Supervisors do not trust subordinates to do their jobs.
19. There is an effort to jockey around to secure power and authority in the organization.
20. Clearly written documents (budgets, schedules, job descriptions) are not used in the organization.
21. Communication flow is neither prompt nor timely.
22. People have no influence over how jobs are to be performed.
23. Job assignments are not challenging for people.
24. My dissatisfaction with this organization is increasing.
25. Management creates policies which hinder good job performance.
26. Supervisors show little respect for subordinates.
27. Mutual back scratching is used to get ahead in the organization.
28. The chain of command is not followed.
29. People do not communicate to others important ideas about improving job performance.
30. Management allows people to participate in only trivial decisions.
31. People are asked to do work different from what they were trained for.
32. I experience dissatisfaction with this organization.
33. My job duties and work objectives are unclear to me.
34. I work on unnecessary tasks or projects.
35. I have to take work home in the evenings or on weekends to stay caught up.
36. My demands for work quality made upon me are unreasonable.
37. I lack the proper opportunities to advance in this organization.
38. Unreasonable time deadlines are set up for the completion of work assignments.

39. I am unclear as to whom I report and/or who reports to me.
40. I get 'caught in the middle' between my superiors and my subordinates.
41. I spend too much time in unimportant meetings which take me away from my work.
42. My assigned tasks are sometimes too difficult and/or complex.
43. If I want to get promoted I have to look for a job with another organization.
44. Work must be rushed in order to complete it on time.
45. I lack the authority to carry out my job responsibilities.
46. The formal chain of command is not adhered to.
47. I am responsible for an almost unmanageable number of projects or assignments at the same time.
48. Tasks seem to be getting more and more complex.
49. I am hurting my career progress by staying with this organization.
50. I lack sufficient time to do the quality of job I want to do.
51. I do not fully understand what is expected of me.
52. I do things on the job that are accepted by one person and not by others.
53. I simply have more work to do than can be done in an ordinary day.
54. The organization expects more of me than my skills and/or abilities provide.
55. I have few opportunities to grow and learn new knowledge and skills in my job.
56. I work under deadlines.

PART III

The Hospital as a Context

Stress in Health Professionals
Edited by R. Payne and J. Firth-Cozens
© 1987 John Wiley & Sons Ltd

Chapter 13
Managing and Coping with Budget-cut Stress in Hospitals

Todd D. Jick

The state of health of medicine is increasingly in question ... as is its own awareness of how deeply mired down medicine is in many facets of its operation. The organization and structure of medical services, the nature of the delivery of services to the populous, the multiple emotional and psychological problems of physicians, the rising incidents of suits against physicians, the prevalence of addiction, alcohol and suicide problems among physicians, and social image of not trusting the medical profession as implicitly as before, all attest to the growing embarrassment of medicine *vis-à-vis* the public. Medicine's integrity is suffering. (Phillips, 1982, p. 49).

One more challenge is currently being added to the medical profession's woes—hospital budget cuts. In their extreme form, these cuts allegedly threaten the quality of patient care, overload physicians and nurses with twice the work and half the staff, and provoke a new set of difficulties for the administration of health care services. Not surprisingly, these new circumstances bring with them a new mix of stressors.

This chapter begins with a brief review of the environmental conditions and economic pressures that led hospitals towards financial restraints. Then, I shall describe the primary stressors experienced by individuals employed in 'lean and mean' hospitals and propose a number of hypotheses of their cognitive origin. Then, in a more prescriptive sense, I will recommend some administrative actions designed to reduce the magnitude of the stressors and/or minimize their impact. The chapter concludes with a summary of the research and administrative challenges ahead.

FINANCIAL MALADIES IN HOSPITALS

Until recently, health expenditures escaped the grasp of politicians and community groups seeking to cut costs. Hospital administrators and overseers shared in the mentality that medical care should be 'priceless', i.e., above consideration of costs since human life and well-being were at stake. However, the astronomical increases in the cost of health care has reversed this attitude dramatically in the 1980s. The cost of sophisticated medical equipment soared as did administrative costs. For example, according to Himmelstein and Woolhandler (1983), administrative costs accounted for 22 per cent or $77.7 billion of all US medical bills. Such activities as billing, accounting, marketing, and institutional planning grew substantially—with 17.7 per cent more personnel performing these tasks between 1970 and 1982.

The era of unlimited expansion, however, came to a grinding halt in the early 1980s when hospitals indeed became a prime target for retrenchment. Cost containment began to compete with disease containment for the attention of hospital administrators and employees. The focus shifted as admission rates dropped, as threats of restricted revenue arose from new medicare payment systems and other private insurers, and as more aggressive outpatient services left hospitals with the more diseased and thus more costly patients. Health care costs had clearly increased at a rate significantly higher than general inflation. In short, in Western countries (particularly the US) governments and employers clamped down on health care spending.

As a result of these conditions, hospitals have been faced with difficult problems of resource allocation and resource generation. Cost pressures have caused hospitals to take a variety of unprecedented actions such as reducing nursing and support staffs, closing selected wings, consolidating support services, eliminating medical services which overlap with those offered by nearby hospitals, and pruning administrative costs in a wide variety of areas.

It has been argued that these cutbacks are typically perceived and experienced by organizations as creating a crisis-like state (Jick and Murray, 1982). Although the degree of crisis for any one hospital can vary considerably, it is fair to say that the health care landscape has inexorably been reshaped as a result of this new cost consciousness. Hospital journals are replete with articles on the subject of financing, revenue generation and cost-cutting. Terminology that had once been used exclusively in the industrial sector has emerged: rationalizing services, productivity ratios, limiting expenditures and capital growth, profit generation, etc. General hospitals now hire 'general managers'.

This new breed of hospital administrator faces the twofold challenge of containing costs and containing the stress associated with cutbacks. The next section will discuss the nature of these stressors and their potential impact on hospitals.

BUDGET-CUT STRESSORS

Many stress studies have misguidedly examined relatively stress-free populations (Fletcher and Payne, 1980; Payne, Jick and Burke, 1982). However, because it is reasonable to expect that employees in retrenching hospitals will be prone to considerable stress and thus more likely to manifest strain symptoms of interest to stress researchers, there is now a valuable opportunity to examine a large population 'at risk'.

Not surprisingly, due to the recency of budget cuts in hospitals, little research has yet been published on how individuals and hospitals respond to these stressful conditions (Jick, 1985; Quick and Quick, 1984), although sources of stress in the medical profession, in general, are reported elsewhere in this book and have been well documented and reviewed by Phillips (1982, pp. 49–100). Commonly identified general causes include 'treadmill living', excessive ambition to get ahead financially and professionally, little vacation time and personal 'space', legal liabilities, and unending pressure and crisis. Anecdotal interviews and evidence of many of these stressors is well described by Medved (1982) and Ashkenas (1979). Interestingly enough, however, none of these analyses and descriptions from before 1982 identify budget cuts and administrative matters as a significant source of stress.

Yet, general interest in organizational decline and retrenchment has grown in recent years. Jick and Murray (1982) linked the crises and decline literature with organizational reactions to externally imposed budget cuts. Fottler, Smith and Muller (1985) studied five health care institutions with differing degrees of crisis to examine whether these hospitals followed the administrative strategies for retrenchment prescribed by the crisis and decline literature. Murray, Jick and Bradshaw (1984) similarly reported data on the tactical responses of six Canadian hospitals to budget cut crises.

In each of these studies, the primary emphasis was on the fiscal and organizational adaptation to budget cuts. Less attention was paid to the 'human side of budget cuts', especially the strains placed on individuals and how that can be minimized or managed. The situation was similar in the 1970s: the onset of 'merger-mania' was initially treated primarily as a financial problem while only later did the literature focus on the stresses and strains of everyone involved.

What then are the sources of budget-cut stress? To begin with, it is important to differentiate between objectively and subjectively experienced budget-cut severity (Caplan *et al.*, 1975; Jick, 1985). Budget cuts—whether threatened, impending, or implemented—have certain objective characteristics; At the most obvious level, some cuts are simply larger than others and thus are likely to produce more stress for organizational members. Fottler, Smith and Muller (1985) assumed, for example, that severe retrenchment would be operationally defined as budget cuts greater than 10 per cent (after accounting for inflation) coupled with substantial personnel loss and curtailment of key services. Essentially, as the objective severity of the threatened or actual cuts increases, it might be expected that there would be more uncertainty of knowing how to respond and thus more experienced stress.

But these objective indices and measures may be only partially useful. It has been well understood that subjective interpretations of budget crisis may indeed differ from their 'objective' severity. The emphasis in stress models on cognitive appraisal and felt/experienced stress attests to the importance of the interpretive step whereby the degree of severity or uncertainty is a matter of individual difference and experience. In other words, a routine budget cut of 5 per cent in one hospital may or may not be perceived as less threatening than a similar size cut in another hospital which has never had to cut costs. It depends in part on the amount of organizational slack. Or, at the individual level, a more senior hospital member of a hospital may be less threatened by staff reduction threats than a more junior employee fearing for his or her job. Thus, the arousing information must be *experienced* and perceived as demand stress (Payne, 1979).

Perceived demands consist of two dimensions: perceived severity and perceived time pressure. A number of hypotheses follow, which are based on anecdotal evidence of probable relationships dealing with severity and magnitude:

Hypothesis 1 The more budget cuts are perceived as large, the higher the likelihood of experienced stress/uncertainty.

Hypothesis 2 The more budget cuts threaten or negatively impact absolute or relative pay, the higher the likelihood of experienced stress/uncertainty.

Hypothesis 3 The more budget cuts threaten or impact staffing levels, the higher the likelihood of experienced stress/uncertainty.

Hypothesis 4 The more budget cuts threaten or create overload by increasing paperwork, the higher the likelihood of experienced stress/uncertainty.

Hypothesis 5 The greater the extent to which cuts are perceived to threaten changes in goals, programs, or hospital survival, the higher the likelihood of experienced stress/uncertainty.

Hypothesis 6 The greater the frequency of cuts, the higher the likelihood of experienced stress/uncertainty.

Hypothesis 7 The less the perceived organizational slack and the fewer the perceived opportunities for alternative funding, the higher the likelihood of experienced stress/uncertainty.

Hypothesis 8 The fewer the management assurances perceived (e.g. regarding job security or department survival), the higher the likelihood of experienced stress/uncertainty.

There is also the issue of time pressure. Presumably, the less the forewarning and the lower the information clarity, the greater the surprise and thus the higher probability of experienced stress and uncertainty of knowing how to respond. On the basis of the above, then, one might posit the following:

Hypothesis 9 The less forewarning information received of impending budget cuts, the higher the likelihood of experienced stress/uncertainty when the cuts finally occur.

Hypothesis 10 The lower the perceived information clarity regarding the nature of impending budget cuts, the higher the likelihood of experienced stress/uncertainty.

Hypothesis 11 The lower the perceived response time available between the mandate to cut and the actual cuts, the higher the likelihood of experienced stress/uncertainty.

Individual differences in the degree to which the time pressure and severity are perceived as stressful largely depend upon one's perceived resources and coping stength (McGrath, 1976). This can be operationalized in terms of (a) the perceived means for coping with the threat, (b) the perceived probability of success if such coping techniques were utilized, and (c) the costs to the individual of such means. In (c), an individual perceives the potential consequences or importance of not meeting the demands both personally and professionally. In light of the above, it is posited that:

Hypothesis 12 The greater the perceived uncertainty of success in nullifying or combating the demands, the greater the experienced stress/uncertainty.

Hypothesis 13 The more important the perceived consequences for not meeting the demands, the greater the experienced stress/uncertainty.

Consider the following case of a nurse whose hospital administration is implementing cost-cutting measures:

> I have come home and cried because I didn't have enough time to do a decent job for my patients. I have complained endlessly to my administrators. All I hear is 'there is no budget for more help. Do the best you can'.... There is nothing more frustrating than to know you have to do patient care and can't because you don't have the time. (Hull, 1985)

As the number of nurses in many hospitals drops to save funds, the workload for the remaining nurses rises commensurately—as does the demand stress.

The strains associated with budget cut stressors are not unique. Experienced stress is manifested in well-recognized behavioral, psychological, and physiological symptoms. Figure 1 portrays this typical set of strain response tendencies and the objective and felt stressors described above. A study of hospital budget cuts (with work-force reduction) (Jick, 1979) found several of these responses among a small but substantial proportion of the hospital staff: increases in voluntary resignations, reduced job satisfaction, weakened loyalty

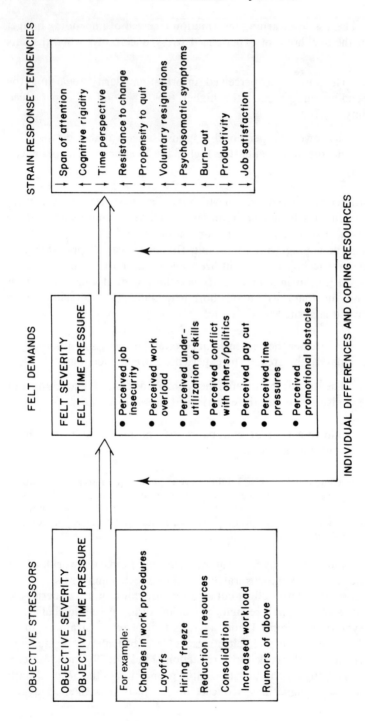

Figure 1 Hospital budget cuts and demand stress

toward the hospital, various psychosomatic and somatic symptoms, and decreased productivity due to reduced effort on the job.

The organizational costs of this stress can be enormous in hospitals, where flawed judgments caused by stress can cause at a minimum, considerable discomfort for patients but, in an extreme, can even lead to fatal mistakes. Errors in judgment and misassessment are of course difficult to trace directly to cost-cutting stress, but such dangers may indeed be all too prevalent in many health care institutions. Anecdotal evidence (Jick, 1985) would suggest that budget-cut stress is associated with a decrease in the health and well-being of both the hospital staff and clients.

What remains open to speculation, however, is the relationship between the perceived degree of severity/time pressure and strain response. The example above would suggest that the relationship is linear, that is, the more severe the crisis and uncertainty, the more debilitating and negative the stress responses. On the other hand, some might argue that the relationship is curvilinear. That is, perceived 'moderately demanding' situations are likely to be associated with 'eustress' or 'opportunity stress', which stimulates stronger motivation, group cohesion, and a generally positive work milieu. Staw, Sandelands and Dutton (1981), for example, posited that threatening situations resulting from common or familiar problems may result in performance increments, while threats arising from radical changes may lead to performance decrements. The nature of the budget-cut threat therefore must be carefully understood. One should not necessarily assume that all the effects will be deleterious.

REDUCING COSTS AND REDUCING STRESS

As fiscal cuts are perceived to be 'at hand' and/or are ultimately realized, then it can be expected that many theatened employees are likely to feel and behave in ways that are detrimental to themselves as well as to the functioning of the organization, although not all individuals will suffer negatively. One can imagine two individuals hit with the same pattern of cuts: one ends up limping along wracked with stress, desperately seeking to get out if possible; the other appears to be maintaining all essential activities or even exhibiting new and original activities while exuding confidence, loyalty, and commitment to the organization. What can be done by hospital administrators to maximize the number of the latter individuals and minimize the former?

The key is to follow two basic principles of cutback management:

(1) Cuts made on the basis of expedience, convenience, arbitrariness, short-term perspectives, or political interests will exacerbate stress in hospitals. Cuts should only be made based on careful priority analysis, rational planning, and both the short *and* long-term view.

(2) 'It's not what you cut but how you cut it!' The most effective cost reductions and savings can still create negative countereffects and/or not be implemented as planned if they are decided upon, introduced, and explained in ways unacceptable to hospital staff.

Although 'success' stories of well-managed budget cuts are far less frequent than tales of demoralized administrators and staff, there are certain techniques that work effectively in most situations. They are fashioned after the two principles above and can minimize perceived uncertainty and perceived demands:

MAXIMIZE DOWNWARD COMMUNICATION

Staff in the dark will become restless, resistant, and discouraged. It is advisable to hold meetings, provide fact sheets, make speeches, and encourage questions, constantly emphasizing the 'why' behind all cuts and actions.

INVOLVE AFFECTED PARTIES AS MUCH AS POSSIBLE

Staff should be involved in cutback decisions where feasible and allowed to participate in establishing new priorities and long-term planning.

RESHAPE EXPECTATION LEVELS TO SUSTAIN MOTIVATION

If spending and staffing levels in the hospital will never be what they once were, say so! But, at the same time, goals that are needed, challenging—yet attainable—should be identified. People should know what they are *working for* while they are retrenching; they should know there is a positive future.

BUILD ON READINESS TO MAKE CUTS, NOT RESISTANCE

For every pound of resistance to cuts there is almost always at least an ounce of willingness or readiness to try something new or do something better. If hospital staff are asked to offer innovative methods that demand fewer resources, they usually have more than enough to offer.

PROVIDE OUTLETS FOR STRESS RELEASE

In stressful times, humor and oddball recreational activities will serve to release pent-up tensions, build group cohesion, and develop a healthy distance from problems often beyond one's control.

BE PREPARED TO TAKE SOME GRIEF

Although it is often uncomfortable and unpleasant to do so, hospital administrators involved in budget cuts must encourage the voicing of negative, hostile feelings and complaints. Small group, face-to-face interaction characterized by 'heat' and anger should also allow for compromises and diffuse angry feelings.

Of course, the most direct means of alleviating damaging stress is by not having to cut costs at all. Fottler, Smith and Muller (1985) and Murray, Jick and Bradshaw (1984) have identified health care institutions that have tried to cope with cost pressures by seeking new revenue sources through more aggressive negotiations with funding agencies or through voluntary contributions. In addition, a growing number of hospitals in the US have begun to market their services actively in order to maintain or expand patient demand—and thus alleviate federal budget cuts. These methods, if successful, can indeed reduce the need for hospitals to change program emphases or restrict services or cut staff or take any other actions that would lead to a higher probability of demand stress.

Realistically, however, many hospitals have exhausted the possibilities of enlarging or shifting the sources of resource dependence. It is for such hospitals that the stress risks are highest and the management challenge the greatest. One can safely conclude that individuals who work in these cutback environments are likely to be at higher risk than those who do not.

WHERE TO FROM HERE: A CAUTIOUS PROGNOSIS

I have argued that the additional stress precipitated by budget cutting on the medical staff and the hospital organization must be delicately managed. The field of medicine must continue to seek not only medical solutions to human disease but administrative solutions to the fiscal 'disease'. In so doing, these administrators will become more and more involved in stress management.

To assist these administrators, I suggested a number of hypotheses to predict relationships between budget cuts and organizational and individual stressors and strains. This domain of budget-cut stress is an ideal opportunity to examine a subject population that is indeed strained (to a large extent), as researchers have been advocating (Payne, Jick and Burke, 1982). Moreover, researchers can apply a traditional model of stress research—objective stressors/felt stressors/felt strains—in a new area. Many of the stressors are in fact similar to classic organizational stressors of overload, role ambiguity, and threatened job security. But the particular mix of stressors and the acute nature of their onset in many situations represent a unique and fascinating opportunity for deepening our understanding of the impact of stress and especially the management challenges for alleviating damaging stress.

The effects of ongoing budget cuts is a relatively unexplored research topic. There is the distinct possibility that funding cutbacks will persist with moderate severity for the next decade in some hospitals, and it is unknown how people react to such prolonged pressures. That is, what are the long-term effects of chronically declining organizations on individual well-being and effectiveness? Will the perceived severity and time pressure diminish or increase as cutbacks become more routine? These are apt questions for future research.

Overall, this chapter intends to promote an exciting new application for stress research. It does so with the expectation that our understanding will be sharpened if we examine: (1) the stressors most often associated with budget cuts; (2) the relationship between objective stressors and cognitive appraisal; (3) the impact of individual differences and coping skills; and (4) the manifestation of strain responses most likely to emerge under conditions of budget cuts.

Business and service institutions of all kinds in Western developing countries have been subjected to particularly intense fiscal pressures in recent years. It is somewhat ironic that a pressure-cooker environment such as a hospital would also experience the onslaught of additional stressors and strains since, by its very mission, it is supposed to be reducing the stressors and strains of its clients. In order to be more effective at doing so in the future, hospitals must realize that they too have become stressed 'patients' who require short-term remedial and long-term preventative actions to help them survive and prosper.

REFERENCES

Ashkenas, R. (1979). *Professional career and its consequences: An exploratory study of academic physicians.* Unpublished doctoral dissertation, Case Western Reserve University.

Caplan, R., Cobb, S., French, J. R., Harrison, R. V. and Pinneau, S. (1975). Job demands and worker health. NIOSH Research Report, Cincinnati.

Fletcher, B. and Payne, R. (1980). Stress and work: A review and theoretical framework, *Personnel Review*.

Fottler, M. D., Smith, H. L. and Muller, H. J. (1985). Administrative strategies for retrenchment in health care organizations: Theory and practice. Paper presented at the 1985 Academy of Management meetings, San Diego, California.

Himmelstein, D. and Woolhandler, S. (1983). Letter to the editor regarding 'Investor-owned and not for profit hospitals', *New England Journal of Medicine*, 22 December.

Hull, J. B. (1985). Hospital nightmare: Cuts in staff demoralize nurses as care suffers, *Wall Street Journal*, 27 March, 37.

Jick, T. D. (1979). Process and impacts of a merger: Individual and organizational perspectives. Unpublished doctoral dissertation, Cornell University.

Jick, T. D. (1985). As the ax falls: Budget cuts and the experience of stress in organizations. In T. A. Beehr and R. S. Bhagat (eds) *Human Stress and Cognition in Organizations: An Integrated Perspective*, John Wiley, New York. pp. 83–114.

Jick, T. D. and Murray, V. V. (1982). The management of hard times: Budget cutbacks in public sector organizations, *Organization Studies*, 3/2.

McGrath, J. (1976). Stress and behavior in organizations. In M. D. Dunnette (ed.) *Handbook of Industrial and Organizational Psychology*, Rand McNally, Chicago. pp. 1351–95.

Medved, M. (1982). *Hospital: The Hidden Lives of a Medical Center Staff.* Simon and Schuster, New York.

Murray, V. V., Jick, T. D. and Bradshaw, P. (1984). Hospital funding constraints: strategic and tactical decision responses to sustained, moderate levels of crisis in six Canadian hospitals, *Social Science and Medicine*, **18**, 3, 211–19.

Payne, R. L. (1979). Demands, supports, constraints, and psychological health. In C. J. McKoy and T. Cox (eds) *Response to Stress: Occupational Aspects*, London International Publishing Corporation, London.

Payne, R. L., Jick, T. D. and Burke, R. J. (1982). Whither stress research? An agenda for the 1980's, *Journal of Occupation Behavior*, **3**, 131–45.

Phillips, E. L. (1982). *Stress, Health, and Psychological Problems in the Major Professions*, University Press of America, New York.

Quick, J. C. and Quick, J. D. (1984). *Organizational Stress and Preventive Management*, McGraw-Hill, New York.

Staw, B. M., Sandelands, L. E. and Dutton, J. E. (1981). Threat-rigidity effects in organizational behavior: A multilevel analysis, *Administrative Science Quarterly*, **26**/4, Dec., 501–24.

Stress in Health Professionals
Edited by R. Payne and J. Firth-Cozens
© 1987 John Wiley & Sons Ltd

Conclusion

If our knowledge of stress amongst health professionals were complete and comprehensive we would know accurately what proportion were experiencing a given number of symptoms, the severity of the symptoms and how long they had been experienced. We would know the rates of different types of symptoms; the proportion which were actual physical symptoms such as headaches, backaches, vomiting, accelerated heart rates, sleep difficulties; the proportion of affective indications of strain such as panic attacks, depressive feelings, tension and anxiety; the proportion that showed themselves as unusual behaviours such as aggressive attacks, drinking bouts, running away from problems; and what proportion were more cognitive in nature, such as making errors, forgetting, poor judgement, faulty reasoning or misperceptions.

We would further know how these symptoms were distributed amongst the different groups of professionals, and whether they were differentially distributed by different hierarchical levels within the profession. For example, do stressed nurse managers suffer more cognitive symptoms than those nurses who deal directly with the patients? We would know whether the size of the hospital altered the frequency of symptoms and their distribution within different professional groups. A complete knowledge base would contain information about which individual difference variables are most strongly related to the development of strain symptoms, so that we would know which groups are most vulnerable. Are women social workers more vulnerable than male social workers in the same kinds of jobs? Are people who are high on internal locus of control less vulnerable? Does it help if you are able to attribute failures to the external world rather than to yourself?

In addition to this knowedge we would also know what were the main causes of these strains and how they differed for the different professions and for different levels within the profession. We would know what parts of the physiological sub-system are most affected by particular stressors. We would know how often people could cope with acute stress and not be damaged, and the point at which regular acute stress becomes chronic strain.

Being able to identify the causes of stress our complete knowledge base would also contain instructions about what to do to change the stressors: how to redesign jobs, decrease workload or allocate it more efficiently, select people who are more resistant to particular kinds of stressors, introduce new technology to decrease the demands of the job. Our 'stress encyclopaedia' would tell us how to introduce such changes without causing excessive strain whilst doing it. It would also tell us how to motivate people to decrease their own vulnerability by creating tailor-made packages of training suitable to particular individuals. Who finds meditation the most effective stress reducer? For whom does physical exercise work best? When are drugs useful? Who responds best to social support, and what kinds of social supports work best for what people?

Those who have read this book will percieve that it addresses many of these issues, but they will also recognize that our present knowledge of stress has more the properties of a primitive map than an encyclopaedia. The book gives an idea of the lay of the land for the different issues outlined above, and enables the reader to decide in which general direction he or she might wish to travel, but the present state of scientific knowledge prevents it from containing a set of precise prescriptions or instructions. After all, we still have no fully reliable way of making people lose weight or give up smoking, and they seem reasonably simple problems compared with understanding the dynamics of interpersonal relationships in complex organizations.

Let us briefly remind ourselves what we do know, however, as well as identifying some of the more outstanding gaps in our understanding. First, what do we know about levels of strain amongst health professionals?

It must not be forgotten that all professionals have lower death rates per age group than blue-collar workers, lower morbidity and lower sickness absence, even though they tend to work more hours. An important question for this book then is, 'Do health professionals experience more strain than other professionals?' Before addressing this, however, it is worth emphasizing that when strained professionals are asked which area of their lives is causing the strain, they are much more likely than blue-collar workers to attribute the strain to their jobs (Warr and Payne, 1982). Work then is an important cause of strain for professionals.

One reason why stress research is growing fast in the health field is that jobs involving caring for people are believed to be particularly stressful. The weight of the evidence presented in this book accords with the view that many people in these professions regularly experience stress which is to some extent at least attributable to the job. The proportion who experience very severe stress which lasts for months or years, however, is probably similar to other professional groups and, as Payne pointed out in Chapter 5 on surgeons, even where there is evidence for chronic stress as in the high levels of urinary cortisol found in the surgeons and the anaesthetists, it is still not clear whether such levels also have clinical implications. Porter, Howie and Levinson in Chapter 3 showed many of their doctors reported regularly feeling pressured, but only 8 per cent of their responses were classified as 'hurried' or 'very pressured'. Scheiber's chapter contains many references on this issue too and there are studies which show physicians to be no more stressed than other professionals (a point also made by Kent about dentists). But our overall impression is that the evidence does indicate the regular occurrence of moderate levels of strain, which appear to occur more frequently than for most other professional workers (e.g. Colligan, Smith and Hurrell, 1977).

Another point evident in the book, however, is that strain levels vary across the different health professions. The proportion of medical students reaching the cut-off point of 'showing minor psychological problems' on the GHQ is 38 per cent (Firth-Cozens's chapter) whereas it is only 33 per cent for psychiatric nurses (Jones, Chapter 10). Both of these are high, however, compared with managerial samples, except for managers working in a plant which was threatened by closure (Banks *et al.*, 1980). Ivancevich and Matteson also show that medical technologists and laboratory technicians have high rates of objective stressors in their jobs, quoting the work of Terborg from the US National Institute of Occupational Health. There is then no simple answer to levels of strain in health professionals. They vary by symptom examined, by professional group, by level in the profession, and even by size of hospital, where larger hospitals tend to have higher rates (Firth-Cozens, 1987). Whilst the picture is by no means fully detailed, this book brings together the most comprehensive collection of data on the issue, and regardless of how health professionals compare with other groups, the data show quite clearly that there are many people showing signs of strain severe enough to affect their job performance and their own well-being: it is an issue of substantive importance for health professionals themselves, and the organizations that employ them.

Given there is strain, which stressors are most likely to cause it?

THE STRESSORS OF HEALTH PROFESSIONALS

Clearly the most common stressor among the health professionals is feelings of overload, whether this is controlled by the organization or institution, as in the case of medical students, physicians in training, medical technologists or social workers, or by the individual, as occurs in private practice such as dentistry or general practice. For the latter groups, the trade-off in worrying more about time is, of course, worrying less about finance.

Several authors have pointed out the potential hazards to patients that can be caused by time pressures in the professional; for example, in his chapter on general practitioners Howie described the possibility of mistakes occurring, and certainly difficulty with decision-making and memory problems at work occur when stress levels are high (Firth and Shapiro, 1986).

The metaphor expressed by some helpers is that it feels as if there is a tidal wave of need which they are constantly battling to hold back before it crashes down. Of course, such endless demands are likely to be exacerbated by financial cuts to services, and the stress of coping with suffering patients on longer and longer waiting lists will affect all levels of health professionals, both in hospitals and in the community, as well as other health occupations such as admissions clerks and administrators.

At the same time it is necessary to hypothesize, as Illich (1975) has done, that the provision of any health service will in itself create its own demand. Thus providing a counselling service for sexual problems will create a demand that may well reflect real need within the community, but which will continue to require resources as more and more clients discover a solution to their needs. If this is true then there seems no way that time pressures can ever be reduced to a reasonable level apart from considerably increasing staffing levels, or by irradicating disease and social problems.

There are clearly differences, however, between the experiences of overload in the various professions discussed, and in different groups within each profession. Thus it appears from Jones's chapter that working with long-stay psychiatric patients engenders less overload than working in other branches of nursing, such as the elderly or intensive care. While for some professions the demands will be constant, and so predictable, for others, such as social work (Rushton, Chapter 9), there can be periods of relative calm followed by a rush on services that cannot always be predicted. Finally, it is clear from Cartwright's chapter and others that women are in an especially unenviable position concerning overload. Like female workers in other professions, it is likely that they are carrying not only their full-time jobs, but also a larger than equal share of family chores. Unlike these other workers, both halves of their lives are spent caring in some way for the needs of others, and any burn out symptoms that might exist in the helping professions would be expected to be exacerbated in women.

A number of writers have pointed out that occupational demands alone will rarely result in inevitable strain (Karasek, 1979; Payne, 1981). There are certainly likely to be other aspects of the job, such as levels of support and discretion which will alleviate or exacerbate the potential stress of overload. Similarly, it has been pointed out by Firth-Cozens and Scheiber that the constant reference to time pressures may be a way to defend against the anxieties of considering other stressors, perhaps more threatening, such as dealing with death and suffering.

Overload, time constraints and the effects of these on personal life are also often given as the principal stressors by trainees within the various professions, though this is a complaint of students more generally (Bjorksten *et al.*, 1983). Other sources of stress during the training phase include feelings of isolation, dealing with death and suffering, and relationships with senior staff who are sometimes seen as providing inadequate feedback or as acting in ways that reduce rather than engender confidence. In his chapter, Kent has described ways that a lack of self-confidence in student dentists can exacerbate the problems faced.

Conclusion

It is clear that all health workers face occupational hazards of one type or another. Many are inevitably in contact with contageous and infectious diseases either by direct patient contact, as with nursing, medicine and dentistry, or indirectly via their blood, urine, etc., as with medical technologists. The chapters by Margison, Jones and Rushton make it clear that, for those working in psychiatry and social work, there is a strong threat of violence which does occasionally manifest itself as actual physical harm and even death.

Although these risks have always to some extent been intrinsic to health jobs, recently it seems there is a more general sense of external threat to those within the health professions. This comes from the public in terms of increased violence, from the government in terms of financial cuts, and from the media who have, in the last few years, produced some highly critical programmes of various aspects of health care. Jones describes the implications of this media interest for workers in a secure hospital, and Rushton shows that it strongly affects social workers concerned with the possibility of child abuse. Perhaps partly as a result of such programmes, health professionals no longer can be so sure of high status within the community and doctors in particular no longer enjoy the infallible omnipotence they could once presume. Alongside this decline in trust, goes the increase in legal actions which affect the medical profession in particular, as Scheiber's chapter makes clear, but also may necessitate all health workers taking out personal liability insurance (Gomersall, 1987).

The public's attitude to the patients who are treated within a particular specialty may rub off to some extent on the professionals that care for them, as Margison describes in his chapter on psychiatrists. At the very least it seems that extra strain may be caused by having to in some sense defend the rights of the patients against public hostility, as Thomson suggests occurs in mental handicap.

The health professions generally are highly labour intensive and are unique among professions in that their 'clients' are also to some extent their 'products'. For this reason relationships, both with colleagues and with patients, are likely to be particularly important. It is clear from many of the chapters that these relationships can be a major source both of satisfaction and of strain. Supportive colleagues are obviously an important antidote to events which are so often potentially laden with anxiety; on the other hand, those who are competitive or critical or lazy will only exacerbate difficult situations.

The patients themselves are clearly an important source of job satisfaction for most health professionals, and Firth-Cozens has shown how in her sample, talking to patients was the most enjoyable part of the medical students' role. This potential buffer against stress will thus be virtually absent in jobs such as medical technologists who have only minimal patient contact. It is likely that this satisfaction arises partly from the feelings of control (as opposed to helplessness) which are engendered by care. The increase in poverty and unemployment and their related social 'diseases' are likely to reduce seriously the health workers' sense of being able to do something positive to help. The helplessness of this position is well summed up in the following poem by Brecht from 'A Worker's Speech to a Doctor':

> Too much work and too little food
> Makes us feeble and thin
> Your prescription says:
> Put on more weight.
> You might as well tell a bulrush
> Not to get wet.

Patients are also a major source of stress, as Kent's chapter on dentists makes clear, and the following extract from an article by Levine (1982) describes both the problem and a less than appropriate method of coping with it.

> There is an ancient joke about psychotherapists which long preceded today's concern about alienation and burnout. A younger analyst, frazzled at the end of each day's emotional wear and tear, enviously observed an older, more experienced colleague who seemed to leave the office at the end of each day fresh and carefree. Screwing up his courage, the younger man finally asked his more experienced colleague, "How can you leave the office so full of energy, and so fresh after listening to all of your patients' troubles all day long?" The older man looked at his younger colleague and said, "Who listens?"

Patients who respond to treatment, who are appreciative and co-operative are clearly going to make a job more satisfying than those who are non-compliant, angry, upset or whose afflictions, as within mental handicap, are likely to improve very little.

Where professions have important differences—such as where nurses deal face-to-face with patients while medical technologists do not, or where doctors hold a medical model of illness while social workers will hold a socio-environmental model—then difficult relationships between professions may often occur. Thus Ivancevich and Matteson (Chapter 12) describe how medical technologists see stress created by medical staff not understanding the pressures under which they work; while, on the other hand, it is likely that medical and nursing staff, having to deal directly with patient's suffering, are more likely to be impatient of anything they see as unreasonable delay.

Differences in power and status between the professions can often create relationship problems, as Margison (Chapter 6) has shown in his description of the multidisciplinary team within psychiatry. Power comes not only from salary differentials but also from the fact that professions such as medicine and nursing have been established from the beginning of the health service whereas others, such as medical technology, clinical psychology or social work, are relatively new and can sometimes experience difficulties finding an influential role in the committees that hold the power.

Change is generally regarded as a source of stress but, considering how dramatic changes have been in health care over the last century, it is perhaps surprising how relatively little alteration has actually occurred within the organization of health services. Although working conditions for staff, such as hours and length of shifts, are infinitely superior to those earlier in the century, there have been very few fundamental changes in the roles played by individuals within the system. Thus, although women doctors now train in numbers approaching equality, virtually nothing has been done to improve the system to allow them to both have families and to practise in hospital medicine. Despite their greater numbers, very few have positions of power within the hierarchy.

However, some change has occurred and more is undoubtedly on the way. Thus fundamentally new approaches to the care of the mentally handicapped were brought about by the realization that they were able to learn and improve (Thomson's chapter). Changes in the demands for services alter as cures are found for various diseases, and Kent has pointed out that one source of stress for dentists is taking place with the decrease in demand that is occurring as personal dental care improves. While maternity services are being removed from the community and placed within the hospital, one of the most dramatic changes to occur is the current move within psychiatry and mental handicap from hospital-based services to the community. This will involve a fundamentally different way of working both with patients and with teams and initially may place considerable strain upon both.

However, the change that is seen as causing considerable strain to health professionals both in Britain and in North Amrica, is that created by financial cut-backs and the 'rationalization' of services (Tyson and Merrill, 1984). As Jick (Chapter 13) describes, large cuts produce various stress symptoms, reduced job satisfaction, and decreased productivity. Clearly in situations where patients' demands for treatment are rising, and staff numbers are being reduced, work pressures will become much greater. Although the decisions of the hospital managers are themselves life-or-death (in that reducing the number of kidney machines, for example, will inevitably mean that certain patients will die) they are sufficiently removed from their customers to ensure that they are not faced with either their anger or their anguish. To know that a service is possible which will save life or reduce suffering and to be unable to provide it, makes the job of a health professional both distressing and unrewarding. As Jick suggests, '... budget-cut stress is associated with a decrease in the health and well-being of both the hospital staff and clients'.

Another area of change, described by Fitter (Chapter 11), is that produced by improvements in technology. Apart from the increased sophistication of monitoring equipment now used by nurses and others, high-powered microcomputers are also changing the quantity and quality of information available for managing the hospital. Both these aspects of technological change have stressful implications for staff, though as Fitter's chapter shows, they can also be used to improve the service to patients and make jobs more interesting.

Having identified the stressors we should now ask, 'What can be done about them?'

WHAT CAN BE DONE?

There are two broad strategies for coping with stress. The first is to change the environment so that the overall stress is reduced. In terms of the demands, supports-constraints model presented in the Introduction, the strategy for this can be guided by asking questions about the demands or requirements of the job. Are the standards too high? Is too much being expected? Are the present goals ever attainable? Are the priorities sensible? If job demands cannot be changed to reduce stress, then one is forced to look at constraints. Can more time be given? Will new technology help? Can staffing levels be changed, or rules altered to allow more efficient practices? If all constraints have been removed or reduced and stress still exists then it is the turn of the social system to suffer examination. Is professional help required to increase trust between people? Can support groups be set up? Can counselling services be provided?

The other broad strategy for dealing with stress is to improve the coping capacity of individuals. This is often done by providing specific techniques such as relaxation or time management, but job rotation and the widening of experience through education and training in professional and management skills are also sound ways of decreasing vulnerability to occupational stress.

Considering first the overriding problems of overload, Reidbord (1983) has suggested that, for medical students at least, education and training should be regarded as a lifelong pursuit of knowledge, rather than crammed within a limited period of time. Moreover, he suggests the usefulness of certain areas of rote learning should be questioned and hopefully reduced, thereby giving more time for experiential learning, group work, and personal growth. Organizational changes in the time structure of training has also been suggested by Cartwright in Chapter 4 on women physicians. She questions the need to produce more and more physicians in the shortest possible time when job prospects are reducing, and recommends that providing the possibility of slower training would allow women to fulfil both family and career aspirations. While such changes for the benefit of women alone are unlikely to happen while they remain with so few positions of power, perhaps it needs to be recognized that a more mature and fulfilled individual, whether male or female, would be of benefit in most aspects of health care.

The reduction of personnel created by financial cut-backs will of course exaggerate overload difficulties, and Jick, in his chapter on budget-cut stress, suggests ways to reduce the deleterious effects so often created by the implementation of these schemes. His overriding recommendations involve maximizing participation and communication of what will be involved in any changes, and being prepared to accept that they will inevitably produce stress reactions. But apart from its concern with budget-cuts, Jick in Chapter 13 also brings out the importance of good management. Poor management is one of the most widely quoted sources of stress by health professionals; good management not only helps people to cope with stress, it actually removes a major cause of it. Fitter's chapter on new technology and health care shows that, while its introduction may create strain, this usually declines with time and experience and its ultimate benefits in terms of reducing overload should then be appreciated.

On a grander level, it may be necessary to 'give back' to patients large areas of responsibility for their personal health care. Although writers such as Mitchell (1984) see this as an inappropriate lowering of care, it may be that the growth of popularity in 'alternative medicine'—which has been more a reaction to anxieties over drug side-effects than to the overload suffered by health workers—can be seen positively as one way to reduce demand for the less serious diseases and allow resources to be re-directed to the more specialized aspects of health care.

It is clear from many of the chapters (for example, Thomson in Chapter 8 on mental handicap workers) that while relationships at work, both with colleagues and with patients, may be a source of stress, they can also be a major source of satisfaction. Thus Rushton (Chapter 9) points out that within social work, weekly supervision can be a very important moderator to stressful experiences, but that poor supervision not only provides no remedy for these, but actually becomes a stressor in itself. Any methods or training which improves supervisory skills and groups relationships would have great potential in helping to reduce the levels of strain.

Training generally is seen as providing the means to reduce many of the stressors discussed in the chapters. Such training can anticipate these problems and provide precise ways of dealing with them. For example, Kent recommends that students should learn interpersonal skills to improve their confidence in dealing with difficult patients, a frequent source of stress for them. Stress management skills can also be successfully taught to groups of workers (Rose and Veiga, 1984), as can patient restraint skills for those who come into contact with violent patients. The use of small groups is seen as a useful way of reducing the stress of dealing with death or suffering (Field, 1984) and more generally special groups may be organized to provide support for individuals who may in some way be a minority; for example, Women in Medicine groups.

The external threat that comes from a lowering of the image of health professionals has already been linked to media programmes which show them in a less than perfect light. However, the media can be used to gain more favourable images as well as to provide information to the public which might dispel myths and reduce their anxiety and so in turn that of the professional helping them. Thus dentists could take proactive steps in encouraging programmes which show the relative painlessness of modern dentistry, and social workers could similarly enlighten the public about how much they actually *prevent* child abuse. Whilst good publicitly is up to the professional body to initiate, members can also take individual action whenever appropriate.

For individuals who find their stress symptoms too severe for self-help, the provision of a counselling service may be necessary. Such services remain rare, at least in Britain, but may increase as organizations appreciate that a reduction in absenteeism and sick leave and a rise in job satisfaction may be associated with their introduction (Cooper, 1986). In Britain, such services have now been provided by two health authorities in London, and the National Counselling and Welfare Services for Sick Doctors has also been implemented to enable doctors to confidentially seek help for themselves or for colleagues about whom they have reason to be concerned.

Such steps may seem small, but they are unusual within professions which are conservative in self-generated change, and may herald the possibility of a future easing of organizational rigidity and the introduction of alternative methods of training and health care which have been incorporated beneficially in younger countries (Pickvance, 1987). Above all, the paucity of research in some areas must be reduced in order to demonstrate the levels of strain that are being suffered by the various groups of helpers. Stress is still not seen or accepted as a common feature of health professionals' work, and relevant research may help to promote a change in the organizational climate towards acceptance that stress exists and towards support for individuals who are particularly at risk. These can only be to the benefit of the professions themselves.

FUTURE RESEARCH ON HEALTH PROFESSIONALS

Several of the authors in this book noted how little research existed on the particular professions they were considering: Rushton on social workers, Jones on psychiatric nurses, Margison on psychiatrists, Ivancevich and Matteson on medical technologists and Thomson on those caring for the mentally handicapped. Indeed, with the possible exception of medical students and physicians, paucity rather than plenty characterizes the state of empirical research. Even for those areas where there are a large number of studies there is the problem that the vast majority of them rely solely on subjective measurements. This state of affairs has been criticized regularly throughout the last ten years of stress research (Kasl, 1978; Payne, Jick and Burke, 1982; Depue and Monroe, 1986). The use of self-report measures of psychological strain is

Conclusion

understandable, since many of the symptoms of stress are psychological in nature and the person is probably the best single source of information about such symptoms. Such experiences as worry, guilt, self-blame, severity of pain, panic are often not capable of objective verification anyway. Other symptoms such as raised blood pressure, smoking, drinking, the making of errors, changes in job performance are often more accessible to other observers. In many research projects, however, even some of these variables are measured by the reports of the subjects themselves. As Bates (1982) showed, doctors' spouses report that their partners appear much more exhausted than the partners admit to the researchers, so personal reports can be misleading, perhaps because of heightened defences involved in some aspects of care as Firth-Cozens has suggested.

Perhaps an even greater dilemma arises from the use of self-reports to describe the nature and severity of stressors. At the individual level it is important to understand the Subjective Environment as indicated in the model in the Introduction to the book (see p. 00). The problem with much research, however, is that it assumes these descriptions represent the Objective Environment reasonably accurately, yet research on perceptions of climate shows that even people in the same jobs or teams do not agree about the nature of their job environment (Glick, 1985). These differences in perceptions amongst people partly stem from real differences in the microclimates that people experience at work—the same supervisor might treat two people very differently—and partly from the fact that personality and values affect perceptions. Payne (1986) shows how trait neuroticism is strongly correlated with symptoms of strain (which is not surprising), but it is also strongly correlated with perceptions of job demands. Thus although high job demands predict symptoms of strain, as would be tested in the typical stress research study, this relationship disappears when trait neuroticism is controlled by multiple regression. Reliance on self-report measures to test such models of stress appears to be an unreliable way of testing them, though in the past it has been the most common way.

A more reliable way of showing the existence of occupational stress is to demonstrate different rates of psychological and physical morbidity in different occupations. It then becomes possible to look for differences in the environment that might lead to these different rates of strain. Karasek (1979) found that rates of strain in jobs of different demands did not differ all that much, but when high demand is combined with low discretion the rates begin to differ considerably. This approach relies much less on subjective reports to assess stressors, though they still constituted Karasek's measures of strain.

As Depue and Monroe (1986) have convincingly shown, however, there is a persistent problem in much of the stress literature because many people in any occupational group will be showing symptoms of physical and psychological ill-health, both because of stressors that have recently occurred in their environments (work or otherwise) and also because they have chronic problems of one kind or another. Depue and Monroe list four broad types of chronic condition which will strongly influence the levels of strain people report at any given moment in time. They are: personality traits such as neuroticism; disorders of affect such as depression; long-standing problems arising from chronic physical illnesses or handicaps; long-standing life difficulties such as family problems, or chronic unemployment. Conclusions drawn about the effects of job stress on psychological strain have been contaminated by the presence of people with these chronic conditions. Depue and Monroe recommend that future studies weed out people with these sorts of chronic problems and study those whose symptoms are more likely to be the result of current stressful conditions.

Whilst this approach makes good sense it adds to the demands on stress researchers. As Schmitt and Colligan (1984) point out, the size of correlations between stress and health is very small. This is partly because ill-health is a low base-rate phenomenon. At any one time only a relatively small number of people report being ill. If the chronically ill are removed from the population under study, then the base rate for illness or strain will be even lower. One way in which this problem can be tackled is to increase the sensitivity of indicators of stress. Apart from improving psychological measures, there is also increasing scope for taking physiological measures. These might give earlier warnings of the presence of strain than can be gained from psychological reports alone. The finding of chronically high urinary cortisol amongst surgeons (Payne, Chapter 5) is one example in the present book, despite the fact that its long-term clinical significance is still unclear. As it becomes easier technologically to collect blood, urine and saliva from subjects it also becomes easier to take multiple measures and these too may enable more sensitive diagnoses to be made. As Depue and Monroe point out, stress might be most easily identified by the presence of variations in response over time, and by the time it takes an individual to recover from a stressor. Stressed people show more variable responses (not necessarily higher levels), and their physiology takes longer to recover to baseline.

While this approach has much to promise Fried, Rowland and Ferris, (1984), demonstrate the need for such studies to be much more carefully carried out in the future. In the past, some researchers have used single measures of blood pressure, uric acid, etc. to assess strain, and single measures are by no means adequate for any of these parameters. The methodological implications of such developments are that subjects will be measured on many occasions over time, and will be used as their own controls. Such studies will, however, be able to trace the effects of a change in stress upon both psychological and physiological variables, and they will include the possibility of intervening to reduce environmental stressors to examine the effects this has on psychophysiological adaptation. Similarly, subjects can be given experience in such things as relaxation and stress inoculation training, and psychophysiological responses to them can be monitored. Such work is already in progress in the treatment of coronary heart disease (Schmitt and Colligan, 1984).

It is evident that few studies of this kind have as yet been carried out on health professionals, but stress research in the future needs to look very different from that of the past. However, health professionals provide an excellent group on which to carry out such work. They regularly experience stress, they work in an environment where the skills for carrying out physiological assessments are readily available, they understand their value—they use them on their own clients in many cases—and they recognize the importance of staying healthy if they are to provide the quality of service their patients need.

REFERENCES

Banks, M. H., Clegg, C. W., Jackson, P. R., Kemp, N. J., Stafford, E. M. and Wall, T. D. (1980). The use of the General Health Questionnaire as an indicator of mental health in occupational studies, *Journal of Occupational Psychology*, **53**, 187-94.

Bates, E. (1982). Doctors and their spouses speak: stress in medical practice, *Sociology of Health and Illness*, **4** (1), 25-39.

Bjorksten, O., Sutherland, S., Miller, C. and Stewart, T. (1983). Identification of medical student problems and comparison with those of other students, *Journal of Medical Education*, **58**, 759-67.

Colligan, M. J., Smith, M. J. and Hurrell, J. J. (1977). Occupational incidence rates of mental health disorders, *Journal of Human Stress*, **3**, 34-9.

Cooper, C. L. (1986). Job distress: recent research and the emerging role of the clinical occupational psychologist, *Journal of the British Psychological Society*, **39**, 325-31.

Depue, R. A. and Monroe, S. M. (1986). Conceptualization and measurement of human disorders in life stress research: the problem of chronic disturbance, *Psychological Bulletin*, **99**, 36-51.

Ferner, J. D. (1980). *Successful Time Management: A Self Teaching guide*, Wiley, New York.

Field, D. (1984). Formal instruction in United Kingdom medical schools about death and dying, *Medical Education*, **18**, 429-34.

Firth, J. A. and Shapiro, D. A. (1986). An evaluation of psychotherapy for job-related distress, *Journal of Occupational psychology*, **59**, 111-19.

Firth-Cozens, J. (1987). Emotional distress in junior house officers. Social and Applied Psychology Unit, Memo No. 826, Sheffield University.

Fried, Y., Rowland, K. M. and Ferris, G. R. (1984). The physiological measurement of work stress: a critique, *Personnel Psychology*, **37**, 4, 583-616.

Glick, W. H. (1985). Conceptualizing and measuring organizational and psychological climate: pitfalls in multilevel research, *The Academy of Management Review*, **10**, 4, 601-16.

Gomersall, J. (1987). Defensive caring, *Changes*, **5**.

Illich, I. (1975). *Medical Nemesis: The Expropriation of Health*, Calder & Boyars, London.

Karasek, R. J. (1979). Job demands, job decision latitude and mental strain: implications for job redesign, *Administrative Science Quarterly*, **24**, 285-308.

Kasl, S. (1978). Epidemiological contributions to the study of work stress. In C. L. Cooper and R. Payne (eds) *Stress at Work*, J. Wiley, Chichester.

Levine, M. (1982). Method or madness: on the alienation of the professional, *Journal of Community Psychology*, **10**, 3-14.

Mitchell, J. (1984). *What is to be Done about Illness and Health?* Penguin, London.
Payne, R. (1980). Organizational stress and social support. In C. L. Cooper and R. Payne (eds) *Current Concerns in Occupational Stress*, J. Wiley, London.
Payne, R. (1981). Stress in task-focussed groups, *Small Group Behaviour*, 12, 3, 253-68.
Payne, R. L. (1986). A longitudinal study of the psychological well-being of unemployed men and the mediating effect of neuroticism. Social and Applied Psychology Unit, Memo No. 778, Sheffield University.
' Payne, R. L., Jick, T. D. and Burke, R. J. (1982). Whither stress research?: an agenda for the 1980s, *Journal of Occupational Behaviour*, 55, 13-25.
Pickvance, D. (1987). Nicaraguan analysis, *Changes*, in press.
Reidbord, S. P. (1983). Psychological perspectives on iatrogenic physician impairment, *The Pharos*, 2-8.
Rose, R. L. and Veiga, J. F. (1984). Assessing the sustained effects of a stress management intervention on anxiety and locus of control, *Academy of Management Journal*, 27, 190-98.
Schmitt, N. W. and Colligan, M. J. (1984). Lack of stress-health relationships: a base rate problem? *Journal of Community Psychology*, 12, 245-52.
Tyson, K.W. and Merril, J. C. (1984). Health care institutions: Survival in a changing environment, *Journal of Medical Education*, 59, 773-80.
Warr, P. B. and Payne, R. L. (1982). Experiences of strain and pleasure among British adults, *Social Science and Medicine*, 16, 1691-7.

Index

Absence, 272
Activator-reaction-consequence model, 234–236
'Active Jobs', 99
Administrative strategies for retrenchment, 261
Adrenaline, 95
AIDS, xxi, 136
Alcohol, 7, 81, 109, 240
Alienation, 120
Ambiguity, 50, 207
Anaesthetists, 98
Anxiety, xviii, 19, 27, 110, 133, 203
Appraisal, xviii, 177, 247
Arousal, 63
Attitudes, 52, 73
  to mental handicap, 154
  to psychiatrists, 111
  to technology, 214
Authority, 97
Autonomy, 170

Back pain, 138
Beck Depression Inventory, 5
'Beginning Psychiatry Syndrome', 108
Black physicians, 77
Blood pressure, 95, 131, 144
Budget-cut stress, 259 ff, 277
Bureaucracy, 153, 197
Burnout, xi, xx, 25, 40, 108, 139, 177, 181, 198
Business management problems, 128

Cardiovascular disease, 99
Career, 34
  choice, 14
Case studies, 217
Caseloads, 174, 186
Catecholamines, 99
Change, as source of stress, 277
Child abuse, 280
Childbearing, 32

Choice of speciality, 72
Chronic problems, 281
Cocaine, 8
  see also Drugs
Cognitive problems, xxi
Communication, 183, 196, 245, 266, 279
Communication skills, 143
Community workers, 154
Compulsiveness, 27
Computer-based information systems, 213
Conflict, 50
Constraints, xvi, 203
Consultation rates, 49, 64
Control, xviii, 52, 92
Coping, xix, 16, 39, 66, 83, 104, 116, 117, 141, 185, 224, 246
  research on, 248, 250
  skills, 18, 40
  strategies, 80, 160, 161, 163, 221, 251, 278
Cortisol, 95, 99
Costs
  hospitals, 260
  reducing, 265
Counselling, 103
  services, 19, 121, 179, 278
Cruciform Effect, 117, 177

Death, 11, 274
Decision latitude, 51, 54
Defence mechanisms, 108
Defences, xxii, 180
Demands, xvi, 96, 103, 203, 262, 274
  supports–constraints model, 278
Dental assistants, 127
Dentists, 6, 127 ff
  female, 132, 135
  level of stress, 145
  student, 132
Depression, 19, 37, 110, 184, 203
Diary card, 57
Discretion, xviii, 92, 170

Divorce, 81
Doctor–patient relationship, 35
Drug abuse, 39, 81
Drug addiction, 92
Drugs, 7, 82, 110
   see also Cocaine

Early experience, 15
EMG, 138
Empathy, 75
Environment, xv
   physical, 153
   see also Subjective environment and Objective environment
Environmental stressors, 220
Ethnicity, 14
Ethnography, 89
Equipment breakdown, 222, 245
Evaluation, 18
Exercise, 142
Exhaustion, 137

Family, 51, 57, 66
   therapy, 31
Fear in patients, 129
Feedback, 18, 157
Female doctors, 109
Female physicians, 31–32
   see also Women physicians
Financial cuts, 273
Financial planning, 40
Financial rewards, xxii
Financial stress, 32–34
Frustration, 19, 56, 193
Future research on health professionals, 280–283

Galvanic skin response, 130
Gender issues, 76
General Health Questionnaire, 5, 202
General practitioners, 45 ff, 211
Grief, 267
Group therapy, 120
Guilt, 15, 78

Headaches, 82
Health complaints, 240
Health hazards, 134, 239
Heart rate, 95, 98, 130
Hospitals, 259 ff
   size of, 273
   special, 197
Hours of work, 194
Hours worked, xxiii
Hypnosis, 143

Identity, 240
Immune system, 250
Impaired physician, 15, 37, 81
Individual differences, xxii, 13, 145, 263
Intensive care units, 212, 214, 215–224
Isolation, 115

Job dissatisfaction, 140
Job satisfaction, 175, 242, 263, 275, see also Satisfaction

Laboratory technicians, 231 ff
   role of, 233–234
Leisure, 48, 51
   see also Recreation, time for
Levels of psychiatric illness, 3
Levels of strain, 272
Levels of stress, 152
   dentists, 145
   medical technical staff, 236–240
   mental handicap, 162, 163
   psychiatric nurses, 199
   social workers, 182
Life cycle, 71, 79
Life events, 133
Loneliness, 79
Longitudinal research, 252

Malpractice, 34–37, 179, 197
   premiums, 33
Maltreatment, 157
Marriage, 28–32, 116
Masculinity, 81
Media hostility, 168
Media interest, 275
Medical students, 3 ff
Medical technical staff, levels of stress, 237
Medical technologists, 231 ff
   role of, 233–234
Mental Health Act Commission, 116
Mental illness, 151
Mentally handicapped, 151 ff
   attitudes to, 154
   levels of stress, 162–163
Minority status, 75

MMPI, 5
Moral error, 90
Morale, 154
Morbidity, xvi, 101
  rates, 272
  see also Psychiatric morbidity
Mortality, xvi, 109, 137
  rates, 45, 272
  ratios, 91, 93
  statistics, 195

National Health Service, xx, 47, 50, 119, 173
Negligence, 36
Noradrenaline, 95
Nurses, 6
  see also Psychiatric nurses
Nursing role and technology, 213, 226-227

Object Relations Theory, 115
Objective environment, xv, xviii
  see also Environment
Objective experience, 51
Organizational change 186, 211
Organizational decline, long term effects, 268
Organizational stressors, 155, 173, 195, 202
Overload, 10, 24, 47, 215, 273
Overwork, 24, 112, 239
  syndrome, 25

Participation, 227, 279
Participant observation, 180
Participation in decision making, 182
Part-time, 73, 176
Patient
  anxiety, 128
  behaviour, 134
  contact, 50
Patients
  and technology, 213, 219, 225
  as a source of stress, 276
  demands for treatment, 277
  fear in, 129
Perceived severity, 262
Perceived time pressure, 262
Personal therapy, 120
'Personal threat', 113

Personality, 26, 46, 52, 54, 60, 62, 94, 131, 159, 183-184, 281, 282
  type A, 52, 62, 243
Pharmacists, 6
Physical demands, 91
Physicians, 23 ff
Physiological changes, 55
Physiological measures, 282
'Planned organizational change', 104
Power, 83, 168, 276
  and women physicians, 73-74
Pregnancy, 136
Prevention, 119
Prison officers, 195
Private life, 11
Promotion of women, 75
Psychiatric illness, levels of, 3
Psychiatric morbidity, 4, 8, 13
Psychiatric nurses, 189 ff
  levels of stress, 199
  role of, 190-193
Psychiatric patients, 10
Psychiatric symptoms, 38, 243
Psychiatrists, 107 ff
  attitudes to, 111
  role of, 107, 122
Psychodynamic view, 160
Psychosomatic symptoms, 240

Recreation, time for, 6
  see also Leisure
Relationships, 12, 113, 275, 279
  between staff, 158
  with clients, 156, 171
  with colleagues, 170
  with families, 158
  with patients, 193
  see also Doctor-patient relationships
Relaxation techniques, 142, 278
Research strategies, 251
Responsibility, 27, 103, 215, 242
  for people, xxi, 51
Role
  ambiguities, 112, 169-170, 207
  conflict, 117, 169, 177, 207, 240
  of laboratory technicians, 233-234
  of medical technologists, 233-234
  of psychiatric nurses, 190-193
  of psychiatrists, 107, 122
  overload, 207
  strain, 77

Satisfaction, 56, 94, 97, 156, 193
  see also Job satisfaction
Satisfaction with training, 219, 222
Scientific orientation, 54
Selection, 17, 65, 119
Self-esteem, 113
Self-help groups, 41
Self-perceived pressure, 60
Self-report, xx, 178
  measures, 280
Sex, 28, 31, 74, 132, 152, 184, 237, 274, 278
  differences, 13, 73
Sexual activity, 30
Sexual problems, 116
Shift work, 51
'Sick doctor' statutes, 121
Size of hospital, 273
Smoking, 39, 83
Social Clock Project, 80
Social orientation, 53
Social supports, 46, 76 102
  see also Supports
Social work
  nature of, 168–169
  team, 175
Social workers, 167 ff
  levels of stress, 182
Socio-economic status, 14
Special hospitals, 197
Spouses, 29, 32, 101
Staff shortages, 155, 196, 265
State–trait anxiety, 5
Status, xxii, 191, 276
Stress, 63
  environmental, 17
  financial, 32–34
  levels of, see levels of stress
  processes, xv
  sources of, 9, 128
Stresslog, 14
Subjective environment, xviii
Subjective experience, 51
Subjective interpretations of budget crisis, 261

Suicide, 13, 28, 38, 82, 109, 111, 140
'Superwoman', 15, 78
Support, lack of, 182
Supports, xvi, 97, 113, 144, 179, 203, 220
  see also, Social supports
Surgeons, 89 ff
Surgery, stressfulness of, 93

Teamwork, 158
  see also Social work team
Technical error, 90
Technology, 211 ff, 277
  and nursing role, 226–277
  and stress, 217, 223
  attitudes to, 214
  effects on patient care, 219
  impact on nurses, 213
  impact on patients, 213
  patients' responses, 225
Therapy
  family, 31
  group, 120
  personal, 120
Time, 23
  for recreation, 6
  pressures, 10, 24, 48, 90, 128, 273
Triangulation, 252
Training, 16–20, 65, 84, 103, 112, 119, 143, 183, 185, 216, 278
  satisfaction with, 219, 222
Type A behaviour, 243
Type A personality, 52, 62

Unemployment, 155, 167, 276

Values, 103

Women, xxiii
  physicians, 71 ff
  see also Female physicians and Female doctors
  students, 13
Workload, 49, 57, 107, 245